COLLECTED STUDIES SERIES

Studies in East-Central Europe 1500–1900
General Editor: Ivan T. Berend

Money, Prices and Power in Poland, 16–17th Centuries

Antoni Mączak

Money, Prices and Power in Poland, 16–17th Centuries

A Comparative Approach

Routledge
Taylor & Francis Group

LONDON AND NEW YORK

1995

First published 1995 by Variorum, Ashgate Publishing

Published 2017 by Routledge
2 Park Square, Milton Park, Abingdon, Oxon OX14 4RN
52 Vanderbilt Avenue, New York, NY 10017

Routledge is an imprint of the Taylor & Francis Group, an informa business

British Library CIP Data
> Mączak, Antoni
> Money, Prices and Power in Poland, 16th-17th Centuries:
> A Comparative Approach.
> (Variorum Collected Studies Series; CS487)
> I. Title. II. Series.
> 943. 8023

US Library of Congress CIP Data
> Money, Prices and Power in Poland, 16th-17th Centuries:
> A Comparative Approach / Antoni Mączak.
> p. cm. -- (Collected Studies Series; CS487). Includes bibliographical references and index.ISBN 0-86078-478-9 (hb.: acid-free paper)
> 1. Poland--Politics and Government--1572-1763. 2. Poland--Politics and Government--To 1572. 3. Poland--Economic Conditions. 4. Europe--Economic Conditions--16th Century.
> 5. Europe--Economic Conditions--17th Century.
> I. Maczak, Antoni. II. Series: Collected Studies; CS487.
> DK4290. M66   1994   94-43313
> 320. 9438--dc20   CIP

ISBN 13: 978-0-86078-478-4 (hbk)

COLLECTED STUDIES SERIES CS487

CONTENTS

This volume contains xiv + 295 pages

PUBLISHER'S NOTE

The articles in this volume, as in all others in the Collected Studies Series, have not been given a new, continuous pagination. In order to avoid confusion, and to facilitate their use where these same studies have been referred to elsewhere, the original pagination has been maintained wherever possible.

Each article has been given a Roman number in order of appearance, as listed in the Contents. This number is repeated in each page and is quoted in the index entries.

INTRODUCTION

A British historian, in order to explain the case of Lithuania, recently proposed the following comparison:

> For British readers, the best way to approach Lithuanian history is to imagine what might have happened if the United Kingdom had been conquered by the French. They should then imagine that Edinburgh had become a city of English culture under French rule, that the English, Irish, and Jewish communities of Scotland had been decimated, and that the Gaelic minority of Scotland had claimed independence under the slogan of 'Scotland for the Gaels'. Stranger things have actually taken place at the shores of the Baltic.[1]

Change French for Russians, for Edinburgh take Vilna (Polish, Wilno; Lithuanian, Vilnius), let the Irish be Poles and let the Jews remain always themselves. A similar, if not exactly the same, story could be told about Lvov (also Lwów and Lviv; Latin, Leopolis) and the several nations claiming it their own. For centuries Vilna was the principal centre of Ashkenazi Judaism and a centre of the Polish cult of the Holy Virgin, while Lvov, in addition to the other ethnic and cultural groups, was *the* centre of European Armenians, and had a world-record number of cathedrals of various confessions.

Over the centuries, the East and West of Europe have presented interesting contrasts, but until recently the 'Westerners' rarely appreciated enough of what was happening in the East; that it was not mere curiosity, but could be of importance for the European 'core' as well. This collection is chiefly about that Eastern part of Europe, but it is not devoted to its ethnic and national problems, past or present.

I was privileged to start my research in history under the supervision of two strong intellectual personalities: Marian Małowist at Warsaw and Michael M. Postan at Cambridge. Both of them were interested in Europe as a whole. Deeply aware of its divisions in the past, they also resented them in their own lifetime. Different as researchers, both were aware and curious of the impact of the past on the present day. Difficult as supervisors (in their students' opinion, at least), they were dedicated to teaching and expressed themselves best when talking and tutoring. Specifically devoted to economic and social history, both had experienced the brutal impact of power politics and became interested in the intertwining of various facets of historical change.

To their memories, with grateful admiration, this collection is dedicated.

*

* *

The present volume contains fifteen papers researched and published over a score of years. Some of these essays are comparative in approach, some analytic and some of a rather synthetic character. The first two, on Baltic commerce substantiate the opinion that much can still be achieved in that particular areas of research. The monumental publication of the Sound Toll Tables was most accomplished before the advent of the computer age and offers only the tip of the iceberg as far as the available source information is concerned. Once the research grant has been allocated, the work completed and volumes published, there is little chance of attracting the liberality of sponsors. However, because of a fortuitous coincidence, the price data registered by the Danish Sound Toll collectors in the late sixteenth and early seventeenth centuries are particularly abundant and of great value. While most of the information that exists about prices in Europe is just sample data or normative material, the value of goods (principally grain westbound and textiles eastbound) had to be declared at the Sound and this was rigorously enforced. The resulting information is of great benefit when made accessible for statistical research.

The second paper presents a very different kind of study, in that a minor occurrence is fortunately supported by a number of independent sources. Whereas article I is optimistic in proving the existence of massive and important source material reflecting the European economy as a whole,[2] article II analyses the complaints against British privateering and some sixteenth-century manuals of commercial arithmetic. These are relatively minor sources of a most suspect character and yet, they could be checked against each other and have proved to be well worth the study.

Notwithstanding these optimistic conclusions on the availability of sources on Baltic trade, the data for quantitative research in the economic history of early modern Poland is very limited. Although the original source material on prices and yields of grain originated from that country, subsequent critical research set doubt upon the accuracy of the data. With missing or unreliable population and fiscal records, the economic history of early modern Poland must unfortunately remain incomplete. This leaves little hope of one day able to produce a multidimensional work, comparable to those on particular regions so characteristic of the *Annales* school. Nevertheless, it does not detract from the unquestionable impact of the Boulevard Raspail upon Polish historical scholarship.[3]

Much of the volume is an endeavour to overcome this substantial lack of a statistical base. Articles IV and V (and to some extent also article III) are concerned with the economy of travelling in Europe. Travel diaries and memoirs have long been appreciated as descriptive, literary sources and often quoted, but only in a haphazard way. They are underestimated as a testimony of transition to an age of more quantitative thinking. In a relatively static world, travellers were best equipped for complex comparative thinking and their curiousity produced astonishing observations, more advanced even than those of fireplace-intellectuals.[4]

More than half the volume examines the structures of power in Poland and elsewhere in Europe. Particular attention has been given to informal power relationships, particularly to political patronage. This has, in fact, only become an established area of research in social and political history, including art and church history, in the last decade. Historians and social anthropologists now overlap in their reciprocal fields of research. However, such a situation did not exist in 1981 when the Trustees of *Historisches Kolleg* in Munich offered me its fellowship with excellent opportunities of work and of organising an international conference of historians to debate this subject.[5] Using professional terminology, one may speak of *cosche* or *Verflechtungen* of the early modernists in Europe and America, whose academic approach is somewhat different to the traditional and who are interested in informal instruments of power like the patron-client relationship. Lately their number has visibly increased.

To the readers of this volume I should make some general comments and corrections. Concerning political patronage, mentioned in my writings from the 1980s, I expressed the opinion that it was very limited if not non-existant in Scandinavia. Recent research, done chiefly in Lund, makes such a hypothesis obsolete. Professors Bengt Ankarloo, Göran Rystad and Eva Österberg together with their colleagues in Lund showed great interest in my research and have corrected some of my opinions.

On the other hand, I would like to reassert strongly two points made in articles VIII, XII and XV.[6] Firstly, I would set the 'turning point' in the history of the Polish-Lithuanian Commonwealth (see article XV) even earlier than the late sixteenth century. The reader may observe a certain hesitance in the text, even an inconsistency. The 'point of no return' is the historian's declaration of faith, a short-hand form of expressing a general opinion on the factors of historical change. Now, I see no roots for the future of centralised government in the power structure of late-fifteenth-century Poland.[7] The statutes of King Casimir decisively curtailed the royal prerogative, after the king had been blackmailed by the *lévee* of the gentry in response to his summons to go to war against the Teutonic Order in 1454. From this, a power structure was created, which was based on local self-government and run by the estate, that is to say, the nobility. The following hypothesis, therefore, seems plausible: the size of the country determined the weakness of the central government and hence the socio-political structure of the estate itself.[8] The answer can perhaps be sought by comparing the Polish case with other similar cases. In this light, the centre-localities paradigm proposed by Michael Braddick seems a useful theoretical framework.[9]

Secondly, I feel even more opposed to the term 'oligarchy' in relation to seventeenth- and eighteenth-century Poland. I do not believe that each *term* ought to reflect directly the *reality* described by it. However, if a term exists to describe the Polish constitutional scene of the late fifteenth and sixteenth century, it is the 'self-government of nobles (in counties)'. The subsequent development, which gathered momentum in the seventeenth century, was nothing more than 'the magnates' patronage' as a principal power relationship. If we cannot manage without oligarchy, then the 'competitive oligarchy' of Robert Dahl would be acceptable.

Notes

1. Norman Davies, 'Strange History of Baltic Exchanges', *The Guardian*, September 27, 1991.

2. The value of Sound Toll price notations was first mentioned and appreciated by the late Professor Astrid Friis.

3. This impact was most visible in the late 1950s and in the 1960s, but 'rue de Varennes' (which was then designated the VIe section of the École Pratique des Hautes Études) evokes a different association.

4. I develop this theme extensively in *Travel in Early Modern Europe*, Polity Press, Cambridge 1995.

5. See Antoni Mączak with the cooperation of Elisabeth Müller-Luckner, *Klientelsysteme im Europa der Frühen Neuzeit*, Schriften des Historischen Kollegs, Kolloquien 9, Munich 1988.

6. For contrasting views from those in article XIV, see Andrzej Wyczański in J.K. Fedorowicz, ed., *A Republic of Nobles: Studies in Polish History to 1864*, Cambridge University Press, Cambridge 1982.

7. This idea came to me from the controversy surrounding the Tudor revolution in government.

8. I develop this theme in a book published in Polish, in *Klientela: Nieformalne systemy władzy w Polsce i Europie, XV–XVIII w.* [Clientele: Informal systems of power in Poland and Europe of the 15th to 18th centuries], Warsaw, 1993; and also a paper read in London in 1993, 'Paradoxes of democracy in Poland, 15th to 18th centuries' sponsored by the School of Slavonic and East European Studies, University of London and the Polish Cultural Institute.

9. Michael Braddick, 'State formation and social change in early modern England: a problem stated and approaches suggested', *Social History* 16/1, January 1991, pp. 1–17. I used this format in 'The state', in M. Aymard and P. Ginzburg, eds. *Einaudi's Storia dell' Europa*, vol. V (forthcoming).

ACKNOWLEDGEMENTS

I am grateful to the following persons, publishers, societies and journals for their permission to reprint the articles included in this volume: Erik Gøbel, Editor of *The Scandinavian Economic Review* (for article I); *Studia Maritima* (II); the Istituto Internazionale di Storia Economica 'Francesco Datini', Prato (III); Editions Privat, Toulouse (IV); Warsaw University Press and the University of Iowa Press (V); Luigi de Rosa, Editor of *The Journal of European Economic History* (VI); Macmillan Press Limited, Basingstoke (VII, XV); Oxford University Press (VIII); Editions de la Maison des Sciences de l'Homme, Paris and Cambridge University Press (IX); Allmänna Förlaget and The Bank of Sweden Tercentenary Foundation (X); Cambridge University Press (XI, XIV); Lund University Press (XII); Gotland Fornsal, Visby (XIII).

I

The Balance of Polish Sea Trade with the West, 1565-1646

I

The balance of trade is generally regarded as a major item only on an obsolete mercantilist agenda where it is discussed rather as an element in an abstract doctrine than as a real economic problem. Polish historians would follow the same line as their colleagues elsewhere if the economic situation of the Polish Commonwealth at the beginning of the seventeenth century did not compel them to lay emphasis on a supposed change in money flows. It has been established beyond doubt that the early seventeenth century was a most crucial period in Polish economic and socio-political development; its importance for Poland was much greater and more portentous than Ruggiero Romano has shown it to be for Western Europe.[1] A deep crisis in the serf-labour economy, Polish towns and cities generally checked in their development, the state weak against external foes and its own magnates—these *signa temporis* were to continue to characterise Polish history until the final days of independence in the late eighteenth century. The Polish experience was uniquely acute because the structural crisis of her economy and the political crisis of the state coincided with the general European depression. In his discussion of the period

[1] R. Romano, 'Tra XVI e XVII secolo. Una crisi economica: 1619–1622', *Rivista Storica Italiana*, LXXIV (1962).

1619–1622 Romano stressed the role played by the money market and the credit system, both so highly developed in the leading countries of the West: in Polish commercial relations, however, while the turnover of goods was lively, the money market retained rather primitive forms.[2] In this context an important change in what had been a highly favourable trade balance must have caused deep disruption to the economic life of the country.

The results of this breakdown are much better known than the causes. Let us begin, however, by sketching in the background. In early modern times western European countries exploited eastern markets, though under conditions of unfavourable trade balances. Aksel E. Christensen and Artur Attman have shown that Baltic countries belonged in the late sixteenth and early seventeenth century to a specie-importing zone.[3] What role was played by Polish (i. e. West Prussian) ports, the most important group of Baltic commercial centres?[4] What was their place in world trade?

II

We propose to approach the problem by going once more to the Danish Sound Toll Registers (STR),[5] and also by attempting to utilize the printed Sound Toll Tables (STT) in a new way.[6] The impressive effort of the Danish editors to produce a meaningful set of trade statistics was accepted by scholars rather critically, and it was pointed out that many important elements in the original

[2] The money market in sixteenth and seventeenth century Poland is much less studied than trade. An important new contribution is Z. Sadowski's study on 'Money and the beginning of Polish Republic's decay': *Pieniadz a poczatki upadku Rzeczypospolitej w XVII w.* (Warszawa, 1964).

[3] A. E. Christensen, 'Sundzollregister und Ostseehandel. Resultate und Probleme', *Conventus primus historicorum balticorum Rigae*, (Riga, 1938), pp. 391–400; *Dutch Trade to the Baltic about 1600*, (Copenhagen, The Hague, 1941), pp. 367–369; A. Attman, *Den ryska marknaden i 1500-talets baltiska politik, 1558–1595*, (Lund, 1944), Chapter V. I am very much indebted to Professor Attman for his valuable remarks and suggestions and not less for his cordial hospitality during my sojourn in Gothenburg in 1967.

[4] These were Danzig (in Polish: Gdansk) and Elbing (in Polish: Elblag) situated in West Prussia, officially called Royal Prussia. The main port of East Prussia, or Ducal Prussia, was Königsberg.

[5] I adopt the abbreviations introduced by A. E. Christensen; see his *Dutch Trade, passim.* STT means here *Tabeller over Skibsfart og Varetransport gennem Øresund*, ed. N. Bang, vols. I, II A, II B, (København, 1906–1933).

[6] Related problems are discussed in papers read at the conference on the history of Central European trade, Marburg/Lahn 1967 and at the Tenth Congress of Polish Historians, Lublin 1969. See, too, my paper 'The Sound Toll Accounts and the Balance of English Eastland Trade, 1565–1646', *Studia Historiae Economicae*, vol. III, 1968 (published 1969).

source had been lost in summary publication. Nor did the original source itself maintain a high or uniform standard of accuracy, since the effectiveness of customs inspection fluctuated heavily.[7] The historian is once again faced with a source both rich and treacherous. Should he ignore it, or attempt to overcome its deficiencies, or simply close his eyes to its shortcomings? While there is no simple solution, we have tried to use methods which would help us to minimise as far as possible the effects of the deficiencies of both the original source and the published edition. We have made particular use of the price information provided for English, French and Scottish cargoes.

Whereas statements concerning quantities of goods passing through the Sound were often inaccurate, the price quotations have been proved to be highly accurate.[8] This permits moderate optimism: at least one feature of the source may be accepted as reliable. For the two periods before 1569 and after 1618 the situation is even better: according to Aksel E. Christensen and Pierre Jeannin higher reliability in the registration of goods was assured in the first period by low customs rates and in the second by extremely stringent customs examination.[9] We have selected four relatively reliable sample years from the STT (1565, 1625, 1635 and 1646) and five with a lower reliability in the registrations of goods (1575, 1585, 1595, 1605 and 1615).[10] We have, of course, taken account of warnings as to the accuracy of registration of the ports of departure and of the origin of cargoes. These strictures are probably particularly important for smaller harbours like Reval or Stettin (Szczecin). For Polish ports and for Königsberg, which together constituted the lion's share of the Baltic trade, this source of inaccuracy does not seem important.[11]

We intend to consider only the prices of goods which were charged duty *ad valorem*. To arrive at a rough estimate of the value of exports and imports it is necessary to select commodities which, firstly, are relatively representative of Polish commerce; secondly, constitute together a high share of total

---

[7] For the most up-to-date discussion of STR and STT see P. Jeannin, 'Les comptes du Sund comme source por la construction d'indices généraux de l'activité économique en Europe, XVIe–XVIIIe siècle, *Revue Historique* (1964), pp. 55–102, 307–340.

[8] Astrid Friis, 'The Two Crises in the Netherlands in 1557', *Scandinavian Economic History Review* I (1953), p. 221. We discuss the reliability of price quotations in the STR and the STT in A. Mączak, 'Sundzollregister als eine preisgeschichtliche Quelle, 1557–1647'. *Jahrbuch für Wirtschaftsgeschichte*, 1970, III.

[9] Christensen, *Dutch Trade*, pp. 318–350; Jeannin, *loc. cit.*, pp. 96–102, 307–309.

[10] 'Falsified' does not always mean 'too low': skippers often used to declare cheap goods in place of expensive ones. It was therefore possible that the quantity of cheap rye was exaggerated at the cost of dear wheat, etc. See Jeannin, *loc. cit.*, p. 97.

[11] Striking differences between Danzig, Elbing and Königsberg in the composition of goods exported and imported suggest that inaccuracies in this respect were not great. Mączak, 'Sundzollregister'.

trade; and, thirdly, occur constantly in the tables. The last condition needs explanation. An important new commodity must always be taken into consideration,[12] but if we are in possession only of sporadic price quotations, it will be hard to get reliable comparisons. It is better to omit such items.

Tables 1–4 below show all the commodities that have been taken into account. Some detailed points about these should be noted first.

Westbound cargoes

Rye is measured in *lasts*. This is the total amount of rye noted in the Sound as shipped from Danzig (Gdansk) and 'West Prussia' (or 'Royal Prussia' in the language of the times)—i. e. Elbing (Elblag). The same is true of wheat. The following are disregarded: barley (very small quantities), buckwheat, flour (more important, especially in the earlier years), malt and grits. The inclusion of these items would not materially change the picture of cereal exports, and price data for them are in any case very scarce.

Wainscots and clapholt are in *hundreds*. For some years we consider not only prices of a *hundred* (which was the most important unit of measure) but also of a *ring* and of a *threescore* (one *Schock*). These prices do not agree, so for each year we have established average values and expressed the quantity in *hundreds*. The price of different units indicates not only different quantities but also different qualities: e. g., some kinds of wainscot were sold in *rings*, some others in *hundreds*. There were enormous differences of price, more apparent in STR than in STT. The average is made up here from substantially divergent elements.[13]

Ashes, pitch and tar are in *lasts*. All cargoes have necessarily been omitted which lumped various items together (e. g. 'pitch and tar'). Until 1585 duty was often levied upon such mixed cargoes without differentiation, but this was seldom the case later on.

Potash is in *shippounds*. In the STT one finds potash in both *shippounds* and *lasts*. A *last* has been reckoned as twelve *shippounds*.[14]

Flax and hemp are in *lasts*. The usual conversion is one *last* to 6 *shippounds*,[15] but because flax in *shippounds* was usually more expensive that in *lasts*, we introduced two prices and multiplied each by a corresponding quantity.

Hides and skins in pieces. Here, too we introduced individual prices and multiplied each by a corresponding quantity.

---

[12] E. g., potash, wool, steel, haberdashery. See Tables 1, 2.
[13] Mączak, 'Sundzollregister'.
[14] Christensen, *Dutch Trade*, p. 443.
[15] Christensen, *Dutch Trade*, p. 442.

Iron. In some columns of STT (vol. II A) bar-iron (*Stangjærn*) is in *shippounds*. *Lasts* in 1615 is a mistake easy to correct by comparison with the STT, vol. II B, p. 244. *Lasts, shippounds* and *hundredweights* could be reduced to a common denominator but since we have fairly exact price data for metals we did not think that appropriate.

There remains a broad margin of different goods of elusive values and variable importance. They played a role in exports, but their inclusion would not change the trend. We shall come back to them.

Eastbound cargoes

Salt and herring are measured in lasts and total imports are covered.

Wines: Rhine wine is in *aumes,* other in *pipes.* Other units of measure are not taken into consideration. A. E. Christensen gives a conversion of 1 *pipe* to 3 *aumes* but we used this only in Table 20. 'Other wines' (i. e. other than Rhine) are put together with brandy and vinegar. As to 'Colonial goods' we considered only those measured in *pounds.* To disregard other units of measure (like pounds, sacks, packs, bundles, etc.) is a necessary but arbitrary operation and the figures we get can therefore only be indices, less reliable than those for other groups. We chose pounds because this unit covered most differentiated goods and applies to the larger part of them. Only for the *pound* unit does one find prices given for every year.

Textiles are in *pieces.* The *piece* is the dominant measure, though one fairly frequently meets *packs,* and textiles from Scotland come in *ells.* In order to avoid errors we eliminated *packs,* whose true prices must in any case have remained unknown. Among textiles in *ells* one can discern certain kinds, usually Scottish, which are relatively expensive, and also very cheap English ones: for example, in 1615 one notes 950 *ells Pleding* worth 178 rixdollars, but 3700 *ells* English *Klædelister* worth only 52 rixdollars. Accordingly, it also seemed prudent to disregard *ells.* Even i 1635, when the English and Scots brought as many as 38,523 *ells* (and 6,000 more were brought by Swedes free of duty) their whole value was estimated at 5,992 rixdollars, whereas textiles in pieces were valued at 511,070 rixdollars. For 1625 corresponding figures are 3,258 and 557,024 rixdollars. The value of textiles in *ells* was clearly trifling.

We have omitted numerous groups of commodities of little importance which lacked regular price quotations. These are trousers and stockings, textile raw materials (wool, cotton, silk, yarn), minerals, hops, oil, olive oil, starch, cheese, soap, glue, ivory, glass, paper, haberdashery (*Kram*), iron, steel, lead, tin, corn. They only appear occasionally. Most of them were imported by the Dutch, so we are deprived of price quotations. A test of the leather trade shows that the prices of a commodity exported from the Baltic cannot be used for the same commodity imported.

Then there is the difficulty of establishing quantities. We may perhaps disregard the well-recognised problem of false custom declarations, and rely on the selection of years of comparable reliability. But the arrangement of the STT as well as peculiarities of the STR make it additionally difficult to compute the bulk of imports. Table 4 a for every tenth year in vol. II A of the STT describes goods according to the port of departure of westbound ships, so that here is no difficulty in recognising Polish (i. e. Danzig + Elbing) exports. Imports raise more problems. Table 3 b describes goods going eastwards in Western bottoms, grouped according to the Eastland ports from which boats were to return. Polish imports in Eastland bottoms must then be computed. They can be estimated on the basis of table 1 b in the STT vol. II A, but we can only take account of Danzig and (very few) Elbing ships and have to exclude the unknown contribution of Lübeck and Königsberg ships. On the other hand, we possibly include Danzig freights serving other Eastland harbours (Table 5 below).

Table 6 below bears on this problem. It shows that for some years the contribution of Eastland navigation was too small to influence significantly the balance of the Polish trade with the West. This is encouraging for our calculations, but we must remember that the role of Easterlings in navigation through the Sound nevertheless varied considerably.

We have discussed the crucial problem of price quotations and price estimates at length in an essay in *Jahrbuch für Wirtschaftsgeschichte*,[16] and our conclusions may be summed up as follows. We agree with Aksel E. Christensen[17] and Astrid Friis[18] that prices declared at the Sound were not formal values, though they were rounded off. They are very diverse, but this merely reflects different market conditions and different qualities of goods from particular regions and ports. So it should be borne in mind that the tabulated price averages are built up from various differentiated local prices using weighted averages, a consideration which is unimportant for corn, but much more significant for wool and flax. Various tests indicated a high degree of conformity between prices and price series gathered from the STR and those from other sources, for example data on rye prices at Danzig and Riga. The price was usually a more trustworthy element in the declaration than the quantity.

The special value of these price quotations is grounded on the very large

---

[16] Vol. 1970: III, Maczak, 'Sundzollregister'.
[17] Christensen, 'Sundzollregister und Ostseehandel'.
[18] Friis, 'The Two Crises'.

number we can use in our samples. We can construct averages based on scores of declarations, sometimes—in the case of grain, for example—on scores of thousands of units; in the case of imported textiles the sample almost equals the total statistical population.

In sharp contrast with most price statistics of the period, the STR enables us to study not only the prices of particular varieties of goods (kerseys or wheat, for example) but also price averages for given groups of commodities (textiles or grains). This has a particular advantage: there is a risk in examining the market without data properly reflecting elasticities of demand. Not much can be deduced if the price of a given kind of cloth rose: customers had a broad choice of other cloths and one cannot readily follow changes of quantity in them all. Conclusions based on the changing prices of one type of cloth may simply be confusing in comparison to conclusions based on an overall trend in textile prices. 'Colonial goods' create their own problem. The classification comprised an extraordinarily heterogenous mass of pepper and Brazilian wood, rice and nutmeg, tobacco, plums and many other goods described in the notes of vol. II A of the STT, an assortment which changed with Dutch and English colonial expansion.

In general, it appears from the differences in unit prices (Table 7 below, line 1) that price fluctuations were partly due to changes in assortment. For instance, a higher proportion of cheap kerseys in the textiles lowered the average even if the price of kerseys themselves remained unchanged. This puts us in a position to examine statistically the problem of the new draperies, so often discussed in a general way. In 1635 the volume index of textile imports to the Baltic (1565 = 100) reached 730. For expensive 'Suffolks' (in the STR decribed as *Kleide,* in the STT as *Klæde*) it was only 242, but for kerseys 964 and for single dozens no less than 4400 (in 1565 there had been only 113 pieces of this last). The result was a very low index of average textile price, only 104, which was much lower than any one of its individual components.

III

Let us now return to our main objective, the balance of trade. A straightforward comparison of imports and exports based on prices at ports of departure (f. o. b. prices) does not of course, reveal the true balance of trade. As Eli F. Heckscher pointed out, the STR provides such f. o. b. prices in east and west ports but says nothing about freight costs and mercantile profit.[19] The balance

---

[19] E. F. Heckscher, 'Öresundtullräkenskaperna och deras behandling', *Historisk Tidskrift,* Stockholm (1944). A practical solution has been proposed in our essay 'The Balance of English Eastland Trade'.

of trade can only be estimated for a given country. The Dutch trade, for example, was carried in its own vessels, which also served foreign merchants. A large part of the English trade was carried in foreign bottoms. Polish trade on the other hand was strongly passive: both freight costs and mercantile profit were negative items in Danzig's and Elbing's balance of trade, since ships and merchants were generally alien and one may calculate the trade balance of Polish ports by using local prices. It is not difficult for exports on the basis of the STR alone, but to deal with imports it is necessary to be able to calculate the differential in prices between western European and Polish harbours.

This differential depended on many factors, such as supply and demand, tariff barriers, freight costs, and the possibility of using a commodity like salt or coal as ballast. Coal was free of duty at the Sound because it could be used in this way. The differential was very variable but it is possible to examine some of the things which determined its size.

For Danzig we can use a price series compiled by Julian Pelc, corresponding to vol. I of N. W. Posthumus's *Inquiry into the History of Prices in Holland*, which, however, refers to Amsterdam and not to the English east coast.[20] Of course, we can hardly use single quotations; what we need are comparable price series for ports in the West and in Poland. We can find such series for rye, herrings and salt (which is bedevilled by questions of different qualities); on the other hand we lack comparable series of prices for raw materials, hides, skins and textiles.

Occasionally light may fall on the problem from another quarter. R. W. K. Hinton quotes a calculation made by John Ramsden, merchant of Hull,[21] concerning cloth price in 1621 or 1622:

'the price of one kersey in Hull	30 s.
merchant's own costs	7 s.
price of one kersey in Poland (i. e. in Danzig)	33 s. 9 d.
the loss	3 s. 3 d.'

'A few years ago', according to John Ramsden, he received 47 s. 3 d. for one kersey. His gain must have been less than 10 s. 3 d., because in a boom year English prices and costs *ad valorem* (duty inclusive) were also higher. Ramsden was eager to stress the depression of trade, so he probably traced a

[20] J. Pelc, *Ceny w Gdańsku w XVI i XVII wieku* (Lwów, 1937); N. W. Posthumus, *Inquiry into the History of Prices in Holland*, vol. I, (Leiden, 1943).

[21] R. W. K. Hinton, *The Eastland Trade and the Common Weal in the Seventeenth Century* (Cambridge, 1959), pp. 17 f.

rosy picture of earlier times and might have overestimated the price formerly received for the cloth. Assuming that the figure of 30 s. also represents the former price, then gross profit in earlier years would have been less than 57.5 per cent, the net profit less than 34.2 per cent. If one rixdollar equalled 4 s. 6 d., the price of a kersey in Poland (i. e. in Danzig or possibly Elbing) in 1621 would be about $7^1/_2$ rixdollars, in England $6^2/_3$ rixdollars. This is quite reasonable. It seems that the trade depression of 1620–21 affected the quantities of English cloths exported to the Baltic countries much more severely than prices. The 6.7 rixdollars derived from Ramsden's account corresponds very well to declared prices of kersey in the STR. In good years, then, there would be about 50 per cent difference in price between English and Polish ports, $^2/_5$ of which would consist of freight costs and duties, and about $^3/_5$ in merchant's profits. The merchant's own marketing costs, other than freight, would add 23.2 per cent to the initial purchase price, so another 20 per cent may be reckoned as freight costs. Of course, these are only estimates. In depression years mercantile profits obviously fell dramatically; if the differential in price became no more than, say, 12.5 per cent, merchants might well lose. We may suppose, as a working hypothesis, that the movements of price differentials in the cloth trade fluctuated roughly similarly to those in the corn trade; sixteenth-century merchants and later mercantilists were aware of a close interdependence between both streams of commodities. One may well ask whether the high elasticity of demand for relatively costly goods like cloth[22] created exceptionally high fluctuations of prices and profits. The STR provides the best evidence and indicates the most exact answer.

Let us now turn to mass-consumption goods like herrings and salt. A comparison of herring prices in Amsterdam (Mathias herring) and in Danzig suggests that the price differential would usually be about 25 per cent. Caution is necessary here because Posthumus also quotes a more expensive quality of herrings (full herring), and if one took this as the basis of comparison, average differentials would be much lower.[23] Prices of salt fluctuated in a different manner. There appears to have been a slight negative correlation between prices and quantities of imported salt.[24] In some years prices in Danzig were actually lower than those in Amsterdam, and in general the difference of prices between the two ports was small.

[22] B. E. Supple, *Commercial Crisis and Change in England 1600–1642* (Cambridge, 1959), pp. 73 f.; Hinton, *op. cit.*, pp. 12 ff.

[23] Posthumus, *op. cit.*, Nos. 44, 45.

[24] Prices and quantities of imported salt for nine sample years between 1565 and 1646 give a clear inverse correlation. But if one examines the full population one can observe such a correlation only for years of extremely high and extremely low imports. It is a risky business to reason from sample years.

These examples and theoretical considerations of elasticity of supply suggest that fluctuations in both profit and freight costs were large. In general, freight costs amounted to around 20 per cent and mercantile profits to around 25 per cent (45 per cent in all) of the f. o. b. price of imported goods.[25]

So far as export prices are concerned, the increase between Baltic and the North Sea ports is less important for our argument here, because Polish, i. e. Danzig, navigation was very weak. Potash in our sample years used to fetch at Amsterdam on average 168 per cent of the Danzig price. For rye there is clearly a relationship between domestic Danzig price and the size of price-increases in foreign markets. In the years of the lowest prices in Danzig the differential (Amsterdam price less Danzig price) was about 60 per cent above Danzig price; in the dearest years only 37 per cent; the mean differential for the forty years discussed was 49 per cent of the Danzig price.[26] There was also some correlation between the price differential and the fluctuations in the volume of grain exported from the Baltic during the first half of the seventeenth century.[27]

Prices estimated on the basis of the notes in the STT relate to goods carried on ships of the same nationality. This means that for example English goods in Dutch bottoms are disregarded. The sample is thus reduced but not necessarily distorted, as English prices did not in fact show any correlation with a ship's colours. It would, however, be otherwise if Dutch goods had been taken into consideration. Dutch merchants knew how to get Polish goods at lower prices. We need therefore to make a significant correction: the value of Polish corn exports should be reduced by a few per cent, as they were heavily controlled by the Dutch. We must also remember that a large part of the corn exported in English bottoms was bought in Elbing, where it was usually a little dearer than in Danzig.

A similar situation may also be expected to have ruled for the import trade. English cloth and colonial goods seem to have been relatively dear. The course of the struggle for cloth markets between English and Dutch merchants shows clearly how difficult it was for the English to compete with the Dutch. The

[25] Maczak, 'The Sound Toll Accounts and the Balance of English Eastland Trade', p. 105.
[26] Maczak, 'Sundzollregister als eine preisgeschichtliche Quelle'. We examined the period 1597–1647, omitting some years which lacked information. 'Low' prices are defined as 30 rds. for one last, 'high' as over 40 rds. For extreme cases the differences are very clear. When prices did not exceed 25 rds., the surplus was 66 per cent, when they exceeded 50 rds. it was only 25 per cent. If we depended only on sample years from STT, we would get a false figure, only 38 per cent. See Note 20. We are indebted to Professor Svend Ellehøj, Copenhagen, who generously allowed us to use his notes on corn prices from STR.
[27] M. Hroch, J. Petráň, 'Europejska gospodarka i polityka XVI i XVII wieku: kryzys czy regres?' *Przeglad Historyczny* LV (1964), p. 5 n. 16.

embargo on the export of precious metals, so passionately denounced by Thomas Mun, does not explain all the problems of English trade. We can check this partly by examining the prices of textiles exported in 1625.[28] Among over 31,000 pieces of textiles (not only woollen cloth) imported to the Eastland in Dutch ships, almost 23,000 were made up of *thirumtej*. One finds *thirumtej* among French goods, and hence one can estimate its average price. For 324 *thirumtejs* the average price is 4.73 rixdollars, and if one includes a cargo of mixed *thirumtej* and *camelot* (an additional 1662 pieces) it is 4.75 rixdollars. This average price is much lower than that of cloths in English bottoms, which is 11.6 rixdollars. A similar situation arose in 1595 when kerseys dominated in Dutch bottoms (1019 kerseys out of 1337 cloths in all). Kersey was a cheap sort of English cloth: the mean price for kerseys was 8.2 rixdollars but the mean price for all cloths was 21.8. For the remaining years, however, one cannot make similar estimates. As the share of the Dutch in the Baltic import of textiles increased, and as their cloth was cheaper than the English, we must assume that our calculations tend to overestimate the true value of Polish cloth imports.

IV

Are the sample years which we have taken from the STT reasonably representative? Aksel E. Christensen indicated from a lastage index alone that it would be better to adopt other years than those ending with 5 (i. e. 1565, 1575, 1585, etc.).[29] We are, however, interested only in the overall size of the Polish sea trade and so we can use a variety of checks on the usefulness of the sample years. We lack price quotations for each year, but we can measure the volume of those goods which roughly determined the scale of the turnover, i. e. rye and wheat exports. Cloth dominated imports, but as we do not know the volume of Polish cloth imports year after year, we must avail ourselves of total imports to the Baltic. The last check is the value of rye exported from Polish harbours.

Deviations from the five-year average (see Table 15 below) are clear for rye and wheat in the middle sample years. But equally, by choosing these sample years we lose two extreme periods, the evident boom of 1618–1622 and the catastrophic slump of 1628–1632. The first embraces years of very high supply of corn and the beginning of a new and very effective customs control. The second is also a peculiar period, influenced by war in Prussia,

[28] STT, vol. II A, p. 176, 372.
[29] Christensen, *Dutch Trade*, Diagram XIV.

early years of reconstruction, and of additional impositions when the Swedes were able to levy their own high customs (*licenten*) on Polish trade off Danzig. The sample years 1615, 1625 and 1635 do not reveal these wide fluctuations, although they reflect fairly enough the average in their own five-year periods. Figures for textiles in the sample years are roughly in line with the fluctuations, though they also tend to understate them (see 1625, 1635, 1646). But, surprisingly, when we consider the value of rye, we see that the price in only one out of nine sample years exceeds its five-year average. 1625 is nearest to its quinquennial average, but this is due to the fact that 1627 is missing from the quinquennium, the year when Prussian harbours were blocked (so the mean figure is over-estimated). The use of some sample years like 1585 or 1646 is simply disastrous. Sharp fluctuations were the norm, an exaggerated reflection of changing harvest yields. The value of exported corn was a determinant of Polish demand for foreign luxury goods, including cloth.

How large are the gaps in our statistics? It is clear that we cannot determine them exactly. The assortment of goods was growing all the time. In imports, as we said, we have been obliged to omit a number of generally unimportant classes of goods—trousers and stockings, textile raw materials and half-finished goods (wool, cotton, silk, yarn) minerals, hops, oil, olive oil, starch, cheese, soap, glue, ivory, glass, paper, haberdashery, iron, steel, tin, stones and grains. Most of these were imported to the Eastland by Dutch merchants. What was the trend of their value? For most of them the years 1625, 1635 and 1646 showed a great increase in volume, which cannot be explained solely by a previous inaccuracy in the source. Take minerals, for example: in 1565 these amounted to only 2,000 lbs, and later they almost disappeared; but in 1625 they reached 58,000 lbs, in 1635, 13,000 lbs, in 1646, 15,000 lbs. Stockings and trousers grew from nothing to 13,600 in 1646. Textile raw materials and half-finished goods grew from about 20 lbs to 10,500 lbs in 1646. Starch grew from one aume to 84 thousand, glue from two lbs to 25,000 lbs in 1646, paper from 220 reams to four thousand in 1655. Other goods grew a little less, others oscillated. Ivory, which had appeared for the first time in 1595 (1,200 lbs), in 1646 reached 5,412 lbs. We do not know its price. After adding up every calculable item we were able to reckon for 1565 an additional 4,000 rixdollars in imports, and 173,000 rixdollars in exports. For 1635 the respective figures are 64,000 and 249,000 rixdollars, and for 1646, 78,000 and 235,000 rixdollars. The proportions for exports and imports are roughly similar to these in our tables. There remained, however, further serious gaps: e. g. in 1646 among exports there were barley, flour, grits (together over 4,000 lasts in volume, worth in Danzig about 40,000 rixdollars), masts, dyestuffs, minerals; among the imports such colonial goods as were not reckoned in lbs—metals, soap, greases, and many small items. It seems that volumes were more important than price levels in determining the balance of trade. The reduction of the export trade surplus was due partly to an enormous increase in the import of colonial goods, but above all to expanded imports of cloth.

V

There is a tremendous difference between trends in exports and trends in imports. Taking 1565 as 100 (customs declarations in 1565 were still fairly accurate), let us compare the sample years 1625, 1635, 1646. The general export index reaches 118, import 489, whereas the export surplus index is only 27. At the same time the corn export index is 121, whereas the textiles import index is 900 and the index for colonial goods (where the basis in 1565 was very low) exceeds even that figure (Tables 10 and 12 below).

As things now stand the picture would not be changed seriously either by amendments dictated by the obvious inaccuracies of our source between 1569 and the customs reform of 1618, or by making allowance for the earnings and profits of Danzig ships and merchants. Even this last item, however, can be estimated. If imports in Danzig and Elbing ships in 1646 reached 76,500 (say 80,000) rixdollars we may estimate the value of exports in Polish bottoms at roughly 120,000 rixdollars, assuming the proportion of imports to exports is similar to that in ships of other colours; following earlier calculations we may also estimate a further 45 per cent, i. e. 54,000 rixdollars, for profit and freight. In all, the favourable balance on this would reach 90,000 to 100,000 rixdollars.

A lot has been written about the export of raw materials and semi-finished goods. Our tables broadly confirm the importance of these trends. Although they excited the curiosity of foreign visitors, notably Italians, and caused deep concern to Polish mercantilists, they were certainly a very lucrative branch of exports, perhaps the most lucrative. Timber (clapholt and wainscots) rose in price spectacularly, as did pitch and, in some years, tar and ashes. It may be argued that price incentives worked thus against the vital long-term interests of the Polish economy, if these lay in the direction of developing home manufactures. The picture was complicated, however, by a shortage of timber in some areas. The centre of Eastland timber exports shifted from Danzig to Königsberg in East Prussia. In 1598 an English traveller, Peter Mundy, did not even mention timber in Danzig and Elbing, whereas he was astonished at the sight of the Königsberg timberyards.[30]

---

[30] *The Travels of Peter Mundy in Europe and Asia 1608–1667*, ed. Sir Richard Carnac Temple, vol. IV, (London, 1925), p. 91: 'Here is the greatest trade For oake tymber, that

With wool the opposite was the case. Although its part in the export trade as a whole was not very impressive, at its peak in the 1640s about 450 metric tons yearly were shipped out. This amounted to about 600,000 fleeces, a third or a quarter of the whole wool output of the exporting hinterland. It was most probably due to this export boom that the wool price index rose in relation to rye by about a quarter during the 80 years discussed here.[31]

Changes in industrial exports were of relatively minor importance though they increased slightly over the whole period. Export of *osmund* iron declined, and after the Polish-Swedish war of 1626–1629, vanished, but only to give way to the more fully-processed export of bar iron and even steel. There was a clear rise in textile exports, foreshadowing a further considerable increase of linens in the second half of the seventeenth century. These phenomena deserve further research, though they are unlikely to reflect changes in the economy far beyond the ports. Iron and steel were produced near the ports themselves, linen was manufactured in Danzig or brought from Silesia, a province then belonging to the Habsburg dominions.

One may conclude that the favourable balance of Polish sea trade with the West was reduced in the first half of the seventeenth century, but that it still remained mostly in surplus (Table 16 below). Violent fluctuations seem typical. This surplus agrees with the apparent total balance of Baltic trade, as reflected by the Sound lastage (after making allowance for freight costs and profits). This concurrence is by no means accidental, because Danzig engrossed the lion's share of the Baltic trade and was the chief exporter of grain. It is important, nevertheless, to remember the substantial differences between the individual Polish ports. As long as the English Eastland Company retained its staple at Elbing the great majority of cloths were brought there, and these substantially exceeded the value of local exports. We have touched on this problem elsewhere in a study of the balance of English trade with the Baltic.[32] Here it suffices to mention that in our sample years Elbing nevertheless surpassed Danzig in iron exports in 1585 and 1605, in flax in 1575 and in 1625 and in wool and linen in 1595 and 1605 (Tables 1 og 2 below). These

I thinck is in all those Countries, viz., beames, wainescott, Clapboard, etts. For there lay such a Number off piles with them on both sides of the River comming uppe to the Citty etts. and other parts adjoyning, thatt I conceave, were they laid together, itt would take uppe a square off Neare 1/2 of an English Mile ... and upon 15 or 16 Foote high, which is an incredible quantity.'

[31] A. Mączak, 'Produzione e commercio della lana nell' Europa centro-orientale dal XIV al XVII secolo, *Studi Storici*, XI: 1 (1970), p. 24 (erratum to be corrected: 1st line, third column—6 in stead of 8). It should be observed that during the seventeenth and eighteenth centuries Polish wool fell at the Amsterdam Mart in comparison with Castillian wool; *ibid.*, p. 25, Table 3.

[32] Mączak, 'The Sound Toll Accounts and the Balance of English Eastland Trade'.

were all goods independent of the Vistula rafting, but still sought for by
the English importers. In the earlier article we concluded that the English
trade balance with the Eastland also remained definitely in surplus. Who was
then the payer, if the Polish ports—and one important Western partner—
England—all enjoyed surpluses? Even without complete data (i. e. full values
of goods exchanged) the debtor is easy to find. The volume of textiles carried
in English ships was 47.5 times greater than that carried in Dutch ships for
1565, 1575 and 1585 on average. For rye the relation was inverse: 60.4 lasts
on Dutch ships for every one on English. This contrast declined steadily; in
our last three sample years, 1625, 1635 and 1646 one gets 1.1:1 for textiles
and 1:17.3 for rye.[33] But throughout, these immense exports from the Baltic
put the Dutch trade balance heavily in deficit.

VI

Our estimates of the trade balance may be compared with some earlier ones.
The earliest were attempted at the very beginning of the seventeenth century,
while modern research has considered the problem from the late fifteenth
century on. Henryk Samsonowicz described Danzig's trade balance between
1460 and 1492 as coming into surplus (Table 18 below). Our experience
would suggest the need for greater caution when there are figures for four
individual years only, but it is highly probable that in the first twenty years
of the sixteenth century surpluses became the rule. The following half-century
then saw the surpluses growing enormously thanks to the increase in corn supply.[34] For the 1580s we have Roman Rybarski's estimates of total Polish
land and sea exports, based on customs records destroyed by fire in 1944.[35]

Some of the contemporary seventeenth-century estimates are also valuable.
Wojciech Gostkowski expressed the view of a well-informed specialist, relating
to Danzig and Elbing (see Table 19 b below). The precise year to which his
calculations refer remain uncertain, so we give two exchange rates of the Polish
zloty (florin, florenus polonicalis) with the rixdollar, for 1620 and for 1621.
Marshall Mikolaj Wolski's estimates are known through the account of Jan
Grodwagner, one of the best Polish mercantilist writers of his time (see Table
19 c below). He tells us that the balance was estimated more than ten years

---

[33] Calculated from STT, vol. II A.

[34] See also S. Hoszowski, 'The Polish Baltic Trade in the 15th–18th Centuries', *Poland
at the XIth International Congress of Historical Sciences in Stockholm* (Warsaw, 1960), pp.
121–125.

[35] R. Rybarski, *Handel i polityka handlowa Polski w stulecin XVI*, vol. I, (Warszawa, 1958),
p. 247 f.

before the book appeared in 1630. The exports of Danzig and Königsberg were estimated at 3.5 million Polish ducats in gold money, the imports at 2.5 million, leaving a balance of 1.5 million. Together with other scholars we suppose that the last figure is a printer's or author's mistake and so we correct it to one million. In a study of the money market in the early seventeenth century Zdzisław Sadowski put forward a hypothesis that from the last years of the sixteenth century the surplus of Polish trade began to dwindle away because of rising import prices.[36] Sadowski does not exclude the possibility that the total Polish trade balance actually fell into deficit.

Lastly Miss Maria Bogucka estimated the balance of trade of Danzig using what is probably the most reliable source, the *Pfahlgeld* registers between 1634 and 1649. For some of the ten individual years discussed she had the full records available, for others only one or two out of the three sets of registers originally kept, but since each of the three *Pfahlherren* was on duty every third week, each register gives fairly accurately one-third of the yearly turnover of goods and the gaps may be readily filled. Miss Bogucka's figures provide an important corrective to the earlier and very inaccurate estimates of Detlef Krannhals.[37]

Table 19 below brings all this data together revalued in rixdollars. It should help us to check our own estimates. Let us notice first that contemporary estimates seem to be confirmed in the light of Miss Bogucka's figures though perhaps Gostkowski has given inflated figures for the period of low corn exports and monetary crisis.

The only year for which we can compare the results of various methods is 1646. Figures from Table 19 d should be higher than these from Table 16, because in the latter Danzig's trade with other Eastland ports and with Scandinavian harbours has been omitted. For Danzig exports (without Elbing) we have got a figure virtually equalling imports. We should complete both by adding about 235,000 rixdollars omitted from exports and 78,000 rixdollars omitted from imports. The gap between the export figures in the two tables then becomes rather narrow: 2,941,000 rixdollars compared with 2,072,000 rixdollars + 235,000 rixdollars + some other inestimable goods. We are left with some 600,000 rixdollars, or rather over 20 per cent of exports, which seems a reasonable share for Danzig's Baltic trade. A comparison of imports

---

[36] Sadowski, *op. cit.*, p. 77.

[37] Maria Bogucka 'Handel baltycki a bilans handlowy Polski w pierwszej polowie XVII wisku', *Przeglad Historyczny*, LIX (1968); D. Krannhals, *Danzig und der Weichselhandel in seiner Blütezeit vom 16. zum 17. Jahrhundert* (Leipzig, 1942), pp. 73 f. Krannhals' figures do not exceed two-thirds of those calculated on the source material by Miss Bogucka. Recently Dr. C. Biernat has maintained that customs declarations do not form a balanced distribution on which lacking data can be estimated, review in print in *Zapiski Historyczne*, 1971 : 2, p. 137.

gives 2,488,000 rixdollars, compared with 2,085,000 rixdollars + 78,000 rix-dollars + some odd thousands, in all about 300,000 rixdollars for internal Baltic trade, or only 12 per cent of imports. Local trade thus seems to provide a relatively larger surplus than that beyond the Sound. With more material available, one could investigate both series of figures broken down by commodities.

Other years than 1646 were more prosperous for Danzig and the figures we have got for our sample years seem at first sight to be too small. But let us remember that the samples chosen for the STT were generally poor. We have checked relationships between the total values of Danzig exports with their chief determinant, the corn trade (see Diagram 2 below): the correlation is high and provides significant evidence for the reliability of the figures in the STT.

VII

Let us now consider the Eastland terms of trade. Much has been written about them, mostly stressing the impact of relative prices on the agricultural system of east-central Europe, but we cannot be sure if in fact in the sixteenth century a greater increase in corn prices than those of industrial goods fostered the increase of grain production by the serf-labour manor, as Stanislaw Hoszowski states.[38] We do not know to what degree the terms of trade could and did influence a lord's decision. This is for us, however, only a secondary question. We are more directly interested in the terms of trade themselves as a factor in the trade balance. Z. Sadowski suggests that a change occurred from the end of the sixteenth century—a relative decrease of agricultural prices analogous to the phenomenon observed by Wilhelm Abel for Germany in the period 1600–1620 and for other Western countries at a later period.[39] Our material enables us to estimate the terms of trade on the basis of the volume of almost all the goods shipped. The only serious handicap is that we can only do it for the sample years. The strengths and weaknesses of our method are evident from what follows.

Total exports and imports are calculated at constant prices, i. e. the average of the three sample years 1565, 1575 and 1585. Then the exports and imports are revalued at current prices × 100, and the sum divided by their values at constant prices. The result will be the outcome of varying price tendencies.[40]

[38] S. Hoszowski in *Historia Polski*, vol. I, 2 (Warsaw, 1958), p. 137.

[39] Sadowski, *op. cit.*, p. 73; W. Abel, *Agrarkrisen und Agrarkonjunktur in Mitteleuropa vom 13. bis 19. Jahrhundert* (Berlin, 1955), pp. 72 f.

[40] The formula runs as follows $\dfrac{100 \times \text{value in current prices}}{\text{value in constant prices}}$. Much depends here on

If it exceeds 100, we witness a general rise in prices: if it does not, it means that prices fell. A simple comparison of indices gives the terms of trade. We can also disaggregate to express individual commodity price trends. Clearly, much depends on the natures of the sample years 1565, 1575 and 1585. A coincidence of high prices and small quantities may heavily distort the result: an average of only three sample years may not give a very firm base.

What were the comparative movements of the Polish and East Prussian terms of trade? Both countries exported and imported similar goods, whose value has been calculated here on the basis of similar average prices. But the relative quantities of the various goods differed considerably in the two areas, and these movements cause important changes in our accounts. As previously stated, inflation was most marked for just those classes of goods like timber which were losing their importance at Danzig but increasing at Königsberg. It was least marked for industrial goods—linen and metals. This agrees with the supposition that in the first half of the seventeenth century prices in Poland were relatively unfavourable for the development of industry. Among imported goods the decisive factor was a relative and even absolute decrease in textile prices, which constituted one half of the total imports, and also in colonial goods, which grew rapidly in importance. Even the relatively high prices of salt and herrings could not redress the balance. In general the thesis of a relative decrease of food prices after 1600 cannot be confirmed. Most important goods— corn, salt and herrings—grew dearer in relation to textiles.

These observations, of course, do not enable us to draw any conclusion about the price structure of the total Polish trade, by land as well as by sea. We lack particulars of hundreds of thousands of knives, scythes and sickles, imported from Steiermark; we lack prices of leather and hides sent in bulk to Leipzig; we cannot appreciate the part played by diverse luxury goods carried overland. The terms of the sea trade alone may have had a crucial importance.

the arithmetical method. The apparently simplest method—to multiply the average price of a class of goods (for 1595, 1615 and 1625 etc.) by the average quantity—proves inadequate. For instance

> 1000 pieces of a commodity at 10 rixdollars in one year,
> 500 pieces   at 20 rixdollars in the second,
> 300 pieces   at 30 rixdollars in the third one.

Using averages one multiplies 600 pieces by 20 dollars and gets 12,000. The other method, of first discussing every year separately, brings 10,000, 10,000 and 9,000, on the average 9,667 dollars. The results of both methods vary in both directions but the second method seems more appropriate. Anyway, yearly fluctuations of prices and goods were so great, that any change of sample must bring about important differences. The differences between Polish and East Prussian terms of trade, as shown in Table 20 below, seem to a high degree due to that factor of statistical technique.

We may recall the vital role attributed to the Danzig trade by seventeenth-century Polish economic thinkers, who pointed out that the bulk of native Polish exports were sent by sea. Most of the furs and hides exported over the Western frontier had come to Poland from Muscovy and Lithuania, the last since 1569 in close union with Poland.

Nevertheless, important or even decisive as it may have been, we must again stress that a favourable balance on sea trade did not mean that the total trade of the country was in surplus. We have mentioned the import of iron tools. Still more important was the import of Silesian, Lusatian, Moravian and Czech textiles. For 1582–1586 Rybarski estimated the import of such coarse or common cloths at 100,000 a year.[41] Although direct proofs of a negative balance are available only for the Moldavian (i. e. Turkish) trade,[42] it seems highly probable that large quantities of precious metals imported through Danzig flowed out again on the land routes. The decline in the export surplus on the sea trade probably meant a sharp overall deficit on the total balance of the country at the beginning of the seventeenth century. But what meaning can the expression 'the country' have in this context?

Leaving aside Lithuania (a vast region of a peculiar and backward economy), Poland was badly integrated; yet from the middle of the sixteenth century onwards one can see deep changes taking place in the corn-exporting areas. Even very distant regions, five or six hundred kilometers from the Vistula estuary and Danzig, began to send corn down the rivers. If one takes into consideration the role played by grain in the total goods supply both on local markets and in exports, it is clear that changes in the quantities and directions of gold and silver flows from overseas were of great importance. Changes in the terms of trade and other factors evidently did affect large estate owners.[43] Did they influence the consolidation of landed property? Did they give rise to major changes in the Polish political system? Did they advance oligarchy and bury the blooming sixteenth-century Polish noble democracy? The borderlands of economic and constitutional history remain to be explored.

[41] Rybarski, *op. cit.*, vol. I, p. 169.
[42] Z. Switalski, 'Clo od wywozu pieniedzy wywozonych za granice Rzeczypospolitej w latach 1598–1659, *Przeglad Historyczny*, LI (1960), 24–30.
[43] W. Kula, *Théorie économique du système féodal. Pour un modèle de l'économie polonaise 16–18 siècles*, (Paris—La Haye, 1970); Sadowski, *op. cit.*

I

STATISTICAL APPENDIX

Contents

I

KEY

–	no data entered in the source
0	data exist, but the figure is too small to be noted
.	no material available
×	the panel must remain empty because of the construction of the table

Diagram 1

Value of Rye Exported through the Sound from Polish Ports, 1557–1647. 5-year averages (the year 1645 omitted)

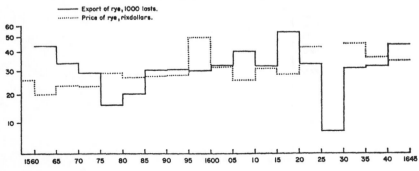

Export of rye, 1000 lasts.
Price of rye, rixdollars.

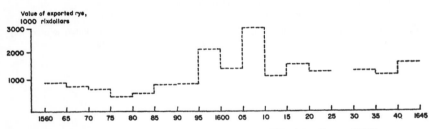

Value of exported rye, 1000 rixdollars

Source: STR supplemented by J. Pelc, *Ceny w Gdansku w XVI wieku* (Lwow, 1937).

Diagram 2

*Value of Rye Exported through the Sound Compared with Total Danzig Exports, 1640–49
(semi logarithmical scale).*

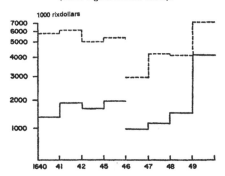

———— Value of rye exported from Danzig and Elbing through the Sound.
– – – – Total Value of Danzig exports according to local custom registers.

Source: STT vol. II A and M. Bogucka, 'Handel bałtycki a bilans handlowy Polski w pierwszej
polowie XVII wieku', *Przegląd Historyczny,* LIX (1968), p. 248.

Table 1

Danzig Exports in Selected Years

Goods	Units of Measure	1565	1575	1585	1595	1605	1615	1625	1635	1646
Rye	1000 lasts	40.5	23.6	13.0	29.1	35.1	31.4	19.2	39.1	32.3
Wheat	1000 lasts	4.1	1.7	0.9	2.1	1.7	1.1	3.1	9.0	11.1
Wainscots	1 hundred	2780	1030	460	520	140	630	70	30	60
Clapholt	1 hundred	570	530	540	1120	520	840	80	50	40
Ashes	1000 lasts	8.2	3.6	2.0	2.6	4.0	3.5	0.4	1.0	0.6
Pitch	1000 lasts	1.3	0.8	2.8	3.9	1.3	1.4	0.5	0.3	0.2
Tar	1000 lasts	1.3	2.3	0.8	0.8	0.7	0.6	0.3	0.2	0.7
Potash	1000 shippounds	–	–	–	–	1.7	0.7	10.8	16.1	13.3
Flax	1000 lasts	1.8	0.8	0.0	0.0	0.1	0.0	0.2	0.2	0.7
Flax	1000 shippounds	0.5	0.7	0.5	0.5	0.2	0.5	1.0	0.3	0.2
Hemp	1 last	0	139	52	52	41	57	22	301	296
Hemp	1 shippound	1321	1064	123	625	65	140	624	298	288
Wool	1 shippound	–	–	0	0	80	40	1030	680	2050
Textiles	1000 pieces	1.4	3.1	0.0	0.1	0.8	–	0.3	9.3	10.6
Osmund iron	1 last	110	110	60	30	10	10	40	0	–
Bar-iron	1000 shippounds	2.9	1.7	1.2	2.0	2.1	0.9	2.5	0.1	5.4
Steel	1000 cwt.	–	–	–	0	–	–	0	0.2	2.1
Hides and Skins	1000 deg.	1.0	0.1	0.1	0.0	1.2	0.2	0.2	4.2	3.8
Hides and Skins	1000 pieces	0.7	–	–	3.0	2.5	–	0.0	3.6	11.7

Source: STT, vol. II A.

Table 2

Elbing Exports in Selected Years

Goods	Units of Measure	1565	1575	1585	1595	1605	1615	1625	1635	1646
Rye	1000 lasts	0.7	0.1	0.5	0.1	0.6	2.0	0.4	0.1	0.5
Wheat	1000 lasts	0.4	0.0	0.1	0.8	0.1	0.5	0.1	0.3	0.6
Wainscots	1 hundred	10	0	0	0	10	0	0	–	–
Clapholt	1 hundred	0	0	30	10	0	10	0	–	10
Ashes	1000 lasts	0	–	0.9	0.2	0.1	0.1	–	0.0	0.0
Pitch	1000 lasts	–	–	1.2	1.0	0.3	0.7	0.2	0.1	–
Tar	1000 lasts	0.0	–	0.7	0.2	0.1	0.0	–	–	–
Potash	1000 shippounds	–	–	–	–	0.0	0.1	0.7	–	0.0
Flax	1000 lasts	–	1.0	1.3	1.2	1.1	0.4	0.7	0.0	0.4
Flax	1000 shippounds	–	0.0	0.3	0.0	1.6	–	0.4	–	–
Hemp	1 last	–	–	231	105	83	126	94	0	–
Hemp	1 shippound	–	–	0	–	–	–	–	–	–
Wool	1 shippound	–	–	–	160	220	140	30	–	–
Textiles	1000 pieces	0.1	0.1	0.0	2.1	1.7	0.9	0.3	0.0	–
Bar-iron	1000 shippounds	0.0	–	2.3	1.9	3.4	0.4	0.5	–	0.2
Hides and Skins	1000 deg.	–	–	0.2	–	–	0.1	–	–	0.0
Hides and Skins	1000 pieces	–	–	–	–	1.1	–	–	–	–

Note: *Osmund* iron was not re-exported from Elbing.
Source: STT, vol. II A.

Table 3

Danzig Imports in Western Bottoms. Selected Years

Goods	Units	1565	1575	1585	1595	1605	1615	1625	1635	1646
Salt	1000 lasts	7.0	1.5	4.2	5.4	5.6	5.0	5.6	2.6	2.9
Herrings	1000 lasts	2.4	0.3	1.6	2.8	3.5	3.2	5.7	3.2	5.1
Rhine Wine	1000 aumes	4.1	1.8	2.3	1.8	4.3	2.1	2.3	0.9	2.2
Other Wines	1000 pipes	0.9	0.4	1.6	3.2	5.2	1.8	4.4	1.7	2.7
Wines in all	1000 aumes	6.8	3.0	7.1	11.4	19.9	7.5	15.5	6.0	10.3
'Colonial Goods'	1000 lbs.	47	30	16	61	215	44	78	1732	875
Textiles	1000 pieces	5.3	8.3	0.6	1.5	6.1	6.8	31.4	38.7	33.6
Hides and Skins	1000 pieces	990	854	131	137	229	237	165	756	187
Leather	1000 pieces	21	19	11	2	7	10	22	65	10

Source: STT, vol. II A, Table 3 b.

Table 4

Elbing Imports in Western Bottoms. Selected Years

Goods	Units	1565	1575	1585	1595	1605	1615	1625	1635	1646
Salt	1000 lasts	0.0	–	0.4	0.2	0.2	0.8	0.1	0.1	0.3
Herrings	1000 lasts	–	–	0.0	0.1	0.1	0.1	0.1	0.0	0.0
Rhine Wine	1000 aumes	0.5	–	0.0	–	–	0.2	–	0.0	–
Other Wines	1000 pipes	0.0	–	0.1	2.0	0.0	0.0	0.0	0.1	0.0
Wines in all	1000 aumes	0.5	–	0.3	6.0	0.0	0.2	0.0	0.3	0.0
'Colonial Goods'	1000 lbs.	–	–	5	19	–	1	1	30	13
Textiles	1000 pieces	0.0	–	19.1	17.6	24.2	21.3	27.1	0.5	2.3
Hides and Skins	1000 pieces	–	–	985	624	817	385	70	–	4
Leather	1000 pieces	–	–	40	5	32	49	30	–	–

Source: STT, vol. II A, Table 3 b.

Table 5

Imported Goods in Lübeck, Danzig-Elbing and Königsberg ships.
1565, 1635 and 1646

Goods	Units	1565			1635			1646		
		L	D – E	K	L	D – E	K	L	D – E	K
Salt	lasts	680	135	232	2727	300	–	1817	918	–
Herrings	lasts	5	95	–	96	4	–	130	277	--
Rhine Wine	aumes	–	–	–	–	–	–	449	–	–
Other Wines	pipes	9.5	37.5	–	510.5	152	–	415.5	985	–
'Colonial Goods'	lbs.	–	–	–	46370	29260	–	36150	68578	–
Textiles	pieces	–	136	–	83	508.5	–	520	192	–
Hides and Skins	pieces	–	5300	–	–	–	–	3432	–	–
Leather	pieces	–	–	–	300	–	–	–	–	–

Signature: L: Lübeck ships.   D – E: Danzig and Elbing ships.   K: Königsberg ships.
Source: STT, vol. II A, Tables 1 a and 1 b.

Table 6

Danzig Imports in Danzig Bottoms. Selected Years

Goods	Units	1565	1575	1585	1595	1605	1615	1625	1635	1646
Salt	1000 lasts	0.1	1.9	1.2	1.4	1.6	0.1	1.0	0.3	1.0a
Herrings	1000 lasts	0.1	0.0	0.6	0.0	–	–	–	0.0	0.3
Rhine Wine	1000 aumes	–	–	–	–	–	–	–	–	–
Other Wines	1000 pipes	–	0.0	–	0.2	0.9	0.3	0.1	0.2	1.0b
'Colonial Goods'	1000 lbs.	–	–	0	–	147	–	1	29	69
Textiles	1000 pieces	0.1	0.0	0.0	0.1	0.0	0.1	–	0.5	0.2
Hides and Skins	1000 pieces	5.3	12.0	4.3	66.0	6.6	24.6	–	–	–
Leather	1000 pieces	–	–	–	–	–	–	–	–	–

a Included 0.1 in Elbing Bottoms.
b Included 0.2 in Elbing Bottoms.
Source: STT, vol. II A Table 1 b.

Table 7

Price Indexes for Textiles and 'Colonial Goods'. Selected Years

	Year	Textiles				'Colonial Goods'			
		Average price	*Klæde*	Kerseys	Single Dozens	Average price	Sugar	Rice	Pepper
Average price for one piece or one pound in Rixdollars	1565	14.0	20.7	5.5	8.5	0.57	0.22	0.04	0.50
Indexes 1565 = 100	1565	100	100	100	100	100	100	100	100
	1575	114	108	125	166	503	142	150	.
	1585	132	162	151	113	241	120	125	.
	1595	154	162	149	118	256	104	.	114
	1605	136	185	140	142	91	.	150	50
	1615	112	197	149	146	212	.	.	58
	1625	124	175	122	132	.	.	.	.
	1635	104	182	147	166	189	.	.	.
	1646	154	211	187	.	202	.	.	.

Source: STT, vol. II A, Table 1 b, 2, notes.

Table 8

Prices of Exported Goods in Rixdollars. Selected Years

Goods	Units	1565	1575	1585	1595	1605	1615	1625	1635	1646
Rye	1 last	26.0	20.0	29.4	35.4	23.0	29.2	53.0	35.0	28.4
Wheat	1 last	[50.0]	45.0	45.0	55.0	56.3	45.0	65.0	59.0	50.4
Wainscots	1 hundred	25.0	21.4	36.3	44.6	42.6	54.5	73.1	100.8	108.1
Clapholt	1 hundred	37.6	36.5	70.2	95.3	97.0	101.0	140.6	205.7	199.0
Ashes	1 last	17.1	22.1	48.6	29.4	41.9	45.5	44.2	30.7	70.0
Pitch	1 last	15.2	13.9	10.7	15.9	15.1	18.9	25.2	41.8	42.2
Tar	1 last	15.0	12.0	8.9	17.4	20.3	21.4	19.0	26.8	14.5
Potash	1 shippound	–	–	–	–	–	10.7	7.6	12.6	9.7
Flax	1 last	55	73	98	70	94	85	64	96	96
Flax	1 shippound	8	16	15	13	18	21	14	16	17
Hemp	1 last	52.0	80.4	48.6	50.0	64.9	46.6	36.9	79.3	61.1
Hemp	1 shippound	7.1	15.6	7.7	8.0	12.1	9.6	8.8	17.5	9.5
Wool	1 shippound	–	–	–	[50.0]	53.0	40.7	47.1	33.0	86.0
Textiles	1 piece	[3.5]	3.5	3.4	2.6	3.4	1.9	2.6	2.4	2.7
Osmund iron	1 last	57.5	53.5	51.3	47.7	38.2	43.4	46.3	60.0	–
Bar-Iron	1 shippound	5.9	6.2	6.1	6.0	5.7	6.1	8.0	5.1	6.4
Steel	1 cwt.	–	–	–	–	10.0	–	7.0	[6.0]	4.9
Hides and Skins	1 deg.	4.2	7.0	11.5	10.0	20.7	–	14.3	16.8	7.1
Hides and Skins	1 piece	1.5	–	–	6.0	[5.0]	–	–	1.9	[2.0]

Source: STT, vol. II A, notes to Table 1 b, 2.

Table 9

Prices of Imported Goods in Rixdollars. Selected Years

Goods	Units	1565	1575	1585	1595	1605	1615	1625	1635	1646
Salt	1 last	8.5	47.3	10.3	16.6	21.1	13.3	16.3	33.6	20.4
Herrings	1 last	22.0	23.8	20.0	43.3	50.1	49.0	46.7	44.8	55.4
Rhine Wine	1 aume	8.4	18.1	11.6	16.9	15.3	13.6	21.2	33.5	23.4
Other Wines	1 pipe	16.4	47.7	14.5	32.4	31.3	34.4	31.2	31.3	27.4
'Colonial Goods'	1000 lbs.	57	280	137	146	52	121	[110]	108	115
Textiles	1 piece	14.0	16.0	18.5	21.6	18.6	15.7	11.3	14.5	21.6
Hides and Skins	1000 pieces	23.0	26.9	26.2	25.9	27.1	21.1	36.3	27.9	38.6
Leather	1000 pieces	70.0	64.6	56.7	82.1	92.5	55.6	62.2	61.3	68.0

Source: STT, vol. II A, notes to Table 1 b, 2.

Table 10

Value of Danzig and Elbing Exports in 1000 Rixdollars. Selected Years

	1565	1575	1585	1595	1605	1615	1625	1635	1646
Rye	1091.2	474.0	396.9	1033.6	821.1	975.3	1038.8	1372.0	931.5
Wheat	225.0	76.5	45.0	159.5	101.3	72.0	208.0	548.7	589.6
Wainscots	69.8	22.0	16.7	23.2	6.4	34.4	5.1	3.0	6.5
Clapholt	21.4	19.4	40.0	107.7	50.4	85.8	11.2	10.3	10.0
Ashes	140.2	79.6	140.9	82.2	171.8	163.9	17.6	30.7	42.0
Pitch	19.8	11.1	42.8	77.9	24.1	39.8	17.6	16.7	8.4
Tar	19.5	27.6	13.3	17.4	16.2	12.8	5.7	5.4	10.1
Potash	–	–	–	–	–	8.6	87.4	202.9	129.0
Flax	103.0	144.0	139.5	90.5	145.2	44.5	80.0	24.0	109.0
Hemp	9.4	27.8	14.6	12.9	8.9	9.9	9.9	28.6	20.8
Wool	–	–	0.0	[8.0}	14.4	7.4	49.9	22.4	176.0
Textiles	[5.3]	11.2	0.0	7.4	8.5	1.8	1.6	22.4	28.6
Osmund Iron	6.3	5.9	3.1	1.4	0.4	0.4	1.8	0.0	–
Bar-Iron	17.1	10.6	21.6	23.4	31.3	7.9	24.0	0.5	35.8
Steel	–	–	–	0.0	–	–	0.8	[1.2]	[10.3]
Hides and Skins	5.2	0.7	1.2	0.0	42.8	–	2.9	77.3	50.4
In all	1733.2	910.4	875.6	1645.1	1442.8	1464.5	1561.5	2366.1	2158.0

Source: Tables 1, 2 and 8.

Table 11

Value of Elbing Exports in 1000 Rixdollars. Selected Years

	1565	1575	1585	1595	1605	1615	1625	1635	1646
Rye	18.2	2.0	14.7	3.5	13.8	58.4	21.2	3.5	14.2
Wheat	20.0	0.0	4.5	44.0	5.6	22.5	6.5	17.7	30.2
Wainscots	0.3	0.0	0.0	0.0	0.4	0.0	0.0	–	–
Clapholt	0.0	0.0	2.1	1.0	0.0	1.0	0.0	–	2.0
Ashes	0.0	–	43.7	5.8	4.2	4.6	–	0.0	0.0
Pitch	–	–	12.8	15.9	4.5	13.5	5.0	4.2	–
Tar	0.0	–	6.2	3.5	2.0	0.0	–	–	–
Potash	–	–	–	–	–	1.1	5.3	–	0.0
Flax	–	73.0	132.0	84.0	132.2	34.0	51.2	0.0	38.4
Hemp	–	–	11.2	5.3	5.4	5.9	3.5	–	–
Wood	–	–	–	[8.0]	10.2	5.7	1.4	–	..
Textiles	[0.4]	0.4	0.0	5.5	5.8	1.8	0.8	0.0	–
Osmund Iron	–	–	–	–	–	–	–	–	–
Bar-Iron	0.0	–	–	11.4	19.4	2.4	4.0	–	1.3
Steel	–	–	–	–	–	–	–	–	–
Hides and Skins	–	–	–	–	[5.7]	–	–	–	0.0
In all	38.9	75.4	227.2	187.9	209.0	150.9	98.9	25.4	86.1
Value of Danzig Exports	1694.3	835.0	648.4	1467.2	1233.8	1313.6	1462.6	2340.7	2071.9

Source: Tables 2 and 8.

Table 12

Value f. o. b. of Danzig and Elbing Imports in Western Ships.
In 1000 Rixdollars. Selected Years

Goods	1565	1575	1585	1595	1605	1615	1625	1635	1646
Salt	59.5	71.0	47.4	92.9	122.4	77.1	92.9	90.8	65.2
Herrings	52.8	7.1	32.0	125.5	180.4	161.7	290.9	143.4	282.5
Rhine Wine	38.6	32.6	26.7	30.4	65.8	31.3	48.8	30.2	51.5
Other Wines	14.8	19.1	24.7	168.5	162.8	61.9	137.3	56.3	74.0
'Colonial Goods'	2.7	8.4	2.9	11.7	11.2	5.4	8.7	190.3	102.0
Textiles	74.2	132.8	364.5	412.6	563.6	441.2	661.0	568.5	775.5
Hides and Skins	22.8	23.0	29.2	19.7	28.4	13.1	8.5	21.1	7.4
Leather	1.5	1.2	2.9	0.6	3.6	3.3	3.3	4.0	0.7
In all	266.9	295.2	530.3	861.9	1138.2	795.0	1251.4	1104.6	1358.8

Source: Tables 3, 4, and 9.

Table 13

Value f. o. b. of Elbing Imports in Western Ships in 1000 Rixdollars. Selected Years

Goods	1565	1575	1585	1595	1605	1615	1625	1635	1646[b]
Salt	0.0	–	4.1	3.3	4.2	10.6	1.6	3.4	6.1
Herrings	–	–	–	4.3	5.0	4.9	4.7	0.0	0.0
Rhine Wine	4.2	–	0.0	–	–	2.7	–	0.0	–
Other Wines	0.0	–	1.5	64.8	0.0	0.0	0.0	3.1	0.0
'Colonial Goods'	–	–	0.7	2.8	–	0.1	0.1	3.2	1.5
Textiles	0.0	–	353.4	380.2	450.1	334.4	306.2	7.3	49.7
Hides and Skins	–	–	25.8	16.2	22.2	8.1	2.5	–	0.2
Leather	–	–	2.3	0.4	3.0	2.7	1.9	–	..
In all	4.2	–	387.8	472.0	484.5	363.5	317.0	17.0	57.5
Value of Danzig Imports in Western Ships	262.7	295.2	142.5	389.9	653.7	431.5	934.4	1087.6	1301.3

Source: Tables 4 and 9.

Table 14

Value f. o. b. of Goods Imported in Danzig bottoms. In 1000 Rixdollars.
Selected Years

Goods	1565	1575	1585	1595	1605	1615	1625	1635	1646
Salt	0.9	89.9	12.4	23.2	33.8	1.3	16.3	10.1	20.4[a]
Herrings	2.2	0.0	12.0	0.0	–	–	–	0.0	16.5
Rhine Wine	–	–	–	–	–	–	–	–	–
Other Wines	–	0.0	–	6.5	28.2	10.3	3.1	6.2	27.4[b]
'Colonial Goods'	–	–	0	–	7.6	–	0.1	3.1	7.9
Textiles	1.4	0.0	0.0	2.2	0.0	1.6	–	7.3	4.3
Hides and Skins	0.1	0.3	0.1	1.7	0.2	0.5	–	–	–
Leather	–	–	–	–	–	–	–	–	–
In all	4.6	90.2	24.5	33.6	69.8	13.7	19.5	26.7	76.5

[a] Included 2.0 in Elbing Bottoms.
[b] Included 5.4 in Elbing Bottoms.
Source: Tables 6 and 9.

Table 15

Textiles and Rye
Sample Years in Relation to Five-Years' Averages

Periods	Import of Textiles		Export of Rye from Danzig		Value of Rye Exported from Danzig and Elbing	
	5-years' averages	Sample years	5-years' averages	Sample years	5-years' averages	Sample years
	1000 pieces	1000 pieces	1000 lasts	1000 lasts	1000 Rixdollars	1000 Rixdollars
1563–1567	10.4	7.7(74)	42.3	40.4(95)	921	840(91)
1568–1572	9.5	×	30.5	×	645	×
1573–1577	10.3	9.8(95)	31.2	23.6(76)	551	479(87)
1578–1582	9.4	×	16.0	×	448	×
1583–1587	26.6	22.0(83)	25.8	13.0(51)	777	378(49)
1588–1592	19.2	×	25.5	×	672	×
1593–1597	23.8	21.8(92)	33.5	29.1(87)	1269	1060(84)
1598–1602	46.4	×	36.5	×	1758	×
1603–1607	15.2	32.8(216)	35.0	35.1(100)	920	835(91)
1608–1612	44.8	×	36.0	×	1129	×
1613–1617	36.2	39.2(108)	33.6	31.4(93)	1050	886(84)
1618–1622	60.8	×	59.0	×	1641	×
1623–1626 1627–1632a	94.8	81.2(86)	23.8	19.2(81)	1125	1098(97)
1633–1637	90.1	72.5(81)	33.5	39.1(117)	1263	1372(109)
1638–1642	74.0	×	41.0	×	1438	×
1643–1647	54.6	71.4(131)	34.0	32.3(95)	1453	932(64)
1648–1652	30.6	×	×	×	1340	×
1653–1655	39.0	×	×	×	771	×

Note: Figures in parentheses indicate the relationship of sample years to the 5-years' averages (in per cent).

a Omitted because of the Polish–Swedish War.

Source: Tables 1, 2, 3, 10, 11, and Diagram 1.

Table 16

Estimate of the Value of Imports. In 1000 Rixdollars. Selected Years

	1565	1575	1585	1595	1605	1615	1625	1635	1646
a Danzig's Trade in Foreign Ships (+ 45 per cent for freight and the merchant's profit)	387.2	428.0	206.6	565.4	947.9	625.7	1354.9	1754.8x	2015.6y
b Danzig's Trade in Danzig Ships	4.6	90.2	24.5	33.6	69.8	13.7	19.5	26.7	69.1
c Danzig's Trade in all	391.8	518.2	231.1	599.0	1017.7	639.4	1374.4	1781.5	2084.7
d Elbing's Trade in Foreign Ships (+ 45 per cent)	6.1	–	562.3	684.4	702.5	527.1	459.7	24.7	83.4
e Elbing's Trade in Elbing Ships	–	–	–	–	–	–	–	–	7.4
f Danzig and Elbing in all	397.9	518.2	793.4	1283.4	1720.2	1166.5	1834.1	1716.2	2175.5

The Balance of Trade

	1565	1575	1585	1595	1605	1615	1625	1635	1646
For Danzig	+1303.5	+316.8	+417.3	+858.2	+216.1	+674.2	−88.2	+559.2	−12.8
For Elbing	+32.8	+75.4	−335.1	−496.5	−493.5	−376.2	−360.8	+0.7	+0.7
Grand Total	+1336.3	+392.2	+82.2	+361.7	−277.4	+298.0	−449.0	+559.9	−12.1

Note:
x Including the value of imported haberdashery = 122,600 rds. Former sample years brought only trifling quotations.
y Including the value of imported haberdashery = 90,800 rds.
Source: Table 13; STT, vol. II A, Table I b (for haberdashery).

Table 17

The Balance of English Trade with Eastland. In 1000 Rixdollars. Selected Years

	1565	1575	1585	1595	1605	1615	1625	1635	1646
Net value of English Exports	187	277	611	681	840	813	632	826	811
Net value of English Imports	164	251	304	531	341	370	268	557	515
Net surplus	23	26	307	150	499	443	564	269	296
Net surplus in proportion to the value of exports (in per cent)	12	9	50	22	59	54	68	33	58

Condensed from A. Mączak, 'The Sound Toll Accounts and the Balane of English Eastland Trade, 1565–1646', *Studia Historiae Economicae*, vol. III (1968), Table IV.

Table 18

The Balance of Danzig Trade in the Second Half of the Fifteenth Century.
In Prussian Marks

Years	Exports	Imports	Balance
1460	60,000	183,000	−123,000
1470	63,000	96,000	− 33,000
1475	96,000	135,000	− 39,000
1492	322,000	245,000	+ 77,000

Source: H. Samsonowicz, *Badania nad kapitałem mieszczańskim Gdańska w II połowie XV wieku,* (Warszawa, 1960), Table I.

Table 19

Data and Estimates of the Balance of Polish Foreign Trade. Sixteenth and Seventeenth Centuries. In 1000 Rixdollars

Years	Exports	Imports	Balance	Remarks
(a) 1581–1585	2600–4530	.	.	Chief export goods, by land and sea
(b) 1620?	6280	.	.	Through Danzig and
1621?	4920	.	.	Elbing only
1620?	2420	.	.	By land only
1621?	1890	.	.	
(c) 1615–1620?	5500–5750	3930–4100	+1570 to 1650	Through Danzig and Königsberg
(d) 1634	4178	2020	+2158	⎫
1640	5806	4170	+1636	
1641	6150	3855	+2295	
1642(e)	5023	4223	+ 800	
1643(e)	5399	3041	+2358	
1645(f)	2984	2456	+ 528	⎬ Danzig only
1646(f)	2941	2488	+ 453	
1647(f)	4205	3400	+ 805	
1648(f)	4072	1800	+2272	
1649(f)	7047	2692	+4355	
1634–1649 on the average	4781	3015	+1766	⎭

Sources:

(a) Estimated by R. Rybarski, *Handel i polityka handlowa Polski w XVI stuleciu* (Warszawa, 1958), vol. I, p. 247 f.

(b) According to W. Gostkowski, 'Sposób jakim góry złote, srebrne w przezacnym Królestwie Polskim zepsowane naprawić . . ., 1622' – in *Merkantylistyczna myśl ekonomiczna w Polsce XVI i XVII wieku. Wybór pism*, ed. E. Lipiński (Warszawa, 1958), p. 155. Years are suggested according to the date of edition; figures differ because of changing course of Polish money.

(c) Marshal Mikołaj Wolski's estimates, according to Jan Grodwagner, *Discurs o cenie pieniędzy teraźniejszej i o niektórych skutkach jej*, 1632, edited in *Merkantylistyczna myśl . . .*, p. 342 f. Wolski became Marshal in 1615; he died in 1630; his estimate surely does not refer to the years of the Polish–Swedish war, 1626–1629; most probably it concerns the period 1615–1620. Those years witnessed a monetary reform, which however did not involve gold money.

(d) According to *Pfahlgeld* registers; M. Bogucka, 'Handel bałtycki a bilans handlowy Polski w pierwszej połowie XVII wieku', *Przeglad Historyczny* LIX (1968), p. 248.

(e) Only two registers are preserved.

(f) Only one register is preserved.

Table 20

Values of Exports and Imports in Current and Constant Prices Sixteenth and Seventeenth Centuries. Index Base: Average for 1565, 1575 and 1585 = Values at constant Prices = 100

Classes of goods	Polish ports		Königsberg	
	1595/1605/1615	1625/1635/1646	1595/1605/1615	1625/1635/1646
Grains	115	136	122	135
Wood	198	354	204	356
Ashes, Pitch, Tar & c.	129	250	111	227
Fibres, Yarn & Textiles	109	169	122	105
Metals	97	123	137	106
Hides, Skins & Leather	293	194	200	162
Exports	125	147	134	146
Salt & Herrings	122	171	103	126
Wines	122	132	123	136
'Colonial Goods'	52	70	95	71
Textiles	98	81	84	83
Hides, Skins & Leather	100	135	118	167
Imports	106	98	101	103

Source: Tables 8, 10, 12 and 14.

Königsberg indexes derived from A. Mączak, *Między Gdańskiem a Sundem. Studia nad handlem bałtyckim od połowy XVI do połowy XVII w. (Between Danzig and the Sound. Studies in the Baltic Trade from the Middle of the 16th to the Middle of the 17th Century)* in preparation.

II

SIR FRANCIS DRAKE'S PRUSSIAN PRIZES. RISKS AND PROFITS FROM THE GDAŃSK-IBERIAN COMMERCE ABOUT 1589

The abundant archives of Gdańsk yield very scant information about the cost and profits in maritime trade [1]. Very few commercial registers and merchant accounts have been preserved and we know from the book by Maria Bogucka that the records of the courts of justice and municipal offices are also very modest [2]. The estimates based on the declarations submitted by the merchants are unreliable because they are founded on fixed prices of merchandise [3]. But the matter is not quite hopeless and it is well worth looking for new sources of information and new methods of research.

In this study we have tried such a new method and drawn on sources known but usually ignored which may, justifiably, arouse a historian's distrust. I have in mind the complaints of Gdańsk merchants, ow-

---

[1] This is a new version of the article entitled *Angielscy kaprowie i gdańscy rachmistrze. W poszukiwaniu nowych źródeł do dziejów handlu* [*English Privateers and Gdańsk Accountants. In Search of New Sources for the History of Trade*], [in:] *Społeczeństwo, gospodarka, kultura (Society, Economy, Culture)*, Studies presented in homage to Marian Małowist for the 40th anniversary of his scientific work, Warszawa 1974, pp. 211 - 222.

[2] M. B o g u c k a, *Handel zagraniczny Gdańska w pierwszej połowie XVII wieku* [*Foreign Trade of Gdańsk in the First Half of the 17th c.*], Wrocław 1970; critical article on the subject by A. M ą c z a k, *Ceny, obroty i zyski w handlu gdańskim pierwszej połowy XVII w.* [*Prices, Volume and Profits in Gdańsk Trade in the First Half of the 17th c.*]. "Przegląd Historyczny", vol. 62, 1971, pp. 280 - 294. A list of writings on the subject of the trade between Gdańsk, and Spain and Portugal has been compiled by M. B o g u c k a, *Handel Gdańska z Półwyspem Iberyjskim w pierwszej połowie XVII wieku* [*Gdańsk Trade with the Iberian Peninsula in the First Half of the 17th c.*], "Przegląd Historyczny", vol. 60, 1969, p. 1.

[3] A. M ą c z a k, op. cit., p. 292. The registers of the Gdańsk Pfahlgeld for 1640 and 1641 give a uniform price of one last of rye — 120 Polish florins; this is valid for all the 930 entries preserved in the source. At that time, English merchants or skippers declared in the Sound that in Gdańsk they had paid various prices for a last, from 24.0 to 41.6 thalers. Cf. A. M ą c z a k, *Sundzollregister als eine preisgeschichtliche Quelle, 1557, 1647*, "Jahrbuch für Wirtschaftsgeschichte", 1970, Teil III, pp. 179 - 220.

ners of goods carried to Lisbon and Sanlucar, and confiscated by privateers — Sir Francis Drake and his companions in 1587 - 1590, and also handbooks on arithmetics and bookkeeping a few of which appeared in Gdańsk at that time [4]. Reservations and questions which these sources must arouse will be discussed further on in a critical analysis. My author's credo which has prompted me to take up this subject is as follows: if a set of those sources shows a mutual concordance of their elements, if the information which can be compared with other material does not show any discrepancy, then it is permitted to assume that the other, uncheckable information is credible.

What do the two kinds of sources say in the matter of the account of profits and losses in the Gdańsk-Iberian trade?

Some years after the taking of Gdańsk prizes, between May and August 1591, the Gdańsk Senate sent several letters to Queen Elizabeth which contained declarations drawn up by the victims, i.e. the merchants and shipowners. Some of the declarations were submitted individually and they contain lists of goods belonging to one owner and carried on several ships; there are also collective complaints concerning the property of several merchants lost aboard the same ship; finally, there are complaints lodged in respect of lost profit in freight. Altogether, 29 letters have been preserved in the London Public Records Office, to which must be added the correspondence both printed and preserved in the Gdańsk Archives [5]. Since we do not intend to investigate the entire dis-

[4] *Elementa ad fontium editiones*, vol. IV: *Res polonicae Elizabetha I Angliae regnante conscriptae ex Archivis Publicis Londoniarum*, ed. C. H. Talbot, Romae 1961. As concerns handbooks we have consulted mainly S. G a m e r s f e l d e r, *Ein New Rechenbüchlein...*, Danzig 1589; i d e m, *Buchhalten Durch Zwey Bücher nach Italianischer Art und weise...*, Danzig 1579; W. S a r t o r i u s de S a d a, *Ein New Künstlich Rechenbüchlein...*, Danzig 1592; also D. B r o d o c h, *Rechenbuch auff den Linien und Federn, nach Preussisch Müntz, Mass und Gewichte*, Danzig 1587; J. L e h m a n, *Künstliche und ordentliche Anweisung der Arithmetica...*, Danzig 1604. Cf. E. W o j c i e c h o w s k i, *Materiały archiwalne, rękopisy i stare druki gdańskie z zakresu księgowości [Archival Materials, MSS and Old Prints of Gdańsk Concerning Bookkeeping]*, "Rocznik Gdański", vol. XV - XVI, 1956 - 1957; *Z historii rachunkowości w Polsce i Gdańsku w wieku XVI. Wybór tekstów [From the History of Bookkeeping in Poland and Gdańsk in the 16th Century Selected Texts]*, ed. A. Grodek and J. Surma, Warszawa 1959 (ibid., in Polish edition of excerpts from Gamersfelder and Sartorius, in particular the entire Gamersfelder journal from the 1570 ed.). Vol. IV of the *Elementa* has serious drawbacks. The registers have been edited carelessly, inconsistently, sometimes downright misleadingly. The editor did not check the concordance of figures so that we do not know when we have a printer's error and when it is the authors of the 16th c. texts that made a mistake. For instance, in document No 86, freight is to amount to 550 ducats, when it should be 540 or the merchant's profit in Lisbon would be only 1850 (not 1860). We assume 550 (i.e. MMCCCC less DXL equals MDCCCLX). There is also an obvious mistake in No 78: 4 rings clapholt + freight make MMXXIIII ducats. In No 85 (p. 136) one line is missing after line 30.

pute, we have not looked for other sources [6]. The main problem is the question whether the information obtained is of use in the study of the calculation of commercial profits.

The control investigation should proceed along two lines: checking the figures by comparison with other sources, and investigating the internal concordance of the source, the connection between the information it provides and the interests of the author. But this method reveals an important theoretical problem, best seen in the question of price, which lies at the roots of a merchant's calculation. If we accept the consistency of the declared figures with data from other sources as the basis for their credibility, then immediately a whole chain of inconsistencies appears before us. The statistics of prices in historical studies are only of approximative reliability. What is the percentage of divergence which does not exceed the limits of probability? When we compare single figures, not two sequences, then a general answer is difficult; but one can argue *e contrario* that complete concordance of data about prices provided by various sources and concerning different deals should arouse suspicion for it is impossible that in reality prices (even concerning similar transactions e.g. export) of a given kind of goods throughout the year or even one month should always be the same. So some discrepancy is a natural thing and ought not to cause reservations. The point is how to interpret those differences [7].

[5] *Elementa*, Nos 71 to 98 including 76A (hereafter only numbers will be quoted). No 99 forwards the complaint by a trumpeteer of Gdańsk aboard a Swedish ship who had been robbed. It is of no value to us. It also contains the correspondence and comments on the complaints written by an English official. Investigation in the Gdańsk Archives did not bring any outstanding results. The relevant correspondence file with England contains the lists of losses suffered by Gdańsk citizens which had certainly been drawn up in Gdańsk (Voivodship State Archives, in Gdańsk, 300, 53/623); it accords very well with the declarations in the *Elementa*; it also contains the losses of the following years (1587 - 1596 jointly) amounting altogether to fl. 129, 479 gr. 3 din. 15. The section *Missiva* contains some letters on similar matters but of secondary value; there are no copies of letters printed later in the *Elementa* after the originals sent to England. They were probably included in the section *Handel* (Commerce) which was burnt in 1945.

[6] It is interesting to note in connection with the Gdańsk—English dispute that it is not the only set of this kind of sources for those years. The English privateers chased everyone who sailed to the ports ruled by Philip II, irrespective of the flag flown by the ship. During an inquiry conducted for some other purpose in Rigsarkivet in Copenhagen we found the *Nomina S.R. Daniae Subditorum, qui ab Anglicis piratis spoliatos esse quaeruntur, et summa petitionis ipsorum* (1592). They are complaints lodged by Danish merchants and shipowners mostly of Copenhagen, from the years 1587 - 1592. Contrary to Gdańsk plaintiffs they accurately calculate the lost capital and interest, yet their claims are couched in general terms. We have failed to find calculations and details similar to those which we shall discuss below. There are only twelve Danish complaints (Rigsarkivet, Copenhagen, Tyska Kansliet, Utlandske Afdeling, England A III, No 84).

[7] More on this subject, A. Mączak, *Die Sundzollregister...*, pp. 191 - 195.

Table 1. Rye Prices in Complaints of Gdańsk Merchants, in Sound Toll Registers and on the Retail Market in Gdańsk, 1588—1589 (in Polish Florins pro Last)*

Year and Month	Elementa No.	Elementa Fl.	Sound Toll Month	Registers Fl.	Market in Gdańsk Quarter	Market in Gdańsk Fl.
A. Rye						
1588 November	95	33.2	November	26.8		
1589 March	79	27.3				
March—						
—April	92	30.8				
	87	40.5				
	87	31.9				
April	88	28.0			II	26—28
	90	30.0				
	94	30.0				
	88	30.5				
	86	30.6				
	96	31.3				
	74	31.4				
	85	32.0				
	88	33.6				
	85	34.0				
	85	35.0				
Early Spring	73	32.3				
	73	32.4				
	74	31.3				
			August	26.8—29.2		
			November	32.7	IV	30—36
B. Barley						
1588 November	93	47.2			I	39.0
					II	42.0
					III	26.0
					IV	23.0
1589 April	84	24.8			I	23.0
	85	27.0			II	26.0
	94	24.9				
	94	34.9				

* S o u r c e s: *Elementa*, see numbers; Rigsarkivet, Copenhagen, Øresundtoldsregnskaber, 1588 and 1589; J. P e l c, note 9, Tables 2 and 3. Data from the Sound are calculated from rixdollar; they represent monthly averages. Calculation is rather difficult. Rixdollar from 1566 on contained 25.984 g of pure silver. Polish grosz in 1588/89=0.695 g, thus 1 rixdollar=37.387 Polish grosz. But in Gdańsk i rixdollar was changed for 35 Polish grosz. On the contrary to J. Pelc, P. S i m s o n think they were two different kinds of dollar (see *Gesammelte Beobachtungen über das Wertverhältnis verschiedener Münzsorten zu einander im 16. und 17. Jhr.*, „Zeitschrift des Westpreussischen Geschichtsvereins", vol. XL, 1899, p. 116). We keep in our article the calculation of Gdańsk (1 rixdollar=35 grosz). Counting the silver proportion 25 984 g, prices in florins and in grosz have to be 6.8%/o higher. Polish złoty (florenus polonicalis, polnischer Gulden)=30 grosz=540 denar. For abbreviation we use: florin=fl., grosz=gr., denar=d., rixdollar=rd., ducat=duc., last=l.

Table 1 shows the prices of rye and barley in Gdańsk taken from various sources. It appears that there is no adequate basis for comparison for the short period under survey (mainly spring of 1589). And yet, when the comparison is possible, the prices in which the Gdańsk merchants calculated their losses correspond to those declared by the English in the Sound and stay within the limits indicated for retail prices in the Gdańsk market.

The connection betweeen the export and retail prices in Gdańsk is something of a mystery. Despite the concordance of trends in export and retail prices, one cannot exclude considerable differences at certain times connected not only with the margin of profit. The municipal authorities were interested in maintaining high prices for the export of grain because they brought profits to the city's treasury and to the influential section of its citizens, while concern for public order dictated moderation in respect of local market prices. One might add that although the declarations about the price paid for grain presented in Elsinore by the English have turend out to be true and accurate, yet various groups of merchants who shipped goods by sea from Gdańsk had probably paid varying prices for them. The Dutch who were freer with cash and credit had many connections in Gdańsk and entered into joint ventures with the local merchants, and also were always strongly interested in the grain trade; they were probably able to obtain goods on better conditions than the English; the Gdańsk merchants, on the other hand — and it is in them that we are mostly interested — were entitled to direct contacts with the hinterland and so could probably obtain merchandise at lower prices. So it is rather surprising that the concordance of prices in the complaints and in the English declarations in the Sound should be so striking. Well, in some cases, the plaintiffs remark that they quote the prices "cum impensis", once even "cum impensis usque per fretum Danicum" (No 79, wheat). So they added the customs duties in the port of Gdańsk, sometimes also the Danish ones, while the prices declared by the English were probably f.o.b. prices.

The fact that there was a considerable difference between the figures in respect of one month or one fleet or even a single ship indicates that the English, French and Scots did not quote either lower or estimated prices. It is the same with the prices declared in the complaints, and it is easy to see these differences in Table 1; the case is the same with wheat (Table 2). So there seems to be no tendency to raise the value of the lost cargo by declaring exaggerated prices. We shall see that, for all this, it is not possible to exclude exaggerated declarations about the size of the cargo.

From the data furnished by the bookkeeping handbooks we shall select only those which concern the years and problems dealt with in the complaints. Are the realities of the merchants' life, proliferating on

Table 2. Wheat Prices (in Fl. pro Last) According to the Merchant's Complaints

Nr.	Date		Price	Notes
72	November 1588		50.8	
			51.5	
74	April	1589	52.9	
			61.0	
76			58.0	
76A	March	1589	59.0	
	April	1589	53.4	
			53.4	
79	March	1589	44.5	*cum impensis usque per fre-*
85	April	1589	50.0	*tum Danicum*
			50.0	
86			52.5	
			52.5	
87			44.8	
			43.4	
			30.3	
			32.5	*viliore triticum*
			51.1	
88			44.5	
			55.0	
89			58.0	+*impensa* fl. 3.5
			58.0	+*impensa* fl. 5.0
			58.0	+*impensa*
			58.0	+*impensa* fl. 5.2
			58.0	+*impensa* fl. 5.2
90			56.0	
97			53.4	
			53.4	
98			56.2	

the pages of the manuals, just so much fantastic fiction or are they fiction based on everyday experience of its authors and disciples?

The answer is difficult; particularly so as an answer both straightforward and generally applicable would be hard to come by. I shall explain it on an example. In one of his arithmetical problems Sartorius gives the following data: His Majesty (the Polish King), his senators and the gentry have altogether 90,000 villages; the bishops and canons have 110,000; parish priests, parishes and monasteries another 6,560 villages; if each village sends 12 soldiers etc ... It turns out from the calculation that Poland would have had two-and-a-half million strong army and more than 14 barrels of gold needed for its upkeep. Fantastic? Hardly anything else. Yet, when perusing various gentry household notebooks from the 16th - 17th centuries called *silvae rerum*, and similar manuscripts of the Gdańsk burgesses, one often comes across such texts. By obviously exaggerating the share of the Church estates, they served anticlerical agitation around 1562 and the following years [8]. The figures from that problem reflect realities but in the sense of the realities of a, say, statistical social consciousness. Sartorius drew his figures from sources which he was entitled to consider trustworthy.

As concerns political arithmetic, ideas most surprising for the modern student were current; but it would not have been reasonable on the part of the author to feed his pupils-merchants fantastic figures concerning prices, costs, time of voyages, rates of exchange, contents of cargoes carried in various directions. Here, handbooks of arithmetic are less useful than manuals of bookkeeping. Their basic contents furnish no absurd information: osmund iron comes from Sweden, flax from Lithuania, raw materials and grain are shipped west in exchange for pepper, wine, cloth and salt. But are these details relevant for the time when in Portuguese waters ships flying the flag of St. George and the arms of Elizabeth were hunting their prizes from Gdańsk?

Again we may refer to the prices of grain. For the year 1589, when Gamersfelder's handbook appeared, J. Pelc [9] noted one last of rye costing from 14 to 36 florins, the first price being blatantly low. If we ignore it, the amplitude will not exceed 10 florins (26 to 36); annual average = fl. 27.9. The handbook gives prices from fl. 26 ort $2^{1}/_{2}$ to fl. 28 gr. 20. We do not know what prices were paid the suppliers at that time, but the export prices in the manuals may be compared with the English declarations about Gdańsk prices submitted in the Sound. Gamersfelder quotes from fl. 24 or 1 to fl. $25^{3}/_{8}$ for one last; the English paid from fl. 30.8 to 34.9, somewhat less in Elbląg [10]. The previous year's prices, which have also to be considered, were lower judging from the autumn Elbląg prices. In spring, i.e. in April 1588, the English would declare the equivalent of even as much as fl. 40 (in thalers), later the prices declared were lower.

I do not see any contradiction in this for, as I said before, the English had to pay more for grain than the Gdańsk merchants who got it directly from the landowners.

Gamersfelder's figures can be checked against other grains. The prices of wheat are in reasonable proportion to those of rye. Barley is estimated at fl. 25 and 27 (and a few orts) while Pelc notes its price varying from fl. 23 to 26, and the year before from fl. 38 to 42 in the first half, and from 23 to 26 in the second. So the prices do correspond. Oats cost

[8] Sartorius de Sada, *Ein New Künstlich Rechenbüchlein...*, p. E. vii, No 93.

[9] J. Pelc, *Ceny w Gdańsku w XVI i XVII wieku* [*Prices in Gdańsk in the 16th and 17th C.*], Lwów 1937, Table 2.

[10] Prices paid by the English as per Sound Toll Registers, Rigsarkivet, Copenhagen, sub anno. Cf. critical appraisal of these figures in A. Mączak, *Die Sundzollregister...* and in *The Balance of Polish Sea Trade with the West. 1565 - 1646,* "The Scandinavian Economic History Review", vol. XVIII, 2, 1970, p. 114 ff.

in the manual some fl. 15 to some 19; Pelc gives the price from fl. 9 to 15, in the year in which the manual was published, and from fl. 13 to 25 the year before [11]. So there is no contradiction here either.

Sartorius' manual should be compared with 1591 and the next year. We shall find less information about prices: rye is variously estimated at fl. 26.72, fl. 32 gr. 22 d. 9 and fl. 40.75. In the retail market the price in 1591 was from fl. 22 to 44, a year later fl. 18 to 29. In two cases the prices quoted by Sartorius for ox hides diverge seriously: 30 marks (i.e. fl. 20) and fl. 106 orts 3. Pelc's figures are scant and wide apart: from fl. 30 to 88.

In Gamersfelder the relation of the thaler to the grosz corresponds to the rate on the Gdańsk market (gr. 34 - 35; Sartorius does not give any figures). Brodoch (of Königsberg but published in Gdańsk) gives gr. 35; Lehmann (publ. 1604) exchanges the thalers in Hamburg at the rate of gr. $36^{1}/_{3}$ to 38, the average being $36^{7}/_{8}$, while in Pelc the thaler is worth gr. 37. The Portuguese ducat was worth gr. 44 both in Gamersfelder and the complaints. One of the latter gives its worth at gr. 42 a rate unfavourable to the plaintiffs. The gr. 50 rate quoted in one of the complaints is at one with the rate in Sartorius; so we may assume that writing in 1591 the plaintiff quoted the current rate of exchange instead of the one from two years before.

So there is a considerable concordance between prices in the chronological series, and in manuals and declarations of losses. This makes it possible to turn to an analysis of the merchants' calculations contained in the last two sources. Let us begin with Gamersfelder. His figures will be converted into grosz in order to avoid the confusion of ducats, thalers and Polish florins. This was not the practice of the Gdańsk merchants but the bills of exchange drawn on Gdańsk were always made out in grosz [12].

Here is Gamersfelder's calculation:

Receipts		Expenditures	
		Gdańsk	
		cost of wheat	46,440
		cost of wainscot	14,580
		total	61,020
		Lisbon	
from sale of wheat		freight for wheat	7,636
	65,142	freight wainscot	11,088
from sale of wainscot	27,324	customs, other costs	950
		total	19,674
		cost of stay	880
		grand total	81,574
total receipt	92,466	profit from voyage to Lisbon	10,892

[11] J. Pelc, op. cit., Tables 23, 16, 48.
[12] N. Posthumus, Inquiry into History of Prices in Holland, vol. I, Leyden 1946, p. 590.

Voyage Home

Lisbon

cost of salt (388,6 lasts)		64,328
other expenses		1,034
		65,362
freight (for 351 lasts)		76,781.75
customs and other costs		3,827.50
		80,608

for salt in Gdańsk	138,294	total prime costs	145,970.25
loss on return voyage	7,676.25		

Here it should be explained that on the home voyage the skipper was forced to throw overboard part of his cargo so that only 351 lasts (90.7 per cent) was brought to port. Altogether, over the whole voyage, the owners of the cargo earned only 5.8 per cent of the capital they had invested. On the westwards voyage they got 18 per cent on wheat, and 13 per cent on wainscot; on the voyage home the loss was of 5 per cent. Had it been possible to avoid the storms in the Bay of Biscay, the pattern of prices would have allowed barely to cover the cost of the return voyage.

A similar calculation in Sartorius seems questionable. Even the voyage from Gdańsk to Lisbon caused considerable loss, not shown by the author, because the value of the cargo in Gdańsk (*Hauptgut*) has been deducted from the sum obtained only after the return. Wainscot, clapholt and tar bring losses, freight for rye is exaggeratedly high (20 ducats, 14 for wheat). On the way home, four-fifths of the sum obtained was brought in cash, but the rest, invested in salt and spices, brought a fivefold profit. It is contrary to all that we know about the trade on route, so this calculations should be rejected.

Calculations in an earlier book by Gamersfelder ("Buchhalten", publ. 1570) are also strictly related to the realities of the time, the year 1569. After the theoretical part comes a model for keeping a journal. It is to be a complete journal covering the time from April 1 to December 29; the entries are interconnected and the author is conducting several business and banking deals as well as private and household transactions. He is also interested in Lisbon. The deals with that port are conducted by Gamersfelder in a triangle whose third apex is a permanent trading partner in Antwerp. He calculated his profit from a wheat deal at 23 per cent, although he must have lost the cost of freight somewhere on the way [13]. On ashes and timber sent to Amsterdam he earned 16 per cent, on rye and wax sold in Antwerp over 14 per cent. The gives the scale of expected profits next to which the journal notes down also the los-

---

[13] S. Gamersfelder, "Buchhalten", journal, July 30: "the sailor charges 7 ducats freight on each last". This item does not figure in the journal and the costs (Unkosten) mentioned do not amount to the relevant figure.

ses and insurance cost which is to compensate the merchant for at least part of his loss.

To return to the complaints lodged by the Gdańsk victims of Sir Francis Drake. Our distrust is aroused not so much by the fear of some fantastic arithmetic on the part of the authors as of downright falsifications in the profit accounts. After all, the Gdańsk authorities to which they swore their declarations were not interested in detailed checking or in limiting the exaggerated claims of their fellow citizens. None of the plaintiffs refers to his ledgers: it seems that bookkeeping did not yet achieve in Gdańsk, at least formally, the rank of a reliable document. Most of the Gdańsk merchants simply determined the quantity and value of the lost merchandise. Councillor Joachim Ehler, who often appears in those cases, seemed to be most interested in claiming overall losses, probably including the profits expected but lost.

Together with his son Augustin he shipped 30 lasts and 30 bushels of rye (No 73). Here is their calculation (conversion figures in brackets).

	ducats	grosze
value of goods in Gdańsk		29,773
value of goods in Lisbon	1,472	(64,768)
freight (à duc. 10 a last)	300	(13,200)
broker's fee and other costs	68	(2,992)
expected profit	1,104	(48,576)
invested in pepper would		
yield in Gdańsk		55,200

So on the way out to Lisbon the capital was to bring a profit of 113 per cent of the value of the goods in Gdańsk, and 41 per cent in relation to the overall cost sustained so far. On the voyage back, although its cost had been included in the former account, the expected profit was under 14 per cent. Altogether, the invested capital was to yield a profit of exactly 20 per cent. The calculation does not show any tendency towards expectation of extravagant profits from imports to Gdańsk which speaks well of its authors.

Another calculation (No 76A) concerns 25 lasts of wheat belonging to Hermann Kleinfeldt and loaded onto three ships. The value of the goods — cum impensis but without mention of freight so it probably means price in Gdańsk — is rated at fl. 1,371 gr. 5; in Lisbon the owner wanted to get for it the equivalent of fl. 2,000. If we accept that in this simplified account Kleinfeldt presented his net profit, then it would mean 146 per cent of the value in Gdańsk; by adding the usual 13 .ducats a last for freight we would have raised the expenditure to some fl. 1,880, and the value in Lisbon accordingly, but the profit would only come to 33.5 per cent. Calculated in this way (with freight added) the price of wheat in Lisbon is low.

Bartholomew Schultz also put his calculation of expected profit (No 86) in detail. He had shipped 20 lasts of wheat and the same amount of rye on three ships; the price of wheat was set at fl. 52.5, of rye at 30.7 a last.

	ducats	grosze
value of goods in Gdańsk		
wheat		49,863
rye		18,360
value of goods in Lisbon		
wheat	1,440	(63,360)
rye	960	(42,240)
freight Gdańsk-Lisbon	550	(24,200)
in Lisbon he would have the sum of	1,850	(81,400)
which invested in pepper and other goods		
would bring in Gdańsk		93,000

Thus, gross profit on the way to Lisbon was to bring, in relation to the price of grain in Gdańsk, 27 per cent in the case of wheat and 130 per cent in that of rye, while the voyage home was to yield 14 per cent, and the overall expedition a profit of 24 per cent. The concordance with the Ehler figures is striking, all the more so as the particular elements of the calculation are different. This means that the profit obtained in the export to Portugal exceeded, after the cost had been deducted, 40 per cent of the invested capital, while the less profitable deals on the way home allowed of only some 20 per cent profit for one voyage [14].

In turn, Joachim Ehler and his son Michael (No 80) sent on two ships:

[14] Mr. Boris Floria has kindly drawn my attention to a somewhat analogous calculation of an English merchant trading between Archangel and Spain, France, England and Hamburg (1585). In result of the very considerable differences in prices, the home voyage was to bring him a very high profit:

wine (Spanish) — price in Archangel higher by	359	per cent
wine (French) —	507	„ „
raisins (Spanish) —	455	„ „
pepper (from Spain) —	35	„ „
sugar (from Spain) —	80	„ „
lead (English) —	79	„ „
cloth (English) —	67 and 78	„ „
paper (French) —	97	„ „
copper (from Hamburg) —	124	„ „
saltpeter (from Hamburg) —	185	„ „
herrings (from Hamburg) —	43	„ „
etc.		

Altogether the value of the cargo in Archangel prices was 194 per cent higher than in the ports of loading. The lack of certain figures makes it impossible to establish similar relations between prices of goods exported from Archangel (hemp, wax, lard). *Pamyatniki diplomaticheskikh snosheniy Moskovskogo gosudarstva s Anglieyu*, ed. by K. N. Bestuzhev-Riumin, vol. II (1581 - 1604), [in:] "Sbornik Imperatorskogo Russkogo Istoricheskogo Obshchestva", vol. XXXVIII, 1883, pp. 217 - 221.

	ducats	grosze
20 lasts of flour and 10 lasts of wheat *cum impensis usque per fretum Danicum*		24,358
wheat in Lisbon was to bring (duc. 72)	720	
flour	720	
freight (duc. 10 a last)	300	
net profit in Lisbon	1,140	
at the rate of duc. 1 = gr. 50		(57,00)
at the rate of duc. 1 = gr. 44		(50,160)

According to this calculation, the profit on the Gdańsk—Lisbon section was to bring 106 per cent of the invested capital (or even 134 per cent at the rate of duc. 1 = gr. 50).

Another calculation by this enterprising merchant (No 78) is not quite clear; the most reliable is the calculation of expected profit from the import of Spanish wine.

110 measures of wine à duc. 15, duc. 1,649 gr. 6 d. 2 (ad summum)		(72,562)
their value in Gdańsk		214,500
expenditure (joint freight for wine and salt)		21,436
net profit	over	193,00

or some 166 per cent of the capital invested in Lisbon.

Another set of information is to be found in the complaints of shipowners, including Gdańsk citizens, who submitted claims also as merchant-owners of the merchandise lost in Lisbon. The shipowners of the "St. Georg" counted on a profit of 998 ducats gr. 20 on the freight (this would have given, à gr. 42 fl. 1,397 gr. 26). On the way back they intended to invest this sum obtained in Lisbon in Portuguese salt which would have brought them fl. 31 a last. It is not known how much salt was there to be. The cargo shipped from Gdańsk amounted to 77 lasts of grain, also some timber and lead which constituted the balast and therefore was not charged with freight (as in No 75; in complaint No 93 the owner of lead declared 189.5 quintals). The price of one last of salt in Lisbon — just under four ducats — is given by Gamersfelder's calculation.

Expenditure apart, the cash collected in Lisbon would have sufficed for the purchase of 260 lasts which could bring fl. 8,060 — a 5.5 — fold profit! In comparing the contradictory estimates by Gamersfelder and the owners of the "St. Georg", we note the very low price of salt envisaged by the former in Gdańsk. For the year 1589, Pelc quotes a barrel of salt *tout court* at gr. 40 to 60, or an average of gr. 50. One last contained 16 barrels so that one last was worth fl. 26²/₃. Spanish salt was the most expensive, although we can compare it in Pelc's only with figures for the 17th century. If other kinds exceeded fl. 26, then fl. 31 is not a particularly high price for Spanish salt. But, in order to save

Table 3. Cargo of the ship "St. Georg", April 1589, According to the Declaration of Ship- and Cargoowners

Merchants	Cargo According to the Declera-tion of		Cargo Value in Gdańsk (According to Merchant)	Freight According to Shipow-ners
	Shipowners	Merchant		
P. Dillinger	1 hundred clapholt	12 rings small clapholt		duc. 46
H. Kleinfeld	5 l. grain	5 l. wheat	fl. 295 gr. 5 d. 15	duc. 65
T. Sievert	10 l. grain	10l. wheat in tuns	?	duc. 130
	plumb	189.5 cwt.	?	no freight
J. Ehler	10 l. grain	10 l. flour in tuns	fl. 405 gr. 29 d. 4½	duc. 120
		5 l. wheat	cum imp. per fretum Danicum	
A. Vogel	10.5 l. grain	10.5 l. barley in tuns	fl. 260 gr. 20	duc. 136. gr. 20
H. Thorbeck	10 l. grain	10 l. wheat	fl. 580	duc. 130
	12 l. wheat	20 l. flour	fl. 720	
	(loose)	2 l. flour	fl. 52	
		1 massa wax	fl. 36 gr. 18	
P. von Doren	5 l. grain	10 l. flour	fl. 252 gr. 23	duc. 65
J. Kemmerling	3 l. grain			
A. Behme	3 l. grain	2 l. wheat	fl. 106 gr. 26	duc. 39
A. Mallein	—	1 l. wheat	fl. 53 gr. 13	—
A. Karsten	8.5 l. grain	8.5 l. barley	fl. 296 gr. 21 d. 6	duc. 85
M. Schultz	—	1 l. wheat	fl. 47	
		1 l. rye	fl. 30 with impensa	fl. 15
pro nave ipsa	1/2 hundred clapholt			duc. 22

the Gamersfelder calculation, as the prices of salt fluctuated considerably, those fl. 13 gr. 4 do not seem impossible. Pelc gives scant information (one or a few figures a year, many years are blank), but salt from Brouage was sold in 1587 for fl. 35.2 a last, and in 1592 for fl. 16 in five cases, in 1593 for fl. 14.4 and 12.8. The minimum prices of salt, without specification of kind, in the years starting with 1585, were: fl. 12.8, 34.7, 21.3, 21.3, 21.3, 16.3, 17.1, 13.9 a last [15]. Contrary to the case, noted above, when the goods were the joint property of the shipowners, freight had to be paid. Gamersfelder assumes 5 ducats, i.e. fl. 29 a last, on the home voyage, which is quite a high figure compared with the price in Lisbon.

It seems that the place where that freight was paid was of consider-

[15] J. Pelc, op. cit., Tables 37 and 39. I converted the figures at the rate of 1 last = 16 barrels, in accordance with the remarks on p. 16 of the introduction.

Table 4. Cargo of the ship "Lilium Gedanense", April 1589 According to the Declaration of Ship- and Cargoowners *

Merchants	Cargo According to Shipowners	Cargo According to Merchants	Value in Gdańsk **	Freight ***
	82 l. rye			duc. 902
	61 l. wheat			duc. 732
	50 clapholt			duc. 23
J. Ehler&Comp.		15 l. rye	fl. 485 gr. 25	duc. 150
A. Kleinfeldt		10 l. wheat	fl. 500	
B. Schultz		12 l. wheat	fl. 629 gr. 17	
M. Bartsch		15 l. wheat	fl. 793 gr. 23 d. 4½ ****	
S. Heine		17 l. wheat	fl. 522 gr. 2	
P. Gisan		8 l. rye	fl. 323 gr. 21 d. 12	
G. Hagemeister		15 l. rye	fl. 525	
T. Sievert		20 l. wheat		
P. Dillinger		6 rings clapholt		
Total		37 l. rye	fl. 3, 778 d. 16½	
		74 l. wheat		

* Source: complaint Nr. 71.
** According to the merchants.
*** According to the shipowners.
**** This is a half of the value of 30 last wheat sent in two bottoms.

able importance: in advance in Lisbon or in Gdańsk after docking. If paid in advance, it would have diminished the capital invested in Iberian merchandise. Although freight is calculated in ducats, Gamersfelder's hero deducts the dues for the goods thrown overboard during the voyage home which means that he has paid after its completion.

The complaint of the owners of "St. Georg" makes possible a comparison of the declarations made by the owners of the cargoes and the shipowners. Table 3 suggests that the false figures in the declaration may have been concealed in the quantities of the goods allegedly lost. On the other hand, it is to the credit of the shipowners that they calculate each ducat at the rate of gr. 42, which is gr. 2 less than the rate given by the merchants and the manuals.

The declarations are considerably though not entirely in agreement. Jacob Kemmerling, indicated by the skipper, is not to be found either among the merchants lodging complaints against privateers, or in the summary preserved in the Gdańsk Archives. Andrew Behme was in reality a partner of Gregory Mallein whom the shipowners' declaration omits. A Martin Schultz also declared his part in the cargo. So the shipowners' declaration is really less weighty. Did the merchants lie? It is possible, although part of the freight may have been paid in advance and so they did not have to declare it. It is not very relevant to our considerations.

A comparison of the declarations of losses enables us to collate the value of goods and cost of freight on the voyage west. The kind of packing (e.g. grain in barrels) does not seem to have any bearing on the cost of transport.

Another complaint, that of the owners of the "Lilium Gedanense" (No 71), does not mention the owners of the merchandise, and only some of them have been found; see Table 4.

The *impensa*, mentioned earlier seem to be the most difficult item in a commercial calculation.

Table 5. *Impensa* in the Sea Transport According to the Declaration of Hermann Thorbeck

Cargo	Quantity	Value	*Impensa*	*Impensa* pro last	% of Value
Wheat	15 l.	fl. 870	fl. 74 gr. 20	fl. 5.0	8.6
Wheat	14 l.	fl. 812	fl. 48 gr. 13	fl. 3.5	6.0
Wheat	10 l.	fl. 580			
Flour	20 l.	fl. 700	fl. 68 gr. 12		5.0
Flour	2 l.	fl. 52			
Wax	1 massa	fl. 36 gr. 18			
Wheat	10 l.	fl. 580	fl. 51 gr. 16	fl. 5.2	8.9
Wheat	10 l.	fl. 580	fl. 51 gr. 22	fl. 5.2	8.9
Total		fl. 4, 210 gr. 18	fl. 294 gr. 23	fl. 4.6	7.0

We shall compare them on the basis of complaint No 89 (Table 5). The sums and the relation to the value of the goods f.o.b. are relatively big in comparison to the figures found in bookkeeping manuals. In the journal of 1569, Gamersfelder estimates:

	fl.	gr.
cost of 40 lasts of rye as per price paid	990	
cost and fees f.o.b.		
Pfundzoll à gr. 5 a last	6	20
Traglohn à gr. 4	5	10
Messerlohn à gr. 1	1	10
Burdingsgeld à gr. 4	5	10
Peingeld à gr. 1	1	10
two dozen mats à gr. 29	1	28
total	21	28

The overall costs amounted to 2.2 per cent, but they were paid in Gdańsk while the expenditure listed in complaint No 89 seems to be of a different nature and concerns transport apart from the sums expended on freight.

It is difficult to sum up the results of all these comparisons. Uniformity was not expected, it would have looked suspiciously like collusion between the claiming Gdańsk merchants. One would hardly expect, too, similar results of trade deals conducted with such big risks. But when the Gdańsk merchant estimated his future profits, he did not take into acount what we would today call an act of God; he was guided, like his fellow merchants, only by his knowledge of the overseas trade, hence the concordance of forecasts.

The meticulous care with which the complaints were drawn up illustrates an important feature of the intellectual and moral make-up of the merchnts, a feature well known from the reading of the business correspondence in medieval and modern Italy, the Netheralnds and other countries leading in commerce. Did the losses suffered at the hand of English privateers contribute to the Gdańsk merchants' withdrawal from the Iberian trade? They returned to it in changed circumstances but only to a small extent [16]. The calculations presented here make it possible to study these matters by comparing the profit per unit of merchandise and the rate of capital turnover in the overseas trade with the relevant figures in the trade with the hinterland. We think that much may yet be learned in this respect from the bookkeeping manuals. Gamersfelder's journal of 1569 suggests that overseas commercial deals brought a higher profit than trade with Gdańsk's hinterland. His hero "Kristoff Unverdorben" who shipped wheat and wax to Antwerp got a 12.6 per cent profit; ash and tar brought him 15.9 per cent, and wheat sold in Lisbon 22.5 per cent. But the price of cloth imported from Antwerp was only some 10 per cent higher in Gdańsk. Local transaction brought, as a rule, less than 10 per cent. Yet, even then deals in local trade and with Poland had a much lower attendant risk. The transport of grain by the Vistula was effected at the risk and responsibility of the suppliers. And at least part of the transaction brought a more rapid profit; even when buying grain standing the Gdańsk merchant paid only an advance sum in the autumn or spring.

By the end of the 16th century the Volpone of Gdańsk would learn his craft diligently, both from practice and from textbooks. He did not have to be ashamed of his progress and if after several decades he decided to withdraw his capital from the overseas trade, he must have had important reasons for doing so.

Translated by Krystyna Kęplicz

[16] Cf. M. B o g u c k a, *Handel Gdańska z Półwyspem Iberyjskim* ..., pp. 3 - 5:

III

Development Levels in Early Modern Europe.
The Evidence of Synchronic Comparisons of Prices and Wages

There is little agreement among scholars about the nature of development and underdevelopment in the preindustrial era. Yet at the same time there seems to exist a consensus that our contemporary experience may not be projected towards earlier centuries. In this sense the basic idea of Paul Bairoch's magisterial work has been commonly accepted. However, nobody believes in general socioeconomic uniformity of development in preindustrial times and consequently there arise at least two sets of questions, one concerning the nature of regional differences of development, and another concerning their measurement, and in particular the measurement of development levels.

The modern world is one of tight international, or interzonal, connections. It would be a loss of time to enumerate examples of mutual dependence of countries even very far away from one another. A big step in this direction has been made in the sixteenth century, not only because of the oversea expansion of Europe but also inside and around Europe. Tight commercial and financial relations are a prerequisite of dependence − or interdependence − of countries; one may guess that during the week to follow our discussion will concentrate upon these inequalities of development arising from, or created by, tightening international connections. However, mutual dependence is not a necessary prerequisite of inequality of development levels.

There are good reasons to argue that in preindustrial times the latter type of economic inequality predominated. Primo, international commerce was still a very imperfect vehicle of economic exchange (in the widest sense of the word). Secundo, there still remained very broad sectors of subsistence economy, if not independent from, yet only indirectly influenced by, international market relations. The nature of the autarchic sector of an economy was very complex; one may rather speak about *sectors* in plural. As Witold Kula has shown, the East European manor was internally divided into subsistence and market-oriented sectors [1] but there were also large areas virtually independent from outer markets, where even lesser towns liked to cover their demand for food from their own fields [2].

It is the first thesis of this paper that backwardness in the period in question may be rooted in a region's dependence on a more developed partner, but more often it is due to a region's commercial isolation.

The nature of preindustrial economies, as well as the character of source material they have left to us, make it extremely difficult to evaluate levels of economic development. There are several indicators often analyzed, like density of population, degree of urbanization, figures of production of some odd items, cereal yield ratios. However, these are often open to doubt and/or the units compared are political (countries, i.e., states). Now, in the early modern Europe a state was only rarely economically uniform, and internal differences were sometimes abysmal (e.g., Gdansk, i.e. Danzig — and Ukraine). What is even worse, quantitative estimates often avail themselves of modern (often anachronistc) geographic or political units. What is "Germany" in the sixteenth century? What use may be of a sixteenth-century figure to "Germany in her 1937 frontiers"? What is useful for long-term comparisons, often loses any sense for the synchronic ones. And these margins of errors [3]!

The richest deposits of comparable figures from the prestatistical era, price series, have been hardly used for development estimates. Prices of wheat, salt, wool, cloths, and other goods in international

---

[1] W. KULA, *Théorie économique du système féodal,* Paris 1970, p. 10 seq.

[2] E.g., in Podlasie, a border region between Lithuania and Poland, new towns chartered in the fifteenth-sixteenth centuries were endowed with thousands of hectars of land (information by Prof. Andrzej Wyrobisz).

[3] Recently Andrzej Wyczański tried to estimate Poland's place among European countries in the sixteenth century. A conclusion one may draw from his interesting and stimulating book is that statistical margins of errors are too wide to make general national estimates truly comparable. A. WYCZANSKI, *Polska w Europie XVI stulecia,* Warsaw 1973.

commerce are fit for drawing diachronic curves but when compared synchronically they inform directly about commercial profits and transport costs. The second thesis let be: price series should be exploited as indicators of economic development.

My initial working hypothesis has been that there are, roughly speaking, two kinds of goods: one earmarked for extraregional commerce, and another consumed at home or sold in the region of production, in the neighbourhood. Prices of each of these groups of products are determined by different factors. In the period in question, distant demand strongly influences prices of silks, woolens, salt, spices etc.; these are textbook examples. Much less is known about determinants of prices of locally consumed goods.

An imaginative dissertation published fifteen years ago in Poland aimed at measurement of demand by comparing local rye/oats price ratios in various parts of the country in two chronological cross-sections (in 1564/65 and about 1620) [4]. The rye: oats quotient indicates intensity of demand for rye, i.e., the principal export commodity, as contrasted to a local-consumption product, oats: where rye prices are relatively high, the demand from abroad must be intensive, and *vice versa*. The author had tried to eliminate any short-time factors, and some subsequent control investigations proved that he was not fully successful in that. And yet his basic idea proved sound and fruitful; I may formulate it a little broader: development can be measured and studied by comparisons of regional price structures.

Economic historians, familiar with principal comodities of international trade, hardly lean over numerous goods of more local interest. Only a few of these products seem comparable; different measures — these sacks, bundles, cartloads — can disarm even the most temerary scholar. Even measurable items like shoes, which used to be among simple "mass products" of preindustrial crafts, can discourage one because of their variety reflected by price-ranges. One may take into consideration only the cheapest brands available in a place. However, may it be taken for granted that what was acceptable as footwear in, say,

---

[4] S. MIELCZARSKI, *Rynek zbożowy na ziemiach polskich w drugiej polowie XVI i pierwszej polowie XVII wieku. Próba rejonizacji*, Gdańsk 1962.

Cracow, was similar and similarly acceptable (and consequently comparable) in Cologne or Modena [5]?

What remains for comparisons are mostly building materials, bricks, shingles and two sorts of nails: shingle-nails and lath-nails (*Lattennägel*). These are easily measurable, sold in large quantities and included into price series by thousands (bricks, shingles, nails) or hundreds and three-scores (shingles, nails). Unavoidably there are some quality differences reflected by particular determinants, like in Hamburg: *Kamper Steine, Rodenberger Steine, Hamburger Steine* and by differential prices [6]; only some of them can be eliminated or ascertained, like "large" "small" or "medium" bricks (or shingles), "double" nails.

Now, what reality is reflected by comparisons of price series of such commodities? When studied diachronically they do not differ from any other series and visualize vicissitudes of building activity in a town. On the other hand, their synchronic differences in space seem to mirror differences of local conditions. Each item tells its own story, more or less different from the other. As far as *bricks* are concerned, raw material may be disregarded; appropriate clay is one of the most common deposits but much fuel is needed under European sun and transport may be difficult and expensive, too. *Shingles* are easier transportable and do not need fuel, yet proper wood may be scarce in some places [7]. *Nails* are products of more complex, sometimes even advanced, industrial processes and invoke both fuel and raw-material factors. However, they are still relatively simple and uniform products as compared with knives, sickles, ploughs or locksmith's goods.

A synchronic comparison of prices of above-mentioned commodities is informative about several factors hardly discernible from each other:

---

[5] See reservations of F. BRAUDEL and F. SPOONER, *Prices in Europe from 1450 to 1750*, The Cambridge Economic History of Europe, IV, Cambrige 1967, p. 415 seq.

[6] *Institut für Wirtschafts- und Sozialgeschichte der Universität Göttingen, Preis- und Lohngeschichtliches Archiv (Elsas-Archiv), Hamburg, Jahrrechnungen des Hiob-Hospitals: Mauersteine,* passim. I am very thankful to Prof. Wilhelm Abel, Prof. Karl-Heinrich Kaufhold and Dr. Dietrich Saalfeld for their friendly aid and co-operation.

[7] On resources of building materials in Europe, cfr. A. WYROBISZ, *Resources and Construction Materials in Preindustrial Europe*, A. MĄCZAK and W. N. PARKER (eds.), *Natural Resources in European History. A Conference Report*, Resources for the Future Research Papers, R-13, Washington, D.C. (1978), pp. 65-84.

1) intensity of building activity, 2) cost of labour, itself depending upon demand and supply of labour force, and upon 3) basic maintenance costs of labourers. High prices of items in question are products of all these components and — with some reservations — may be taken for positive indicators. However, these very reservations are of importance; I shall return to them in due course.

Prices of bricks from twelve cities from between Rhine, Danube, Vistula, and Dniester region (Lwow) may serve for a case study. Compared horizontally they present somewhat of an area of high prices including Frankfurt (Main), Speier, Würzburg, Gdansk and Hamburg; Utrecht and Augsburg are rather cheap as well as Munich. In the East, Vienna matches Leipzig, Cracow and Lwow, and lags behind Warsaw. Brick prices in Gdansk, a fast developing industrial and commercial centre, in the second half of the sixteenth century equal the highest ones in Central Europe and do not yield to those in Frankfurt or Speier (from the 1620's several series are discontinued).

Tiles (a control-item) confirm the relative cheapness of building ceramics in Utrecht: in 1550/59 to the 1590's a thousand of roof tiles costs there (on the average per decade) from 49.2 to 61.5 grams of silver, while in Vienna they are 73.2 to 80.0 grams, in Cracow slightly more, and in Gdansk almost exactly three times more (108.5 to 183.9; 154.6 on the average).

Shingles' prices are not available in the West and in Gdansk. Vienna and Klosterneuburg testify about price levels comparable to Cracow and Lwow: slightly below the former and above the latter.

Also shingle-nails in Austria (the same two cities) are sold for similar prices. The prices of lath-nails are known from more places. Utrecht is once more astonishingly cheap, but also in Würzburg (where bricks are so expensive!) one can get lath-nails for nuts in comparison to Cracow and Lwow, and particularly to Warsaw. Is it not characteristic that regional price differentials of bricks and nails seem to be inverse in Würzburg (most probably representative for the Rhine-Main region) and in Poland? Certain data from yearly accounts of royal domains in Poland which do not constitute a price series seem to confirm a rule that nail prices are more sensible to lively market conditions than bricks and shingles.

Let me now turn to other sets of figures, better known because of

massive research done in particular by Wilhelm Abel and Charles Ver-
linden and their collaborators: craftsmen wages expressed in cereals
(here: in rye). For obvious reasons bread would be a better common
denominator but there are almost no price figures for it from most
places. Wilhelm Abel's price relatives (a day-work salary in kilograms of
rye) have been checked and also completed for the subsequent period
1600-1649.

When real wages are discussed one cannot ignore short-term
changes; grain prices were highly elastic and their fluctuations determined wages decisively. Levels of wages in West German cities were
low both in comparison to Antwerp and to Austria or Poland. Figures
we have for Leipzig are questionable: *Zimmermann* is rather a master
carpenter than a journeyman (*Knecht, Geselle*), so his pay is about 1/3
higher. However, even indipendent from gaps in records, vertical
(chronological) fluctuations are deeper than the horizontal (synchronic)
differences. Even the fifty years' averages are therefore open to doubts
and of limited reliability. So, at this stage it may be only concluded that
real wages are differently determined form, in some cases inversely
proportional to, prices of building materials.

A wealth of informations about prices of consumables and directly
about living costs is contained in expense sheets of travellers. Open to
strong criticism and difficult to be evaluated when unique, such expense sheets become outspoken and talkative when they can be cross-
checked [8].

Among numerous items of expense sheets there are some repetable
and to a large degree comparable. Comparable, of course, in a
framework of each particular journey. A traveller's consumption habits
and his purse-potential, number of his men and horses must make a
constant although they are subjected to varying pressures in each region
visited. A trivial factor heavily distorting the picture is exhaustion of

---

[8] I discussed this subject in *Un témoin des prix européens à la fin du XVIe siècle, Mélanges en
l'honneur de Fernand Braudel, Histoire économique du monde méditerranéen 1450-1650*, I,
Toulouse 1973, pp. 327-336 and in *Preise, Löhne und Lebenshaltungskosten im Europa des 16. Jahrhunderts. Ein Beitrag zur Quellenkritik,* Wirtschaftliche und soziale Wandlungen im saekularen
Wandel. Festschrift für Wilhelm Abel zum 70. Geburtstag, II, Die vorindustrielle Zeit: Aussera-
grarische Probleme, Hannover 1974, pp. 326-344.

purse during a long journey. Fortunately this is by no means very common thanks to good services of merchants-bankers: a traveller when about to go abroad used to provide himself with bills of exchange or bills of credit drawn on particular bankers resident of cities he intended to visit [9].

Much depends on they way of boockkeeping. Albeit both very detailed and officially confirmed (by original bills and by inspecting officers) expense sheets of envoys must not be necessarily more useful than more indirect opinions and notes of a Fynes Moryson or a John Lauder of Fountainhall. Usually the repetitive items are dinner, supper (including bed), in German records: *verzehrt,* in Danish: *aftens maaltid, middag,* etc. There arise numerous doubts as to the nature of single items and many of them must remain disregarded. It is a particularly happy occasion when expenses of bed and table are separated from those of the stable. Each group reflects a different reality. But what reality?

A bill for bed and meals depends upon quality of services done: a single room? a single bed (a big issue in sixteenth-century Germany where two guests usually shared a bed)? locks? a privy? Also number and skills of servants of an inn, quality of food and number of courses, pewter or wooden dishes, silver, glass or faïence, linen or silk napkins (or no napkins at all) shaped the overall price. Michel Montaigne and his contemporaries devoted much attention to such things upon which depended their health, spirits and prestige.

The horses might have been less discriminative; their provender surely depended less upon local cuisine and because of that our scanty information about maintenance costs is of particular value. It directly reflects local prices of fodder components (hay or straw, oats) plus service costs. No imported goods were involved and therefore a comparison of inn- and stable-expenses is of some interest.

The statistical series in question are of very particular character. Low figures may signify either moderate costs of quality food and

---

[9] I discuss these mechanisms in great detail in a book on daily life of travellers in Europe, 16th-17th centuries *Życie codzienne w podróży po Europie w XVI i XVII w.*, Warszawa² 1980 and in *Tourists and Bankers in the XVIth and XVIIth Centuries, Studi in memoria di Federigo Melis*, IV, s.l. 1978, p. 349-360.

III

lodging or (what more common) rather primitive living conditions. Very
often the cheapness of a hostelry was product of both moderate prices
of basic food and primitive service, furniture, rooms etc. Travellers
were hardly temperate and discreet about these subjects and loved to
enlarge upon them. True, their impressions did not reflect the living
conditions and living costs of people native of a country but their world
still was not equipped with Hilton hotels and even the most wealthy
lords and princes did not avoid the hardships of journey through "barren", "wild", underinvested regions. And even if a prince was rather
sure he would sleep each night in a bed, travel chronicles were being
written by courtiers much more sensitive about these problems. Travel
diaries of Philippe le Beau and Charles-Quint through Spain serve as a
good example and may be contrasted against the court's experience in
more developed landscapes between, say, the Upper Rhine and the
Netherlands [10].

* * *

Participants of a round-table discussion are not expected to supply
final solutions; they should rather suggest questions and trends of inquiry. Now, I believe that alongside the discussion of large contrasting
blocks, be they "core" and "periphery" or "metropoly" and "colo-
ny", one should study more complex and gradual phenomena of the
development/backwardness opposition. Wherever the great international commerce is involved, and wherever one can contrast to one
another large distant areas, an opposition seems sharp. An inverse approach proves that some indicators of development change only gra-
dually. Notions like "the core" and "the periphery" are of a relative
nature in that a peripheric area has its own developed core-region, often (always?) connected with, and depending on, the higher developed,
dominating regions abroad or overseas.

A feeler of diverse price series and particularly a comparison of

---

[10] See *Collection des voyages des souverains des Pays-Bas*, ed. M. GACHARD, Bruxelles 1876-
1882, I-IV, passim.

them suggests that for the period in question there is no clear "moder-n" conjunction like "the development equals high standard of living of the population". Expense sheets of travellers seem to be the most sensitive known aggregate inicators of living standards and living expenses. They inform about locally acceptable quality of life of propertied classes. Where cities' network is dense, one gets quality service (sensu largo) every day (or rather every night), and index in question becomes an index of urbanization. Travellers may complain but high expenses rather exactly reflect, and are proportional to, consumption standards. But beware! A step aside from the trade (and tourist) route and there may be a wilderness: no food, no lodging. But exactly the density of roads, inns, the supply of travel services is an indirect but rather faithful indicator of development, whatever this notion may signify.

The more strange is the striking contrast of travel expenses and of wages expressed in grain. Where a gentleman traveller enjoys the best treatment, the wage earner gets his meagre equivalent of six to ten kilograms of grain per working day. Where — as in Poland (beyond the principal cities) and in East Germany — inns are less than modest, and travellers are reminded to keep their straw-bed (or rather bedding) away from cows that share the lodging, the workers' real wages are much more substantial.

These were the two sides of the phenomenon of relative dearth of food in better developed regions. The traveller simply noted higher food cost, approved of its better quality and/or complained against high taxes and rents that were supposed to be at the roots of the dearth. A journeyman, a worker — on the other hand — disposed of a strictly limited budget and did or did not meet both ends.

One of the most difficult questions is to divide various factors contributing to the price level: density of population, natural conditions, food imports, intensity of money economy etc. All these factors are interdependent but still in certain countries and at certain times some of them seem to dominate. Any such division must be — in a sense by definition — only rough and approximative but I do not think it to be totally hopeless.

May I present one more set of indicators: money wages of labourers whose salary consisted mostly from food, shelter and some clothes

(Figs. 4 & 5). The most appropriate and most common case are the milk-maids (cow-maids): poorest-paid unskilled women. Wherever there is information about the wages, their nature is strictly comparable. Milk-maids are getting some money (once, twice or four times in a year, but not for day-work) plus shoes, shoe soles, skirts, shirts, kerchiefs etc. There are several types of women's jobs but they are usually easily discernible. In Speyer there are *Viehmägde* and *Schweinemägde,* and occasionally a *Nebenmagd.* In Polish manors there are cow-maids (*ancillae, dziewki*) and also girls and an "old lady", a supervisor and manager of the garden and dairy farm, a much better paid and influential person. In Poland about 1565 total value of money paid to cow-maids plus the above-mentioned clothes made up 1/6 to of 1/4 the value of food supplied to a working person. However, these foodstuffs were not necessarily market goods, so in practice they often had very little real value. On the other hand, a milk-maid's income consisted also of windfall and regular tips, perhaps some minor pilfered foodstuffs and other goods. Important is that a couple of coins earned by a milkmaid were not to be spent on basic food. The sum was determined to a certain degree by supply of, and demand for, labour: mobility of labourers was limited but there was no *Gesindezwangsdienst* (compulsory employment) in Poland. The very fact of great and regular regional differences of these wage-supplements in money prove that they had to attract labour hands. Generally speaking, a chart of these supplements reminds of a zero-sum strategy of games: each figure is a compromise between contrasting interests of landlords and their manor-managers, and of the labourers.

The highest figures of the chart concentrate near to Gdansk (about 100 Polish *grosz,* i.e., 0.815 grams of silver in 1565). Figures for Ruthenia, in the S-E corner, are schematic (always 60 grosz. Another high figure (80) derives from Spiš (German: Zips), a region neighbouring to Upper Hungarian (i.e., Slovakian) silver and copper mines. Islets of higher wages concentrate in neighbourhoods of larger towns and along the Silesian border. In Little Poland dominate 36 to 48 grosz; in Great Poland the minimum is somewhat lower; in Mazovia one gets about 30 grosz only. Another set of data derived from Church estates confirms these results for 1582. Another confirmation concerns oxherds from the same Royal domains. A schematic chart of *relative* money supplements

for milkmaids (figures to the left of *) and oxherds (behind the asterisk) all over the country may look as follows:

Royal Prussia 200-400*250-370
Great Poland 100-160*100-200 Masovia 100*100
Little Poland 120-180*100-140
Ruthenia 200*200

High index figures for Ruthenia can be explained by demand for
labour in the neighbourhood of thinly inhabited Ukraine; in Royal
Prussia on the Lower Vistula husbandry was much more intensive,
cities prosperous and growing (Gdansk!), serfdom — at that time —
mild, and still tolerable labour services; intensive demand for labour
hands in that area manifested itself in rather high (money) price of
labour while small good made in Gdansk or imported through it were
on the spot cheaper than elsewhere in Poland. The saddle of a synchronic curve extended between Gdansk and Ruthenia needs a few
words of interpretation. In Masovia landed property was comminuted,
towns rather miserable in comparison with Great Poland and Royal
Prussia. Small farms and tiny estates of petty squires did not press for
labour. Great seasonal and permanent emigration (the latter embracing
all classes from the landless poor to townspeople to petty noblemen
and clergy) and low level of salaries signified misery. A similar demographic expansion plus high wages would have and opposite meaning.

A phenomenon marginal in itself like money seems to be a very sensitive indicator: in the neighbourhood of larger towns figures used to be
higher (Poznan and some centres of clothmaking industry in Great Poland; Cracow). In general, the higher figures the more flourishing a region. And what about the other countries?

In Speyer the average yearly salary of a milkmaid, 1560-1565,
equalled to 135.5 grams of silver (or 155.7 grams, value of the allowance in kind included); in Leipzig one got in 1573 113.7 grams silver.
A Frisian farmer, Rienck Hemmema, whose detailed business accounts
have been studied by H. Slicher van Bath, was paying sparingly
(labourers escaped from his farm) but still a *kleine meid* was getting
(1570 to 1573) ca. 110 stuivers, a shirt and shoes, i.e., 81.1 to 89.4
grams silver whereas a *groote meid* (and this probably was comparable
to other milk-maids or *Viehmägde*) could count, depending on silver

value of the stuiver, for 206.4 to 227.6 grams [11]. The highest pay in Poland, near to Gdansk, equalled 106.0 grams (130 grosz), the lowest comparable was only 19.6 grams (24 grosz).

* * *

All these diverse and dispersed sets of figures do not permit to draw a map of development (and backwardness) in early modern Europe. The network of information is not dense enough, nor is its nature well enough clear. However, it seems to promise some solutions in the future when more types and more dense information are collected from various areas. What is particularly important and promising: each set of figures informs sparingly, often very sparingly, but from a different angle. Wages calculated in grain (bread) and in silver tell different tales and there are reasons to discuss them both ways. Last but not least, one cannot make a step towards understanding the early modern type of development in Europe without understanding the circulation of money. Comparative models of prices and wage relationships for many countries and regions may be a convenient, operative and effective approach.

---

[11] B. H. SLICHER VAN BATH, *Een fries landbouwbedrijf in de tweede helft van de zestiende eeuw*, Agronomisch-Historische Bijdragen, IV, Wageningen 1968, p. 114 seq.

Silver Equivalents of Prices: LATH-NAILS
(grams of silver per 1000)

	Utrecht	Würzburg	Vienna (medium)	Vienna (large)	Klosterneuburg (large)	Leipzig	Cracow *	Warsaw *	Lwow *
1550-9	·	16.0	18.4	20.7	19.0	·	18.9	·	24.2
1560-9	7.22	25.2	17.5	27.3	25.3	·	29.0	39.5	31.8
1570-9	8.16	24.0	18.2	·	25.0	31.3	30.5	38.5	43.2
1580-9	13.50	26.4	·	·	·	26.7	34.5	37.5	39.7
1590-9	·	25.0	·	·	·	28.3	34.8	37.4	40.8
1600-9	·	27.5	·	·	24.8	41.2	43.8	48.5	42.2
1610-9	·	28.1	·	·	·	41.2	36.5	51.3	35.3
1629-9	·	30.0	·	·	39.0	·	35.1	58.3	46.3
1630-9	·	29.0	28.1	32.1	37.4	40.2	37.5	62.2	45.7
1640-9	·	26.1	24.8	·	38.9	45.2	43.8	66.2	41.7
1550-99	(9.63)	23.3	(18.0)	·	23.1	(28.7)	29.5	(37.3)	35.9
1600-49	·	28.1	·	·	32.6	42.2	39.3	57.3	42.2

* Original data for three-score.

RYE EQUIVALENTS OF DAILY WAGES: CARPENTERS AND MASONS

(kilograms of rye)

	Antwerp j.* mason	Hamburg j. mason	Augsburg j. mason	Munich j. car- penter	Leipzig car- penter	Vienna j. mason	Kloster- neuburg j. mason	Gdansk j. mason	Gdansk j. car- penter	Cracow j. mason	Lwow j. car- penter	Lwow j. mason
1550-9	10.0	8.7	10.4	.	.	20.8	.	12.3	14.7	14.0	.	.
1560-9	15.6	7.9	9.2	.	15.9	12.2	8.1	.	14.8	16.9	(27.4)	27.4
1570-9	16.1	6.4	6.6	.	8.7	7.3	.	17.3	15.2	11.2	(9.3)	9.8
1580-9	12.2	8.4	7.8	.	8.6	13.9	9.3	17.6	15.8	18.6	(22.4)	31.4
1590-9	11.0	7.5	6.5	.	8.4	9.3	14.3	16.1	12.9	17.8	.	.
1600-9	.	11.5	6.9	.	10.8	10.9	.	17.5	17.5	6.7	(14.2)	25.3
1610-9	.	13.6	6.6	.	8.4	12.3	6.7	10.7	15.2	6.7	12.0	19.8
1620-9	.	9.2	4.5	(5.8)	25.6	13.0	22.4	8.8	7.7	.	18.1	27.8
1630-9	.	11.6	5.1	(10.3)	10.9	7.5	13.3	14.5	12.5	.	6.2	10.8
1640-9	.	13.7	10.7	(7.3)	18.0	10.7	14.8	11.7	11.5	6.9	9.0	12.7
1550-99	13.0	7.8	8.1	.	10.8	12.7	(10.6)	15.8	14.7	15.7	.	(22.9)
1600-49	.	11.9	6.7	(7.8)	12.0	11.3	(14.3)	13.4	12.8	(6.8)	(11.9)	19.3

* Journeyman.
Mostly summer wages (wherever available); in Gdansk, Cracow, Lwow – data from II and III quarter.

SILVER EQUIVALENTS OF PRICES: BRICKS

(grams of silver per 1000)

	Utrecht	Frankfurt/M.	Speier	Augsburg	Würzburg	Munich	Vienna	Leipzig	Gdansk	Cracow	Warsaw	Lwow
1550-9	44.6	98.8	67.8	74.8	78.8	32.8	35.0	·	61.1	46.6	·	38.5
1560-9	·	118.6	94.6	86.5	107.3	55.7	45.5	·	125.0	46.2	51.2	46.2
1570-9	59.9	122.7	116.9	78.4	120.4	54.1	45.0	50.8	106.7	48.6	69.3	43.9
1580-9	54.6	124.2	132.2	79.6	77.8	51.9	48.1	47.7	114.2	46.4	62.5	42.1
1590-9	102.2	86.6	131.4	·	109.8	59.2	48.2	46.7	88.7	52.5	79.0	45.5
1600-9	·	85.5	132.1	88.6	118.4	63.4	62.8	51.3	84.7	57.5	99.9	50.5
1610-9	·	107.5	127.3	99.3	116.3	64.9	62.6	72.4	169.5	50.2	101.3	50.5
1620-9	·	·	·	·	·	87.2	92.6	·	151.7	64.4	76.9	74.4
1630-9	·	·	·	·	·	112.2	87.6	·	168.1	68.9	115.1	79.4
1640-9	·	·	·	·	·	108.0	78.4	·	177.3	78.2	151.1	85.0
1550-99	65.3	110.2	108.6	79.8	98.8	50.7	44.4	(48.4)	99.1	48.1	(65.5)	43.2
1600-49	·	(96.5)	(129.7)	(94.0)	(117.4)	67.7	76.8	(61.8)	150.3	63.8	108.9	68.8

Rye Equivalents of Daily Wages:
MASONS & JOURNEYMEN-CARPENTERS in Strasbourg
(kilograms of rye per daily pay)

1551-75	12.9
1576-1600	8.3
1601-25	13.3
1626-50	9.3

Attention!

In price series for Gdansk, Cracow, Lwow and Warsaw decades begin with 1 (1551, 1561 etc).

In price series for Vienna and Klosterneuburg years 1619 through 1624 are omitted.

Averages open to particular doubts are in parentheses.

Silver Equivalents of Prices: SHINGLES
(grams of silver per 1000)

	Vienna	Kloster-neuburg (small)	Cracow **	Cracow *	Lwow *
1550-9	26.9	27.6	20.0	23.4	31.5
1560-9	2.4	28.6	23.0	26.3	37.0
1570-9	27.7	27.8	22.4	28.4	32.0
1580-9	26.2	26.0	23.5	28.8	27.5
1590-9	25.7	26.9	27.8	35.8	30.8
1600-9	26.7	27.4	.	45.1	27.7
1610-9	25.1	25.7	.	39.3	24.8
1620-9	31.6	25.2	.	38.6	29.3
1630-9	23.3	23.9	.	38.3	31.2
1640-9	23.4	23.7	.	44.8	32.0
1550-99	27.0	27.4	23.3	28.5	31.8
1600-49	26.0	25.2	.	41.2	29.0

* Original data deal with three-scores.
** Shingles sold per three-scores are ca. 20% more expensive.

Prices and wages have been calculated in silver or in rye according to information contained in standard editions of price series:

for *The Netherlands*, N. W. POSTHUMUS, *Inquiry into the History of Prices in Holland*, I-II, Leiden 1946-1964;

for *Leipzig, Frankfurt/M., Würzburg, Speyer, Augsburg*, M. J. ELSAS, *Umriss einer Geschichte der Preise und Löhne in Deutschland vom ausgehenden Mittelalter bis zum Beginn des neunzehnten Jahrhunderts*, I-IIA-IIB, Leiden 1936-1949; cf. note 6;

for *Poland*, S. HOSZOWSKI, *Ceny we Lwowie w XVI i XVII wieku*, Lwów 1928; J. PELC, *Ceny w Gdańsku w XVI i XVII wieku*, Lwów 1937; IDEM, *Ceny w Krakowie w latach 1369-1600*, Lwów 1935; E. TOMASZEWSKI, *Ceny w Krakowie w latach 1601-1795*, Lwów 1934; W. ADAMCZYK, *Ceny w Warszawie w XVI i XVII wieku*, Lwów 1938;

for *Vienna* and *Klosterneuburg*, A. F. PRIBRAM, *Materialien zur Geschichte der Preise und Löhne in Österreich*, I, Vienna 1938;

for *Strasbourg*, A. HANAUER, *Etudes économiques sur l'Alsace ancienne et moderne*, I-II, Paris-Strasbourg 1876-1878.

Professors Pierre Jeannin, Othmar Pickl, Marzio Achille Romani, Ekkehard Westermann kindly aided me with valuable information which only partly and often indirectly could be turned to account in this essay.

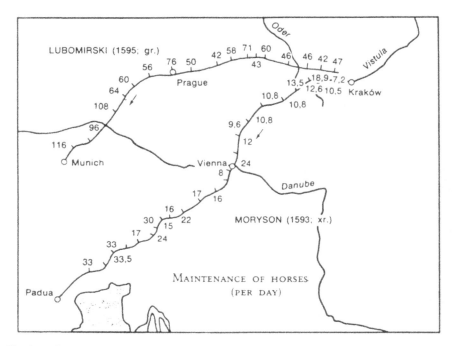

Fig. 1. — Costs of maintenance of horses per day: Stanislaw Lubomirski, 1595, in Polish *grosz*; Fynes Moryson, 1593, in Imperial *Kreuzer*. From A. Mączak, *Preise, Löhne*, cit.

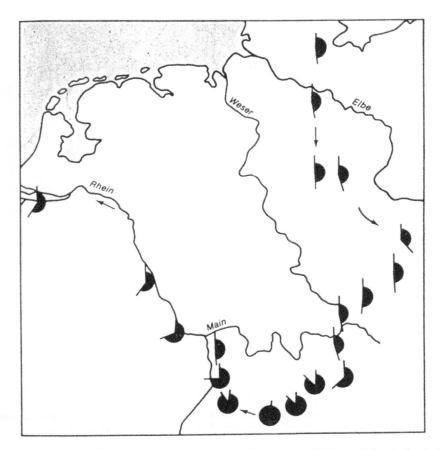

Fig. 2. — Daily expenses of a Würtenberg embassy to Westminster, 1595, in relation to the most expensive day: in Stuttgart (full ring). From A. Mączak, *Zycie codzienne w podrózach po Europie w XVI i XVII wieku*, Warszawa 1980, p. 87.

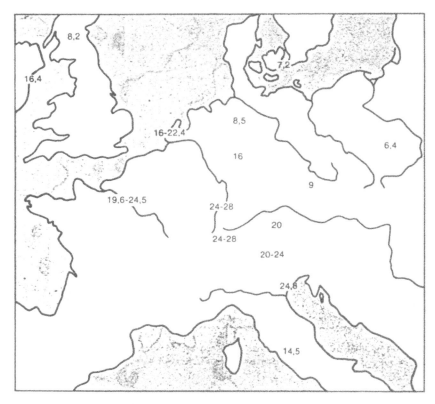

Fig. 3. — Motyson's own estimates of the dinner's (+ overnight) cost in various parts of Europe; I omit the less reliable data for England, 1590's. From sources quoted for figs. 1 & 2.

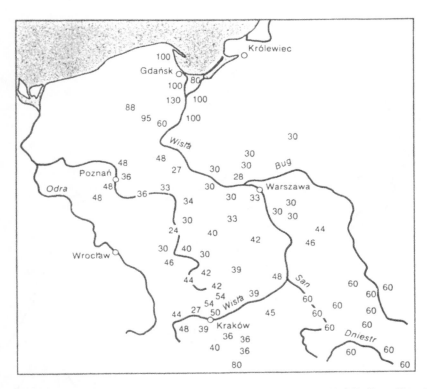

Fig. 4. — Money salaries of cow-girls (royal estates, per year in *grosz*, 1564/65). From Mączak, *Preise, Löhne,* cit.

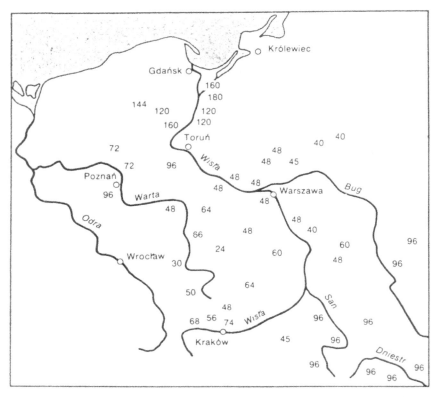

Fig. 5. — **Money salaries of shepherds (royal estates, per year in *grosz*, 1564/65). From Mączak,**
***Preise, Löhne,* cit.**

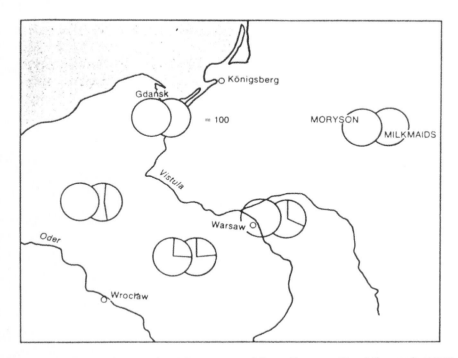

Fig. 6. — A Comparison of relative daily expenses of Fynes Moryson with relative yearly money salaries of cow-maids in Poland.

IV

Un voyageur
témoin des prix européens
à la fin du XVIᵉ siècle

Les historiens qui analysent les conjonctures et autres phénomènes économiques ont l'habitude d'insister tout particulièrement
sur les changements s'effectuant dans le temps. S'ils sont cons-
cients des liens qui s'unissent dans l'histoire, le temps et l'espace,
qui se pénètrent indissolublement, ce sentiment ne suscite le plus
souvent que de vagues réflexions. Le temps, c'est la durée et le
changement. L'espace, ce sont les routes (et le manque de routes).
Lorsque le chercheur se penche sur le problème que posent les
différences dans l'espace, il doit fort souvent se demander ce
qui peut remplacer dans les trois dimensions spatiales l'outil
commode — trop commode, peut-être — qu'est la série chrono-
logique ? Nous essayons d'abord de comparer les prix et de les
analyser et nous savons déjà bien des choses sur la densité de la
population, mais nous sommes encore bien loin d'une synthèse
comparative. En attendant qu'elle soit élaborée, questionnons les
contemporains, adressons-nous ne serait-ce qu'aux voyageurs. « Syn-
chronie ? Un coup de sifflet et voilà le film arrêté. Tous les per-
sonnages du drame restent à leur place. Le globe terrestre tourne
toujours, mais les hommes et les choses restent immobiles. Mais dans
cette vision synchronique du monde il apparaîtra immédiatement
que des régions, des économies, des sociétés ne sont pas au même
point, au même niveau du développement. Parfois elles ne sont
ni de la même époque, ni de la même durée. » [1]
Il n'est pas possible de réaliser cette pensée de Fernand
Braudel dans une courte esquisse analytique. Mais si l'on tient
à le faire, l'*Itinerary* de Fynes Moryson peut fournir un bon point
de départ [2]. Au cours de la période très importante bien que
brève, comprise entre 1591 et 1597, ses notes de voyage et ses
réflexions synthétiques nous conduisent à plusieurs reprises à
travers les deux principaux « isthmes » qui relient le Nord à l'Italie. Désintéressé, curieux de connaître le monde, s'intéressant aux
langues étrangères et convaincu que « the variety is the most

of pleasing thing in the World », Moryson a traversé plusieurs fois l'Allemagne, le Danemark, la Pologne, la Moravie, la Bohême, les pays des Alpes, le nord des Pays-Bas, il s'est aussi embarqué pour le Proche-Orient où il a visité la Palestine et la Syrie, parvenant finalement à Constantinople. Seules les très grandes villes retiennent longuement son attention. L'Italie l'éblouit. Il s'y départit de son style concis, décrit en détail les monuments, les coutumes, la vie quotidienne. Il n'oublie pas en général de noter les prix de l'avoine, le coût des repas, le nombre des lieues faites dans la journée et les pièces de monnaie qui passent entre ses mains. Après avoir accompagné Moryson jusqu'au but de son voyage, le lecteur pourrait ne pas l'apprécier à sa juste valeur. Ce voyageur ne manifeste en effet son esprit de synthèse que lorsqu'il commence à donner des conseils à ses successeurs. Nous n'y trouvons pas seulement des *nationum proprietates* stéréotypées, mais aussi des observations originales que nous chercherions en vain chez les autres auteurs.

Les problèmes qu'il soulève dépassent malheureusement le cadre de cette esquisse très brève. Nous concentrerons donc notre attention sur une seule question, remettant les autres à une autre occasion.

Que valent les impressions d'un touriste qui ne s'arrête que pour changer de chevaux, dîne, ne consacre dans ses notes qu'une seule phrase aux hommes d'une région donnée et poursuit sa route le jour même ou le lendemain ? Ce sont précisément les voyageurs de ce genre qui façonnent l'idée stéréotypée qu'on se fait des peuples et des pays. Moryson [3] lui non plus, n'a pas échappé à cette règle générale. Sachons-lui cependant gré de la manière méticuleuse dont il a noté les petits riens quotidiens, contrôlons — quand il est possible de le faire — ses informations et permettons-lui de nous parler de ce qu'il connaît le mieux. S'il ne fait pas de doute qu'un touriste sait bien moins de choses sur un pays que les habitants de ce pays, ses observations ont cependant une valeur comparative. Là où les recherches précises font défaut et où le manque de sources les rend impossibles, les observations et les notes succinctes d'un voyageur peuvent servir de guide à l'historien et donner plus d'ampleur à ses investigations.

C'est en effet aux questions les plus simples qu'il est parfois le plus difficile de répondre ; on explique avec peine, après quelques siècles, des questions qui sont évidentes pour chaque touriste contemporain.

.*.

Suivons donc notre voyageur en partant de l'embouchure de l'Elbe où il a débarqué venant d'Angleterre. Arrivé à Stade — écrit-il — il a pris un repas à l'auberge allemande, qui lui a coûté 4 1/2 shillings de Lubeck. A l'auberge anglaise de Stade, il aurait payé 8 pence pour ce repas. Dès la première phrase, nous trouvons un problème monétaire. Lorsque Moryson quitte l'Allemagne du Nord, il fait usage, au Danemark de shillings danois, à partir de la Prusse Royale, de groschen polonais, en Moravie, de groschen moraves et en Bohême, de groschen tchèques. En Autriche, il a des kreuzer dans sa bourse, et ensuite des soldi et autres menues monnaies italiennes. En Allemagne du Sud, il dépensera des batzen, et aux Pays-Bas, des stuivers, etc., etc. Comment réussissait-il à se servir de ces diverses pièces de monnaie et comment un historien doit-il expliquer ces faits ?

La menue monnaie, surtout les pièces de cuivre, avaient cours dans des régions bien plus restreintes que les monnaies lourdes, surtout celles dont la renommée était établie. Moryson, qui sait parfaitement calculer la valeur des angels anglais en reichstaler et en ducats de Venise, explique très simplement le mécanisme du crédit et des transferts d'argent. Il n'a aucune difficulté à calculer la valeur réciproque des petites monnaies et s'empresse d'indiquer les profits et les pertes qui résultent de leur échange. Ceci nous permet de suivre son exemple [4]. Comme unité de base nous avons choisi le kreutzer impérial (xr), généralement connu dans tout l'Empire. Prenant exemple sur notre voyageur, notons ses dépenses. Voici un tableau présentant les prix qu'il payait généralement pour ses repas.

Les différences régionales sont évidentes. Les pays les plus chers en Europe — tout au moins à ce point de vue — sont : la Rhénanie, le Palatinat (pour être plus précis : les environs de Francfort), la Thuringe (Halberstadt et la région des mines de Mansfeld) ; ensuite l'Allemagne du Sud avec la Suisse, les Pays-Bas et l'Italie du Nord (l'Etat de Venise). Les régions de la presqu'île situées entre le Pô et Rome sont un peu moins coûteuses. En Autriche, Styrie et Carinthie, le niveau de prix est le même qu'en Allemagne du Sud. Les prix sont assez bas sur les bords de la Baltique et les plus bas se rencontrent au centre de la Pologne, mais en partant de là ils s'accroissent rapidement lorsque le voyageur approche de Vienne. Le tableau qu'il nous en brosse répond à ce que nous savons d'une façon très générale des prix européens (seul le prix du froment a déjà été analysé plus à fond). Quelles conclusions pouvons-nous en tirer ? Demandons-nous d'abord si les services que Moryson payait dans les divers pays sont comparables.

Il s'efforçait de voyager commodément. Nous éliminons d'ailleurs les cas où il était obligé de limiter ses dépenses et ceux où il dépensait plus qu'il n'avait l'intention de le faire. Il payait en général son dîner et son souper. Dans l'Angleterre de Shakespeare, le *dinner* était le repas de midi, le *supper* celui du soir [5]. Dans les notes de Moryson, le coût de ces deux repas ne diffère pas régulièrement. Le *supper* est fort souvent plus cher que le

PRIX D'UN « DINNER » OU D'UN « SUPPER » [5]

Région	Prix « A »	Prix « B »
Danemark	7-8 3/4	8-8 3/4[a]
Stade-Lubeck	10	
Allemagne du Nord		4 1/2 (?)
Frise Orientale	7 1/2-11	
Basse Saxe	7 1/2-11	
Thuringe (Halberstadt-Mansfeld)	28	
Saxe (Torgau-Leipzig-Dresde)	15-18	
Worms-Francfort/Main	24-32	
Allemagne Centrale		16
Franconie	24	
Haut Palatinat	18-20	18-20[b]
Allemagne du Sud		20-26 ; 24[c]-28
Strasbourg-Heidelberg	24	
Innsbruck	24	
Haut Rhin	24	
Suisse	24	
Grisons (et environs)	15-22	
Paris et région de Rouen	25	
Normandie		16 (?)
Angleterre		jusqu'à 32
Ecosse		8
Irlande		16 1/4
Veneto (Venise, Padoue)	15-22	22
« Italie Centrale »	8 1/2-22	7 1/2-10 3/4
Prusse Royale (Gdansk-Elblag)	8-10	
Leczyca-Cracovie	2 1/2-4[d]	
Silésie Polonaise	12-16	
Pologne (en général)		4-6 ; 8-12
Moravie	8-11 3/4	
Bohême	13-23	12
Autriche Inférieure	14-24	
Styrie-Carinthie	9-24	

dinner, alors que le *breakfast* est moins coûteux et parfois inclus dans le prix du coucher. Il arrive aussi qu'il coûte autant que les deux autres repas. Le voyageur, désireux de poursuivre sa route aussi rapidement que possible, se contente parfois d'un seul repas copieux, ou bien il considère que seul le prix de ce repas est digne d'être noté. Que signifient par conséquent les différences de prix que nous présente le tableau ? Ne reflète-t-il que les prix différents des produits alimentaires et la valeur du travail fourni pour les préparer ?

La question est bien plus complexe. Il ne fait pas de doute que c'est le prix des produits qui compte, mais compte également leur offre. « No countrey in Europe affordes victuals at a lower rate » a noté Moryson à propos de la Pologne (nous en parlerons

encore dans la suite) et il a répété les données que nous trouvons dans ses notes sur Leczyca et la région de Piotrków : « Here
we invited two Polackes to dinner, yet both together spent onely
foure grosh and a halve for us and them, for we had ten egges
for a grosh, and all other victuals very cheape » (I 134-135 ; IV 72).
Le coût minime de ces repas était donc dû à l'absence de victuailles plus somptueuses ou d'un bon morceau de viande [7]. La façon
de s'approvisionner en denrées alimentaires est également symp-
tomatique. Dans l'Etat de Venise, le marché des produits alimentaires surprend Moryson qui note : « all victuals being sold
in small portions, according to the smallest money, yea, the very spices, which in the shoppes are put in papers, ready beaten...
particulary at Paduoa, the markets abound rather with variety,
than quantities of meat » [8].

Dans le journal de Moryson ne s'ébauche pas seulement la
division de l'Europe centrale en riche et pauvre, mangeant bien
ou moins bien. Nous avons évidemment l'Europe de la bière
et l'Europe du vin. Même les chevaux peuvent s'en apercevoir.
En se rendant à cheval de Cracovie à Vienne, notre voyageur
anglais se souciait des sabots de son cheval ; en Moravie, il a
noté : 6 xr pour la bière utilisée pour laver les sabots du cheval,
alors qu'à Leoben, c'est-à-dire en Styrie, il a employé à cet
effet de la lie de vin pour 4 xr [9]. Lorsqu'on parle des différents
frais d'entretien, de la qualité des repas et de la vie des voyageurs,
il est toujours question de vin. Dans les pays du Nord, le vin
accroît sensiblement le prix des repas. En Bohême, le vin coûte
plus cher que le reste du repas (I 34). Là où il est bon marché
(comme dans le Palatinat, I 37), Moryson en boit tant qu'il pourrait avoir pour ce prix deux dîners sans boisson.

En Europe, les voyageurs boivent beaucoup en règle générale.
Un Anglais (qui avait à cette époque le droit d'emporter 20 livres
sterling, I 122) ne doit pas — selon Moryson — prendre pour
exemple les Allemands « who drinke and banquet as much abroad
as at home, nor the Italians, who live they among Christians and
Paggans, yet cannot restraine their incontinences, nor the Polo-
nians, who being perhaps the sonnes of Castellani... commonly
spend more prodigally in Italy, and like places, then at home,
so as many times they spend their whole patrimony abroad »
(III 374). Boire fait partie d'un rite, façonne le rythme de la
vie. Moryson, économe mais pas avare, doit s'y plier. En Allemagne et aux Pays-Bas, il participe aux *Schlaffdrunck* qui durent
longtemps, fatiguent et coûtent très cher. Aux Pays-Bas du Nord,
les boissons, et surtout le vin, sont grevés d'impôts qui pèsent
lourdement sur le budget de tout étranger qui ne se contente pas
d'eau (I 101 ; III 470 ; IV 33).

En accompagnant Moryson dans ses pérégrinations en Europe,
d'une auberge à l'autre, nous avons la possibilité de faire quelques

observations. L'Anglais, habitué aux auberges confortables, note les coutumes continentales. En Pologne [10] et en Bohème, la viande est préparée « out of doors » (II 29). En Pologne ce sont les épices qui dominent dans le goût de la viande et du poisson. Bien que Moryson ne soit pas hypersensible (il est capable d'apprécier un bon repas même s'il est servi de façon très fruste), ses notes succinctes ne permettent pas de mettre en doute que c'est en Italie que la vie est la plus agréable et la plus confortable.

Moryson cesse d'être sobre de mots lorsqu'il énumère les fromages, la volaille, les viandes et les poissons mis en vente sur le marché de Padoue. Dans l'auberge — il l'écrit avec admiration — les draps, les nappes et les essuie-mains sont d'une finesse extrême. Il est évident qu'il est dans l'intérêt de toute la société de servir les touristes. Les étrangers n'y habitent pas seulement dans les auberges. L'hôtesse padouane de Moryson « had a house like a Pallace », elle, servait les touristes à des prix peu élevés, leur fournissant les draps de lit, préparant la viande qu'ils achetaient eux-mêmes (dans ce pays, les repas sont une question trop sérieuse pour que l'achat des victuailles puisse être confié aux femmes ou aux serviteurs, I 148) [11].

Sur les terres polonaises, la situation semblait être tout autre. Moryson conseille d'y emporter son propre lit, ces commodités faisant défaut dans les auberges en dehors des grandes villes (III 471). Il est évidemment plus commode de faire le voyage à cheval et de le vendre ensuite avec profit en Italie, mais comment se passer d'un lit ? Ne généralisons cependant pas trop hâtivement. En Prusse Royale (c'est-à-dire dans la région située entre Gdansk et Torun) les voyageurs sont également fort bien accueillis. Les logements sont propres et bien tenus, on leur fournit des draps qui sont ensuite changés chaque semaine [12]. Il existe également en Prusse une coutume peu ordinaire : on y rapporte aux voyageurs dès leur arrivée, et ensuite une fois par semaine, de l'eau chaude pour qu'ils puissent se laver les pieds ! (IV 33).

.*.

Le coup d'œil du voyageur, du touriste — soulignons-le encore une fois — induit souvent en erreur. Il fixe et contraint à généraliser des phénomènes et des observations purement individuels. Il permet cependant de tirer certaines conclusions d'une façon incomparablement plus simple — et pas toujours moins exacte — que ne pourrait le faire la technique des recherches économiques. Voici comment Moryson résume ses impressions : « And in truth, myselfe having in Poland and in Ireland [13] found a strange cheapnesse of all such necessaries, in respect they want, and so more esteeme Silver, this observation makes me of opinion much

contrary to the vulgar, that there is no more signe of a flourishing, and rich commonwealth, then the deare price of these
things (excepting the yeeres of famine), nor any greater argument
of a poore and weake State then the cheape price of them... »
(IV 70).

Aujourd'hui, les points de vue de Moryson se heurteraient
également à l'opposition des maîtresses de maison, mais l'écono-
miste et l'historien y décèlent une observation exacte bien que
fragmentaire des phénomènes qui leur sont connus. Nous sommes,
pourtant, encore éloignés de la formule élégante de François
Quesnay : « ... Disette et cherté est misère. Abondance et cherté
est opulence... »

.•.

Il est difficile de dissimuler la disproportion choquante qui
existe entre la série de conclusions qui peut être tirée du tableau
présenté et de la carte annexée et les pièces à conviction fort
modestes et unilatérales. Nous traitons donc toute la question
comme une hypothèse qui nous engage à poursuivre des recherches, et nullement comme un jeu. En effet, partout où il a été
possible de soumettre dès maintenant à certaines vérifications
les notes de Moryson, celles-ci sont parfaitement d'accord avec
les autres données relatives au niveau des prix de détail [14].

Il n'est cependant pas facile de définir exactement ce qu'expri-
ment ces chiffres et ces schémas. Les régions de l'Europe, dès la
fin du XVIᵉ siècle, étaient liées par l'échange de marchandises :
produits alimentaires, articles de grand luxe, biens durables et
biens se détériorant rapidement, et dans cette Europe il n'y avait
pas de pays où *tout* était soit bon marché, soit très cher. Cela
est également valable pour les produits alimentaires, ne serait-ce
qu'en Pologne où le prix des épices dépassait le prix du poisson
qu'elles accompagnaient, pêché dans un étang voisin (IV 69 ; 71).
Par conséquent, si nous obtenons en fin de compte un aperçu
aussi régulier, ces chiffres sont des indices — ou tout au moins
des symptômes — du rythme des échanges de détail, de la vita-
lité de l'économie et, peut-être, de la portée de l'échange des
monnaies ou en employant la terminologie de l'époque — de la
wealth of nations. Lorsque Fynes Moryson revint de son dernier
voyage, il aurait pu lire ce que Alonso de Herrera avait écrit à
ce sujet : « C'est par les monnaies des métaux inférieurs que l'on
peut le mieux juger de la fertilité et de l'abondance d'un pays,
car par elles, s'achète, au détail et au jour le jour, ce qui est
nécessaire à la vie quotidienne » [15].

Moryson n'est pas une exception, il n'est pas le seul voyageur
qui ait noté systématiquement ses dépenses. En plus des données
que nous fournissent les voyageurs, nous pouvons également recueil-

lir les témoignages de bien d'autres contemporains, ne serait-ce que des ambassadeurs de Venise, si largement, mais incomplètement consultés par les historiens.

NOTES

1. F. Braudel, Histoire opérationnelle. Publié en polonais : F. Braudel, *Historia i trwanie*, Varsovie, 1971.

2. Nous nous servons de l'édition : F. Moryson, *An Itinerary, containing his ten years' travel...*, éd. anonyme, Glasgow 1907-8 (4 vol.). Cf. aussi Shakespeare's Europe... Unpublished Chapters of Fynes Moryson's Itinerary, being a Survey of the Condition of Europe at the End of the 16th Century, éd. C. Hughes, Glasgow 1903. Moryson a déjà une assez riche bibliographie, cf. des livres de B. Penrose, particulièrement *Urbane Travellers*, Philadelphia, Pa., 1941. On a surtout discuté des problèmes culturels (cf. J.C. Whitebrook, Fynes Moryson, Giordano Bruno and William Shakespeare, *Notes & Querries*, CLXXI, 1936, pp. 255-260 ; personne ne s'est penché sur ses observations économiques.

3. Pour abréger, les autres renvois concernant l'« Itinerary » seront insérés dans le texte.

4. Sur la conversion des monnaies et les conditions de change il y a tout un chapitre fort abondant. Moryson vit dans un monde « trimétallique » dont il décrit le fonctionnement plusieurs fois. Vu l'abondance des informations sur l'or et l'argent dont dispose l'historien, ce coup d'œil sur une bourse pleine de petite monnaie de cuivre et d'argent est fort intéressant. N.B. Moryson — anglican, attire l'attention sur le rapport entre l'abondance de la petite monnaie et l'omni-présence de l'aumône ; il discute les conséquences du manque de monnaie de cuivre sur le niveau des prix en Angleterre (IV 96, voir aussi IV 71). Les problèmes de la divisibilité de la monnaie et de son influence sur les échanges et sur les prix se dessinent d'une façon multiple.
C'est à M. Christopher Smout, qui m'a aidé par sa profonde connaissance de la littérature, et aussi à la Bibliothèque du British Council à Varsovie, qui m'a fourni des ouvrages, que j'adresse mes remerciements.

5. Il nous a fallu omettre les informations détaillées relatives à la méthode de conversion des monnaies. Les données les plus importantes sont tirées du chapitre déjà mentionné (note 4). On les a vérifiées avec les manuels. Les chiffres sont exprimés en kreitzer (kreutzer) — xr.

A — d'après les notes quotidiennes de Moryson,
B — d'après son opinion plus générale,
a — ou 6 shilling lubeckois, « reckoning three for beare (c. à d. beer) apart » (III 471). Autres prix à Helsingör et Frederiksborg ; à Roskilde 7 shilling danois (I 122-123).
b — aussi la Bohême à l'ouest de Prague (vers Nuremberg).
c — à Innsbruck.
d — IV 72, 471 — voir un dîner trop modeste à Leczyca.

6. « With us the nobility, gentry and students go to dinner at eleven before noon and to supper at five, or between five and six... The merchants dine and sup before twelve at noon and six at night, especially in London... », W. Harrison, *The Description of England*, éd. par G. Edelen, Ithaca 1968, p. 144.

7. Mais Moryson près du riche centre minier de Mansfeld (Thuringe) manquait aussi de viande et ne mangeait que des œufs.

8. Il vaut la peine de souligner qu'en Italie (Padoue, Florence), à Paris, mais aussi en Palestine, on achète la viande à la livre, tandis que dans le Nord Moryson note le prix de quantités plus importantes, comme le « quart », ou la « demi-pièce », etc...

9. On ne peut traiter ici des prix du fourrage, bien qu'ils ne soient pas moins

représentatifs que les prix des repas. Moryson a voyagé à cheval de Cracovie à Padoue et d'Italie en Lorraine.

10. Un demi-siècle plus tard, Peter Mundy nous donnera une description détaillée des auberges prussiennes. Depuis quatre siècles les hôtels sont en Pologne un problème non résolu ; pour les étrangers ce n'est souvent qu'une curiosité. La discussion sur ce sujet entre John Barclay et Lucas Opalinski est intéressante. Ce dernier explique le défaut d'équipement des auberges par les coutumes des nobles polonais, qui ont l'habitude de voyager avec tous leurs meubles et leurs tapisseries.

11. Un indice caractéristique de la généralisation des services hoteliers en Italie est l'existence des repas à prix fixe : « al pasto — that is by the more at a set rate (seldome exceeding three Giulii) », IV 101.

12. En Italie aussi on fournit les draps de lit, mais dans ce pays Moryson préférait mettre un caleçon de lin, par crainte des maladies vénériennes.

13. On pourrait considérer cette phrase comme une première tentative de comparaison entre l'Irlande et la Pologne — problème toujours digne d'attention.

14. Soulignons ici, sans entrer dans le détail, l'analogie frappante entre les prix polonais notés par Moryson et le niveau des salaires (ou de leur partie monétaire) des domestiques de ferme dans les mêmes régions. Les deux phénomènes dans une certaine mesure permettent de saisir les cadences différentes de la circulation de la petite monnaie à l'échelle régionale. Cf. à ce sujet ma communication au colloque polono-hongrois de Poznań en Juin 1971 : *Les échanges commerciaux comme facteur d'inégalités économiques. Les territoires polonais au XVIᵉ-XVIIᵉ siècle*, Le problème mérite d'être étudié à part.

15. Alonso Herrera, *Libro de agricultura*, Alcala 1539 (1598), p. 351vᵒ-352, cité par F. Braudel, *La Méditerranée et le monde méditerranéen à l'époque de Philippe II*, vol. I, p. 478.

CARTE

Les secteurs foncés des cercles montrent le rapport entre les prix de repas dans une région donnée et le prix le plus élevé (cercle entièrement foncé). On a indiqué les itinéraires et les dates des voyages de Moryson.

Cette carte n'est qu'une esquisse impressioniste. Sa précision est limitée tant par les conditions graphiques que par les écarts de prix dans le cadre de territoires même restreints. Pour la même raison on a omis le cercle correspondant à la traversée de la Thuringe (de Sangershausen à Erfurt) par Cobourg jusqu'à Bamberg. En Lorraine et en Champagne Moryson voyageait à pied, après avoir vendu son cheval, pour ne pas attirer l'attention des brigands (mais sans succès !). Faisant semblant d'être pauvre il se comportait d'une façon différente et ne notait pas les prix des repas. Moryson souligne l'uniformité des prix en Italie — grossièrement : entre Rome et la vallée du Po — ce que symbolise notre cercle placé aux environs de Florence. Notre « Guide Moryson » indique aussi des endroits dignes des étoiles du « Guide Michelin », quoiqu'il nous informe mieux sur les prix que sur la qualité de la cuisine.

Les données des diagrammes pour l'Angleterre et l'Ecosse sont très vagues. Il a fallu omettre l'Irlande, où « le repas » noté par Moryson coûte 1 shilling (c. à d. 16,25 xr, ou 58 % du prix rhénan). Si on considère ce prix de repas comme « typique », cela nous semblerait très cher. Les prix alimentaires sont peu élevés en Palestine et Syrie (II 61), mais le manque d'auberges correspondant aux auberges européennes, la cuisine fort différente et la nécessité de faire semblant d'être pauvre (rappelons la Champagne des années 1590) rendent difficile toute comparaison.

FIGURE 1.

V

OBSERVATIONS ON WEALTH AND ECONOMIC DEVELOPMENT IN RENAISSANCE AND BAROQUE TRAVEL LITERATURE*

This study will deal with observations of European travelers in the sixteenth and seventeenth centuries, with their impressions, their critical criteria and their biases, as revealed in what they perceived to be the social disparities of the time. As writers and travelers, the authors of these accounts were almost by definition well educated, though not leading intellectuals or, in most cases, specialists in the matters they were observing. In spite of their education, they were also frequently faced with phenomena, the explanation for which would have required from them a totally different training and experience. Nonetheless, their attitude toward the economic, social, and political problems of the nations they visited constitute valuable source material for historians today.

As members of industrial societies, we assume the world to be constantly changing. Though the optimism proclaimed by many apostles of some variety of "progress" is counterbalanced by dismal, though equally diverse, prophecies of doom, no one today imagines the world as being static. But the situation was very different in a period when the rate of population growth was low, increase of labor productivity was slight, and the absorptive power of the market fairly stable. Demographic catastrophies, the effects of military operations, and local laws were more important forces for change than strictly economic variations or alterations in production and consumption. In a situation where static elements dominate, the national wealth already accumulated is of greater economic importance than the current national product at any given time, which represents a variable element. Their term "wealth" — that

This article was first published in *State and Society in Europe from the Fifteenth Century to the Eighteenth Century*, ed. Jaroslaw Pelenski, pp. 231-244, Wydawnictwa Uniwersytetu Warszawskiego, Warszawa 1985. © 1985 by Wydawnictwa Uniwersytetu Warszawskiego and the University of Iowa. Reprinted by permission.

terme mal défini de nos jours, according to J. B. Say — corresponds more closely to our notion of abundance, and not to our habit of expressing everything in statistics and of separating the economic from other phenomena in a modern state.

The comments on Provence by Jakub Sobieski (1588—1646) will serve to illustrate the problem. He was a well-educated statesman (the father of the later King of Poland, Jan III) who traveled widely and knew several languages. In 1611, passing through Provence from Spain to Italy, Sobieski wrote:

> This is the region of France that was defined by Julius Caesar with a word [i. e. province] for its excellence. He is believed to have said that among all provinces this is *the* province, and he took such a liking to it that it became his favorite place of residence; and rightly so, for in all France there is no country so rich in cities, towns and people, so lavish with all kinds of spirits and so happily situated. The sea is about and there are cheerful rivers, almond groves, orange and lemon orchards, vineyards thick-set and exquisite, people — and especially the fair sex — exceptionally comely; even peasant women in their sleekness and fair complexion can rank with any gentle women and even old hags are not so ugly as elsewhere. There are many holy shrines and the bodies of the saints rest in many places. One may be shown the grave of St. Anne there. Two Marys are laid to rest in a single town. In another, St. Martha, the sister of St. Mary Magdalen, has been buried. In a small town called Tarascon lies the body of St. Mary Magdalen herself. Here lies St. Lazarus... there, the woman of the company who lifted up her voice and said: „Blessed is the womb that bore thee and the breast that you sucked" [Luke, 11:27]. They may show you many other saints' bodies, as well as relics and holy places. The air in Provence is good, very temperate; although the country is warm, hotter than other provinces, yet the people live long and diseases are not so common as elsewhere. [1].

This description, exceptionally detailed for Jakub Sobieski, contains several points worth mentioning. Although the beauty of Provençal women and the multitude of Provençal relics may not seem of any great importance to a country's economic development, Sobieski's comments do have a point to which I shall return later.

Sobieski's comments also prove not to be unique. Antoine de Lalaing, a courtier of Philip the Fair, and his companion during journeys round the Netherlands, Germany, France and Spain, wrote that Cologne was a town *"riche, puissante, marchande, fort peuplée, bien pavée, bien murée de gros murs matérielles et sumptueuses decorée."* Further on he describes the relics of saints; his estimate of their number (including the remains of eleven thousand virgins of St. Ursula), reaches twenty-three to twenty-four thousand; "the land is so holy here that it does not accept

[1] Jakub Sobieski, *Dwie podróże Jakuba Sobieskiego ojca króla Jana III odbyte po krajach europejskich w latach 1607—1613 i 1638,* ed. E. Raczyński (Poznań, 1833), p. 129.

other bodies, even those of innocent children."[2] The multitude of the relics of Cologne are a measure of that city's worth, both in this world and the next.

Among the occasional observations on wealth and poverty that are scattered in the texts of travel accounts, one can distinguish certain common features: one is the assumption that a country's wealth is usually centuries old and its converse, that the very antiquity of the civilization contributes to its prosperity. The latter idea was most clearly expressed by Thomas Coryat, who tried to prove that the populations on the left bank of the Rhine and on the right bank of the Danube were denser than on the opposite banks because these territories had once belonged to the Romans.[3] In turn, the duration of prosperity or poverty is, according to him, the consequence of such constants as climate.

Jean Bodin and Giovanni Botero were regarded as the two greatest authorities on such matters. Their views, especially those of Botero, deeply influenced the travelers' imaginations. A great variety of suggestions concerning climate, quality of soils, law systems, waterways, density of population, languages, etc., the validity of which could be tested by a traveler surveying a given country, afforded an educated man considerable freedom of choice. Botero's determinism did not dampen the enthusiasm of anyone.

From the end of the sixteenth century a considerable body of literature was published to prepare travelers for their tasks. These tasks were regarded as education and preparation for public service. Various "instructions for foreign travel" gave readers what were purported to be the most important items of information. From among the hundreds of questions that the travelers were expected to answer, we can select a dozen or so from a questionnaire compiled by Albert Meyer, the German author of a pamphlet translated into English in 1589.

> Whether the place be much or little frequented of travellers and merchants, or else desolate, or almost desolate... Whether it be of any name and fame, for power, wealth, force, multitude of people or not... Whether the people live long... or else die in their youth, or riper yeres, yea or not,... The beauty, pleasantnesse, fertilitie, barrenesse, of the region soile, grounde, fields, etc... The natural goodness of the soile, the harvest and increase of all sort of fruits... The quantitie of grasse and hay. ....The fare and dyet of the region. ...The industrial studies... of the inhabitantes. ...The waightes and measures...[4]

[2]Collection des voyages des souverains des Pays-Bas, ed. M. Gachard, I (Bruxelles, 1876), pp. 256, 334. These are the impressions of foreign travelers in Cologne. Even less impressionable Protestants could hardly help being plainly astonished.
[3]Thomas Coryat, Crudities hastily gobled up in five moneths travells... (1611), (Glasgow, 1905).
[4]Albert Meier, Certaine briefe and speciall Instructions for Gentlemen, merchants, students, souldiers, marriners etc... (London, 1589).

This meticulous questionnaire, full of those "yea or nots," could not have been followed to the end; not even Arthur Young could cope with it. It reflects well, however, a range of interests and a scientific attitude that was diametrically opposed to that of the majority of travelers. For example, most inquisitive explorers made detailed notes on ancient or later inscriptions, or described medals and ancient coins seen during the trip. In the second half of the seventeenth century, a new generation of travelers-naturalists grew up, who looked for plants and minerals (another lengthy questionnaire for their needs was compiled by Charles Linné). Yet the majority of travelers jotting down their observations had to learn how to look and had to select the necessary information according to various criteria. The instructions enumerated things worthy of interest and suggested ready-made patterns of observation.

A rich profusion of diverse remarks makes it very difficult to come to some definite conclusion as to which elements were considered by these authors simply as curiosities and which were meant to represent an overall image of a country's wealth, particularly as regards the most obvious discrepancies among social groups and classes. Here a traveler's judgement would greatly depend on his family background. Thus, if a Polish magnate expressed his abomination for the peasant-like manners of the Dutch, his comments might simply reflect the contrast between the social structures of Poland and of the Netherlands. Foreigners from Western Europe in their turn were astonished by the disparities among social classes in Poland. Yet the travelers in general never doubted that the wealth of a country should be measured by the prosperity of the richest persons in it. The notion that the condition of the poorer classes, especially the peasantry, was more indicative of 'general wealth, was very slow in gaining acceptance. This does not mean, however, that all travelers left the living and social conditions of the peasantry unnoticed, but it was more apt to be connected with their interest in taxation systems. The following are reflections on Normandy by Peter Heylyn, a well-known author of manuals on world geography and of surveys written in the form of travel guides.

> For my part I could never yet find, where the great wits of theirs [i.e. inhabitants of Normandy] lay... For what with the unproportionable rents they pay to their Lords, on the one side, and immeasurable taxes laid upon them by the King, on the other, they are kept in such a perpetuated course of drudgery that there is no place for wit or wisdom left amongst them. Liberty is the Mother and the Nurse of those two qualities... [5]

It is worth noticing that Heylyn concentrates upon the peasants; this is exceptional as most authors directed their attention primarily

[5]Peter Heylyn, *A Full Relation of two Journeys: the one Into the Main-Land of France, the other Into some of the adjacent Ilands* (London, 1565), p. 6.

to the nobility, Heylyn's typically English commentary ("Liberty is the Mother...") is supplemented with other explanations for Norman poverty, first of all, pettifoggery. Finally, Heylyn draws a parallel between Normandy and Norfolk (with references to Ortelius and Camden), the soil and the long coast constitute the basis for the analogy, yet "the *country* of Normandy and the *people* of Norfolk, are somewhat richer." The political system and want of freedom deprive the country of its natural wealth, for in Normandy "you would think the grain has a desire to kisse the earth his mother, or that it purposed by making it self away into the ground, to save the Ploughman his next years of labour." [6]

Serfdom and poverty of French peasants have been favorite topics of English travelers since the times of Sir John Fortescue. "Commons and plebeians..." runs a note about the French by Sir John Reresby, a Royalist who, in 1654, set out for the Continent to await better times, of whom. I may say, so as to the peasants, they are certainly the most miserable, slavish people in the world..." That is why, he adds, Charles V called the King of France "*Rex asinorum*, his subjects not being less passive than that sluggish animal, under those weighty burthens imposed upon them." [7]

Such a comment suggests reliance on some general belief rather than direct experience. Champagne is described .in a survey of France by John Elliot as follows:

...the pepole active and given to good husbandrie... the townes wealthy, the villages well inhabited, and to be breefe, they want nothing necessary for mans life... Howbeit the people of Champagne are somewhat teastie and self-willed... The husbandmen of Poictow are slie, will deceave a man with pratling, their pedlarly speech, dull wittee lubbers, malicious, disloyal, and smally to be trusted, lovers of brablings and novelties: but such as inhabite the Townes are utterlye of an another disposition, they are tractable, courteous... Angoulême. The inhabitants of this countrie are quicke witted, standing upon their reputation, stout, great boasters, taking small delight in trafikke, living for the most part upon their rents... [this must have referred to the squires]. The peasant dull witted, rude and clownish, given to toyle... [8].

In these and many similiar passages one finds genuine information woven in with stereotyped platitudes and common prejudices. It might be worth examining the influence peasant uprisings of the first half of the seventeenth century might have had on common opinion regard-

---

[6]*Ibid.*, pp. 7 ff. Emphasis mine.
[7]John Reresby, *Memoirs and Travels of...* (London, 1904), p. 4. [Caspar de Tonde] D'Hauteville, *An Account of Poland* (London, 1698), Chapter XXII, also includes remarks about Polish peasants.
[8]John Elliot, *The Survey or Topographical Description of France...* (London, 1592), pp. 46—71.

ing the character of the French peasant — Sir John Reresby, for example still considered him as "passive as a donkey." The reign of Charles I and its aftermath produced a widespread opinion that the English were "rebellious."

Among the mass of prejudiced, stereotypical, and simply superficial information we can discern some attempts at genuine comparative study. An outstanding example is "An Itinerary" of Fynes Moryson, whose accuracy and reliability of judgement has already been noted.

> The Husbandmen in Germany [wrote Moryson] are not so base as the French and Italians, or the slaves of other Kingdoms, but much more miserable and poore than the English Husbandmen: yet those of Prussia, a fat and fertile country, come nearest to the English in riches and good fare.[9] The other being hired by Gentlemen to plough their grounds, give their services at low rates, and pay so great rent, to their Lords, as they have scarcely meanes to cover their nakedness with poore clothes, and to feed themselves with ill smelling coleworts and like meate. In Moravia incorporated to Bohemia, and lying between it and Polonia, the husbandmen are meere slaves... Also I understood by discourse, that the Marquesse of Anspach in Germany hath many meere slaves for his husbandmen. But all other in Germany are free, howsoever without doubt they be greatly oppressed not only by the Gentry, but also by the Churchmen. ...And it is probable that the neighbourhood of the Sweitzers, who rooted out their Noblemen, and got liberty by the sword, makes the Gentelmen of Germany lesse cruell towards the poore clownes. For either upon their cause, or for the fertility of the Country, no doubt the clownes in Suevia and other places neare Sweitzerland, live much better then in any other parts; as likewise in places neere Denmarke and Poland, admitting slaves generally, the poore people are more oppressed then any where else .through Germany... And I shall in due place, shew, that in Denmark and in Poland, the people are mere slaves, so as the Gentlemen and Lords recken not their estates by yearly rents, but by the number of their Bawren (or clownes) who are all slaves.[10]

His choice of countries — Poland, Denmark, Moravia, and Swabia — indicates that Moryson followed his own inclinations. Although his remarks dealt directly only with the situation of peasants, they have an obvious relationship to the total economic conditions in the countries as a whole[11]. The relationships between the *corvée*, serfdom, and the wealth of the community is as recognized today as it was by Moryson,

---

[9]"Prussia" means here the Vistula Fens between Gdańsk (Danzig), Elbląg (Elbing) and Malbork, a well-developed, rich, almost "Dutch" country.
[10]Fynes Moryson, *An Itinerary Containing His Ten Yeeres Travell*, IV (London, 1908) p. 33 ff. The author traveled in the years 1591—1597, but published his survey in 1617. Although quoted by many scholars, Moryson has not so far been fully appreciated as an observer of economic phenomena. See my article "Un voyageur--témoin des prix européens à la fin du XVe siècle", *Mélanges en l'Honneur de Fernand Braudel*, I (Toulouse, 1973), pp. 327—336.
[11]However, in the seventeenth century the authors still had considerable difficulty in comparing living conditions in the countryside. Even fairly accurate accounts of these conditions in particular countries cannot provide more general comparative inferences. Moryson's studies, though based on rather superficial observations, are

though his contemporaries tended to prefer a psychological explanation — laziness.

Laziness was often emphasized by foreign travelers in Ireland and Spain, although each otherwise presented problems unique to itself. "Irish idleness" was considered to be different from the Spanish version probably because the English (who provided the greatest number of surveys of Ireland) were as a rule unfriendly, even hostile, to that country.

> O, what a slavish servitude doe these silly wretches endure [wrote William Lithgow] the most part of whom in all their lives have never a third part of food, natures clothing, nor a secure shelter for the winter cold. [Husbandry in this country was] bad and uncivill: husbandmen do not wish to learn anything, they are unfamiliar with the harness so they tie the plaugh to horses' tails. All rebels should be hanged, and law and peace will ensure [Lithgow concludes]...[12]

In Spain, according to the same author, live "the most penurious Peasants in the world... whose quotidian moans, might drew tears from stones. Their Villages stand... wanting Gardens, Hedges, Clothes, Barnes, or Back-sides: this sluggish and idle husbandry, being a natural instinct of their neighbour or paternal Moors." [13] But these comments reveal less of the personal aversion or disgust toward the Spaniards that Lithgow so emphatically manifested in his description of the „wild" Irishmen. [14]

An analogous paragraph from Moryson's description of Ireland may help clarify his way of thinking. "The Irish thus given to Idleness, naturally abhorr from Manuall Artes, and Civill trades to gain their owne bread..." He observed that local fishermen would only go fishing after their bread had run short.

> And in my opinion [he continued in his characteristic style] this idleness hath bene nurished by nothing more... than by the plenty of the land, the great housekeeping, drawing the people from trades, while they can be fedd by others without labour. This experience hath shewed of old, as well in England, where the greatest robberies were commonly done, by idle servingmen swarming in great houses, as in the more northerne parts, and in Ireland, where the multitude of loose Followers hath of old beene prone to fight their Lords quarrels, yea to rebell with them. Whereas no doubt the exercise of trades, and the Custome of industrie to live every man of his owne, are a strong establishment of any Comon Wealth.

really exceptional in this respect. Examples of numerous literary commentaries on the subject may be found in James Howell's *Instructions for forraine Travell...* (London, 1642).

[12] William Lithgow, *The Totall Discourse Of The Rare Adventures (1632)* (reprinted in Glasgow, 1906), pp. 431 ff.

[13] *Ibid.*, pp. 445 ff.

[14] One realizes how much depends on the author's attitude (whether from national sentiment or personal preference), as e.g., the remarks of Lithgow (*op. cit.*, p. 433) compared with those of a chronicler of Charles V's travels, on the bosoms of Irish women. Cf. *Collection des voyages des souverains*, III, p. 283.

Land should be distributed among the tenants and turning from farming to the raising of sheep should be prohibited, as it was in England. [15]

Unfortunately, Moryson did not travel to Spain, but we have numerous comments on that country from others who did. In the seventeenth century, Spain had become a favorite subject for travel surveys of a philosophical bent, for the country had for a long time been considered something of an enigma. Spanish idleness was believed to have derived from Arabic influence, as Lithgow's commentary implied. As in other countries, snap judgements were also made about Spain to explain psycho-social features and what was found to be the behavior of various social groups of classes. It can be observed that the gravity, haughtiness, and leisured pace of the hidalgo became "idleness" when it referred to the Iberian peasant.

Laurent Vital, an alert and inquisitive chronicler accompanying Charles I (subsequently, Emperor Charles V) in his journey from the Netherlands to Spain, wrote the following comments about Asturias:

...croy que si les gens y estoient aussy dilligens à labourer comme par dechà [i. e., in the Netherlands, Vital's native country] et cultiver ses terres, qu'ilz auroient, sans comparaison, trop plus de biens qu'ilz n'ont: mais il ne leur chault de labourer, sinon seulement ce qui leur convient pour gouverner eulx el leur mesnye, car ilz sont la pluspart fondez sur gentillesse, jasoit ce qu'ilz soient pauvres, et se dissent tous estre nobles en vertu de certains priviléges qu'ilz ont acquis des roys de Castille... Mais, combien qu'ilz soyent anobliz, si ne sont-ilz guaire enrichiz...[16].

The provinces of Spain were considered exotic and exciting because of the contrasts of scenery and character. The country presented a cadence of changing landscapes, alternating barrenness with richness and fertility. The changing contours of the land and, above all, the alternating scarcity and profusion of water, intensified the contrasting effects. The following remarks were written in Alcaniz, near Valencia, by Barthélemy Joly, an almoner and adviser of the French King in the early seventeenth century:

Partout ilz ent tout de mesme, vivans en loysir et faineantise, ne s'adonnans à aulcunes oeuvres manuelles ny à aulcune science, si ce n'est de vieilles histoires de leurs roman... Tous ce pais [i. e., Aragon] est si sec qu'il est presque tout deshabité et là où il nya de l'eau, les peuplades sont le long d'icelle, aussy frequentees et habitees comme elles sont rares et en petit nombre[17].

It is difficult to compare surveys of Spain: too much depends on the sensitivity and biases of the various authors. A radical inflation of prices and changes in the economic and political conditions of Spain in the seventeenth century prompted many travellers visiting it to reflec-

[15]*Shakespeare's Europe. Unpublished chapters of Fynes Moryson's Itinerary*, ed. C. Hughes (London, 1903), p. 200.
[16]*Collection des voyages des souverains*, III, pp. 93 ff.
[17]"Voyage de Barthelemy Joly en Espagne (1603—1604)". *Revue Hispanique*, XX (1909), pp. 530, 470.

tions that comprised both the *loci communes* of what might be called contemporary political science and their individual impressions; it is very difficult to separate the two. Nonetheless, occasionally we come across surveys characterized by freshness of insight, as for example, the diaries of two little-known Polish travelers.

Jakub Sobieski was both fond of travels and knew how to describe his impressions well. When visiting a country, he tried to discern the mood of the country and understand its people. Leon, he wrote, is "a country barren and, due to its desert, melancholy for anyone trying to cross it." Asturia is

> a country as disagreeable for traveling as the Kingdom of Leon, if not more; one feels like spitting while going through those mountains, rocks and deserts, and the only thing that causes some pleasure is the necessity of traveling along the coast, so that one can always see the sea, the rocks and the mountains... Near Lisbon [however] the country is surprisingly cheerful and beautiful, full of orchards, gardens, orange, lemon and olive groves, with vineyards all around.

Sobieski's miserable experience in the "sordid country" on the road to Seville was rewarded by the splendid scenery of Andalusia: "as soon as we entered Andalusia, our eyes, weary with wilderness, were rewarded by the beauty, cheerfulness, wealth, and fertility of the country... In contrast to the desert and sand through which we had been traveling for a week, we believed we had entered a paradise... [18]

Another anonymous Polish traveler, who visited numerous European countries at the end of the sixteenth century, was particularly impressed by Spain, considering it first of all as surpassing the others in „abundance."

> If anyone says that it yields no bread because all bread comes from us [i.e., from Poland], I will tell him that this is not so because the land is infertile but because no one will plough the soil... The population is sparse, for nearly everyone goes to work in foreign lands. It is no secret how many Spaniards remain in Italy... Thus no one should be surprised that they have little of their own bread, for there is no one to grow it; they prefer to buy it, since it is easier to earn money than to till the soil. But look at their own treasures: they have their own gold, good and highly valued...

His impressions from Seville, where he saw the unloading of merchant ships comming from the Indies, eclipsed anything he had experienced in Castille and Aragon which lacked both trees and water.

> I saw many ingots of silver, fewer of gold, and such an amount of oxhides that they were heaped high all around the town; then, there were quantities of various spices, foreign goods... The people, to my mind, are very wealthy, for, although there is a profusion of all things they are also very expensive; tradesmen charge extraordinarily high fees as well: a shoemaker, as I know from my own experi-

18 J. Sobieski, *op. cit.*, pp. 105, 106, 109, 112.

ence, would not even touch a shoe for a real, the equivalent of four of our pennies. [19]

It is easy today to impute naïveté to a traveler who, coming from a distant country and dazzled by the wealth of Andalusia and all the treasures brought from the Indies, did not realize the gravity of the economic situation in Spain at the turn of the sixteenth century and would not swallow all the wisdom of *arbitristas*. I am quoting these impressions as an example of the clash between two civilizations: a man coming from a primarily agricultural country, characterized by a slow development of commercial enterprises meeting face-to-face a diametrically opposite environment. The account of his visit to Genoa in the same diary provides an even better illustration. "All those people possess some kind of Mercurian quality; no one wishes to learn more than to write, to read, and to count. Reckoning is regarded as the greatest skill, and all around the town you will neither see nor hear anything but business contracts, calculations, *cambia* and various kinds of transactions... All people are exceedingly avid of gain." This passage also implies that financial transactions and the habit of reckoning were more deeply rooted in Italy and England than in Poland by the sixteenth century. [20]

Thirty years later, a courtier accompanying Prince Władysław, the son of Zygmunt III, King of Poland, who travelled incognito to Genoa, visited some palaces of the nobility and was astonished by the small size of their kitchens. He wrote "that small kitchen made the palace itself so large," and further on he assumed that "the people seem to be parsimonious, they prefer to do what will serve their posterity and make their country more elegant. It is just the reverse of our own ways, for we build a kitchen larger than the house we live in miserably, and so all our profits go down the drain [*in cloacam*]." A surprisingly similar remark was made by Moryson, a man of quite different background:

And this is most certaine, that they [i.e., the Italians] inifinitely passe us in the expences about their gardens... in chapels, and other buildings, of which things some yeeld them fruite, the other last perpetually: for they bestow money in stable things, to serve their posteritie, where as our greatest expences end in the casting out of excrements, which makes me lesse commend our expences in great provisions of meate, as well as feasts as daily diet[21].

It was very unusual for an Englishman of that time to criticize English food but it remains that people coming from beyond the Alps

[19] *Anonima diariusz peregrynacji włoskiej, hiszpańskiej i portugalskiej (1595)*, ed. J. Czubek, (Cracow, 1925), pp. 65, 96.
[20] *Ibid.*, p. 55.
[21] *Obraz dworów europejskich na początku XVII wieku... skreślony przez Stefana Paca*, ed. J. K. Plebański (Wrocław, 1854), p. 102; Moryson, *op. cit.*, IV, 94.

were amazed by the magnificence of Italian architecture. And England was at the time rebuilding itself in brick and stone.

Criticizing one's own society, which has its origins in the experiencing of a much wealthier one is a motif which reappears very frequently in the diaries of Polish travelers. From the opposite geographical point of view, that is, looking at the transalpine countries from Italy at the time when the Renaissance mode of life was just beginning to be accepted there, the attitude was somewhat different, For example, Niccolò Machiavelli could write in 1507 the following remarks about the wealth of Germany:

> Perchè li populi in privato sieno ricchi, la ragione è questa: che vivono come poveri non edificono [scil. the palaces], non vestono e non hanno masserizie in casa, e basta loro abundare di pane di carne, e avere una stufa dove rifuggire il freddo: e chi non ha dell'altre cose, fa senza esse e non le cerca. Spendosi in dosso due fiorini in dieci anni, e ognuno vive secondo il grado suo e queste proporzione, e nessuno fa conto di quello li manca ma di quello ha di necessità e le loro necessità sono assi minori che le nostre [22].

This ideal picture of a Sombart type of *Nahrungswirtschaft* was developed by Machiavelli in greater detail and actually explained Italy rather than Germany. Moreover, at least in the case of Northern Germany, the account was excessively simplified — one needs only compare it with the impressions noted by Machiavelli's contemporaries — his friend Francesco Vettori or Cardinal Luigi d'Aragona. [23]

This approach became very popular throughout the sixteenth century and consisted in classifying societies *a priori* as either "frugal" (being a positive characteristic) or "prodigal." This distinction was both moral and mercantile, and was essentially the same as that manifested for example in the polemics on Mandeville's "The Fable of the Bees" more than a century later.

In the seventeenth century still another shift in reasoning seems to have taken place. It might be defined as a transformation of rationalism. A diversified, "expressionistic" mode of interpreting the experience of other countries (the mode which was to reappear later in altered form during the Romantic era), viewed with a new approach based on objective economic analysis. Though this approach apparently can be observed most often among English diarists, at the same time, it must be observed that other travel accounts have not yet been examined from the point of view of influence on and from mercantilist thought. And

---

[22] Niccolò Machiavelli, *Rapporto delle cose della Magna. Fatto questo Ritratto sopra le cose della Magna*, in: N. Machiavelli, *Arte della guerra e scritti politici minori a cura de Sergio Bertelli* (Milan, 1961), pp. 209 ff.

[23] Francesco Vettori, *Viaggio in Allemagna di...* (Paris — Florence, 1837), passim; *Die Reise des Kardinals Luigi d'Aragona durch Deutschland, die Niederlande, Frankreich und Ober-italien, 1517—1518, beschreibt von Antonio de Beatis*, ed. L. Pastor (Freiburg in Br., 1905), passim.

yet, such an experience used to take a strong hold upon intelligent people's way of thinking.

Fynes Moryson, travelling through some poverty-stricken small towns in central Poland, noted:

> ...myselfe having in Poland and in Ireland found a strange cheapnesse of all such necessaries, in respect they want and the more esteeme silver, this observation makes me of an opinion much contrary to the vulgar, that there is no more certaine signe of a flourishing and rich commonwealth, then the deare price of these things (excepting the yeeres of famine), nor any greater argument of a poore and weake State, than the cheape price of them.

The accumulation of wealth possessed by the upper classes ("kings, noblemen and merchants") tends to increase demand, as may be seen in England: "all things for diet and apparell and our very wanton desires, are sold at a much higher prices than in former ages, because riches make us not able to want any thing of serve appetite, at what price soever it is sold." [24]

Moryson's observations would have been heartily applauded by John Ray, M.D., F.R.S., who, seventy years later, while travelling from the Netherlands to Italy, wrote the following remarks about Holland:

> ...that the dearness of this sort of provisions is an argument of the riches of a town or country, these things being always cheapest in the poorest places... All manners of victuals, both meat and drink, are very dear, not for scarcity of such commoditties, but partly by the reason of great excise and impost wherewith they are charged, partly by the reason of the abundance of money that is stirring there[25].

Inflated ground rents and high prices of land raise the wages, because "were not the poor workmen and labourers well paid for their pains, they could not possibly live." [26] An inquisitive traveler of those times was able to collect a rich assortment of information about prices and wages, supply and demand, and many other questions concerning the market.

The clash between two contrasting modes of observation may be discerned by comparing the remarks on Provence by Jakub Sobieski quoted above with those of John Locke who visited the same country in 1676. According to Locke, the country was

> ...however commended, wherein I have seen more barren ground than fruitful, and yet had passed the best part of it. The people too, if one may judge by their clothes and diet, had, like the country, 5 acres of poverty for one of riches, for I remember at Aix in a gardiner's house, where we found them eating their

[24]F. Moryson, op. cit., IV, p. 70.
[25]John Ray, Travels through the Low Countries, Germany, Italy and France... (London, 1732) (Ray traveled in 1663), p. 44. I discuss more thoroughly the remarks of Moryson, Ray and others in "Prices, Wages and Living Costs in Sixteenth-Century Europe. An Essay in Source Criticism" in Festschrift für Wilhelm Abel (in press).
[26]Cf. also Charles Wilson's penetrating remarks about taxation.

Sunday dinner was noe thing but slices of congeald bloud fried in oile which an English gent, was with me would needs fast, though to the turning of his stomach [27].

The period between the two surveys was one of economic and social depression for that part of the Mediterranean coast, of *misère et banditisme* according to an expression of Fernand Braudel. [28] In addition the English gentleman was probably more disposed to look into a tenant's cooking pot when traveling abroad than he was when at home. [29] Finally, the difference of attitude was also in part due to their differences in background and in part to the disappearance of some features that had fascinated the Polish nobleman earlier.

The approach of Moryson, Ray, or Locke now appears to us as being much more realistic than Sobieski's profusion of relics, beauty of nature, and comeliness of women, but under the surface Sobieski, too has something to tell us. "There are lots of holy places," he wrote; the distribution of relics in Europe certainly presents a very diversified picture. The greatest number of important relics can be observed in the countries with the oldest traditions. This was not because the most eminent members of the Church had once lived there, but because the Dark Ages saw in the West the appearance of the most extravagant of the relics. This was so in Provence as well as in Cologne where, it was believed, the soil was permeated with holiness. Julius Caesar's fondness for Provence could also be seen as a contribution to its "wealth," because it symbolized the durability of Provence's civilization. Longevity of the inhabitants and salubrious climate are also symbols, whose significance in the times of primitive medicine was much greater than it is today. [30]

These vivid and suggestive descriptions of the countries' wealth tend to be understood with reference to the way we perceive things and experience. Quite frequently a single episode, e.g., the anonymous Pole and the shoemaker in Seville will tend to dictate our conception of prices and the standard of living in some country at a given time. Sometimes a stray piece of information about salary or some scene observed in a street become grounds for far-reaching, generalized assump-

[27] *Locke's Travels in France, 1675—1679...*, ed. J. Lough (Cambridge, 1953), p. 88.
[28] Fernand Braudel, "Misère et banditisme", *Annales, Economies, Sociétés, Civilisations* II (1947), pp. 129—142.
[29] Incidentally, one cannot always rely on travelers' impressions concerning the local diet. Jakub Sobieski was deeply shocked at seeing scrambled eggs with slices of Ravaillac's flesh fried in his host's pan. If the scene had been in Warsaw, and Sobieski were a French diarist, the French public would be convinced even today that Poles are devoted cannibals.
[30] It is worth remarking that in today's world the mortality rate is as good an index of the relative prosperity of nations as is *per capita* income.

tions. [31] It is in this way that the sixteenth or the seventeenth century as seen through a traveler's eyes becomes a historical scene at the same time so distant and so astonishingly close to our own. The Renaissance and Baroque travelers were also very diverse in type, though the mode of thinking peculiar to a given epoch can be revealed from a traveler's immediate reaction to some novel or surprising circumstance, or the nature of the personal impressions he wishes to share. For this reason, sources of this kind may be useful for the examination of modes of perception and argumentation in a given period and the conscious or unconscious values and criteria of evaluation. Travelers' memoirs are also occasionally accompanied by accounts of the traveler's expenditures; these might also prove to be invaluable evidence for the prices of goods and services. [32] For these reasons, the cultural historian would do well to share the investigation of these sources with scholars from other disciplines, particularly psychologists and economic historians.

[31] The mistake of inferring the wealth of a country from the signs of luxury displayed by the rich is universal. In underdeveloped countries today the splendor of fashionable districts often screens the poverty of *favellas* from the sight of tourists.
[32] This evidence is discussed in many papers mentioned above, notes 10 and 26, and in my paper prepared for the International Congress of Economic Historians (Copenhagen, August, 1974).

VI

Money and Society in Poland and Lithuania in the 16th and 17th Centuries

1. INTRODUCTORY REMARKS

The only safe conclusion one can draw about the social distribution of money in early modern Poland is that it was not uniform. If a scholar poses more searching questions he encounters a wide gap in the sources available to him. This is the main reason why it is still impossible to produce a Polish monograph that would match Frank Spooner's work on the French monetary system.[1] One can only hope that in time some new way of using this fragmentary material will be found or, less probably, that some fresh evidence will be unearthed. The principal records of the state treasury have been lost, and there is scarcely any valuable information on coining. One must rely on secondary information which can only lead to hypothhetical rather than firm conclusions. However, and this may be a justification for taking up this particular topic, there is abundant evidence on the role played by money in the relationships between men and between social groups.

As this is a *sujet-fleuve*, on which some limitations must be imposed, I shall focus my attention on rural rather than urban

---

[1] F. SPOONER, *L'Économie mondiale et les Frappes Monétaires en France 1493-1680*, Paris 1956.

society, and in particular on the nobility. First, this is a more unusual approach than concentrating upon towns and commerce; second, and most important, I strongly believe that the way in which the nobility, and in particular the high nobility (the *magnates*), lived and spent their money played a crucial role in the circulation of money both on a national and a local scale. These are the reasons for the particular structure of my paper, which is designed to stress the characteristic features of the social and economic structure of Poland and Lithuania.

2. THE SUPPLY OF MONEY

The student of the Polish monetary system must pay particular attention to the balance of trade, and in doing so he is likely to be influenced predominantly by what was happening in Gdańsk (Danzig) and Elblag (Elbing). In Gdańsk he will find abundant — if often doubtful — statistics for prices and quantities of goods, whereas there is little similar evidence available for inland areas.

The flow of precious metals through the country can be broadly sketched as follows.[2] During the 16th century the sea trade brought a high percentage of money to the country. A huge relative surplus of exports diminished at the turn of the century and even dwindled away in some years of the critical first half of the seventeenth. The balance of inland trade was less favourable for the country's economy. Little can be learnt about trade with Silesia, in which commerce with Bohemia, Austria and Saxony was concentrated. It seems that the Polish trade balance was mainly passive in that direction, because of the large quantities of cloths and haberdashery which she imported. Only oxen were an important export item, but the massive export of oxen to Silesia, Saxony and the Rhine was ended by the Thirty Years War.

---

[2] M. BOGUCKA, *Handel zagraniczny Gdańska w pierwszej połowie XVII wieku* (Le Commerce extérieur de Gdańsk dans la première moitié du XVII⁰ siècle), Wrocław 1970. Miss Bogucka's conclusions are based on toll registers from Gdańsk. (When the titles of books or papers are translated into French a French summary and a French title are included). A. MĄCZAK, *The Balance of the Polish Sea Trade with the West, 1565-1646*, « The Scandinavian Economic History Rewiev », 1970, based principally on the Sound toll registers.

Money and Society in Poland and Lithuania in the 16th and 17th Centuries

Much less evidence is available about the trade balance with Muscovy. Wax and furs were exchanged for industrial goods, some of which (or even most) were re-exported from the west. In east-west transit commerce it is generally very difficult to calculate the involvement of the country's economy in the continental trade.

It was the south-east, or Oriental, trade that drained Poland of the money which it earned through the Baltic. No customs figures are available but every scrap of evidence suggests a heavy export of gold and silver. At the end of the 16th century Poland introduced a special duty on the export of gold and silver, which was perceived only on the Turkish frontier. The situation was illustrated by individuals like John Sanderson, a pilgrim and merchant who was well informed about conditions in Constantinople: « Divers merchaunts are come latelie out of Poland; they have brought wyer, lattin plates, knives; nether coniskins nor tinne, but most redie mony ».[2a] Mountain robbers in the Carpathians trimmed their caps with English golden Nobles, which were obviously also destined for Turkey.

Various factors that will be discussed later caused changes in the Polish trade balance. Baltic exports, which were predominantly grain and timber, fluctuated according to supply rather than overseas demand. Prices, on the other hard, were highly dependent on general European trade cycles and in the second half of the 17th century the fall in the value of exports was a result of both diminishing quantities and unfavourable prices. However, the decrease in the export surplus was due primarily to the rise in imports, and imports are closely connected with the social distribution of profits from foreign trade and with the social distribution of income in general.

This was even more true for the import trade from the Turkish dominions. In the war with Turkey Poland became more and more dependent on oriental luxury goods that became fashionable among the gentry. The expensive silks (also imported from Venice), Persian carpets, arms and armour, as well as spices which poured

---

[2a] *The Travels of John Sanderson, Works issued by the Hakluyt Society*, 2 Series, vol. LXVII, 1930, p. 169.

into Poland through both the Baltic and Turkey, had no equivalents in Polish commodities.

Although indirect and never satisfactory, there is abundant evidence that for the country as a whole the era of an active balance of trade ended in the first decades of the 17th century and that the fateful 1620's marked the beginning of a prolonged period of a passive trade balance.[3] Recent research has produced sets of economic statistics marking the vicissitudes of the country's economy, which were always expressed in terms of the changes in the balance of foreign trade. The coining policy and the money market of most of the 17th century gave rise to serious problems in the supply of gold and silver, which resulted in a permanent monetary crisis.

This demand could hardly be met by local silver mining. The output of silver from the Olkusz mines did not exceed 0.3 tons per year between 1574 and 1577 and reached its peak, i.e. 0.8 to 1.3 tons annually, between 1606 and 1609.[4] These quantities were, however, smaller than the changes in the yearly balance of sea trade. Almost all the non-commercial items on the Polish balance of payments are to be written on the debit side of the account sheet. Contemporary opinion was troubled by the tributes which were paid to the Tartars in order to prevent their incursions, and the question of the *annates* and other payments to Rome was constantly raised by Polish Protestants and even by some anti-clericals Catholic.

Foreign travel was another debit item. Foreign travellers were by no means rare in Poland but they were not heavy spenders. Fynes Moryson, who visited this country in the 1590's, stressed the cheapness of food there (with the exception of spices, which were more expensive than the meat or fish they seasoned) and the

---

[3] A. MANIKOWSKI, *Zmiany czy stagnacja? Z problematyki handlu polskiego w drugiej połowie XVII wieku* (Le Commerce de la Pologne entre 1660 et 1700 - période de stagnation ou de transformation?), « Przegląd Historyczny », vol. LXIV, 1973, fasc. 4; A. MĄCZAK, *op. cit.*

[4] D. MOLENDA, *Produkcja srebra w Polsce w XVI i XVII wieku* (Silver Production in Poland in the 16th and 17th centuries), *Społeczeństwo, Gospodarka, Kultura* (Society, Economy, Culture. Studies in Honour of Marian Małowist), Warszawa 1974, p. 228 f.

poor living conditions outside the larger towns.[5] At the same time foreign travel could be a disastrous drain on a nobleman's purse. The Grand Tour or several years of study at a foreign university, became obligatory for young men from the upper stratum of the nobility from the mid-sixteenth century and was fashionable until the late seventeenth at least. It is important to note that even the richest magnates tried to limit such expenses; fathers were motivated not only by such moral reasons as frugality but also by often justifiable suspicious of their sons' tutors. However, it is very amusing to read of how one of the greatest European landlords, Prince Christopher Radziwiłł, ordered a tutor to re-make his young master's clothes in Munich in the German fashion.[6]

All figures can be misleading, but even a rather frugal Grand Tour was equivalent to the income from one or more estates. In two and a half years in Munich, Stanisław Lubomirski, the son of a rising magnate, spent with his modest group of servants about 4,950 *zloty*, which was equivalent to the income from about ten medium sized villages. Less wealthy noblemen spent less but even so the financial burden of foreign studies could be a crushing burden on their estate. Two young orphans called Goździe, spent 3,815 *zl.* during their journey to Strasbourg and Leiden between 1595 and 1599. During these four years, their guardian was able to raise 5,800 *zl.* from their estate, so foreign travel swallowed up about two-thirds of that sum.[7] A traveller, however, had to be virtually independent of his family's trusteeship in order to be able to spend really large sums. This was the case with Prince Boguslaw Radziwiłł who spent hundreds of thousands of *zloty* during his long military and political apprenticeship in Germany, France and the Netherlands: between 1642 and 1644 the managers of his Lithuanian estates sent to him abroad 230,000 *zl.* (i.e., 77,000 ducats), which amounted to almost half of his fabulous income.[8]

---

5 F. MORYSON, *An Itinerary, containing his ten years' travel...*, Glasgow, 1907-1908, *passim* (in particular vol. II p. 29, III p. 471, IV p. 33).

6 M. ZACHARA, T. MAJEWSKA-LANCHOLC (eds.), *Instrukcja Krzysztofa II Radziwiłła dla syna Janusza* (Krzysztof Radziwiłł's Instruction for His Son Janusz), « Odrodzenie i Reformacja w Polsce », vol. XVI, 1971, p. 179.

7 Biblioteka Polskiej Akademii Nauk, Cracow, MS 3262.

8 Archiwum Główne Akt Dawnych, Warszaw, Archiwum Radziwiłłow, XXIX 24.

3. FOREIGN TRADE AND LUXURY CONSUMER GOODS

Any attempt to calculate the G.N.P. or amount of money circulating in the country would have a margin of error so wide as to call into question the very value of such calculations especially if they cannot be verified against other independent evidence, as Andrzej Wyczański, who tried to compute the value of foodstuffs produced in Poland (i.e., excluding Lithuania the Ukraine and Ruthenia) around 1580 was well aware. His results may, however, be useful for comparison with the value of expensive consumer goods at the same time, which leads us directly to the main subject of this paper.[9] It is worth comparing Wyczański's estimates with some rather conservative import statistics showing the demands of particular social classes.

Table 1 contains estimates of the principal consumer goods which were imported by both land and sea to Poland around 1580.

TABLE 1

ESTIMATES OF CLOTH AND WINE IMPORTS TO POLAND IN THE 1580's

Goods		Quantities	Average Price	Value (zl.)	Comments
Cloth,	Silesian	100,000 pieces	8 *zl.*	800,000	Prices estimated according to retail quotations in Polish towns
	Moravian, Lusatian, Czech	13,000 »	12 »	156,000	Prices estimated according to retail quotations in Polish towns
	Dutch, English & other; Baltic imports	20,000 »	32 »	620,000	Prices estimated according to retail quotations in Polish towns
Wines,	Baltic imports only	7,000 ohms	+	87,000	Baltic imports estimated according to prices in ports of departure +45% for freight & merchants' profit

A. MACZAK, *Między Gdańskiem a Sundem. Studia nad handlem bałtyckim od połowy XVI do połowy XVII w.* (Between Gdańsk and the Sound. Studies in the Eastland Trade, 1550-1650), Warszawa 1972, p. 96 ff. Rearranged.

[9] A. WYCZAŃSKI, *Studia nad konsumpcją żywności w Polsce w XVI i w pierwszej połowie XVII w.* (Etudes sur la consommation des vivres en Pologne au XVI° et pendant la première moitié du XVII° siècle), Warszawa 1969, p. 218.

These figures are by no means a complete estimate of luxury and semi-luxury imports. One cannot specify the quantities of Hungarian wines or the value of imported spices. 1,663,000 *zl.* — the total of the table — is therefore a very conservative figure for expensive imports, and could easily be raised to two millions. For the same period Wyczański's estimates of agricultural produce was 45,000,000 *zl.* + 20 per cent for industrial products and services, total = 54,000,000 *zl.* Both groups of figures refer to roughly the same western provinces of the Polish-Lithuanian state, although some of the imports were sent through Poland to Lithuania. One may also assume that expensive imported goods in the 1580's lowered the G.N.P. by 4 per cent.

Who were the consumers? They were obviously only a narrow stratum of the population. Wines were at that time still an extravagant rarity and not all noblemen drank them often. Silesian cloths were more evenly distributed. They were given as payment in kind to manorial managers or clerks; they are to be found in the inventories of lesser nobles and even of average townsmen. It is important that all these features changed quickly during the following decades; and this is the only factor we may be sure of. In the 17th century imports of "colonial goods" (i.e., spices, sugar etc.) gained in strength. « Within my memory », harangued Sir Ivan Mieleszko, the Castellan of Smolensk at the 1587 *Sejm* (Parliament session), « there were no such titbits ... Hungarian wines were unknown, malmsey was only little tasted, one drank mead and good old aquavit, but there were plenty of pennies ... ».[10] However, after the lifetime of that conservative gentleman successive generations of noblemen consumed more and more foreign luxuries. Table 2 shows the development of "colonial" imports to Gdańsk, Elbląg and Königsberg.

The composite (weighted average) prices of colonial goods, as expressed in silver or any constant currency, hardly changed. In a period when prices rose dramatically (until the 1620's at least) they became increasingly cheaper and probably more evenly

---

[10] J. U. NIEMCEWICZ (ed.), *Zbiór Pamiętników o dawnej Polsce* (A Collection of Memoirs on Old-Time Poland), Puławy 1822, p. 80.

TABLE 2

IMPORT OF "COLONIAL GOODS" TO GDAŃSK, ELBLĄG AND KÖNIGSBERG
(three-year averages for selected years)

Ports	1565/'75/'85	1595/'05/'15	1625/'35/'46	1675/'85/'95
Gdańsk	31,000	156,000	928,000	2,490,000
Elbląg	2,000	7,000	15,000	2,000
Königsberg	0	10,000	228,000	487,000

See Table 1. Rearranged. Included only goods expressed in pounds (other goods could not be compared). Based on the Sound toll registers.

distributed. But this was by no means an even distribution. Wczański's studies of the consumption of foodstuffs suggest that we are discussing not so much the consumption habits of various social classes, but rather of separate consumer groups. It is obvious that the lord himself ate better than his servants, but at the same time a servant's fortune at table depended heavily on the quality of the house, to which numerous 18th century memoirs, as well as Wyczański's figures bear witness. The increase in the consumption of expensive foods may possibly be explained by the fact that firstly, these goods were purchased by more people so their distribution became more uniform; secondly, the tables of the wealthy were better set in the 17th than in the preceding century; and thirdly there were more wealthy households than before, but the rest of population did not eat better.

Everything we know about social change in these times speaks against the first explanation, although the growing wealth of a few commercial urban centres, like Gdańsk, Elbląg, Toruń and some smaller ones should be stressed. On the contrary, the gap was widening between the richer landowners and the rest of the population, in particular the peasantry and lesser gentry. The mass of the urban population was also divided, the majority sharing the fate of the declining rural classes. The courts of the increasingly wealthy magnates and noblemen, then, attracted considerable, and sometimes even large, numbers of servants, retainers and "clients". As a further illustration we need only quote pages from Thorsten Veblen's *Theory of Leisure Class* or the comments made by Lawrence

Stone or Hugh Trevor-Roper.[11] So one may accept our second and third explanations: that there were more and larger courts with many, greedy and hungry dependent consumers. This applies to food consumption, clothes, servants' and retainers' liveries, and even to arms and uniforms purchased in bulk for private troops. Very probably the social and economic polarization of society led to an increased demand for imported goods. Many retainers and commoners fared better than other people, who lived independently of the nobles' courts.

Another reason why this social development contributed to the consumption of imported goods, was the relatively close links between the large landed estates and the Baltic ports. Those goods that were inaccessible for the independent small or middle landowner proved relatively or even absolutely cheaper for the magnate, who sold his grain and timber at favourable Gdańsk prices and bought cloth, spices, and wines, there, so avoiding the retailers.[12]

All this helps to explain why even the highly active balance of sea trade did not cause a spectacular rise in prices in Poland.[13] The influx of precious metals did not saturate the economic system, for the unique structure of the demand for and supply of luxury goods directed a large share of the surplus abroad.

4. THE MAGNATES INVOLVED IN EXPORTING AND IMPORTING GOODS

I have mentioned the direct contacts between the large inland estates and the Baltic coast and its ports. Only a few inland towns prospered from this trade, for usually most of the money acquired from the sale of grain was spent on the spot, in Gdańsk, or Königs-

---

11 L. STONE, *The Crisis of the Aristocracy, 1558-1641*, Oxford 1965, pp. 201-217 & al.; H. R. TREVOR-ROPER, *The General Crisis of the Seventeenth Century*, « Past & Present », vol. 16.

12 W. KULA, *Théorie économique du système féodal. Pour un modèle de l'économie polonaise 16ᵉ-18ᵉ siècles*, Paris-La Haye 1970, p. 94.

13 This was the question raised by E. F. Heckscher in connection with A. E. Christensen's research on the Sound toll registers. See A. ATTMAN, *The Russian and Polish Markets in International Trade, 1500-1650*, Göteborg 1973, p. 118 ff. for a report on the controversy.

berg, on foreign goods or the products of local industry. In this way the inland towns were excluded from commercial dealings as neither their commercial skills nor transport facilities were needed. So what happened to the money?

One must rely upon available evidence, although the phenomenon was very widespread. The early 17th century provided the extreme case of Albrecht Władysław Radziwiłł, a Lithuanian magnate, who sent some 40 to 250 *lasts* of rye annually down the River Niemen to Königsberg. Five account sheets in *zloty* kept by his managers for the years 1626-1629, 1631 and 1634 provide the following figures (total for five years):

TABLE 3

THE CASH BALANCE OF PRINCE ALBRECHT WŁADYSŁAW RADZIWIŁŁ's COMMERCIAL CONTACTS WITH KÖNIGSBERG
(overall figures for 1626-1629, 1631, 1634; in *zloty*)

Income from sales	57,046	Tolls & customs	2,952
Income from freight	26,992	Salaries of the crew	5,929
		Other expenditures	3,688
		Total transport costs	12,569
		Purchases of cloth & other	
		textiles	13,867
		Fruits & spices	4,483
		Other foodstuffs	4,329
		Salt	12,327
		Other goods	2,734
		Total purchases	37,740
Total gross income	84,038	Debts paid	26,469
Total deficit	1,449	Interest on debts	8,709
Grand Total	85,487	Grand Total	85,487

(Based on an unpublished M.A. thesis by MARIA BRZOZOWSKA, *Rafting on the River Niemen and Commercial Contacts of the Radziwiłł Manors with Königsberg in the First Half of the 17th Century*, Warsaw 1970).

Of course the business was not a total loss. Purchases amounted to 44.9 per cent of the total gross income; debt and interest payments accounted for 41.2 per cent. If the Prince sank deeper and deeper into debt, it was due to heavy purchases. The balance sheet, however, does not reveal the entire state of affairs. It includes 5,197 *zl*. for the cash income of Princess Mirska (in 1634), but shows she made purchases totalling only 1,263 *zl*. and had no debts (or at least did not pay them). This means that money did not flow up the river. Much of it found its way into the pockets of Königsberg and Elbląg merchants; only about 3.5% was paid to customs officers and another 11.4% went for the salaries of numerous sailors and their skippers or covered losses caused by accidents. Foodstuffs were brought from home in large quantities so that they could be sold in Königsberg or left until the following year.

All these costs were covered by the freight rates, and the magnates seemed to hold a monopoly over the river Niemen. A.W. Radziwiłł gladly provided space on his boats for his less well-to-do neighbours' timber or ash. In years of poor harvests, shipping remained profitable only through hiring out river boats. When harvests were abundant, less room was available for customers. On the average, the income from freight was twice that of the overal transportation costs.

The next table (4) represents the cash for the transport of grain and other goods from another large estate down the river, this time from the extreme south-east corner of the Vistula Basin. Again it was the case that Sieniawski's steward brought from Gdańsk in cash not more than 6.5% of the gross income. Freight

TABLE 4

THE CASH BALANCE OF ADAM MIKOŁAJ SIENIAWSKI's
COMMERCIAL CONTACTS WITH GDAŃSK
(estimative data for 1715, in *zloty*)

Income from sales		27,930	Tolls, customs & bribes		4,820
Income from freight		41,600	Salaries of the crew		6,143
			Market value of food supplied		
			for crew		7,271
			Operation costs		1,576
			Alms & Holy Masses		46
•			Other expenditures		70
Total gross income		69,530	Total transport costs		19,926
Total net income	ca.	4,500	Purchases of goods	ca.	45,000
Grand Total	ca.	65,000	Total expenditures	ca.	65,000

(Estimated according to J. BURSZTA, *Le commerce entre Sieniawa s/San et Gdańsk... à partir de la fin du XVIIe jusqu'à moitié du XVIIIe siècle*, « Roczniki Dziejów Społecznych i Gospodarczych », vol. XVI, 1954, in Polish with a French summary).

services were more important here than the sale of the estate's products and 60% of the gross income was obtained from rafting.

A third example occurred much later, and reflect a different situation, that of a lord interested in getting cash, and also different times. 1772 witnessed the First Partition of Poland and in Spring 1773 river shippers faced a unique situation; the Prussians were occupying Royal Prussia, and although Gdańsk remained Polish, it was separated from the rest of the country and burdened by heavy tolls. The shipping manager of Princess Ludwika Lubomirska had to pay tolls and customs to officers of all the three foreign powers: Austria, Russia and Prussia, and from his notes it is difficult to distinguish the times when he paid tolls from those when he was a victim of the extortion practised by imaginative and greedy soldiers. In contrast to the previous accounts, the debts are trivial and Princess Ludwika obviously had little interest in industrial imports (besides those mentioned above, there was

TABLE 5

THE CASH BALANCE OF PRINCESS LUDWIKA LUBOMIRSKA's
TRANSPORT OF GRAIN, POTASH AND POPPY SEED TO GDAŃSK, 1773

Cash taken from home	3,000	Tolls, custom & bribes	7,317	
Income from sales	77,772	Crew salaries	6,426	
Ships (etc.) sold	1,072	Manager's salary	1,384	
		Food for the crew	561	
		Other sailing expenses	224	
		Repairing of ships	291	
		Weighing and measuring	358	
		Maintenance of granaries	122	
		Purchases of:		
		Cloth & other textiles	904	
		Spices	8,355	
		Wines	7,238	
		Herrings	990	
		Belts (?)	756	
		Total purchases	19,599	
		Debts paid	2,873	
		Remaining expenses	1,000	
		Unclear items	2,502	
		Total expenses		42,667
		Cash brought back home		37,790
		Paid to the Princess' treasury		387
Grand Total	81,844	Grand Total		81,844

(Biblioteka Jagiellońska, Cracow, MS 6603-11).

also some tin, iron, cotton wicks, ropes, cheap pottery, a kettle . . .), and sought spices and wines (the Hungarian goods were probably easily obtainable at home). For our purposes, it is important to note that 49% of the income was brought home in cash.

Prince Bogusław Radziwiłł has been already mentioned as a heavy spender abroad. Table 6 shows some entries concerning his business in Königsberg which support what we have already stated.

One of the very few existing account sheets for lesser magnates,

TABLE 6

SOME ENTRIES FROM THE CASH BALANCE OF PRINCE BOGUSŁAW RADZIWIŁŁ's ESTATES' TRANSPORT OF GOODS TO KÖNIGSBERG, 1643-1644
(in *złoty*)

1643	Income from sales ('forest goods')	20,130			
			Transport expenses (part of?)		1,200
			Crew salaries		200
			Manager's salary		200
			Manager's board and lodging in Königsberg (10 weeks)		200
			Manager's necessary expenses		267
			Messenger to Königsberg		20
			Debts paid		8,044
1644	Income from sales:		Cash expenses for lard &		
	'forest goods'	12,649	other food for crew		1,734
	rye	6,817	Manager's food for 10 weeks		300
			Debts paid		3,846
			Paid to a Jew for preparation of 'forest goods'		4,220
			Purchases in Königsberg:		
			Silverware	2,153	
			Copperware	6	
			Salt	4,760	
			Spices	500	
			Kitchen battery	213	
			Tin	255	
			Table cloths (Dutch)	386	
			Wine vinegar	45	
			Codfish	16	
			Lock	15	
			Glass (incl. freight)	77	
			Storage in Königsberg	379	
			Total purchases		8,805
	Total	19,466	Grand Total		18,905

(Archiwum Główne Akt Dawnych, Warszaw, Archiwum Radziwiłłow XXXIX, 24).

or rich squires, that of Castellan of Bełz for year 1618, does not permit us to make a clear assessment of his rafting expenses and profits. It is, however, illuminating because it illustrates the complex nature of the money circulation connected with grain exports from far inland. The Castellan brought grain (mostly rye) from Lublin — an important inland commercial centre — and from a small township, Bełżyce, which he sold wholesale in Gdańsk, where he bought herrings, then wine in Toruń, to sell them then in Warsaw and Lublin.[14]

What is most important, all the existing balance sheets reveal that the ports were great sources of money. The second source was the great fairs which were held in Jarosław, Lwów (for the South-East) and Poznań or Toruń (for the North-West). In terms of social classes, then, the principal route for the money supply was the more or less direct connection between the merchants of Gdańsk (also of Königsberg, of Riga etc.) and the great land-owners of the hinterland.

We are now confronted with new questions. A comparison of the meagre sums brought back from Baltic ports, with the large sums spent by the magnates leads us to seek other sources of money and I shall return to this problem later. We must also ask what happened to this money and we must, therefore, see the courts of the nobles as the centres of money circulation.

5. THE NOBLE COURTS AS CENTRES OF CONSUMPTION

There is a clear contrast between manorial accounts and inventories, on the one hand, and the expense sheets of the great noblemen's courts, in which innumerable small entries abound, on the other. The accounts are strictly divided into cash and goods sections and in most of these sources nothing that has been left unsold is expressed in cash terms. The goods section is by no means marginal, on the contrary, keeping cash expenses low seems to be the principal rule of husbandry.[15] What can be obtained from

---

14 Biblioteka P.A.N., Cracow, MS 3262, p. 148.
15 W. KULA, *op. cit.*, chap. III & VI.

one's own estates, was usually abundant; what had to be purchased with ready money was always scarce.

Precious metals of all kinds were a sign of prestige. They were still used in the rather mediaeval way which in the West was slowly giving way to a more economical lifestyle.[16] The cultural change that occurred in Western European countries during the 1620's, hardly touched the Polish Republic. Whereas the English aristocracy disbanded their retinues and even thought of limiting their personal expenditure, their Polish counterparts still, and perhaps increasingly, displayed splendour of a rather anachronistic sort. Even Italian, French, and Dutch-educated magnates followed local traditions in order not to offend public opinion. From the mid-17th to the mid-18th centuries in particular, the Polish Baroque way of life strongly deviated from Western patterns.

Polish noblemen travelling abroad during the 17th century were often puzzled by the sober way of life of Italian nobles who were obviously rich but less ostentatious. The best example is that provided by the Jesuit tutor of the brothers Grudziński after their long (1655-1659) Grand Tour through the European Continent. « The strange Home Behaviour of Lords and Gentleman in Italy and in Spain » — runs the title of a special paragraph devoted to this problem. « One does not see the great fortunes they have (*e contra* among us). Although they have numerous coaches, in towns they use only two horses, except for long journeys ... Saddle and harness even for the most expensive horses are only occasionally decorated with gold and silver thread ... Servants are paid weekly and not given board. Even their Lordships make do with little, even the Pope used to eat for some three Giulii. Banquets are very rare and served to a very limited number of participants. They squander courageously for confectionery ... Nobody keeps a large orchestra, only one or two musicians. They do not sit long at the table, either for drink or for conversation. Servants eat at their own expense, they do not hobnob with each

---

16 H. R. TREVOR-ROPER, *op. cit.* The Author's remarks on extravagant spending in the royal courts also apply to the Polish magnates' courts.

other. In Rome servants often do not live with their lord, only some do ».[17]

It would not be difficult to find contrary evidence, but the tutor's (and most probably also his master's) way of thinking seems to reflect a true cultural gap between the societies. A quarter of a century later, King John III Sobieski summed up his first impressions of Austria in a letter sent to the Queen. « ... if they [i.e., the Austrians] will judge us on our appearance, they will think us *pour plus riches que ne fut Crésus, et pour plus magnifiques de ce siècle*, the livery of our servants [chamberlains], pages and lackeys more than beautiful, our horses richly dressed, our houses ... decorated with cloth of gold ... They, however, have not a single mottle of silver on their horses, their clothes are simple (half German, half Hungarian), their carts are simple; no pages, no lackeys seen as yet. The Prince of Saxony was yesterday in a simple red garment, with a crimson sash and simple thrum ... ».[18]

Nevertheless the Polish heavy cavalry, the hussars, wearing leopard skins over the half-cuirass, with their long lances and decorative wings, were able to inflict a decisive blow to the Turkish army and relieve the siege of Vienna. It is well known, however, that the immense booty from the Vizir's camp outside Vienna greatly contributed to the Polish nobles' growing taste for the Oriental. « Tents, carts they are all mine — the King was happy to inform his French wife in the next letter — *et mille d'autres galanteries fort riches ... Il n'y a point de comparison avec ceux de Chocim* [an earlier victory, 1673, over the Turks]. Several quivers decorated with rubies and saphirs alone may be valued at several thousands ducats ... ».

But it is time to follow the Poles back to their homes. If the Polish nobleman cultivated traditional social virtues, it was not a continuation of mediaeval ways. The rapid concentration of

---

[17] Biblioteka im. XX Czartoryskich, Cracow, MS 3031, p. 579. Cf.: « And in those countries [*i.e.*, Italy] *frugalitas* is more appreciated among people than *prodigalitas*; among us the other way around ... », writes an expert pilgrim and traveller Michael Radziwiłł ("the Orphan"), 1603. Archiwum domu Radziwiłłów, ed. by A. Sokołowski, Kraków 1885, p. 60.

[18] JAN SOBIESKI, *Listy do Marysieńki* (Letters to Mary), ed. by J. Kukulski, Warszawa 1970, pp. 509, 520.

landed property in many parts of the country uprooted many country gentlemen and increased the social differences between the propertied classes. Both old and new members of the upper stratum of landowners, who can be only partly identified with the members of the Senate (i.e., the Upper House), now needed more *noble* retainers than ever. A research programme on the subject is now in progress and we cannot draw on representative figures but it is beyond doubt that service of this kind increased during the 17th and most of the following century. This was of crucial importance for the distribution and circulation of money.

Servants in the lord's home were paid only partly in cash. Part, and often most, of their salaries consisted of free board for themselves and for their own servants as well, while a limited number of their horses were maintained in the lord's stables. The more important the position of a retainer the less formally dependent he was on the lord. The richer the mansion the more nobles it housed, including the sons of neighbouring gentlemen who learned how to behave properly and nobly, and earned their lord's favour for life. They received hardly any salary in cash but, if they succeeded in satisfying the lord, they were often given land for rent or some other reward. An influential magnate had numerous means of rewarding lesser noblemen without paying them directly. But still the pay-roll of courtiers represented an important item in the great noble's court expenses. In the latter part of the period under discussion the lords' obligations were increasingly shifted on to the state: their *clients* were given lucrative, or simply prestigious and attractive, offices and honours.

5. THE STATE AND ITS CREDITORS

At this point we touch on the role of the state. If, as Professor Habakkuk has observed, eighteenth-century England as reflected in aristocratic memoirs looked like a federation of country houses, the Polish « commonwealth of Gentry » was one, at least from the middle of the 17th century.[19] Central institutions were less

---

19 H. J. HABAKKUK and A. GOODWIN (ed.), *The European Nobility in the Eighteenth Century*, London 1963 (quoted from Harper Torchbook ed., 1967, p. 4).

developed than in many other kingdoms and the king had restricted opportunity to appoint new men. Commoners were virtually excluded from competition for appointments but there was much social climbing among the nobility. The treasury was empty and creditors of all sorts were reimbursed with royal estates or single manors, or at least were repaid directly from the gross income of the estates. This system, which was once quite common in Europe, was particularly widespread in Poland until the late 18th century. Civil servants were paid poorly or not at all, and gained their daily bread and butter by nibbling at parties. Higher officials were given Royal estates for life or for a period and became what might be called shareholders in the state. Such « payment in kind » instead of money was an important social factor. When the king appointed a newcomer, the successful climber soon became as good a magnate as any other. Rewarding in kind perpetuated the social and political system more strongly than any custom of purchasing honours, as was so widely developed in England, France, and, principally, in Spain and in the Italian dominions of the Spanish Hapsburgs.[20]

In Poland nobody expected the state to pay its larger debts in cash, for only the leases of customs posts or salt mines approximated to any payment in cash.[21] This might look very similar to the financial practice of absolute states, were there not now and then a particularly glaring feature to stress the difference. This difference is clearly reflected in the different system of financing ambasadors. In countries like Denmark every envoy prepared a detailed list of his expenses, and supplied proofs such as inkeepers' bills, and his declaration was duly inspected. In Poland an envoy was generally expected to cover his expenses out of his own purse but could expect that his obligations would be paid back in the form of honours, influence with the court and of course with

---

[20] This system became a bone of contention between both Houses in the 1550's and 1560's. The Senators were and remained principal possessors of royal estates.

[21] Salt mines were part of the most desirable leaseholds and contributed to the pecuniary gain of their possessors. Small payments were discharged in cash, often by directing the payee to a particular source of revenue (a royal estate, a salt mine, a customs house). Also stipends were often connected with a source of revenue.

royal estates conferred either for a time or for life. These details were commonly known and were explained with particular clarity by a Polish nobleman of Livonian ancestry to a German traveller from Franconia, when they met in a Stettin inn. Heinrich Denhoff had been sent as an envoy and was paying for his own funds. If successful, he would be granted « *aine Starosday mit 20,000 f.* », i.e. a royal estate of 20 thousand *zloty* yearly value, for three years, or even for six and more.[22] And this was by no means an exception.

6. THE SIZE OF MONETARY TRANSACTIONS

I believe that one may distinguish a general, if unwritten, rule that governed the use of money in relations between men outside the sphere of production and commerce. Money seemed to be indispensable in the exchange of petty goods and services, but it was much less so in large-scale transactions involving goods. The more direct and informal relationship between people, the lesser the role played in it by money. Some examples drawn from areas beyond the traditional sphere of discussion on money circulation will illustrate this.

Only a few account books of great noble households are available, although many may still be buried in the archives. Often they do not offer complete information on the expenses and incomes of the estates, simply because they represent the circumstances of one particular treasurer, and either one learns about a particular manor, or else about the lord's own household (the court). For my purposes the latter sources are of much greater value.[23] What were the sources of income or — to be more exact — the origins of the money coming into the lord's coffers? We already know that the direct sale of grain and "forest goods" did not bring him ready cash. And here I would stress a factor whose importance is not fully realized by students of Polish economic life in the 16th and

---

22 PHILIPP MAINHOFERS, *Reise-Tagebuch* . . ., [1617], « Baltische Studien », vol. II, 2, 1834, p. 99.

23 Only manorial accounts have been much used by scholars; other evidence remains virtually untouched, since research has concentrated, until very recently on agriculture.

17th century: the leasing out of whole estates. This seemed to be the easiest way to accumulate income in the form of ready money and also to increase incomes.[24] Two representative cases illustrate this. Krzysztof Opaliński, a rich and highly cultured, ambitious magnate, was badly in need of ready money in the autumn of 1644. « Et haec causa », he wrote to his brother, « I am leasing out in order to have money when I need it . . . Now, after I have a yearly income and after putting out [estates] for three more years I have a feeling there will be a jingle. Last year was only a test but still it brought 70,000 more than my expenses (although you rebuke me), and has shown such an income that what had used to bring ten thousand, now fetches fifteen, sixteen, and some estates even twenty ».[25] And now to Krzysztof Radziwiłł, one of the richest Lithuanian landlords. His controllers had found that two estates, Newel ans Siebierz, when put out to lease might bring at least twice as much as before. « This brings an advantage that instead of dispensing cheese in order to get salt and salt to get cheese, now even in the first year Newel and Siebierz are making at least 6,000 or even more (all expenses included) . . . and still two servants [i.e. managers, now estate farmers] will serve at no particular expense ».[26]

Leaseholders could not work miracles and neither can they all be accused of being careless farmers; they were compelled to run the estates so that they yielded cash rather than income in kind. When they sent grain or timber down the river, these most probably were not sufficient to purchase all the luxuries that were so dear to the magnates' heart. The only large income entries in all the cash balance sheets I have inspected were, however, land annuities. The scope and importance of this practice and its fate in the 18th century deserve close study. The evidence I present

---

[24] If my thesis on leases is valid, it opens new questions that ought to be answered by comparative research on estates belonging to the Church, and the State, as well as to private owners.

[25] R. POLLAK (ed.), Listy Krzysztofa Opalińskiego do brata Łukasza (Krzysztof Opaliński's Letters to His Brother Lucas), Wrocław 1957, p. 240, 6 October 1644.

[26] Krzysztof Radziwiłł to his son Janusz, 29 November 1636, Archiwum Głowne Akt Dawnych, Archiwum Radziwiłłów IV 25, 324, 682.

here is limited, but the account sheets belong to some of the richest and most influential of the great nobles.

The cash balance book of Chancellor Jan Zamoyski (1579-1582), omits the income from his own estates. The Chancellor had then reached the peak of his political influence, but his landed properties and income were only in its prime (Table 7). In 1598 (Table 8) his fortunes were much greater and his expenses were no longer affected by war conditions. The lists ought not to be compared directly, because the Chancellor omitted most items connected with the family and his own living expenses. Two items may however, be stressed: travel costs and the repayment of debts.

Travel contributed strongly to the development of the money sector of the economy. There was a tendency to avoid spending money when travelling through the country, but with questionable success. Noblemen took with them their own beds, tapestries, and even food. Servants prepared the inns and the lord's own cooks prepared his food. This was because a travelling nobleman

TABLE 7

CHANCELLOR JAN ZAMOYSKI's CASH BALANCE, 1579-1582
(in *zloty*)

Ready cash	2,137	*In opera pia* (small alms given to the handicapped, to students, wounded soldiers, Muscovite prisoners)	361
Income from leases of Royal estates	29,166		
King's grants for covering war expenses	29,703	Grants to the Church	782
Income from ecclesiastical estates	515	Family expenses	11,183
Loans	15,879	Clothing	1,321
Grants from noblemen	3,395	House utensils & furniture	4,884
clergymen	984	Servants' salary	3,005
burghers	619	Food and drink	27,421
Jews	162	Personal expenses of the Chancellor (medicines, soap, threads & needles, laundry, barber etc.)	1,839
Total grants	5,162		
Small income (19 items)	6,383	Light	237
Other income	6,448	Taxes	4,247
Total income	95,393	Repayment of debts	2,791
		War expenses	36,344
Total deficit	3,047	Other expenses	95
Balance	98,440	Total expenses	98,440

(From A. TARNAWSKI, *Działalność gospodarcza Jana Zamoyskiego*, Lwów 1935, checked with Archiwum Główne Akt Dawnych, Archiwum Zamoyskich 2519).

TABLE 8

CHANCELLOR JAN ZAMOYSKI's ESTIMATES OF EXPENSES
FOR THE PERIOD 11th JANUARY THROUGH 24th JUNE 1598
(in *zloty*)

Repayment of debts	29,342
Maintenance of courtiers	3,293
Wine	1,500
Spices	1,180
Maintenance of troops and horses	6,117
Craftsmen and buildings	3,186
Taxes	5,115
The *Sejm* (Parliamentary session)	10,000
Small expenses (living costs of two retainers)	155
Reserved for other expenses	4,000
Total	63,888

(A. TARNAWSKI, *op. cit.*, p. 300. Taxes signify land annuities paid for royal estates leased by the Chancellor; however, he paid only less than half of what was legally due from him).

had to take into consideration the scarcity of facilities available along the road; on the other hand the custom (or fashion) of travelling with one's own carpets, furniture and food probably discouraged innkeepers from investing in their business. However, travel always meant spending money. Lesser nobles had to buy everything on the spot and were always worried about the cost of living. The fabulously rich enjoyed, and must have displayed, impressive wealth. Travelling to the *Sejm* session (which from the end of the 16th century was held mainly in Warsaw) was at the time a large — or even the largest — item on a lord's expense sheet. This was also usually an important political event. Every magnate had to appear with a proper, and splendid retinue in order to show his wealth and power. According to a contemporary estimate, which probably rather exaggerated the figure, the 1585 session cost Chancellor Zamoyski the equivalent of 16,000 ducats; in 1598 his treasurer's estimate amounted to a third of that sum: in 1601 the Chancellor took with him 31 sacks of coins worth about 6,000 ducats, almost half his ready money at that time. In the 17th century such expenses grew more than proportionally to the inflation of the Polish currency.[27] What we have said about

---

[27] Chancellor Jan Zamoyski's business activities have been throughly studied by Tarnawski (see Table 7).

Money and Society in Poland and Lithuania in the 16th and 17th Centuries

TABLE 9

SUMMARY OF JOHN ZAMOYSKI's EXPENSES
FROM 19th JULY 1647 THROUGH 1st JULY 1648

	per cent
The Lord's voyages and his messengers etc.	10.5
Servants' salaries	11.4
Alms, gifts, payments in kind	11.0
His Lordship's horses, also those to others as gifts	3.6
Mansions, houses in Cracow and Lublin	1.1
Craftsmen	1.3
Payment of debts, purchases of landed estates, redemption of securities	26.9
"The Law" (various legal expenses)	4.5
Trifles (iron, wax, paper, fuel etc.)	1.3
One quarter of the income from leases of royal estates (in fact, much less)	1.3
The Academy (a college in Zamość)	1.4
Beer	0.3
Loan from a Zamość burgher (money taken by His Lordship when starting on a journey)	20.6
Payments to clergymen and to ecclesiastical institutions	4.8

Total expense	376,803 *zl.*	100.0
Total income	241,620	64.2

(Archiwum Główne Akt Dawnych, Archiwum Zamoyskich 2519, p. 119. Some items are obviously missing, e.g., military expenditure. The Table gives an idea of the treasurer's method way of grouping expense items).

TABLE 10

SUMMARY OF JOHN ZAMOYSKI's EXPENSES
1st MAY 1649 THROUGH 1st JANUARY 1653

	per cent
His Lordship's travelling expenses abroad	25.1
His Lordship's travelling expenses, mostly through Poland (on his way back)	2.6
Salaries	12.1
Military expenditure	15.1
To merchants for textiles, spices and furs	10.4
Legal expenses	6.9
Interest paid	4.7
Hungarian wines	4.0
Debts paid	3.5
Rent on leases of royal estates	2.8
Gifts	2.6
Monthly pay to household troops, artillerymen, foresters and others	2.3
Other items	7.9
Total expenditure	875,574 *zl.*	100.0

(Archiwum Główne Akt Dawnych, Archiwum Zamoyskich 2159, p. 123. Here, in contrast to Table 9, the entries have been regrouped and selected and minor items omitted. There are mistakes in the adding up of the expense total that do not alter the result. From midsummer day 1649 to the end of the 1650 the "yearly income" from lease rents was only 55,120 *zl.*; 77,261 were withheld. Expenses during that time were 219,628 *zl.* The treasurer believed that the royal estates might give his lord less than 162,000; income of about 140,000 is lost because of the Cossack uprising. Total debts were more than 775,000; *Ibidem*, p. 140-146).

Prince Bogusław Radziwiłł's spending abroad may be repeated about Chancellor Zamoyski's grandson and heir, Jan. From 1 May 1649 to 30th December 1652 his expenses for foreign travel amounted to 27.7% of his income and about 80,000 ducats, about twice as much as he was willing to spend on war in that critical period of the Cossack uprising and Tartar raids.

There were usually several important items of expenses: the lord's prestige expenses, his usually generous gifts to noblemen, and last but not least his private army that was always present on important occasions. After the first « free election » of the king in 1573, the army was all too often used either to bring pressure to bear or else to balance the other lords' displays of power. A foreign professor at the Academy of Zamość, Robert Bruce expressed his amazement in his report sent to Queen Elizabeth of England in 1598: « The Senators beare theire owne charges, and therefore are at wonderfull expense in their greate traynes which followe them ... », and his outrage: « It is a matter of greate daunger in theire Dietts, Conventes and iudgements, that according to the auncient custome of Northerne nations whose reason is in theire fyste, they comme into the Senate armed, where considering the deadly feude of greate famelyes ... it is a wonder they comme not to strokes to the manifest ruine of the state ... ». He mentioned a rival of Chancellor Zamoyski, the Palatine of Kiew, « whoe came to the Diet with 7000 horse ». « The Chancellor must keep many men by his side, bestow upon them, honour them, what means very much expense. He has this Diet on his own shoulders ... If he came here not so *potenter*, everything would look poorly », stated his friend, the Crown Marshal, to the King in 1585.[28]

This might lead to the extreme conclusion that large landowners played a crucial and decisive role in the system of money circulation throughout the country. They pumped large quantities of money from abroad (through their leaseholders), and either spent it abroad,

---

[28] *Relation of the State of Polonia and the United Provinces of That Crown Anno 1598*, ed. C. H. Talbot, in the series: « Elementa ad Fontium Editiones », vol. XIII, Romae 1965, p. 95; A. TARNAWSKI, *op. cit.*

mostly on luxury goods, or else introduced precious metals into circulation inside the country.

A detailed register of cash expenditure kept by the Duke of Ostróg's treasurer in 1635-1637, contained four and five figure entries under income, while the expenses were much smaller. Between 6 May an 26 June 1636, 20,000 *zl.* (i.e. 3,630 ducats) were spent, in 419 instalments of an average 48 *zl.* Between 1 February and 28 March of the following year 40,525 *zl.* (also a single item of income) were spent on 622 items that is an average 65 *zl.* In fact the items were usually even smaller and consequently more numerous. Average figures were artificially enlarged by putting together the « weekly maintenance » of the court, which was usually 650 to 750, but often up to a thousand *zl.* Also soldiers' pay was noted as a single entry (about 500 *zl.* per month).[29]

Philanthropy in Poland and Lithuania was not regulated by state laws, but was organized mainly on mediaeval lines by town corporations; only Gdańsk adopted, on a limited scale, such Dutch social inventions as workhouses. In a predominantly Catholic country the rich constantly gave alms, usually small coins. It is very difficult to trace this pious expenditure in the sources (see, however, *opera pia*, Table 7).[30] During the centuries in question a particular kind of almsgiving was developing: a wandering friar, called the *kwestarz*, or the charity collector, visited with a cart all the mansions and country residences in the neighhbourhood of the monastery. This was to become one the most characteristic features of the "old life", which was later recalled by many a nostalgic diarist and writer. The collector's success and reputation depended on his social talents; he was often a hard drinker (this may have been his occupational disease) and a conversationalist who could also offer sound advice. His success was measured by the number of sacks of grain, flitches of pork or lard, and heads of calves or sheep with which he returned to the monastery, and much less often did he collect any money.

---

29 Archiwum Państwowe Miasta Krakowa i Województwa Krakowskiego, Archiwum Sanguszków, 104, p. 55 ff., 114 ff.

30 In the late 18th century Prince Adam Jerzy Czartoryski, neither an overpious nor generous person, had an alms-purse always at hand. K. KOŹMIAN, *Pamiętniki* (Memoirs), Warszawa 1972.

Still more generous charity resulted in the foundation of churches, and monasteries, and the building of chapels. These pious endowments were subject to the general rules of economic behaviour. The nobleman was likely to bestow on an ecclesiastical institution his land, and timber, and other building materials as well as the labour of his serfs, but not money. However, money was usually needed to pay the artists', architects', sculptors', or painters' fees. Also if a nobleman wanted to buy a Holy Mass, he was expected to pay cash.[31]

7. The Credit and Short-Term Fluctuations of the Money Supply

The part played by credit in the expenses of noble households also deserves consideration. The credit market is too big a problem, and still too little studied, to be treated here. I shall therefore mention only some striking features of the credit market so far as it affected agriculture, landownership, and the social aspects of money circulation.

The student of rural in pre-industrial Poland is often tempted to believe that credit was more widespread than the circulation of ready money. His observations would strongly support the statements of R. H. Tawney in his introduction to Thomas Wilson's *Discourse upon Usury*.[31a] In extreme cases — and these were by no means rare — credit (or usury) offered peasants the only, if dearly bought, chance of survival. This happened in particular when seed was scarce, when food was exhausted before the harvest or in times of plague. But credit was hardly ever cheap and the peasantry was at the mercy of usurers of various kinds. Probably the least merciless was the lord himself who, after all, was interested in keeping peasant households running. More dangerous were the lord's stewards, who often practised usury, the village inn-keeper or the miller, who was usually the village potentate, if he was

---

[31] Julian U. Niemcewicz, recalling in the early 19th century his childhood in western Lithuania, tells of his overpious father who distributed little purses of money right and left to pay for Masses.

[31a] R. H. Tawney (ed.), Thomas Wilson, *A Discourse Upon Usury*, London 1925.

not too dependent on the landowner. At the turn of the 16th century, estate administrators seem to have been alarmed at the indebtedness of the tenantry. The surveyors of the estates of the See of Włocławek inquired into their tenants' debts. Both the evidence they collected, and that concerning other estates, has shown that many tenants were deep in debt and — what is even more important — that some tenants were also making substantial profits as village usurers. Credit relationships greatly contributed to social change in the countryside and enabled shrewd village Shylocks to accumulate a fortune.[32] Perhaps on the lowest level no money was involved; what a tenant needed was not cash but rather seed, a tool, or an ox. Even clothes were often made at home or exchanged for other goods within the village; although little or no evidence remains of such agreements on a national scale, there was from the turn of the 16th century a marked decline in the market for cheap clothes, which were previously sold mostly to the peasantry and poor townsmen. Tenants lived on the margin of a money economy: state taxes were not as heavy as the dues demanded by the lord, and the lords were much less interested in their tenants' meagre ready money than in their labour and rent in kind. Only the next stage of accumulation involved money, and this is true both for the usurer and for the lord.

Where the usurer was a pedlar (often a Scotsman) or a merchant, his role in money circulation does not need any explanation; if he was another tenant or a steward, his wealth led, or forced, him to enter deeper into the money economy. This was a requirement of consumption, production and investment as well.

It is deplorable that so little is known about short-term fluctuations in the manorial economy in Poland before the middle of the 18th century outside the largest estates. I suspect that on some estates at least, the landowners pressed their tenants harder in the leaner years, even if they came to the rescue of those in

---

32 A. Mączak, *Folwark pańszczyźniany a wieś w Prusach Królewskich w XVI/XVII wieku* (La ferme domaniale et le village en Prusse Occidentale aux XVIᵉ-XVIIᵉ siècles), « Przegląd Historyczny », vol. XLVII, 1956, p. 373 ff.; Idem, *Kredyt w gospodarce chłopskiej na Żuławach Malborskich w początku XVII wieku* (Credit and Peasant Husbandry in Malbork Fens in the Early 17th Century), *ibidem*, vol. LI, 1960, p. 285 ff.

TABLE 11

GRAIN FROM THE DEMESNE LAND AND GRAIN FROM RENTS
IN THE ESTATE OF TAPIAU, 1550-1695

(sample years only)

		Index of Demesne Crops (average year = 100)	Index of Grain from Rents (average year = 100)	Grain from Rents in relation to Demesne Crops
I. 1550-1621	5 Good Harvest Years	134	115	136
	5 Mean Harvest Years	98	99	186
	5 Poor Harvest Years	68	86	253
II. 1626-1695	4 Good Harvest Years	135	106	209
	4 Mean Harvest Years	106	108	271
	4 Poor Harvest Years	60	86	382

(Approximate figures from H.H. WÄCHTER, *Ostpreussische Domänenvorwerke im 16. und 17. Jahrhundert,* Würzburg 1958, p. XII f. Period I was characterized by peace and predominance of demesne economy [ratio of demesne crops to grain rents = 4478 : 8950 *Scheffel* of grain]; Period II was that of wars and other plagues, until 1660, and of diminishing demesne economy [analogous ratio was on average 2625 : 10501]).

real distress. Table 11 shows the results of a case study concerning the estate of Tapiau in Ducal, in Eastern, Prussia. There is much better evidence for this region and rural conditions were about the same as in Poland. I have available, however, only sample data for every fifth year from 1550 to 1695. It emerges from the table that in mean years — when grain prices were high — the stewards extracted relatively more grain from tenants. This brought great hardship to the serfs and to the lords and at the same time the opportunity to make profit; profit in money this time. The same was true for the other end of the social hierarchy: on the national scale the proportion of great landowners engaged in the Vistula trade was much larger in lean than in fat years.[33]

Credit was also used by the magnates on a very large scale as a tool of their domination over the lesser nobility. The nobles had great need of credit institutions in which to place their money and from which to borrow easily and on reasonable terms. Neither the merchants in towns nor the Church could fulfil this role, particularly in more remote regions. In the 17th century Jews were deeply involved in the money business, but as borrowers. The great landlord was therefore the best banker: his fortune was

---

[33] A. MĄCZAK, *Export of Grain and the Problem of Distribution of National Income in the Years 1550-1650,* « Acta Poloniae Historica », vol. XVIII, 1968, p. 80 f.

a safe pledge and he could not misuse his power because any clear betrayal of the creditors' confidence might bring disaster to his influence as a politician. At the same time, as we have seen, he needed cash and was willing to give a fair interest rate, and often combined his business with other social and political interests. A creditor — or rather customer — was likely to win favours from his powerful neighbour.

Table 12 represents the scale and social distribution of lending and borrowing among the nobility during the annual fairs in Lwów, when most of the business for a large area of Ruthenia was carried on. The Church, Jews and Christian townspeople played a secondary role. The largest transactions were between magnates themselves; when they entered into business with nobles of medium fortune, ten times more often than not they were borrowers. And they did not bother about petty credit transactions with the lesser nobles, although they lent some money to them.

Once more the great landowner appears as the driving force behind money circulation. However, I have previously stressed that he dispersed the large sums he earned from his crops. This time it is the other way around: both small and large sums placed with the great landlord accumulated and were invested often, if not always, on a large scale.

One of the principal investments was the purchase of estates. The system worked as follows: the creditors of the preceding

TABLE 12

CREDIT BUSINESS AMONG THE NOBILITY AT LWÓW FAIRS, 1676-1686
(in 1000's *zl.*)

	Creditors		
	Magnates	Middle Nobility	Lesser Nobility
Debtors			
The Magnates (called *Illustrissimi D-ni*)	6,359	6,070	2
The Middle Nobility (*Generosi*)	616	6,333	21
The Lesser Nobility (*Nobiles*)	200	8	34

(M. WĄSOWICZ, *Kontrakty lwowskie w latach 1676-1686* [Les contrats de Lwów de 1676 à 1686], Lwów 1935. 1000 *zl.* at that time equalled about 83 ducats).

TABLE 13

TRANSACTIONS OF PROPERTY
AMONG THE NOBLES AT LWÓW FAIRS, 1676-1686
(in 1000's *zl.*)

	Sellers		
	Magnates	Middle Nobility	Lesser Nobility
Purchasers			
Magnates	97 (2)	79	— (1)
Middle Nobility	38 (2)	161 (36)	4 (29)
Lesser Nobility	—	1 (6)	3 (70)

(M. WASOWICZ, *op. cit.*). Smaller estate in parentheses.

table become sellers of property, and debtors became purchasers. The net balance (Table 13) is favourable for the greater nobles and unfavourable for the middle nobility: the magnates purchased twice as many estates as they sold. This in balance amounts to 9.3% of the whole turnover of the larger estates during the Lwów fairs. So one may conclude that the further extension of the large estates, which was one of the most important features of the period in Poland and Lithuania, was at least partly financed by the principal losers, the middle nobility. This conclusion, however, varies from region to region. It cannot be at present proved for some regions and was most probably a particular characteristic of only the 16th and 17th centuries.

8. THE REGIONAL DISPERSION OF MONEY

Until now I have discussed the Polish money economy in general, omitting any regional differences. These differences, however, were most probably an important factor in the money market. I shall leave aside the network of great international fairs, since for my argument the relative degree of saturation of small money in specific regions is of greater importance. The student of Polish economic history can only dream of such ample evidence as that discussed by J. G. da Silva in his chapter on the spread of precious metals from Seville,[34] and must try to approach the subject from another angle. The sources are not sufficient to allow us to construct reliable indices of living costs. Furthermore, such an index would not make any sense when money was in many respects a secondary factor. There is, however, a windfall set of figures available concerning the salaries of milkmaids, oxherds and others working on the royal and ecclesiastical estates. The largest series of such data is for 1564-1565 for royal estates all over Poland, including its South-Eastern regions as far as concerned manorial farms. It can be checked for some years by records of ecclesiastical estates and also by less exhaustive and valuable evidence of later surveys.[35]

The sources leave no doubt that pay in cash was only a part of a salary. The *familia* were fed at the farm, some were provided with modest accomodation, and usually some clothing, linen or other payment in kind was added, too. Payment in kind usually varied enormously according to the status of the employee or worker. In contrast to compensation by money and clothing, we can only calculate very roughly the exact value of foodstuffs given to servants and workers. One should remember, however, that not every food item was a market commodity; in other words, there was not necessarily a choice of consuming or selling. Neither can one overestimate the importance of waste, theft and unequal distribution of small daily privileges in the demesne farm community. By definition these factors cannot be included in our calculations but one must aware of their existence and of the role they played in everyday country life. When spread on a map the network of figures makes a regular pattern: the highest salaries are mentioned in Royal Prussia, on the Lower Vistula, near Gdańsk. Rather schematic, uniform figures from the survey of Ruthenia (the South-East) are about two thirds of the maximum level of

---

[34] J. G. DA SILVA, *En Espagne: développement économique, subsistance, déclin,* Paris-La Haye 1965, p. 59 ff.

[35] Here I have summarized the first part of my paper *Preise, Löhne und Lebenshaltungskosten im Europa des 16. Jahrhunderts. Ein Beitrag zur Quellenkritik,* Wirtschaftliche und soziale Strukturen im saekularen Wandel. Festschrift für Wilhelm Abel zum 70. Geburtstag, Bd. II, Hannover 1974, pp. 322-326. See also charts p. 340 f.

the Prussian data. The single high figure appears in Spisz, a district beyond the Tatra Mountains, which was connected with the Upper Hungarian (i.e., Slovakian) mining region. There are also pockets of higher wages around bigger towns, and generally higher figures are to be found by the Silesian border. If one takes the minimum figure (Sieradz) as a basis at 100, the highest, that of Gniew in Royal Prussia, reaches 540. In more general terms, one finds 100 (index figure) for Masovia, 100-160 for Greater Poland, 120-180 for Little Poland, 200 for Ruthenia, and finally 200-400 for Royal Prussia. Even here the differences are impressive.

I interpret these figures on the assumption that compensation in money and some clothing was instrumental in attracting labour. In conditions of serfdom the margin of mobility was not so narrow as many believe. There was a seasonal migration of rural labourers from Masovia towards Prussia and Silesia, which together with the fact that the names of servants regularly changed, shows that there was also a certain mobility and a limited freedom of choice for labourers within the village.

What in fact determined the level of compensation? The case of Ruthenia was described by Jan Rutkowski as follows: the expansion of the borderland economy and a relative shortage of settlers in Podolia and Wolhynia raised the price of labour.[36] In Prussia, on the other hand, it was not only the towns which attracted labour. On the Vistula marshes many peasant farms could not be run without several hired servants and numerous seasonal workers. It was in general a period of rapid development for Royal Prussia when the deep wounds of the wars between Poland and the Teutonic Order were healing, the boom in the export of grain and the spectacular growth of the Gdańsk agglomeration were beginning. The high compensation of rural workers in Prussia bears witness to its prosperity.

Let us turn to the area bridging Prussia and Ruthenia. The overpopulation of poor Masovia was caused not so much by high

---

[36] J. RUTKOWSKI, *Pańszczyzna i praca najemna w organizacji folwarków królewskich w Prusach za Zygmunta Augusta* (Corvée and Hired Labour in Royal Manors in Prussia in the Times of King Sigismond August), reprinted in *Studia z dziejów wsi polskiej XVI-XVIII w.*, ed. by W. Kula, Warszawa 1956, p. 123 f.

population density as by a peculiar property structure. Numerous petty noblemen each ruled over only a few serfs; farms were small, and soil was sand. Since the factors of "land" and "population" are constant, small agricultural units create less demand for labour: the Masovian population therefore spread, colonized "The Desert" (*Wildniss*) on the southern confines of Ducal Prussia, populated large parts of other provinces and systematically exported seasonal labour. Had the compensation been high, our verdict would have been prosperity. Such was the case of Ruthenia, but the low Masovian wages signify misery.

If money compensation was an attraction, its level had to be fixed so that the lord could find it still favourable and the milkmaid (oxherd etc.) earn a socially acceptable wage. I have noted some demographic and social factors that influenced wages, but one must remember that their real value was determined by the general level of prices. In order to keep servants from running away and to attract them in the following year, farm managers supplied them with small sums of money, in particular before fairs. These figures then form very complex indices of the economic situation: the higher an index the better developed the region and the larger the role of a money economy.

9. THE SOCIAL DISTRIBUTION OF MONEY AND CHANGES OVER TIME

These relationships and differences were a constant factor in the economy. In 1615-1616 milkmaids were paid 120 *grosz* per year on a Royal Prussian estate, whereas their counterparts throughout Masovia received only 40 to 60 *gr.* (most often 48 *gr.*). A dramatic crisis between 1620 and 1622 did not undermine this; the relative scales for salaries in Prussia remained high. However, there may have been important changes among several social groups. In Prussia, for example, the higher paid members of the *familia* seemed to fare relatively, or even absolutely, better after the debasement reforms (Table 14).

TABLE 14

WAGES AND PRICE INDICES FOR SELECTED ROYAL PRUSSIAN ESTATES
1565, 1615 & 1624

	Absolute Figure 1563, in *grosz* *	1565	1615	1625	Estate **
Deputy Steward (*podstarości*)	800	100	225	375	G
	720	100	300	417	S
Estate Clerk	600	100	200	250	G,S
Manor Manager & His·Wife	240+140	100	200	211	S
Smith (working in the centre of the estate)	300	100	120	200	S
Cowherd	180	100	.	111	G
Swineherd	100	100	.	120	G
Milkmaid	100	100	.	140	G
Price of Rye		100	127	227	
Price of Shoes		100	302	373	
Grosz in One Rixdollar	33	100	128	227	

(Wages: *Lustracja województwa pomorskiego 1565* [Survey of Pomeranian Woiwodship 1565], ed. by S. Hoszowski, Gdańsk 1961; *Lustracja województw malborskiego i chełmińskiego 1565* [Survey of Woiwodships of Malbork and Chełmno 1565], ed. by S. Hoszowski, Gdańsk 1961.

Prices: J. PELC, *Ceny w Gdańsku w XVI i XVII w.* [Les prix à Gdańsk aux XVIe et XVIIe siècles], Lwów 1937).

* Yearly money wage.

** G for royal estate of Grudziadz; S for Sztum.

General inferences should not be drawn from these figures. The pay of town officers often took the form of a fixed rent and proved to be a handicap and the overall result was inverse to the one we have indicated for the Prussian estates. On the other hand, where day labour was paid for, and where it coincided with a growing demand for labour, the outcome might have been quite favourable to workers and journeymen. But in the countryside where full pay also included food, fuel and shelter, the monetary crisis meant something else; it did not bring danger of starvation but changed the demand for small consumer goods. One may also suspect that the social hierarchy of such limited groups as the employees of estates and manors must have been changing. Otherwise how can we explain the fact that low-income (and socially wretched) groups lost so much in a relatively short time?

10. THE TERRITORIAL LIMITS OF A MONEY CIRCULATION MODEL

The social relationships presentend above must not necessarily be limited to Poland and Lithuania. The crucial feature of my argument is the role played by the great landowners, so one must look at all those countries where great landownership not only predominated but was also more or less directly involved in export and import trades. Although the merchants of the sea ports tried and often succeeded in maintaining the monopoly of contacts with foreign customers, I suspect that this had many other consequences, such as the dependence of the lesser nobles on the great ones, patron-client relationships etc. But here the similarities decrease, for these secondary features were conditioned by the size of the country (for only in a big country with distant ports were lesser nobles so dependent on the magnates for the sale of their produce) and by the state, the weakness of which was a reason for the magnates' political and social predominance. And where else did there exist so great a country with so feeble a government? Poland in fact was the only country that could be described by Montesquieu in a paragraph of his *Esprit des Lois*:

« It [i.e., Poland] has scarcely any of those things which we call the movable effects of the universe, except corn ... Some of the lords possess entire provinces; they oppress the husbandmen, in order to have greater quantities of corn, which they send to strangers to procure the superfluous demands of luxury. If Poland had no foreign trade, its inhabitants would be happier. The grandees, who would have only their corn, would give it to their peasants for subsistence; as their too extensive estates would become burdensome, they would divide them amongst their peasants; every one would find skins or wool in their herds or flocks, so that they would no longer be at an immense expense in providing clothes; the great, who are ever fond of luxury, not being able to find it but in their own country, would encourage the labour of the poor. The nation, I affirm, would then become more flourishing, at least if it did not became barbarous; and this the laws might easily prevent ».[37]

It seems, then, that the role played by money best explains the economic system in question, and offers insight into social structures as well. There are few economic problems that are not social problems as well. Montesquieu presented a counterfactual hypothesis that we may perhaps be able partly to test. Several years after 1626 the Swedish invasion had cut off grain exporters from their traditional markets, and after 1772 heavy Prussian tolls discouraged the trade. The reorientation of the rural economy, the revival of towns and the development of industry from the mid-eighteenth century are phenomena that require a long-term study that would include their 16th and 17th century ancestry.

---

[37] CH. L. DE MONTESQUIEU, *The Spirit of the Laws*, translated by Th. Nugent, New York-London 1966, vol. I, p. 339.

Confessions, Freedoms, and the Unity of Poland-Lithuania

One merit of the study of early modern Polish statehood is that it can suggest questions rarely asked elsewhere. This is fortunate, but has been by no means fully exploited as yet. The system of authority and power in the Commonwealth (*Rzeczpospolita*[1]) consisted of similar building blocks, and was created upon similar principles, to those known everywhere in Latin Europe. During the fifteenth century the estates were shaped; the relationship between them and the king was sealed by articles of government (*Herrschaftsverträge*): the estates enjoyed their representative institutions which at the top level (the Sejm) included the king himself as the first among the 'estates in parliament' (Polish: *stany sejmujące*).[2] The fundamental freedoms forged in the crucial period until 1572 included an early habeas corpus (in Poland: *neminem captivabimus nisi iure victum*, in several charters before and in 1534); a clearly formulated *Quod omnes tangit* (here: *nihil novi…*); and finally the principle *De non praestanda oboedientia* — in its early version in 1501 and as a constant norm (included in the king's oath) in 1573.[3]

Gottfried Schramm sees in fifteenth-century Poland, Bohemia and Hungary a peculiar east-central European type of the early modern State.[4] Its development was interrupted by the Habsburgs in the last two countries, and it survived only in Poland. The Polish constitution was thus not so much a unique phenomenon, but rather the relic of a perished species once characteristic of the area. While I endorse this thesis I wish to stress some special conditions which were shaping the Commonwealth: the nature of the ties that bound it together. In relation to most states this question is hardly asked, their coherence being taken for granted. However, the political and administrative structure of Poland was rather peculiar, and factors of unity and dangers to it deserve equally serious discussion.

It is a thesis of this paper that the *Rzeczpospolita* became so peculiar among *Ständestaaten*[5] because of a particular coincidence of socio-political phenomena. The principal among these contributing factors, or phenomena, may be enumerated as follows: firstly the size of the country; secondly its loose network of communications and the feeble urban development of its distant periphery; thirdly the passive political attitudes of the towns, together with the domination of the nobility in the society of orders; and finally the particular social and property structure of the noble estate. Let me discuss first some topographical and geopolitical realities of the country.[6]

The Commonwealth may be regarded as the biggest *Ständestaat* ever. While built up piece by piece from numerous Polish principalities and finally shaped by a grand merger with the Grand Duchy of Lithuania as the fruit of several unions from 1386 to 1569, it already by the late sixteenth century possessed quite a coherent structure. The *Rzeczpospolita* extended over 990 000 square kilometres (1634) of areas as different as the extensive Ukrainian steppes on both banks of the Dnieper, and the intensive, advanced husbandry characteristic of the Vistula fenlands.[7] There were no convenient transport routes connecting distant parts of the country: the Vistula became during the sixteenth century a very busy highway, but — like both principal Lithuanian rivers, the Niemen and the Dvina — it primarily linked grain- and timber/ash-exporting areas with great foreign trade centres located on the country's borders. The rivers did not bind the country together: rather they bound its regions to foreign markets.

There was no single urban centre of the country, neither in Heinrich von Thünen's economic, nor in a political sense. Riga, Königsberg, Gdańsk (Danzig), Elbląg (Elbing) and Breslau (Wrocław), all of the important foci, either had a quasi-independent status or were situated outside the country. Cracow, Warsaw and Vilna were chiefly royal residences blossoming when the court was there. National importance was also shared by Toruń (Thorn) on the Vistula, as well as by Poznań (Posen), Gniezno and Lublin (all three because of their great fairs); yet in the eastern part of the Commonwealth there was no urban centre of any real economic importance, even if between 1500 and 1650 the urban network grew much denser: from little over seventy to about 920 boroughs.[8] However, as an anonymous pamphlet (1790) put it, 'we have few towns in Lithuania which may be called "towns"'.[9]

In general, regional economies were complementary only to a rather insignificant degree: foreign trade of various sorts dominated over internal. It would be difficult to indicate significant *economic* ties to explain the cohesion of the Commonwealth. This can be said about the 'third estate' as well. I would risk a thesis that for all practical purposes it hardly existed. Unlike in the fourteenth and earlier fifteenth centuries, from the mid-fifteenth century the burgher elites did not try any longer to form a common consensus, to influence national politics, or to struggle for common rights. Their passive attitude towards the early Sejms — whatever were its reasons — proved fatal to the freedom of the burghers and of their towns.[10] Common undertakings and agreements in the sixteenth or seventeenth centuries remained marginal and strictly confined to economic issues. What could be done in favourable conditions one might see in Royal Prussia, where three great and numerous smaller royal towns were represented respectively in the two chambers of the Royal Prussian estates assembly (*Ständetag*). And yet, the country and its body politic were impressively coherent. How then was this body politic formed?

Until summer 1569 Lithuania was a hereditary grand duchy of the Jagiellonian dynasty and several times in the fifteenth century it almost severed itself from Poland. It must be stressed, however, that the grand dukes were not despotic and that as kings of Poland they were not able to use Lithuania as a power base of strong rule in the rest of the country (the Crown), that tactic so often used by European rulers.[11] Lithuania was not a rich country: she had to be supported by Poland in conflicts with her neighbours, and did not furnish a rich treasure-chest to draw from for an active royal internal policy in Poland. Moreover, what is probably still more important, there was developing there a strong and influential stratum of great nobles, less and less dependent on the grand duke's grace. The last Jagiellon, Sigismund Augustus (ruled 1548–72), used to take shelter in Vilna when he preferred to be absent from the Polish Sejm's militant Chamber of Deputies.[12] But when he wished to conclude the real union between the two countries, he had to break resistance to it from boyars and *knyaz'ya* by incorporating important western and southern parts of Lithuania (parts of Podlachia, Podolia and the whole Ukraine) in the Crown of Poland.[13]

One ruler over several countries with their respective estates systems was a relationship typical of the Renaissance. All the most successful ruling families — the Habsburgs, Hohenzollerns or Valois, as well as the kings of Denmark — skilfully used their noble and commoner subjects who originated from one principality as their officials in the other ones. In the vicinity of Poland, the Hohenzollerns proved veritable masters in the struggle for power with the estates; their principal tool was the dependent and dependable 'fourth estate' of *Räte* and other officials.[14] The profit in having officials independent of the estates, and enthusiastically co-operative in curbing them, was obvious; this is why the estates used to struggle for the *ius indigenatus*. That privilege of naturalisation, so dear to the nobility, was directed against aliens and/or commoners. The practice of *ius indigenatus* in Poland has been little researched. What is known about it principally relates to movement between the Crown and Lithuania, or between the Crown and Royal Prussia.[15] The problem is much more general, however, and touches upon several most important questions. How was unity created from numerous principalities which had still had a separate existence in the early fourteenth century? How did Lithuania conform to the Polish pattern? What was the nature of citizenship of the Commonwealth? And finally, who was the sovereign of the Commonwealth: the king or the estate of the nobility? It is not possible to produce satisfactory answers to all these questions in this chapter; on many points I must confine myself to hypotheses, having chiefly in mind what may be summed up as factors of unity and dangers to it.

Let me turn now to the freedoms of the nobles. It has hardly been sufficiently emphasised by historians that already in the fifteenth century the nobility of various parts of the Polish Crown had a liberal tendency to share their freedoms with the newly-incorporated brethren: for example, the petty nobles of all the Masovian fiefs, as well as the nobility of parts of Prussia recovered from the Teutonic Knights. Different regional systems of common law had a tendency to assimilate to each other, and what was found good for Great Poland was also introduced to Little Poland, and so forth. According to the Act of Union sealed in Lublin, freedoms of the Polish noble estate, being at the heart of the whole Polish constitution, were to be shared from 1569 by the Lithuanian brethren as well. In the sixteenth and seventeenth centuries the tendency would be somewhat reversed by the popularity and spread in the Crown of the Lithuanian law, as well of the *Ius terrestre nobilitatis Prussiae correctum* of 1598.[16] It is of importance for my argument that this diffusion of legal and customary norms occurred in an informal way and reflected the common will of the nobility, and not the unifying intention of the monarch: county dietines (*sejmiky*) simply took these norms as a basis of their legislation, and local courts of justice availed themselves of them in jurisdiction.

And yet, for all practical purposes local government — or rather the nobles' self-government — in the counties worked rather differently in the core parts of the Crown on the one hand and in Lithuania or the south-eastern borderlands on the other. The king was left no sufficient means and prerogatives to maintain a working and dependable corps of officers. Large areas of Lithuania and Ruthenia were served by poor technical and social communication networks which made the periphery administratively almost independent. This was an unusual political victory of the periphery over the centre whose mechanism ought now to be explained: it was crucial for that precious balance and unity which at first created what is now often called 'nobles' democracy' (and what they preferred to call '*monarchia mixta*')[17] and which later constituted a power system based principally on patronage by the magnates. It was characteristic of the Polish constitution from the sixteenth to the eighteenth century that some basic traditions and/or precedents had been established long before they began yielding unexpectedly portentous results. An important case was the article of the Statute of Warta (1423) later headed *de sculteto inutili aut rebelli*: in the next century it would become the principal legal basis for the expropriation of tenants and a massive build-up of demesne farms.[18] In a similar way, some early practical solutions were soon becoming deeply rooted traditions. Two of them seem particularly important: the regional self-government of the nobility and the lifetime tenure of officials and dignitaries. At the constitutional level the eight decades after the extinction of the Jagiellons in 1572 brought about a fundamental change in the structure of power in the *Rzeczpospolita*, yet one may risk the thesis that the political system had been pregnant with it already from the mid-fifteenth century. It only needed the keystone of the whole structure — namely the king — to be weakened, and the decentralisation process could start without delay. To express it briefly and in more general terms: to govern efficiently the king had to be sure of his patronage, both as a system of appointing dependable officers and dignitaries, and as the power to reward with perfect freedom their loyalty or to punish them for disobedience.

Now, the king of Poland was limited in both these prerogatives. In the first place, in order to appoint local officials, he had to choose from among candidates submitted to him by the dietines — and these were more and more (but not yet fully and not everywhere) dependent upon local bigwigs. In the second place, he was not much less restricted in his appointments of high dignitaries: he simply could not disregard prominent families even if they tended to oppose his policy — characteristic is the case of the Calvinist Radziwiłłs. In the third place, the king's means of demonstrating his displeasure were limited — Chancellor and Grand Hetman of the Crown (the principal army commander), Jan Zamoyski remained comfortable in both these offices even after he had lost His Majesty's favour.[19] The absolutist tendencies of Sigismund III (1587–1632) were very closely studied by the late Professor Władysław Czapliński. The King indeed did his best: he nominated only senators loyal to him as his deputies (*senatores residentes*). By that means he avoided being effectively controlled by that body.[20] And yet there were but few of his nominees who long remained loyal to their king after they had become, if not independent of his grace, at least little sensitive to his disfavour.

In the Vasa period (1587–1668) the royal household, the court, was becoming more and more the nucleus of a faction than the centre of power and authority. The progress of that tendency is visible when one compares two seventeenth-century civil wars: the Sandomierz or Zebrzydowski *rokosz* (1606–9) and the rebellion of Jerzy Lubomirski (1665–66). An independent Chamber of Deputies — independent from the magnates filling the front chairs in the Senate — could be the prerequisite of a strong monarchy: Sigismund Augustus had finally learned that lesson.[21] And yet, precisely his policy had proved how difficult it was to rule against, or even just without, strong support from the great nobles. Without any major constitutional change, the centre of political gravity shifted from the Sejm to the county *sejmiki* where the gentry was much more dependent on local potentates of senatorial rank, and could be manipulated much more easily. Its growing political dependence followed a relative loss of economic position of the squirearchy in relation to the great landowners.[22] This signified a clear tendency towards the decentralisation of politics: the state was slowly but consistently becoming a federation of great country houses with their inevitable alliances and conflicts (but not bloody feuds!). However, no partner in that game was seriously intending to slice off for himself an independent territory.[23] Noble privilege seemed to have created a firm ground for the political and constitutional unity of the Commonwealth. Let us then now proceed to consider whether that unity was endangered by confessional diversity.

Neither late medieval nor early modern Poland was a country of confessional uniformity; with the progress of time it became unique in its diversity. Catholics dominated in the west of the country, while Lithuania and the Ruthenian parts of the Crown remained Orthodox. Originally (1386) only Catholic boyars had been granted full freedoms in Lithuania, but their counterparts in Poland were never discriminated against because of their adherence to the Eastern Church. The Reformation was to change that relatively simple picture. A large part of the Catholic gentry chose the Reformed creed. According to tentative estimates by Wacław Urban, around 1572 Calvinists and Catholics each accounted for about 40 per cent of participants of the Cracow county dietine, while Polish Brethren (Arians) made up the other 20 per cent.[24] In some parts Lutheranism became popular. Particularly in the early decades of the Reformation, some other branches of Protestantism were also influential, like the Czech and the Polish Brethren. Early successes of Catholicism in Lithuania paved the way for Protestantism there as well. A convulsion comparable to that of the Reformation was the Union of Brest (1596) which created the Greek Catholic (or Uniate) Church. Quite unexpectedly, its impact became even greater than that of the Protestant Reformation; I will return to it.

Some other religious groups were also well represented and/or for some reason important: the Jews, the Armenians, the Muslims, and from the mid-sixteenth century also the Mennonites. Each of them constituted what may be called a particular estate based upon its religious freedoms and economic peculiarity.[25] The Jews were subjected to the royal jurisdiction and paid a lump-sum general tax; they enjoyed broad self-government in towns, and from the last quarter of the sixteenth century until 1764 had their central assembly, the *Vaad* or Sejm of the Four Provinces. However, it should be noted that more and more Jews lived in small towns and in the countryside, some of them, from 1539, also under the private jurisdiction of noble landowners, and that Christian burghers of numerous royal (but not private) towns were granted privileges *de non tolerandis Iudaeis.*[26] Armenians in Poland tended to be merchants specialised in the oriental trade and established in principal centres of that commerce (Cracow, Lublin, Lwów, Zamość, and so forth); in 1519 they were granted a special status and from that time ruled themselves according to a twelfth-century Armenian legal code.[27] Mennonites spread slowly from the north to the south-east of the Crown, seeking their favourite marshy lands for reclamation and improvement. They were never granted a general privilege, but because of their well-known skills and efficiency were much sought-after and as readily promised confessional independence.

Only Scots could not be associated with any particular confession. The gentry liked them as breakers of the commercial monopolies of established merchants, but their legal status was apt to be ambiguous: some of them formed separate classes of taxpayers defined as *szot* (pronounced 'shot', that is, 'the Scots', but loosely also signifying 'pedlar': with cart, with horse, or with basket only). However, some Scots established themselves as fully legitimate merchants and even entered the ranks of town patriciates (or for that matter became professional officers). While the attitude of other population groups towards them was in many respects similar to that displayed towards the Jews,[28] Scots were never associated with a particular religion. A voluntary contribution paid by many of them for King Charles II's cause suggests in a sense their ambiguous status.

This complex confessional matrix, to make it understandable, should be displayed against a map of the Commonwealth. Did confessional divisions contribute to territorial or political separatisms as well? Or was the *Rzeczpospolita* a cultural mosaic, and did the coexistence of various confessions create its particular coherence? Neither conclusion seems fully justified. Religious or ethnic groups not represented in the nobility may well be left undiscussed: they did not belong to the *corpus politicum* of the Commonwealth; the only important exception is that of German townspeople. So our next question should be: was the Reformation leading towards a division of the Commonwealth?

I am prone to answer that question negatively. While Protestantism remained until, say, the end of the sixteenth century popular with the gentry, it was only in one case associated with local freedoms. But this was the important case of Royal Prussia: let me concentrate upon that country for a while.[29]

The Prussian political elite consisted of two bishops (Chełmno [Kulm] and Warmia [Ermland]), the patriciates of three great cities (Gdańsk, Elbląg, Toruń) and noble dignitaries — all of them sitting or represented in the Council (it was also called the Senate). Deputies of lesser boroughs and of the gentry sat in the lower Chamber. The higher elite was particularly jealous of Prussian liberties even after that country had been in 1569 fully incorporated into the Crown. Only during a short period of strong tension between the dignitaries and the gentry (in the 1560s), which was also a period of enhanced self-awareness of that latter estate, did the gentry seem willing to pay the price of Prussian autonomy in order to free themselves from the yoke of local oligarchs.[30] The upper stratum of that estate was strongly in favour of the status quo, that is to say of autonomy, because incorporation into Poland seemed to threaten them with *executio bonorum regalium*, that is, for all practical purposes, with the confiscation of royal estates run, or even owned, by them under various legal titles. Also the greater cities stood firm for the rights they had got during and/or immediately after the Thirteen Years War (1454–66).[31]

Various values were regularly adduced by the partisans of Prussian autonomy, but the monopoly of the German tongue (*die teutsche Zunge*) in its politics was probably invoked most often. While the Polish language was broadly known both by the nobility and the burghers, including the town elites, its use in the estates' assembly was by many regarded as a dangerous prejudice to local freedoms. Even Latin was banished as a substitute establishing a precedent, possibly even more dangerous because Prussian patriots could hardly allege that they did not understand it! The Reformation brought them a big new issue: the Lutheran creed became regarded as one more characteristic element of the Prussian liberties along with the German language. The equality of the Augsburg and the Catholic confessions was from 1557–58, the date of the royal charters of religious freedom for the three greater cities, an item characteristic of the Prussian constitution, a part of its *ius indigenatus*.[32] Already from 1526 the gentry from the county of Chelmno, mostly Polish-speaking, substantiated their denial of tithes with arguments of obviously Lutheran origin.[33]

The interplay of religion and ethnicity in Royal Prussia may be summed up as follows: for members of the *corpus politicum* who were primarily attached to, and associated with, the German language and culture, there was in the mid-sixteenth century (and even after) no other way than the Protestant one. On the other hand, closer ties with the Crown, either because of family origins or because of the language, seemed to offer a broader choice in confessional matters: cultural background did not determine the confession. During the 1550s and 1560s the Crown (that is, Poland) was not necessarily associated in the minds of Prussians with Catholicism. And yet, during the subsequent high tide of reconversions to the Roman creed, in the last quarter of the sixteenth century and the early seventeenth, the Poles (or Polish-speaking Prussians) seemed more prone to change their confession than did their German-speaking brethren.[34]

Even this particular case of Prussia does not support a thesis that confessional diversity endangered the unity of the Commonwealth. Quite the contrary. The province never worked out a common Lutheran organisation: in such a structure there was no keystone but the monarch. However, Sigismund Augustus, albeit hesitantly, would not in the end accept that solution. Protestants from all over the country, when in danger from Catholic-dominated courts of justice or mighty lay and ecclesiastical lords, could seek their haven in the three great Prussian cities. These also became centres of Protestant education and learning because of their *Gymnasien*. On the other hand, in the first half of the seventeenth century, when Protestantism was already in retreat (and Königsberg did not radiate its religious influence so brightly as before), Lutherans from Royal Prussia were seeking patronage and support from the mighty Calvinist Radziwiłłs of Lithuania. To a certain extent the same is also true of other Protestant centres: the urban ones, as well as the residences of great Calvinist lords.

Whatever cohesion Protestant communities were able to create, its general political and cultural importance petered out *pari passu* with the progress of Catholicism. And there is no doubt that the Roman Church was strengthening its administrative structure. It is commonly accepted by Polish historians (I believe Professor Włodzimierz Dworzaczek was the first to express it) that the Reformation failed in Poland primarily because the Catholic Church was in the nobles' minds so firmly associated with the State. With the Commonwealth, I would add, not with royalty. And the Commonwealth was — themselves!

The cohesion and durability of that peculiar political structure of the *Rzeczpospolita* may be explained by the strength of centripetal, or the absence of centrifugal, forces, or both. The state administration and royal prerogative were clearly not responsible for the unity of the country. Were external, foreign magnets absent from the field of Polish politics? I would risk a hypothesis that the Commonwealth of nobles derived its cohesion and force of resistance against external dangers more from the republican spirit of its citizens than from the efficiency of its institutions. The identity of the noble nation included a fair share of xenophobia. Professor Janusz Tazbir has elaborated that theme thoroughly and explained how religious intolerance of the Counter-Reformation era, which was not given full scope *inside* the noble estate, flourished in the form of a xenophobia against the Muslim, Orthodox or Lutheran neighbours, and did not even spare the Habsburgs.[35]

Until now everything in my argument has seemed to point to the essential unity and a tranquil, even liberal, cohesion of the Commonwealth. That could hardly be the whole truth, so we must now return to the problem which the Commonwealth failed to solve. This was the question of the Ukraine which — in the mid-seventeenth century — was personified by the Cossacks.[36]

The Cossack rebellion of 1648 provided a clear sign that the system had reached an insurmountable obstacle. The insurrection led by Bohdan Chmielnicki (Khmel'nyts'kyi) has been recently subjected to serious research, chiefly by American scholars.[37] This topic, crucial for the national consciousness of the Ukrainians, is still too little studied in the broader context of the *Rzeczpospolita*. It is characteristic that for the first time the hitherto liberal attitude of the Polish state to the nobles and similar social groups in peripheral or newly-acquired territories, reached its limit. Unlike the petty gentry of Royal Prussia and Livonia, the *Panenadel* in Lauenburg and Bütow (incorporated 1637 and ceded to Brandenburg in 1657), even the *ziemianie* in Lithuania subjected to the magnates, the Cossack elite could not acquire recognition of their noble status.[38] Other petty nobilities did not threaten to throw the social system out of balance: they were not warlike and often were more or less formal vassals of great lords, either ecclesiastical, or secular, or royal stewards (*starostowie*). At their best these petty nobles were their patrons' loyal clients.

Not the Cossacks in Zaporozhia. They were regarded as trouble-makers whose element was war or brigandage on that immense 'Wild Plains' sector of Europe's steppe frontier. But regarded by whom? Frank Sysyn is right in arguing that in the seventeenth century the nobility of the four palatinates established themselves as an entity — the four 'Rus' palatinates — who claimed special privileges and charters under the Union of Lublin. A theory of contract was evolved of a free union of 'Sarmatian' Ruthenians to 'Sarmatian' Poles at the Union. In short, a political community with a common heritage was emerging in these territories. The theory of contractual relationship of the élite of the four eastern palatinates was expressed most often over the issue of the rights of the Orthodox Church. This produced a fusion of the defense of Orthodoxy, of Rus' historical rights, and of regional constitutional privileges.[39]

It was quite normal for particular provinces (that is, dietines) to complain that their rights were being disregarded, and to claim certain preferences. But in the south-east, several conflicts entwined themselves in the early seventeenth century in a hopeless, tragic knot. The Union of Brest, unpopular with several groups of Orthodox Christians, created lasting tensions over, and struggles for, church property. Conflicts in the triangle of Orthodox, Uniates and Catholics were gaining momentum.

The Zaporozhian Cossacks were a complex social group organised on military principles. Unlike the Russian Cossacks, the Ukrainian ones were to evolve into the leading stratum of a complex society and polity. From the turn of the sixteenth and seventeenth centuries there emerged from their ranks several outstanding leaders, and at least one charismatic one — Chmielnicki. Polish policy demanded that these unruly warriors be obedient to great nobles who were governors of the region, and that when ordered they defend the Commonwealth against the Tatars. The Commonwealth's reason of state demanded that they did not provoke the Ottoman Empire directly or indirectly (that is, by unnecessarily attacking Tatars in their own den). On the other hand, all Cossacks expected to be inscribed into a register and paid regularly. These reciprocal demands for various reasons could hardly be fulfilled.

Internal Ukrainian problems cannot be entered into here. However, it is clear that the Ukraine raised problems which did not emerge elsewhere in Poland or Lithuania. But there was a community created, which remained heterogeneous in relation to the Polish nobility, and there were social and economic issues aggravated by religious ones. Ethno-cultural (or national) factors deepened the gap between the Sejm's polity and the expectations of the Cossack elite.[40] In the second quarter of the seventeenth century the latter became, as a body, outspoken advocates of the Ukrainian people or nation. They even became the leading force and cadres of what grew into the Cossack Hetmanate, a short-lived statehood, subsequently so important for Ukrainian national awareness in the later nineteenth and twentieth centuries. If Poles could not accept the Cossacks' conditions, and were left to suffer ignominious defeat at their hands on the battlefield in 1648, this was due to several factors. Neither the Chamber of Deputies nor the magnates could recognise the Cossacks as a noble group with special status. The magnates in the south-east were particularly hostile towards the independence of Cossacks: it would imperil (in fact even annihilate) their rule over their own tenants, and introduce a distinct and competitive element within their territorial oligarchy.

Political antagonisms became even fiercer because of a cultural division characteristic of that period. The upper crust of the nobility in the Ukraine and Podolia Polonised itself and converted to Catholicism, while the Uniate Church was losing ground among the populace and some nobles to the profit of Eastern Orthodoxy. In his biography of Palatine Adam Kysil (Kisiel), Professor Sysyn depicts and analyses the then endeavours of a patriot — in the sense of the word then current — to keep the country together and bring both parties to the negotiating table. Only at the eleventh hour, when the third partner, the tsar, had already won, and the Commonwealth was entering on its long ordeal, did the treaty of Hadiach seem to offer a last chance. It

> provided for the restructuring of the Commonwealth into a triune state, including a Rus' Principality or Duchy. ... The agreement recognised the abolition of the Union of Brest in the Rus' Principality, assured toleration for Orthodoxy throughout the Commonwealth, granted Senate seats to the metropolitan and three bishops, and reserved some of the major posts in the Rus' Principality for Orthodox nobles.[41]

Thirty thousand so-called 'Registered Cossacks' were to be paid; and the Zaporozhian Hetman was to command a standing army of ten thousand. He was also to be named Palatine of Kiev, which represented a major encroachment into the royal prerogative. But I agree with Sysyn that the most important article of the Hadiach agreement was that promising ennoblement of one hundred men from each Cossack regiment.

Hadiach remained an empty promise of a better future for both interested parties: it was negotiated with one group only from

VII

among the Cossack elite; its conclusion was followed by fierce
rivalry among candidates for the Hetmanate and bloody struggles in
the Ukraine. The common Cossacks' not unjustified distrust of the
Commonwealth (which was in their area represented by ruthless
magnates) led them inevitably into the hands of the Orthodox tsar.
And that sealed the Ukraine's fate for over three centuries.[42]

For the Commonwealth the outcome meant not only a territorial
loss: a truce signed in Andruszów in 1667, and finally the 'eternal
peace' with Russia in 1686, gave to the tsar the right to intervene on
behalf of the Orthodox Church and Orthodox citizens of the
Commonwealth.[43] This signified a major shift in the balance of
power in Eastern Europe and had portentous consequences for the
whole region of Poland–Lithuania–Rus'. In this sense, the inability
to solve what had seemed merely a local socio-confessional problem, led eventually to a major crisis of the *Rzeczpospolita*: its very
sovereignty soon came under threat. Thereby was sealed Poland's
exit from the circle of European powers and, in a few more decades,
also from that of sovereign states.

Notes

1. The commonwealth or *Rzeczpospolita* (= *res publica*, republic) was a
   term embracing both Poland (also known as the Crown [*Korona*]) and
   Lithuania.
2. Because of the limits of space, only the most necessary references can
   be included here. For general information see the articles and references
   in *A Republic of Nobles. Studies in Polish History to 1864*, ed. Jan K.
   Fedorowicz (Cambridge, 1982). The estates of the Sejm were: the King,
   the Council (*Senat*), and the Chamber of Deputies (*Izba Poselska*).
   Incidentally, it has not been remarked on by anybody that the last
   Herrschaftsvertrag in Poland was signed as recently as 31 August 1980 in
   Gdańsk by the representatives of the workers on strike and those of the
   government of the People's Republic. This agreement had all the
   characteristics of such a document; the strikers, or at least their leaders,
   consciously defended citizens' rights in the Republic as a whole, a
   defence which found eventual expression in many of the twenty one
   articles formally agreed upon.
3. Stanisław Grodziski, 'Les devoirs et les droits politiques de la
   noblesse polonaise', *Acta Poloniae Historica*, xxxvi (1977).
4. Gottfried Schramm, 'Polen–Bohmen–Ungarn: übernationale Gemeinsamkeiten in der politischen Kultur des späten Mittelalters und der
   frühen Neuzeit', *Przegląd Historyczny*, lxxvi (1985).

5.   Several generally accepted notions concerning the early modern *Ständestaat* have been recently called in question: its 'dualistic nature' (German: *Dualismus*) by Volker Press, and the idea of a 'society of orders' by William Beik. It is true that these notions may be misleading when interpreted literally, that is, as brief definitions; but they reflect some realities absent from other systems, and therefore are useful when applied carefully.

6.   I have discussed the role of the Commonwealth's dimensions in a paper read at a conference in Gotlands Fornsal, Visby, in August 1986 on 'The Commonwealth of Poland–Luthuania in the Late Seventeenth Century: An Essay in Interpretation of Space' (forthcoming). Most topics touched on in this paper have been in some way developed in other recent publications of mine aimed at explaining the particular socio-political mechanisms of early modern Poland in comparison with those of other European countries. This explains the rather numerous references to my papers.

7.   Cf. Henryk Rutkowski, 'Terytorium', in: *Encyklopedia historii gospodarczej Polski do 1945 roku* (Warsaw, 1981) ii, 384–406, for the best, albeit concise, discussion and bibliography of the territory and historical geography of Poland. On the conditions of transportation see Adam Manikowski's entry 'Transport' (ibid., 415–19, with bibliography at 429f).

8.   The best general presentation of the history of Polish towns prior to the Partitions is Maria Bogucka and Henryk Samsonowicz, *Dzieje miast i mieszczaństwa w Polsce przedrozbiorowej* (Wroclaw, 1987). (Cf. also the same authors' contributions in *A Republic of Nobles*.) Lithuanian towns have, however, been mostly disregarded, though see Stanisław Alexandrowicz, *'Miasteczka Białorusi i Litwy jako ośrodki handlu w XVI i pierwszej połowie XVII w.'*, *Rocznik Białostocki*, i (1961).

9.   *Materiały do dziejow Sejmu Czteroletniego*, ed. Janusz Wolonski, Jerzy Michalski, Emanuel Rostworowski (Wroclaw, 1955) i, 362; quoted by Bogucka in *Dzieje miast* 352. Equation of Polish and/or Lithuanian small towns with villages in Western Europe was not so rare: see ibid., and Jean le Laboureur, *Histoire et relation du voyage de la Reyne de Pologne et du retour de Madame la Maréschalle de Guébriant* (Paris, 1648) 179.

10.   The political behaviour of Polish urban elites remains somewhat of a mystery, although some hypotheses have been launched. Cf. Juliusz Bardach, 'La formation des assemblées polonaises au XV siècle et la taxation', *Colloquium Lustrum V, Anciens Pays et Assemblées d'Etats* lxx (1977).

11.   Antoni Mączak, 'Dänemark und Polen-Litauen in der Neuzeit: Probleme und Perspektiven der vergleichenden Forschungen' (summary of a paper in Polish), *Zapiski Historyczne* (1982) 179–80; idem, 'Le rôle politique de la noblesse autour de la Baltique', in *Pouvoir et institutions en Europe au XVI siècle. De Pétrarque à Descartes*, ed. André Stegmann, vol. ii (Paris, 1987) *passim*.

12.   An admirable analysis of the King's parliamentary strategy and tactics has been given by Konstanty Grzybowski in *Teoria reprezentacji w Polsce epoki Odrodzenia* (Warsaw, 1959).

VII

13. Juliusz Bardach, 'Krewo i Lublin. Z problemów unii polsko-litewskiej', *Kwartalnik Historyczny*, lxxvi (1969) 3.
14. Cf. F.L. Carsten, *The Origins of Prussia* (Oxford, 1954); on the tactics of Duke Albrecht in Prussia, see also Walther Hubatsch, *Albrecht von Brandenburg-Ansbach, Deutschordens-Hochmeister und Herzog zu Preußen, 1490–1568* (Cologne/Berlin, 1960) 193ff. The case of Prussia is the more important in that the state had to be fully reorganised after that part of the Teutonic Order became a secular duchy in 1525.
15. See Bardach, 'Krewo i Lublin'; on the *inus indigenatus* in Royal Prussia, cf. Wojciech Ketrzynski, 'Cromers Rede über das preußische Indigenat', *Altpreußische Monatsschrift*, xvii (1880) 349; Antoni Mączak in *Historia Pomorza*, ed. Gerard Labuda (Poznan, 1976) 374–6. Cf. also Henryk Litwin, 'The Polish Magnates, 1454–1648: The Shaping of an Estate', *Acta Poloniae Historica*, liii, vol. ii. i (1986).
16. Juliusz Bardach, 'Statuty Wielkiego Księstwa Litewskiego: pomniki prawa doby odrodzenia', *Kwartalnik Historyczny*, lxxxi (1974) 4; Zbigniew Zdrojkowski, 'Korektura Pruska: jej powstanie, dzieje oraz jej znaczenie w historii polskiej juryzdykcji i myśli prawniczej', *Czasopismo Prawno-Historyczne* (1961) 2. For the privileges of the nobility in Royal Prussia, see Gerard Labuda, 'Przyczynek do walk wewnątrzklasowych szlachty kaszubskiej w XVII wieku', *Rocznik Gdański*, xiii (1954) 29ff.
17. See the interesting discussion of terminology and substance in a still unpublished paper by Jaroslaw Pelenski: 'Poland-Lithuania, 1454–1573: Nobility Democracy or Tripartite Mixed Government', read at the Third Conference of Polish and American Historians, Poznań, 1979.
18. H. Grajewski, 'Artykul statutu warckiego o przymusowej sprezedązy solectw', *Czasopismo Prawno-Historyczne* (1969) 1.
19. Wojciech Tygielski has shown Jan Zamoyski as a most successful broker between his clients and the King. When he was deprived of the King's grace (but not of his office and profits), the Chancellor lost much of his power to procure posts and profits for them, but still remained formidable in defending his clients: 'A Faction Which Could Not Lose', in *Klientelsysteme im Europa der frühen Neuzeit*, ed. Antoni Mączak (Munich, 1988).
20. Władysław Czapliński, 'Rządy oligarchii w Polsce nowożytniej', in his *O Polsce siedemnastowiecznej. Problemy i sprawy* (Warsaw, 1966) 152–8.
21. Grzybowski, *Teoria reprezentacji*.
22. I substantiate this argument in 'The Conclusive Years: The End of the Sixteenth Century as the Turning Point of Polish History', in *Politics and Society in Reformation Europe. Essays for Sir Geoffrey Elton on his Sixty-Fifth Birthday*, ed. E.I. Kouri and Tom Scott (London, 1987) 521–5. For a more theoretical approach see Witold Kula, *An Economic Theory of Feudalism* (London, 1976). Kula's 'terms-of-trade' figures for various groups of landowners have been disputed by Professor Leonid Żytkowicz, but this does not affect the substance of Kula's argument.
23. It is true that in 1655, during the Swedish invasion of the Commonwealth, Princes Janusz and Boguslaw Radziwiłł declared their intention to sever the Grand Duchy of Lithuania from Poland under Charles X Gustav's protection; but they found little support for that project among the gentry and it shortly became obsolete.

24. Wacław Urban 'Skład społeczny i ideologia sejmiku krakowskiego w latach 1572–1606', *Przegląd Historyczny*, xliv (1953). The best discussion of the Reformation among the Polish nobility is still Gottfried Schramm's *Der polnische Adel und die Reformation, 1548–1607* (Wiesbaden, 1965).
25. A detailed survey of the legal status of religious groups is to be found in the standard manual of Polish legal history, edited by Juliusz Bardach, *Historia państwa i prawa Polski* (2nd edn. Warsaw, 1966); on ethnic-confessional groups as *sui generis* orders of society, see Ireneusz Ihnatowicz, Antoni Mączak, and Benedykt Zientara, *Społeczeństwo polskie od X do XX wieku* (Warsaw, 1979) 342–53.
26. See Gershon David Hundert, 'Some Basic Characteristics of the Jewish Experience in Poland', *Polin*, i (1986) 28–35, for suggestions and bibliography.
27. Stanisław Kutrzeba, 'Datastanagirk Mechitara Gosza i statut ormianski z r. 1519', *Kwartalnik Historyczny*, xxii (1908) 658–79.
28. Dr Adam Manikowski has produced an unpublished MA thesis at the University of Warsaw in which he compares diverse group attitudes to the Jews and to the Scots; but interest in the history of the Scots in Poland is most unfortunately fading away.
29. Kazimierz Slosarczyk, 'Sprawa zespolenia Prus Królewskich z Koroną za Jagiellonów, 1454–1572', *Roczniki Historyczne*, iii (1927); Anna Dembińska, *Polityczna walka o egzekucje dóbr królewskich w latach 1559/64* (Warsaw, 1935). The crucial role of the Palatine of Marienburg (Malbork), Achatius von Zehmen, has been presented by R. Fischer: 'Achatius von Zehmen, Woywode von Marienburg', *Zeitschrift des Westpreußischen Geschichtsvereins*, xxxvi (1897). The cause of Prussian autonomy is represented by the monumental *opus* of Gottfried Lengnich, *Geschichte der preußischen Lande königlich-preußischen Antheils...* (9 vols. Danzig, 1722–55).
30. Marian Biskup, *Trzynastoletnia wojna z Zakonem Krzyzackim, 1454–1466* (Warsaw, 1967).
31. Idem, in *Historia Pomorza*, 69.
32. Karol Górski, 'Problematyka dziejowa Prus Królewskich, 1466–1572', *Zapiski Historyczne*, xxviii (1963) 2.
33. Schramm, *Der polnische Adel*, 16f.
34. On national or regional awareness in both parts of Prussia, cf. Theodor Schieder, *Deutscher Geist und ständische Freiheit im Weichsellande. Politische Ideen und politisches Schrifttum in Westpreußen von der Lubliner Union bis zu den polnischen Teilungen, 1569–1793* (Königsberg, 1940); Erich Maschke, 'Preußen. Das Werden eines deutschen Stammesnamens', reprinted in his *Domus Hospitalis Theutonicorum* (Bonn, 1970) 158–87; Stanislaw Herbst, 'Świadomość narodowa na ziemiach pruskich w XV-XVI wieku', *Komunikaty Mazursko-Warmińskie*, no. 1/75 (1962) 3–10; Janusz Mallek, 'Powstanie poczucia krajowej odrębnosci w Prusach i jej rozwój w XV i XVI wieku', in his *Dwie części Prus. Studia z dziejów Prus Książecych i Prus Królewskich w XVI i XVII wieku* (Olsztyn, 1987) 9–17.
35. Janusz Tazbir, *La République nobiliaire et le monde* (Wroclaw, 1986) *passim*.

VII

36. The term 'Ukraine' has various meanings. Historians representing the Ukrainian tradition often use it in its present-day sense; in the seventeenth century it described the lands of the Dnieper region: cf. F. Sysyn, *Between Poland and the Ukraine. The Dilemma of Adam Kysil, 1600–1653* (Cambridge, Mass., 1985) xiii. It is used here in that latter meaning.

37. See Andrzej Kaminski, 'The Polish–Lithuanian Commonwealth and its Citizens: Was the Commonwealth a Stepmother for Cossacks and Ruthenians?', and Frank E. Sysyn, 'Ukrainian–Polish Relations in the Seventeenth Century: The Role of National Consciousness in the Khmelnytsky Movement', both in *Poland and Ukraine Past and Present*, ed. Peter J. Potichnyj (Edmonton, 1980); Frank E. Sysyn, 'The Problem of the Nobilities in the Ukrainian Past: The Polish Period, 1569–1648' in *Rethinking Ukrainian History*, ed. Ivan L. Rudnytsky (Edmonton, 1981) 29–102; idem, *Between Poland and the Ukraine*. Cf. the essay in comparative history, embracing also nobilities in Livonia, Poland, Hungary and Moldavia, by Orest Subtelny, *Domination of Eastern Europe. Native Nobilities and Foreign Absolutism, 1500–1715* (Kingston/Montreal, 1986). Notwithstanding its title, Subtelny's book focuses on the late seventeenth and early eighteenth centuries.

38. On Prussia, cf. Labuda, 'Przyczynek'. On the *Pannadel*: Richard Cramer, *Geschichte des Landes Lauenburg und Bütow* (Königsberg, 1858); see also the introduction to *Inwentarze starostw lęborskiego i bytowskiego z XVII i XVIII wieku*, ed. Gerard Labuda (Toruń, 1959). A bibliography of the Livonian *Ritterschaft* may be found in Subtelny, *Domination of Eastern Europe*, 226f. On *ziemianie* in Lithuania there is an unpublished Warsaw Ph.D. thesis by Witold Sienkiewicz.

39. Sysyn, 'Ukrainian–Polish Relations', 69.

40. Sysyn, *Between Poland and the Ukraine*, 203.

41. Sysyn, 'Ukrainian–Polish Relations', 69.

42. On the future of the Ukraine in the framework of the seventeenth century and the Petrine Empire, see Subtelny, *Domination of Eastern Europe, passim*.

43. Zbigniew Wojcik, *Traktat andruszowski 1667 roku i jego geneza* (Warsaw, 1959).

VIII

From Aristocratic Household to Princely Court
Restructuring Patronage in the Sixteenth and Seventeenth Centuries

INTEREST in the patron–client relationship is growing among historians of early modern Europe. However, it is doubtful whether the time is ripe for historians to tackle wider topics or to draw general conclusions concerning patronage over large areas or even early modern Europe as a whole. Large gaps exist in our knowledge of patronage. A conference held in Munich in October 1984 provided us with a great wealth of material and showed the diversity of methods employed by historians, but it also demonstrated the difficulty of finding common denominators for the phenomenon in question. In my opinion, it also revealed the inadequacy of the vocabulary employed by historians for the study of clientage.[1]

1. Patronage: historical sources and the anthropologist's vocabulary

While historians now seem better informed than ever before about the progress of anthropological research on clientage, they do not share the propensity of social scientists for building theoretical systems; the conclusions drawn by historians are mostly either tentative, or strictly limited in time and space. It is true that patronage phenomena all over Europe displayed many similarities, especially in their external

---

[1] A. Mączak (ed.), *Klientelsysteme im Europa der frühen Neuzeit* (Schriften des Historischen Kollegs, Kolloquien 9; Munich, 1988). I use 'clientage' and 'patronage' virtually as synonyms, preferring the latter. As the term 'patronage' has several traditional meanings, 'clientage' will be used wherever the danger of confusion may arise.

This article was first published in *Princes, Patronage, and the Nobility. The Court at the Beginning of the Moderm Age, c. 1450-1650*, ed. R.G. Asch and A.M. Birke. © 1991 by Oxford University Press. Reprinted by permission.

forms—phraseology, customs, and rites. However, the patron–client relationship seems to have played different, even contrasting, roles in various local/regional systems of authority and power. The papers and discussions of the 1984 Munich conference on clientage show how complex those human relationships were, and also that this complexity was rooted not so much in the patron–client (or patron–broker–client) relationship itself, but rather in its socio-political matrix. This chapter is not a comprehensive survey of early modern patronage in Europe; it intends to do no more than comment on recent historical research in this area and on some notions introduced by social anthropologists.

My initial thesis is that patronage was a quasi-universal system in the sixteenth and seventeenth centuries. It may be understood as a routine way of exercising power and authority at a time when the public and the private were not yet clearly separated. While this is not a particularly revolutionary insight, few historians have drawn the following conclusions from it, namely that:

(1) such a common phenomenon should be systematized and its various forms and/or uses compared with each other.

(2) countries in which this phenomenon is visible in an extreme form—for example, where we find an especially high or especially low frequency of patronage, or where it fulfils unusual functions—should be studied more closely.

Unlike contemporary Europeans, early modern Europeans were prone to take clientage for granted. It was their medieval heritage, a somewhat softened and usually less ceremonial form of vassalage.[2] It corresponded to the medieval and early

---

[2] A recent paper by J. Russell Major is likely to trigger off a broad discussion on the 'transition from feudalism to clientelism' and on the nature of the latter. Against the author's argument about the importance of the *homagium* ceremony and the allegedly unavoidable ceremonial kiss, it could be argued (1) that there were deep regional differences in Europe (cf. Spain, where the kiss was a widespread Muslim custom) and that (2) putting one's palms into those of the seigneur is an obvious and generally accepted sign of dependence; the significance of the kiss seems more ambiguous. Cf. J. R. Major, ' "Bastard Feudalism" and the Kiss: Changing Social Mores in Late Medieval and Early Modern France', *Journal of Interdisciplinary History*, 27 (1987), pp. 509–35.

modern idea of society as consisting not of a sum of individuals, but rather of a structure based on hierarchy, kinship and corporation.

A hypothesis which, in my opinion, is also worth examining concerns the relationship between some forms of clientage and the money economy. This relationship has, to my knowledge, never been discussed by historians; however, when we analyse pre-industrial societies we may remember what Sir Edmund Leach has written about the 'variety of media of exchange which circulate in different social spheres but which are not interchangeable in any straightforward fashion'.[3] This applies exactly to my subject. To what extent the intensification of money circulation ousted, superseded, and/or modifid client-age networks is an open question. I believe that *modified* is the most appropriate term, but it would be worth studying the role of money in the patron–client relationship of the early modern era.

Historians, unlike some social anthropologists,[4] used to be little interested in clientage itself. They are rather prone to study its role in socio-political mechanisms. However, two very general notions proposed by anthropologists on the ground of their field-work seem to me adequate to the early modern material as well: the concepts of clientage as used by political scientists and by anthropologists.[5] These concepts ɔoth approach the relationship in question from the client's ɔide. The first one defines the client as a sort of social climber or at least a person striving to gain some profit and/or object of value. The spectrum of possible variations in clientage may be best explained by the other usage of the term. Clients, as analysed by the social anthropologist, more often than not need their patrons in order to secure the fundamental means of material existence, or even survival, for themselves and for their families in a difficult social environment.

In order to express it briefly, and to avoid lengthy and

[3] E. Leach, *Social Anthropology* (London, 1982), p. 162.
[4] Some of them may call themselves 'cultural anthropologists' but I use the distinction proposed by Leach, *Social Anthropology*, pp. 24–37.
[5] A. Weingrod, 'Patrons, Patronage and Political Parties', *Comparative Studies in Society and History*, 10 (1968), pp. 376–400; R. Theobald, 'The Decline of Patronage Relations in Developed Societies', *European Archives of Sociology*, 24 (1983), pp. 136–47.

clumsy terms, I will call these two types of relationships the 'political clientage' and the 'poor man's clientage'. Of course, the two forms of that relationship were not always clearly separated, and as far as court society is concerned, political clientage was by no means always more important than poor man's clientage. My suggestion is that we ought not to lose sight of the latter form of clientage which in some parts of Europe was a mass phenomenon. Some clienteles were composed of people for whom finding the basic food and shelter were rather more important than striving for advancement and power. We also find an intermediate, or rather a transitional, link between both types of patron–client relationships, which may be called the 'upstart's clientage'. I shall return to this in the final sections of this chapter.

A parallel set of terms, proposed by a historian,[6] refers to *offensive* (that is, active, acquisitive) and *defensive support* requested by clients from their patron. In some cases requests of acquisitive character correspond to political patronage, but this by no means signifies the equivalence of the two terms.

It may be fruitful also to classify early modern governments according to the part that patronage networks played in them. Factors to look at would include the structures of these networks, as well as their strength and dynamism. Such a perspective, focusing upon real power relationships instead of on institutions and formal prerogatives, is especially useful in discussing the principal constitutional alternative of the period: whether to be for or against absolutism. Political clientage is found in both 'pre-' and 'proto-absolutist', and 'republican' or 'parliamentary' systems, but it is likely that its scope and specific character were symptomatic of, or even responsible for, the development of the power system.

2. The royal perspective on patronage

It is tempting to present the evolution of patronage as a simple trend towards making it a monopoly of the crown or of central government. Recent research on patronage, however, especially in England and France, but also in Poland, has produced

---

[6] W. Tygielski, 'A Faction Which Could Not Lose', in Mączak (ed.), *Klientel-systeme*, pp. 177–201.

more subtle conclusions about the conflict between the aristocracy and the crown, and the part played by patronage in it. Royal attitudes and strategies concerning patronage may be provisionally summed up as follows:

(1) in general, aristocratic patronage is detrimental to royal authority; it should be restricted or abolished;
(2) particular aristocratic clienteles may either weaken or temporarily strengthen the government, and are to be treated accordingly;
(3) the king and his leading ministers may build up their own 'government clientele' network (or networks) in order to use this most reliable relationship to buttress central government and weaken rival factions;
(4) in general, patronage saves the state money; its abolition would ruin the state's finances.

The majority of European rulers followed these or similar principles to a greater or lesser degree. However, both policies and results varied greatly from country to country, depending roughly upon what may be called the 'bureaucratization' of the system of government in question, and upon the role played in it by aristocratic local power bases.

3. The court, the country, and patronage

Most historians of continental Europe are rather reluctant to accept the court versus country interpretation of what is known as the crisis of the seventeenth century. However, this interpretation offers a clear frame of reference and corresponds to the way in which the early modern subjects of our research understood their world. It should be coupled with a patronage-based interpretation of early modern power systems and a functional analysis of the court itself.

The prince's court strove to gain a monopoly of opportunities for social and economic advancement among the nobility as well as other ambitious groups.[7] This was possible only where the aristocracy's regional power bases had been destroyed and the other nobles somehow deprived of their independence. Royal policy in many countries from the

---

[7] J. von Kruedener, *Die Rolle des Hofes im Absolutismus* (Stuttgart, 1973), pp. 48–52.

fifteenth to the seventeenth centuries may be interpreted as one of actions directed against the regional power bases of chiefs of aristocratic factions. The degree of political centralization in early modern states could be evaluated accordingly. However, centralization—or a monopoly of patronage—was the prince's ultimate goal rather than a political reality.

This conclusion may be drawn, for example, from Victor Morgan's criticism of Lawrence Stone's view of patronage in Elizabethan and early Stuart England. Instead of a gradual ('linear') decline of patronage 'as the influence of the State increases', Morgan is inclined to see changes of a structural nature, in particular an increase in the brokerage functions of patrons.[8] This is true, but it also signifies the parallel coexistence of diverse clientage networks, often similar to each other as far as the direct patron–client relationship was concerned, but sometimes fundamentally different in their socio-political functions. These differences depended upon the political position of the patron: whether he cultivated relative independence from the king or tried to establish a close relationship showing loyalty and submission. The latter attitude usually placed the patron somewhere close to the court.

The court's role varied according to one's vantage-point: for the prince, it was the scene of splendour and prestige but also the site of government and central administration. (The balance of these functions and the degree to which they could be separated have rarely been studied in detail.) The members of the court were both royal servants/officers and private entrepreneurs. Their most profitable business was brokerage.

The economic basis of patronage was complex. The system thrived especially well wherever and whenever it was supported by public revenues. It was the nature of court brokerage to

---

[8] V. Morgan, 'Some Types of Patronage, Mainly in Sixteenth- and Seventeenth-Century England', in Mączak (ed.), *Klientelsysteme*, pp. 91–115. This paper contains a comprehensive bibliography. However, Lawrence Stone, against whom Morgan's argument is directed, is principally interested in the aristocracy whose *traditional* patronage in the century before the Civil War was in decline. Stone's argument has recently been supported by Sharon Kettering, 'Patronage and Politics during the Fronde', *French Historical Studies*, 14 (1986), pp. 335–41.

limit access to the source of the distribution of offices and dignities. The broker then used these opportunities to strengthen his position at court itself and, indirectly, his influence in the country.

The true test of the reliability and strength of patronge networks was a rebellion; it exposed any internal tensions. To elucidate this, I shall briefly sum up the results of some recent research on three major rebellions.[9]

4. Patronage and revolt

In his essay on William of Orange, H. F. K. van Nierop casts doubt upon the prince's ability to use his patronage network as an effective tool of rebellion.[10] The noble society of the Netherlands in the mid-sixteenth century displayed most of the typical features of clientage: the vocabulary of *fidélité* and 'friendship', the traditional custom of godfatherhood, and widely developed brokerage.[11] The highly urbanized social landscape of the Netherlands probably did not allow for even quasi-independent clientele networks among the high nobility. Nierop emphasizes the official functions of the nobles. At least in Holland they 'were first of all officials; most noblemen were officials; the majority of officials belonged to the nobility'.[12] This to a large extent explains why their clienteles were so sensitive to their patrons' political position, their relationship with the court and the *landvoogt*, and consequently why they were so unreliable. Clearly, the nobles of the Netherlands did not fulfil the high expectations of *fidélité*, emphasized so strongly by Roland Mousnier:[13] their clientage relationship

[9] I concentrate on this subject in one chapter of a collection of essays, 'The Clientèle: Studies in European Societies, Sixteenth to Eighteenth Centuries' (forthcoming in Polish).

[10] H. F. K. van Nierop, 'Willem van Oranje als hoog edelman: patronage in de Habsburgse Nederlanden?', *Bijdragen en mededelingen betreffende de geschiedenis van Nederlanden*, 99 (1984), pp. 651–76.

[11] Ibid. 671 on adopting a patron's Christian name for a client's son; p. 672 on clients addressed as 'friends' (*vriend*), 'cousins' (*neve*), and for 'familie'.

[12] H. F. K. van Nierop, *Van ridders tot regenten. De Hollandse adel in de zestiende en de eerste helft van de zeventiende eeuw* (Hollandse Historische Reeks, 1; The Hague, 1984), p. 156.

[13] Together with the new generation of scholars of patronage, mostly Anglo-Saxon, Nierop rejects Roland Mousnier's theory of patronage (cf. 'Willem van Oranje', pp. 662, 675).

was based upon their patrons' official position, that is, their close relationship with the court in Brussels.

What happened to patronage networks in England during the Civil War and the Protectorate? The 'revisionist' historians have emphasized the importance or even primacy of patronage as a motivating factor in early Stuart politics.[14] My impression is that much less is known about the Civil War and the Protectorate. Jack H. Hexter asks 'Is there indeed evidence of a single consequential instance in which a "client" acted at a patron's behest in a way in which he would not have acted otherwise? If there is, I have not seen it.'[15]

This may be correct, but it raises a much more general question: was (political) patronage a tool used to break the backbone of less powerful men and make them act against their conscience? Or is it a system that works well either when 'the issues are not abundant' (to use Hexter's expression),[16] or when there is a fundamental consensus between patrons and clients. The latter case is not unusual because often, though not invariably, the patronage system is not visibly oppressive (or at least its oppressiveness must not be perceived as such by the client!).

Some remarks by Mrs Lucy Hutchinson may elucidate various possible situations. She was by no means impartial, but had a great gift of synthetic observation. Referring to the year 1641 she wrote: 'At that time most of the gentry of the country were disaffected to the parliament; most of the middle sort, the able substantial freeholders, and the other commons, *who had not their dependence upon the malignant nobility and gentry*, adhered to the parliament'.[17]

---

[14] Bibliography, sub specie patronage in Morgan, 'Some Types of Patronage' (above, n. 8).

[15] J. H. Hexter, 'Power Struggle, Parliament and Liberty in Early Stuart England', *Journal of Modern History*, 50 (1978), 1–50, p. 19.

[16] Cf. J. H. Hexter, *The Reign of King Pym* (Cambridge, Mass., 1941), p. 75 (cited by Kettering, 'Patronage and Politics [above, n. 81]). There is a broad consensus among historians on the fundamental difference between patronage and political (religious) issues in the mid-17th and mid-18th cents. Therefore the study of the 'structure of politics', in the sense of a Namierization, is not an appropriate method for approaching the Long Parliament.

[17] *Memoirs of the Life of Colonel Hutchinson (. . .) Written by His Widow Lucy . . .*, ed. J. Hutchinson (London, 1906), pp. 100 f. (italics by A. Mączak).

She also mentioned the particular case of her late husband:

At that time Sir Henry Ireton was in the country, and being a
kinsman of Mr Hutchinson's and one that has received so much
advantage to himself and his family in the country by Sir Thomas
Hutchinson's countenance and protection, *that he seemed a kind of
dependent upon him*, and being a very grave, serious, religious person,
there was a great league of kindness and good-will between them.[18]

Ireton removed 'projectors and those of corrupt interest
that were in the commission of the peace', and replaced them
with 'better affected' persons, including Mr Hutchinson. This
is another face of that 'world turned upside down': a former
client obviously becomes a strong patron, everything being
undertaken in a mood of mutual understanding, piety, and
high-mindedness.

But this was an emergency situation, a civil war. It is not
clear to me what happened thereafter to patronage networks
in England. For instance, did the military governors take over
the old clients' networks or create new ones? Or did the
puritan victory mark a rapid and general decline in patronage
relationships? If this was the case, how did patronage re-
emerge in the Restoration era? I cannot offer answers to any of
these questions. I raise them because they are important for
our more general understanding of clientage and have been
little researched by the specialists.

The Fronde has recently been analysed by two American
scholars of the younger generation, William Beik and Sharon
Kettering.[19] Their conclusions cannot be adequately summarized here. Beik proposes an interesting analysis of the
structure of French—and indeed any early modern—society. I
do not share his criticism of the term 'society of orders' but, in
my opinion, his interpretation of 'social classes' fits the early
modern reality very well.[20] His investigation of the rule of
Louis XIV seems to me innovative as well as forcible.

---

[18] Ibid. 98 f. (italics by A. Mączak).

[19] S. Kettering, *Judicial Politics and Urban Revolt: The Parlement of Aix 1629–1659*
(Princeton, 1978); W. Beik, *Absolutism and Society in Seventeenth-Century France. State
Power and Provincial Aristocracy in Languedoc* (Cambridge, 1985); S. Kettering, *Patrons,
Brokers and Clients in Seventeenth-Century France* (New York and Oxford, 1986); cf. also
her recent paper on the Fronde (above, n. 8).

[20] *Absolutism*, pp. 6 ff. 'By "classes" I mean groups whose social and economic
interests are necessarily antagonistic to one another because of their differing

Sharon Kettering's article on the Fronde stresses the importance and effectiveness of patronage bonds in the service of both parties involved. In fact, while some earlier students of the Fronde overlooked the role of patronage, she makes this problem her principal subject. As far as patronage is concerned the French political crisis is fundamentally different from the English one:

> French clients could follow the dictates of their political conscience when the issues were important enough and find a new patron whose politics they shared . . . A client could sever a personal bond with a patron whose political goals or opinions differed from his own, and attach himself to a patron whose political views he shared.[21]

The question is, how often in mid-seventeenth-century France was political conscience indeed separable from a more pedestrian personal interest? In many cases the flexibility or revokability of clientage bonds was probably put to good use by clients, according to their assessments of future political development, that is, their estimates of the relative strength and reliability of potential patrons. Obviously, although driven into a corner, Cardinal Mazarin was still reliable and powerful enough successfully to distribute honours and offices in the provinces and so attract hesitating, or curb rebellious, subjects. This signified that the crown continued to enjoy high prestige (in the broad meaning of the term). At least as far as the *robins* were concerned, the main bond between them and the crown was based upon the process of nomination to office and a patron's role was usually that of broker. The Fronde compromised patronage resting on a local base—that of relatively independent, or oppositional aristocrats. It prepared for the triumph of absolutism.

---

relationships to resources, power and the fruit of labour' (ibid. 7). However, this reopens the problem of the antagonistic or solidaristic nature of clientage bonds. Beik's approach to early modern clientelism has been rightly described by Claudio Rosso as 'un marxismo problematico e aperto'. 'Stato e clientele nella Francia della prima età moderna', *Studi storici*, 28 (1987), p. 75.

[21] 'Patronage and Politics' (above, n. 8), p. 437.

5. France and Poland: two contrasting scenes

Recent studies of the structure of politics in seventeenth-century France[22] have revealed an interaction between two types of patronage, contrasting with each other in formal terms but almost indistinguishable in reality: one based upon the patron's office, and another which may be called 'mighty-neighbour patronage'. The Fronde in fact demonstrated some of the virtues of all types of patronage. It is a paradox that the crisis was eventually defused by the cardinal's massive build-up of new clienteles. Yet this was an Indian summer of mighty-neighbour, aristocratic patronage in France. Its collapse led to the dismantling of all relatively independent patronage networks of any political significance.

The commonwealth of Poland-Lithuania was a contrasting case. There, and particularly in its eastern regions, a combination of constitutional and societal factors created mighty-neighbour patronage networks which were the dominant political force in the provinces, the magnates being the principal brokers standing between them and the king. The latter was the fountainhead of benefices which were accessible virtually only through the brokerage services of the magnates. In order to explain what, in my opinion, may reflect the power brokerage competed with the waning influence of the assemblies of the estates and the increasing power of royal officials (*intendants*, *Hofräte*, commissaries, etc.); in Poland-Lithuania the magnates' power of brokerage was gaining an ascendancy against the direct co-operation between the diets (local assemblies of the nobility) and the chamber of deputies. In the seventeenth century the chamber and the diets ceased to be independent assemblies of the nobility—*populus nobilium*. In order to explain what, in my opinion, my reflect the political thinking of petty or even great noblemen in the late seventeenth and eighteenth centuries, I quote a British text which asks

whether the Liberties of the people are not more likely to be safe in the hands of the friends to a personage who has the greatest landed

---

[22] Both American scholars only roughly follow the systematic method introduced by Sir Lewis Namier. Dr Kettering's *Patrons, Brokers and Clients* is clearly inspired by it.

property in the Kingdom . . . or in the hands of a Gentleman who
(. . .) may be said to be . . . greatly inferior, both in point of weight
in this Kingdom and knowledge of its true interests as also in
knowledge of the World, and of Mankind in General?[23]

'Greatly inferior gentlemen' had a less and less independent
voice, even in local politics, especially in Lithuania. On the
other hand, the magnate was by no means a supreme ruler
even over his client-nobles and constantly had to keep them
satisfied and ensure them of his power of protection. During
the late seventeenth century the state was becoming something
of an informal federation of patrons: essentially it supported
their clienteles. The magnates' households, or rather courts
(*dwory*, as they were called) played a role similar to that which
Norbert Elias and his followers attribute to Versailles, the
Residenz in Munich, or Vienna's *Hofburg*. The elective
character of the monarchy meant that the magnates' families,
rather than the king, were seen as the most stable factor and
consequently attracted the loyalty of lesser nobles.

6. Regional diversities of patronage systems

It would not be justified simply to put European varieties of
patronage somewhere on a scale between these two contrasting
models: Poland-Lithuania under the Wettin dynasty and the
France of the *Roi Soleil*. Local traditions, political events, the
size of a state, etc., together gave rise to diversified patronage
and court-and-country relationships, which also changed
greatly over time. A question still remaining to be asked is why
in some countries—in Scandinavia above all, and in Prussia—
patronage never seemed to have flourished. Its weakness in
bureaucratic structures that were shaped in the seventeenth
century may be ascribed to the initial weakness of aristocratic
clientage networks.

In general, the matrix of patron–client relationships was
determined by the prince's court, the type of bureaucratic
system, and the position of potentates (aristocrats, magnates)
within their neighbourhoods (their local/regional power

---

[23] Robert Butcher to the Gentlemen of Launceston, 1754. Quoted by
H. Wellenreuther, *Repräsentation und Grossgrundbesitz in England 1730–1770* (Stuttgart,
1979), p. 237.

bases). In most countries local/regional power bases were in decline: central state institutions were able to control local affairs (often availing themselves of the ministers' own patronage networks). In Poland-Lithuania a constellation of factors—in particular, the size of the country—created perfect conditions for the consolidation of local patronage bases.[24] The other side of that development was that magnates' courts flourished. The final result calls for a cultural anthropological approach: the landed gentry in Lithuania in the early eighteenth century cultivated an extravagant mixture of noblemen's dignity and clients' servility.[25] A dedication devised by a courtier in Hanover could just as easily have been written by a contemporary nobleman-bootlicker in provincial Poland, Lithuania, or Ukraine:

Wenn Gott nicht Gott wäre, wer sollte billiger Got sein als unser Fürst?[26]

---

[24] I have elaborated this argument in 'The Commonwealth of Poland–Lithuania in the late seventeenth century: an essay in interpretation of space', in S.-O. Lindquist (ed.), *Economy and culture in the Baltic 1650–1700* (Acta Visbyensia 8; Visby, 1989), pp. 7–20.

[25] This point has been elaborated in my paper 'Conventions of the Lop-sided Friendship' to appear in a volume on friendship, edited by Roy Porter.

[26] Quoted by von Kruedener, *Rolle des Hofes*, p. 30: 'If God were not God, who could more reasonably expect to be God than our Prince?'

IX

Vicissitudes of feudalism in modern Poland

The main thesis of this chapter is that feudalism took a rather peculiar shape in early modern Poland; that it exerted its influence for a longer time than in most European countries; that it strongly coloured capitalist relationships in the nineteenth and twentieth centuries; and that some recent socio-economic phenomena are still curiously reminiscent of early modern feudalism.

I cannot comment at length upon the origins of feudalism in Poland and its development in the Middle Ages; this has been done many times.[1] At the turn of the fifteenth and in the early sixteenth century, the Polish economy, society and state show traces which are familiar to every student of Central and Western Europe. Only from that period did the public institutions of Poland (and since the Union of Lublin, 1569, of the Commonwealth of Poland and Lithuania) begin to change and to take a turn quite different from that characteristic of Western Europe, and in fact different from almost all other European countries.

In 1948 the Marxist notion of feudalism was still little in use in Poland, but some historians wished to adapt the concept of 'feudalism' (until then connected principally with the high Middle Ages in the West) to Polish conditions. Tadeusz Manteuffel then observed that Polish–Lithuanian society from the sixteenth century settled into a shape familiar to students of Carolingian times.[2] This conclusion has been neither accepted nor contradicted by any scholar since. However, it ought to be regarded as an important suggestion of some peculiarities in what might be called the periodization of social relationships. While basic economic conditions of life, and lord and peasant relationships in the Commonwealth, did not deviate from those characteristic of the neighbouring countries, the internal structures of the Noble Estate and of their state were taking distinct forms. This opinion has been endorsed recently by Perry Anderson. According to him, 'the feudal State it [Poland] produced provided a singular clarification of the reasons why Absolutism was the natural and normal form of noble class power after the late Middle Ages.'[3] And absolutism had no chance in Poland.

It is difficult to explain thoroughly why this was so. Counter-factual reasoning has found no place in Polish historiography, either economic or political. However, several arguments may be outlined here. The factors involved were both accidental and structural in nature. Descendants of Wladyslaw Jagiello (died 1434) had no clear hereditary rights to the throne, and had to haggle for the consent of the nobility by means of generous charters for the whole Noble Estate. After the dynasty died out in 1572, the free election of kings shattered the power of the throne and deprived the royal person of much of his inherited charisma. In the meantime there were powerful structural factors at work. In the fifteenth and sixteenth centuries few rulers escaped problems with the Estates. The Polish Estates were atypical in that townspeople played virtually no role. As Gottfried Schramm has pointed out, this was not a uniquely Polish situation.[4] But Poland was a vast country and her kings did not keep her divided into separate *pays légaux*, and therefore were unable to play off one against another as did the Hohenzollerns. Unlike successful European princes, the Jagiellons were more often than not short of cash and – what is much more important – they never built an efficient fiscal machine.

Nobody has seriously and thoroughly discussed the consequences of particular social hierarchies and structures for the development of the Commonwealth. The multitude of gentlefolk should be regarded as a secondary factor: petty noblemen never played an active political role and might be compared to simple freeholders or to Prussian *Freie*. They enjoyed fully only their legal freedoms and shared (some only in part) the fiscal ones, but the biggest assets – duty-free exports and imports of goods – were turned fully to account only by the greatest landowners.[5] On the other hand, the lesser nobles were in search of social promotion and could easily be exploited by their bigger neighbours as servants and officials. In the given political structure the king did not take as much advantage as the magnates from the squires' willingness to serve. The highly democratic parliamentary system was not matched by similar equality of wealth and prestige. A recent study of the power elite of Poznan and Kalisz *voievodships* (counties) between 1587 and 1632 (the reign of Sigismund Vasa), has revealed the existence of about 280 officials, from top-rank senators of national importance to petty judges and judiciary officials, as well as repeatedly re-elected members or speakers of the regional Diet.[6] The top nominations depended on the king himself, but the ruler could not elevate upstarts in the face of a popular decision in the local Diet or against the wishes of the whole elite group. Lesser officials were duly elected by the whole body of noblemen. In the long run, this power elite gained politically at the expense both of the king and of their constituency. Less successful landowners were able to carry on exerting political power if they enjoyed prestige due to their firm establishment in their area. However, the whole group was clearly acquisitive and successful on the land market.

During the whole early modern period and in most parts of the country, landed property was increasingly concentrated. This took place not only where there was no substantial core of noble landed estates of large size already in the later middle ages (Prussia, Masovia).[7] During the late sixteenth and early seventeenth centuries the middle stratum of the gentry was decimated and in some parts subsequently as good as wiped out, or rather bought up. Lesser nobles were made dependent upon their wealthier neighbours and this meant the breakdown of the political independence of the gentry. The parliamentary power struggle that in the 1560s had seemed to be fully won by the Executio-Iurium movement for the rights of the middle gentry (or the lesser strata of the power elite?) was eventually determined at the district level and by socio-economic factors like profitability of landed estates and market in landed property.

Political equality within the Noble Estate was doomed by the vitality of the clientage. As Tadeusz Manteuffel saw it,

> the disruption of authority suffered by Poland at the turn of the sixteenth century...caused, first, the independence of the great lords; secondly, their taking over of governmental functions within their estates; thirdly, the creation of a personal relationship between the magnates and the gentry based on the pledge of loyalty (servingmen bound to their masters by the ceremony of handshake), sometimes also strengthened by tenure for life by the grace of the lord; fourthly, the spread of conditional property in the form of endowments granted to the handshake-servants.[8]

All of this was strongly reminiscent of the feudal forms of the high Middle Ages in the West rather than of the changes which in modern times were leading the more advanced societies to capitalism.

The legal and constitutional system made a particularly important contribution to this development. Whereas the great lord was becoming 'not so much a citizen of the Commonwealth as the absolute ruler over a territory, sometimes large, sometimes less so, within its borders', the freedom of the king to choose his ministers and other dignitaries was strictly limited to persons of already high economic and political standing. The leaders of the House of Deputies in the sixteenth century were likely to be promoted to senatorial rank and to be granted royal domains as leaseholds for life. Such a system was detrimental to the 'democracy of the gentry', as Polish historians call it. In the seventeenth century grass-roots political movements degenerated into anarchic rebellions (*rokosz*) and were to a large extent manipulated by the magnates. The clientage was not without its virtues on a local level and in matters of law and order but turned out disastrously in the sphere of national politics. There are good reasons for connecting all of this with the size of the country, with its weak system of communications[9] and with sharp divergences of regional political and defence interests. Whereas kings were elected for life, the local potentate not only seemed to be, he *was*, the backbone of stability for his clients and lesser neighbours. The Radziwills, the Sapiehas, and a score of their peers were as dynastically strong as any family upon one of whose members had been bestowed the crown and the sceptre.

Too little attention has been paid to the system of operation of institutions in Poland–Lithuania or to the social structure of bodies of officials. The Commonwealth lacked mechanisms which contributed to the consolidation of states in early modern Europe. Royal servants with large judicial and administrative powers (*starostowie grodzcy*) were already in the later sixteenth century losing their particular status and becoming as good representatives of local power elites as any other local dignitaries. The precious balance of local and central influences so characteristic of the English Justices of the Peace was never the lot of their counterparts in Poland–Lithuania. And officialdom there never settled into a corporative shape like, say, *parlements* in France. Officialdom never carried on internal struggles between various bodies of different social standing, so characteristic of France and typical of all states where bureaucracies were composed of simple commoners, patricians and true nobles.

Between 1772 and 1795 the Commonwealth endured three partitions culminating in the disappearance of the state from the political map of Europe. There has been much discussion among Polish historians concerning the origins, causes and the inevitability of the partitions. From the mid-nineteenth century each generation of Poles has taken over this problem, translated it into their own terms, used it for their particular goals, as well as studied it according to the rules of scholarship. Nowadays there is more oral than printed discussion. Should we focus upon the whole history of the Commonwealth from the vantage point of its sorry ending? Many Polish historians believe that we should not; no Czech, they argue, studies the Bohemian sixteenth century as a road leading to the White Mountain in 1620.

So far as the fate of feudalism is concerned, two principal sets of questions emerge. First, how the Polish nobility adapted themselves to the new power systems they had to live with, and to subordinate to; second, how the society and economy reacted to capitalist impulses in the nineteenth century. Both questions can hardly be answered in two or three paragraphs. Most Polish–Lithuanian magnates easily turned into aristocrats and courtiers in Berlin, Vienna and St Petersburg, thanks to their wealth, connections, and to what might be called *horror vacui*: they were simply needed as pillars of society in the territories acquired by the partitioning powers. Unless they became security risks because of their Polish patriotism, they were safe from persecution. On the other hand, they were expected – at least by conservative circles – to employ their wealth and prestige in the national cause. While Polish aristocrats lost their political power with the dissolution of the Commonwealth (they could win it only as individuals within the framework of a partitioning monarchy, and there were outstanding cases of such success), they remained socially and economically well established. Unlike the landowners in Upper Silesia, none of their Polish counterparts owned deposits of minerals worth mentioning, so they concentrated on agriculture, forestry and connected industries. If one may risk a generalization, the aristocrats – or rather great landowners – were more prone to risk commutation of labour services and emancipation of tenants than lesser owners. To make a long story short, ownership of large landed estates provided the most important assets although it did not make the landowners immune to crises. Inherited prestige, conservative patriotic myths[10] and wealth brought to that group certain political profits even during the 20-year period of independence (1918–39). Polish industry, heavily dependent upon foreign capital, needed both money and big names; the latter were readily available.

The last chapter about this social group is still to be written: perhaps it will be a study of the remarkable social adaptability and highly differentiated fates among a once ruling class. Probably the most outstanding case is that of the Radziwills who are, in their numerous branches, great landowners in Africa, socialites in the United States, as well as citizens of the People's Poland, professional intellectuals, and active members of Independent Trade Union *Solidarnosc.*

Less wealthy landowning groups found it more difficult to cope with political and economic hardships from the eighteenth century onwards. In 1777 in Prussia and 1781 in Austria, and 1864 in Congress Poland, feudal ownership of land and the personal dependence of tenants and the landless poor upon their lords was abolished.[11] While general and rapid reforms had to be forced by the state upon reluctant landowners, many among them were seeking their own optimal solutions. For lesser owners even commutation of services could be fatally expensive. Started from the mid-eighteenth century by enlightened landlords, commutation was tried in the following decades even by some of the less wealthy as an act of the lord's grace towards his tenants and as a private contract. As a rule, landlords tended to maintain a profitable and flexible ratio of services and money rents according to their own current needs and their tenants' economic potential. In some places, the proximity of early centres of industry made strict forms of serfdom and labour services obsolete. Political changes in the period 1772–1815 left hardly a corner untouched. For example in parts subdued by Prussia the sudden accessibility of credit, hitherto unknown, led the Polish gentry into bankruptcies: they had borrowed heavily but did not use their loans for productive investment, and unexpectedly wound up broken by the terms of payment (Napoleon took over from the Prussians all these claims).

Hard lessons were not ignored (even if bankruptcies were generally attributed to Prussian slyness). Transformations in the management of estates corresponding to commutation of services, enclosures and the emancipation of peasantry, which in some parts of the West had been spread over centuries, in Poland (and in some other Eastern countries) occurred over just decades or even had to be accomplished almost at once.

We cannot discuss here the process of primitive accumulation of capital or the particular traits of capitalism in Poland. What remains to be told is the fate of the petty gentry. That very numerous social class seemed to have little to lose, and yet it lost much. Once unruly voters and retainers of the magnates, petty noblemen (having no serfs) lost their voting rights in 1791. After the partitions, new rulers were reluctant to acknowledge their noble status. In the Kingdom of Poland (Congress Poland) there were hundreds of villages inhabited almost exclusively by petty noblemen unable to prove their noble status. On the other hand, successful capitalists were striving for hereditary titles and coats-of-arms. The noble life-style dominated over the bourgeois one, and the struggle between these value systems is one of the basic themes of Polish literature of the post-1863 era. The fate of the gentry, poorly equipped to cope with the political reality of the late nineteenth century, with structural changes in agriculture and agrarian crises, and unable to find appropriate positions in capitalist society, contributed to a curious idealization of the loser, the unsuccessful and of the misfit idealist. This trend, in Polish literary tradition, is by no means extinguished.[12] Reliable quantitative data concerning the 'social genealogy' of the intelligentsia have been produced only recently and a discussion is now under way, but it seems very likely that it was the noble myth and ethos, more often than not unmatched by personal wealth and chances of social advancement, that was instrumental in creating that social stratum.

In the countryside, enfranchisement reforms did not create anything approaching social equality and they left barely touched some remnants of the feudal system. These were the perseverance of the near-subsistence sector of the economy, and the continuation of ancient social relationships, independent of progressive bourgeois legislation (the *Code Civil* of Napoleon was in force in Congress Poland). Subsistence farming was not in itself feudal, of course, but its remarkably wide diffusion and intensiveness created major obstacles to the development of capitalism and contributed to the preservation of feudal, or rather semi-feudal, bonds. An even more powerful obstacle to the development of capitalism was a peculiar gap between the estate (successor of the manorial farm) and the (peasant) farm. The reforms only modified a little, but did not remove, differences of social conditions. It was much easier for a town bourgeois to settle down as a landowner (and from the mid-nineteenth century the differences between noble and commoner landowners were narrowing) than for an enriched farmer to become recognized as a person 'of quality'. In general, the Polish peasant would not recognize himself in the literary portrait of his French counterpart painted by Honoré de Balzac.

In independent Poland all differences of orders and all hereditary titles were duly abolished. Peasant political parties and farmers' co-operatives led in many respects to the social emancipation of the peasantry. They could hardly improve the structure of land ownership. The enfranchisement of the peasantry had robbed them (directly or indirectly, there were portentous regional differences) of a part of their land, and during the late nineteenth century there continued a trend towards greater polarization of peasant property. In 1921, 24.9 per cent of land under cultivation belonged to dwarf-farms of less than 5 hectares (64.7 per cent of all agricultural properties). Only 1.8 per cent of owners had farms of 20–100 hectares, and 0.6 per cent of over 100 hectares (respectively 10.3 and 27.2 per cent of cultivated land). The agrarian reforms of the 1920s and early 1930s did not bring about much change, although 2,423 thousand hectares of large property were subdivided and sold to 630,000 small owners. All of this contributed to some of the principal causes of the very limited development of a market economy. According to M. Kalecki and L. Landau in 1934, only 54 per cent of the national income passed through the market (65 per cent of consumed income). The market consumption of peasants and labourers was only a little over 22 per cent of their total consumption.[13]

All of this should be borne in mind when we pass to the next – and up to now the last – chapter of the history of feudalism in Poland. We do not argue that some sort of system of that kind was reintroduced in Poland in the later 1940s, but that some socio-economic features, characteristic of pre-capitalist times, reappeared as sometimes secondary but hardly unimportant attributes of the new order.

The post-war land reform of 1944–5 wiped out the landlord class and subsequently was executed with excessive zeal, so that numerous *kulak* owners of much less than 50 hectares found themselves landless. A short if violent wave of forced collectivization succeeded but few of the collective farms were to survive the deep 'thaw' of October 1956: only 17 per cent, about 1,530 in all. And yet, in spite of the violent fate of the country during both World Wars, in spite of two reforms of landed property, of changes of the frontiers of the nation and despite collectivization, one element in the agrarian economy remains constant: the persistence of small farms. In 1921, farms of up to 5 hectares constituted 65 per cent of all farms; in 1950 in the People's Poland they formed 57 per cent of individual farms; in 1970 the corresponding figure was 59, and nine years later 60, per cent.[14] The government tried to cope with the social and economic consequences of these facts in various ways. It tried to impose taxes in kind and compulsory deliveries of grain, and to compel farmers to sell to the state various kinds of crops and animals through sophisticated contract systems.

The student of the feudal economy can easily perceive analogies between some of its characteristics and contemporary Polish agriculture. One needs only a certain degree of generalization. Whereas there were once thousands of feudal owners of peasant and demesne farms, today state agrarian farms (PGR) are run by the state, the same state which pursues particular policies towards private farmers. There is a close analogy to a particular trait characteristic of the relationship between the state and the (independent) trade unions. This was clearly brought home in the summer of 1981 by Bronislaw Geremek: *Solidarnosc* has a particular scope and forms of activity because it represents its members on a nationwide scale not against numerous employers (as has been the case under capitalism) but against a single employer.

This single partner with a voice decisive in all legal and economic matters disposed of a powerful and monopolistic, if clumsy, agro-business system. And yet it could not (and cannot, because this is current history) use methods familiar to the owner of serf-labour manors. He did not dispose of the field labour of farmers, it is true, because he needed it in rapidly developing industry. Also, the mechanization of agriculture in the twentieth century has changed the situation: in serf-labour times demesne farms depended heavily upon the quality and quantity of farmers' tools and draught animals.

And yet the state faced problems very similar to those the early modern Polish landowner had to solve. The uneasy living together of large state-owned and subdivided private farms was in many respects analogous to conditions made familiar to English-speaking scholars by Witold Kula's *Economic Theory of Feudalism*.[15]

First, the state strives to take over the largest possible part of agrarian produce. During the six-year plan (1951–6), alongside buying up of grain, it introduced compulsory deliveries. In 1953 they reached (according to Anderzej Jezierski) 85 per cent of peasants' 'marketable' grain (total produce less seed and household consumption), 51 per cent of potatoes, and 50 per cent of pigs or cattle.[16] Although some of these figures seem lower than in the eighteenth or early nineteenth centuries, strict comparisons would not make sense here.[17] On the other hand, the structural analogy between compulsory deliveries and feudal rent in kind are clear. In this connection one may recognize the gradual evolution of the purchase system by the state as one more commutation of the rent in kind: in 1955 compulsory deliveries made up 70 per cent of grains taken and bought by the state from peasants; in 1970 only 27 per cent. For potatoes, corresponding figures were 84 and 38.[18] After obligatory deliveries had been abolished in 1971, the problem of rents was reduced to that of the differences between the prices paid by market customers and those fixed by the state.

Secondly, both critics of the system and the 'establishment' of the post-Gierek era fluently condemn the wastefulness of that system, and the sorry, miserable results of costly investments in state-owned farms. Once more the student of contemporary Polish agrarian policy should be reminded of its ages-old antecedents. This policy is hardly irrational, or rather it has its particular social rationale. The absurdly inflated apparatus of agro-business and easily tolerated corruption may be interpreted as manifestations of the helplessness and low efficiency of the economic system. However, they are successful as a means of passing the heavy costs of maintenance of thousands of local state servants onto the shoulders of both producers and consumers. Exactly the same has been said about the monumental administrative systems of early modern large estates. And yet both systems were 'rational' only when they remained closed to themselves. Once exposed to competition with their more efficient rivals, they could hardly evade exposure of their fallacies.

The third analogy is more of a societal than an economic nature. Notwithstanding their motivation and official rationale, until recent years (the late 1970s) there remained multiple forms of debasement of the social position of the peasantry. Together with private craftsmen and shopkeepers, private farmers were deprived of a free health service, and of a social security system equal to that of state-employed people;[19] in 1976 they were not granted rations of sugar equal to allocations for the rest of the population. In the early fifties private village industries had been wiped out thoroughly and state-owned plants or state-controlled co-operatives were never able to fill that gap. There is more than a shadow of analogy between that decision and the liquidation of tenants' mills, village ironworks and independent shops in the late sixteenth/early seventeenth centuries.[20] The landlord strove at monopoly of grain turnover and was taking over the lucrative sector of village industry. In both cases there was a tremendous waste of the means of production. In the twentieth century this has led to grave market shortages and in recent times even to ecological problems.[21]

Long after the ruling Polish United Workers' Party renounced mass collectivization, the administration and particularly the local administration, remained reluctant to strengthen the farmers' rights to their soil. This has been proven in 1979 by Waldemar Kuczyński,[22] and strongly confirmed in 1980–1 by the dramatic struggle of small farmers for plots that had been taken away from them.

Whereas in the seventeenth or eighteenth century the landlord had good reasons to subordinate tenant farming to his own demesne farming because it made him the owner of almost the whole product of his estate, a roughly similar tendency on the part of the state was obviously fallacious. Without much success, it was strongly countered from several quarters as being contradictory to national interests. In both spheres – of agrarian policy and of social privilege – one may trace analogies to feudal, or rather pre-capitalist, relationships. In both, that relapse borders upon the ludicrous because principles of socialism have been accepted by the nation and expectations of welfare still run high.

One more analogy with the pre-industrial, pre-capitalist economy can be drawn in respect of the money economy. Both the, say, seventeenth and the later twentieth century deviate from the yardstick of 'free-market economics'. And both deviate in the same direction. In pre-partition Poland money was operational in regulating the contacts of the landed estate with its outer world; it secured to the landlord the means of paying for conspicuous (mostly imported) luxury goods and it was necessary for pursuing his political goals. Inside the estate, marked prices hardly served for measuring the value of goods that were not for sale.[23] Kula has exposed the sophisticated and/or brutal means used by estate administration against any contacts by tenants with markets and customers outside the estate's borders. Some scholars are prone to call that a particular deviation of mercantilism, in the service of the sovereign landlord.

Now, until 1980, by interpreting the official propaganda one might argue that the state commercial policy was based on principles of mercantilism: the development of exports and production for exports, imports limited to vital necessities plus goods and machines, stimulating the national economy and its foreign trade potential, reasons of state being the guiding principle.[24] Revelations of the 1980s totally destroyed this image. In many respects a close comparison of foreign trade priorities in different ages simply makes no sense. However, if one employs the Marxist criterion of class interest, in both cases one can easily trace important common features: foreign trade strategy directly serves the ruling group. In the seventeenth century, against the protests of economic thinkers, along with a monumental monetary crisis and the petering out of foreign demand for Polish grain, imports of silks, woollens, spices and other luxuries were increasing. After the dramas of December 1970 – shipyard workers' protests, the Gdansk-Gdynia massacre and the fall of Mr Gomulka – the import policy was much more sophisticated and complex. However, there is no doubt that individual decisions, the location of new enterprises, the selection of contracting parties, and the choice of goods for import were to a large extent determined by subjective – in contradistinction to the public – interests. On the other hand, it is easy to be carried away by colourful anecdotes.

In order to avoid that danger, let us keep to facts and administrative decrees. A good key to understanding how the group privileges of the 1970s worked is ruling 58 of 11 July 1975 of the minister of foreign trade and maritime economy[25] 'concerning the release from customs inspection of goods carried by some persons crossing the state frontier': 25 categories of state and party dignitaries *and members of their families* were exempted. A close examination of their list (still secret) may lead to better understanding of the composition of power elites. The historian is struck by the similarity of that charter to clauses of the Statute of Piotrkow (1496), that exempted the nobility from export duties on their own needs. It has already been stressed that such a privilege was vitally important only for the upper stratum of that order.

In the same article in *Zycie Warszawy* several other privileges are enumerated, such as a 'right' to unrepayable loans of up to 500,000 zloty, the opportunity to buy foreign currencies at beneficial rates, free redecoration and refurbishing of homes. Popular wisdom easily throws in further benefits: special shops, coupons for sought-after goods, and so on. The fantasy of the people can hardly compete with the vivid imagination of the administration.

Popular consciousness does not endorse such practices. This is the key to analogies and differences between the periods compared. What in the *ancien régime* issued from the very essence of the society of orders in its particular Polish form, is perceived today as a manifestation of corruption, as a caricature, or both. This is due to the short constitutional experience of the inter-war period, to a prevailing myth of the nature of Western societies, and also to a true (if rarely conscious) acceptance of general principles of socialism. It is in this light that the gap between theory and reality becomes so dramatic.

The Polish public cannot compare these facts with manifestations of power abuse abroad. One knows little about the Mafia, Camorra and the abuse of political power in the Mezzogiorno; here and there some arguments, which in feudal conditions were normal or acceptable, in certain conditions rouse popular indignation. This is particularly true of political patronage and judicial immunity.

Ruling 58 was one such privilege of immunity granted to the whole Estate (family members included!). Unlike the old Polish nobility, strictly hereditary and formally closed, the privileged group of today reminds one rather of a *Beamtenadel* of absolute monarchies. This corresponds well with the strong centralizing tendencies of the People's Republic. There are numerous proofs of individual immunities as well: public prosecutors overlook some misdemeanours, malfeasances and felonies, and many similar things have been said and written recently about judges. This makes a particularly stark contrast with the value of quotas of fines that the ministry of justice was imposing upon particular Courts of Justice; justices were appreciated according to their financial achievement ... [26]This was roughly similar to the practice of manorial courts which treated fines as a form of feudal rent. The ruling group did not forget to secure some privileged rights to acquire land in the form of secret but ruthlessly enforced reservation of purchase rights on most sought-after residential quarters and resorts. Virtually nothing has been disclosed about tax immunities.

Political patronage needs much serious research hitherto impossible to pursue. In the Florence of the *Duecento*, in sixteenth-century Scotland, in Lithuania two centuries later, clientage constituted the cornerstone of the political systems. It was petering out where absolutist institutions developed or parliamentary democracy was established. Wherever either royal power or societal control weakened, the field of activity was open for clientage, for cliques and various other informal hierarchical groups. They find the best soil where public substance can be exploited. A biographer of Mayor Richard Daley of Chicago has shown how the Democratic 'machine' dominated and exploited the municipal administration.[27] Contributions to the 'machine' were rewarded by municipal jobs or commissions. This remote case shows that the exploitation of public resources and opportunities by political groupings are widespread and characteristic of various systems. So far as the two ages of Poland's society and state are concerned we come back to the comparison of the archetype and its caricature. The nobility was well aware that theirs was the state, and that they were the state. A much more narrow group, later called the magnates, divided up a large share of state property (income from Royal Domains first of all) and did it according to law. After 1945, the economic activity of the state increased the sphere open for corruption and in the past decade exploited it out of all proportion.

These recurrences of and relapses into the past in the domain of power, find their counterpart in the reactions of the people. Readers of the press in Poland in 1981, already familiar with information about Latin American peons or Portuguese small farmers struggling for land, were astonished to find scanty but strange news about private farmers in Poland seizing pieces of land belonging to state farms. After the first wave of strictly censored information in the mass media, some newspapers reported that local authorities 'have been obliged to reconsider all applications of private farmers concerning restitution of [their] land that had been seized illegally or with glaring injustice...'[28] Another newspaper reported the land hunger of small farmers from Swiebodzin, bordering upon a state farm extensively cultivated on about 24,000 hectares. The conflict was described in a form well known to the student of early modern agrarian history.

These analogies with a remote past – and are they only superficial? – are leading to situations in which the public interest is identifiable with that of the farmer and antithetical to that of the power elite. The earliest and the loudest manifestation, the *cause célèbre* of agrarian conflicts, took place in the autumn of 1980 in the south-east corner of the country in the Bieszczady Mountains. A peculiar sit-in strike of farmers protested against a large *chasse gardée* for VIPs laid out some time before, and protected by severe game laws. 'The Ustrzyki strike is known all over the world,' wrote a poet-protester in January 1981, 'The brave people of Bieszczady shall sweep away all the filth and dirt.' Its author, a former machinist and party instructor, was fired from his job in a state farm (which was in 1980 over £500,000 in the red), and became a prominent member of the solidarity of private farmers'. Ghosts of the Sheriff of Nottingham and King John, and the spirit of Robin Hood, were hovering over Bieszczady Forest, in AD 1981.

Awareness of a particular moral–political insanity is widespread, if one may conclude from letters to editors of the more open and outspoken newspapers and journals: 'A cynical interest group, appearing as Pomet [an enterprise] is building its settlement of "second homes" (so called *dachas*) in the Wielkopolska National Park, against the law and two decisions of the Ministry... It appears that these gentlemen, who may be compared to ancient *feudal nobility* hold cheap the restoration', wrote an outraged reader in September 1981.[29]

Does that mean that feudalism ought to be overthrown once more, after the blows dealt to it by the nineteenth-century emanicipation and reform legislation of the independent Republic, and the *coup de grâce* of the land reform of 1944–5? There is something in that, but by no means everything. If one accuses the participants in power and privilege of feudalism, it is nothing but an inversion of an interpretation much liked by the 'establishment' itself. 'Every society has an explanation for evil. In the West it is largely a religious one. In the Communist societies the official explanation is largely a secular one: "remnants" of influence from the prior social order or "class enemies" are blamed for anything that goes wrong.'[30] In Poland there is an intellectual tendency to trace some features of the 'national character' from early modern traditions of nobility.[31]

Corruption and abuse of power are as good a subject of study as any other and ought to be explored thoroughly as a basic and an applied practical problem. One should not confine oneself to them alone, just as one cannot explain the nature of the British state and society (or can one?) from the fact that there even a princess pays for her own tickets for public entertainment.

'At the root of all the evil in our economy are market shortages,' wrote a columnist in October 1980.[32] This was an overstatement of a truth, as always when one uses the emphatic words: everything, always. He was right that such shortages 'undermine public morals'. I have tried to show how the 'morality of market gaps' does not only open the way for mass misdemeanours. However, it would be a mistake to examine these problems only as economic evils; all these anachronisms, manifestations of a 'renewal', or remnants of feudalism are closely connected with the structure of power.

'*Polonia hodie iacet et laborat*', wrote Philipp Oldenburger in 1675, 'Which Esculap will step forward who may find a medicine for this malady?'[33] One hopes he will be a family doctor.

NOTES

1 Cf. J. Fedorowicz *et al.* (ed.), *The History of Poland until 1863* (Cambridge, forthcoming).
2 T. Manteuffel, 'Problem feudalizmu polskiego' (The Problem of Polish Feudalism), *Przeglad Historyczny* 37 (1948), pp. 62ff.
3 P. Anderson, *Lineages of the Absolutist State* (London 1975), p. 298.
4 G. Schramm, 'Adel und Staat. Ein Vergleich zwischen Brandenburg und Polen-Litauen im 17 Jahrhundert', paper presented at conference of West German and Polish historians in Toruń, April 1981 (in press).
5 A. Maczak, 'Money and Society in Poland and Lithuania in the Sixteenth and Seventeenth Centuries', *J. European Econ. Hist.* 5, 1 (1976), pp. 77ff.
6 E. Opaliński, *Elita władzy w województwach poznańskim i kaliskim za Zygmunta III*

(The Governing Elite in the Poznan and Kalisz Voivodship under Zygmunt III) (Poznań 1981), chap. 1.

7 A. Mączak, 'Zur Grundeigentumsstruktur in Polen im 16 bis 18 Jahrhundert', *Jahrbuch für Wirtschaftsgeschichte* (1967).

8 Manteuffel, 'Problem feudalizmu polskiego', p. 62.

9 U. Augustyniak, *Informacja i propaganda w Polsce za Zygmunta III* (Information & Propaganda in Poland under Zygmunt III) (Warsaw 1981), *passim.*

10 There were also more or less radical, or populist, anti-myths, particularly popular with partisans of peasant political groups. An early protest song from the 1830s ('Hail, lords and magnates') became a sort of anthem of the peasant movement until very recently. One stanza ran as follows:
The landlord class is like an old harlot
Who has lost all her charms...
We won't be allured by the grace of that old hag.

11 J. Blum, *The End of the Old Order in Rural Europe* (Princeton 1978), and my comments concerning his treatment of Poland in *J. European Econ. Hist.* 8, 3 (1979), pp. 777–81.

12 Cf. essays by Professor Janusz Tazbir, in particular 'Pochwa "nieudacznika" i nagana kariery w literaturze polskiej' (Praise of the Unsuccessful and the Rebuke of Success in Polish Literature), *Spotkania z Historia* (Warsaw 1979), pp. 239–52; this essay has unleashed an interesting and fruitful literary discussion in *Kultura.*

13 *Mały rocznik statystyczny, 1937*, p. 66; for Kalecki and Landau's calculations see p. 60 and bibliography in footnote.

14 *Mały rocznik statystyczny, 1937*, p. 64; *idem., 1958*, p. 110; *idem., 1981*, p. 157.

15 W. Kula, *An Economic Theory of Feudalism* (London 1976).

16 A. Jezierski, *Historia gospodarcza Polski Ludowej 1944–1968* (Warsaw 1971), p. 198.

17 The best recent monograph on the servile farm in early nineteenth-century Poland is that of J. Kochanowicz, *Pańszczyźniane gospodarstwo chłopskie w Królestwie Polskim w I połowie XIX w* (The Servile Peasant Holding in the Kingdom of Poland in the First Half of the Nineteenth Century) (Warsaw 1981).

18 *Mały rocznik statystyczny, 1971*, p. 182.

19 On the other hand, in the late 1970s farmers became heavily assessed for compulsory social security charges without adequate benefits. This led to general dissatisfaction and local farmers' protests.

20 Cf. B. Zientara, *Dzieje małopolskiego hutnictwa zelaznego. XIV-XVII wiek* (The History of Iron founding in Malopolska in the 14th–17th Centuries) (Warsaw 1954), pp. 190ff.

21 On the grain trade in early modern times, see Kula, *An Economic Theory.* After 1945 the destruction of village mills based on water power and using small dams probably contributed to the inadequacy of the water supply in the Polish countryside. Shortage of water – dry household wells – is very common and has become one of the principal problems of Polish agriculture and cattle breeding. It is being increased by some recent ill-considered industrial projects, chiefly strip mines.

22 W. Kuczyński, *Po wielkim skoku* (After the Great Shock) (Warsaw 1979). In 1981 this book was reprinted by an official publishing house in Poland.

23 Kula, *An Economic Theory*; A. Maczak, 'Preise, Löhne und Lebenshaltungskosten im Europa des 16 Jahrhunderts', *Wirtschaftliche und soziale Strukturen im saekularen*

Wandel. Festschrift für Wilhelm Abel zum 70 Geburtstag, Vol. II. (Hanover 1974), pp. 322–6; see p. 326 for a comparison of regional salaries in the twentieth and sixteenth centuries. The late Professor Jan Rutkowski made a penetrating analysis of these questions in his unfinished work, *Badania nad podziałem dochodów w Polsce w czasach nowożytnych*, Vol. I (Research on the Division of Incomes in Poland in Recent Times), (Krakow 1938).

24 For a different approach to contemporary 'mercantilisms' see I. Wallerstein, 'Socialist States: Mercantilist Strategies and Revolutionary Objectives', paper presented to 5th Annual Conference on Political Economy of the World-System, Madison, Wisc., May 14–16, 1981.

25 *Zycie Warszawy*, 31 October–1 November 1981. Article by W. Markiewicz, 'The Equal and the More Equal. Ruling No. 58'.

26 *Polityka*, No. 22 (30 May 1981). Article by S. Sołtysiński, 'The Court of Justice is a Business'.

27 M. Royko, *Boss. Richard J. Daley of Chicago* (New York 1971).

28 *Zycie Warszawy*, 7 September 1981; *Dziennik Ludowy*, 8 September 1981.

29 *Kultura* (13 September 1981), letter to the editor. 'Restoration' (*odnowa* literally, renewal) is a key word in contemporary Polish political parlance; it means the return to the proper 'Leninist principles' in state and party politics on the one hand, and the (equally vague) rule of justice, democracy, and common sense in economic leadership on the other. Some journalists, tired of that much-repeated word, asked; 'Did what is about to be restored ever exist?'

30 Ross Terrill, 'Gang of Four in Satan's Role', *International Herald Tribune* (2 October 1980).

31 J. Tazbir in *Kultura* (16 August 1981).

32 *Sztandar Młodych* (2 October 1980).

33 P.A. Oldenburger, *Thesauri rerum publicarum pars secunda* (Geneva 1675), p. 73.

X

Executio Bonorum and *Reduktion*: Two Essays in Solutions of the Domain-State Dilemma

Two notions mentioned in the title of this paper should be explained: *executio bonorum* and the "dilemma." Invited to describe the Polish view of the history of the Riksdag to my distinguished colleagues, I have chosen to examine rare traces of factors of great importance to both countries, otherwise so different from one another in their social and constitutional traditions.

A dilemma common to both countries and, for that matter, to most European states became painfully apparent in the 16th century: how to adapt to fast-rising demands for defence and/or expansion while their mediaeval fiscal systems were still based, in principle, on revenue in kind. In most instances, the dilemma was transformed into the question of how to convert that revenue into cash and how to use the royal (state) domain as security for credit and for the political loyalty of the society's top stratum without losing that domain altogether.

The political struggle for and against the *reduktion* became one of the leading motives of Swedish seventeenth century history and was preceded by and for some time ran parallel to the continuing distribution of revenue from the domain. This can be regarded as a major social and political issue, i.e. social distribution of landed property and, for that matter, of power. I do not intend to dwell upon the question of *reduktion eller kontribution* in Sweden, to use the terms coined so aptly by Prof. Sven A. Nilsson. What I shall try to do is explain how a similar dilemma was resolved in the Commonwealth of Poland-Lithuania or, more accurately, the reasons why it remained unresolved. The most appropriate term depends on the perspective preferred.

In Poland, this issue is known as the parliamentary struggle for the *executio bonorum*, i.e. implementation of the statute in which King Alexander in 1504 promised in his own name and the name of his successors not to alienate any more of the royal domain and to restore goods already alienated.[1]

---

[1] The literature on the subject is monumental. However, citing it would be irrelevant in this brief, comparative essay, so I shall limit myself to the most recent publications in symposium languages. Cf. J. K. Fedorowicz et al. (eds.): *Republic of Nobles. Studies in Polish History to 1864* (Cambridge, 1982), pp. 99, 109, 119.

The movement began gaining momentum in the Chamber of Deputies from around the middle of the 16th century and reached its critical stage in *sejm* (i.e. parliament) sessions in 1562/63 and 1564.

The general historical matrix was similar in both countries in question and in most European states at that time.

Firstly, the early modern state needed a more efficient fiscal system than the existing one. It is enough to mention the progress of expensive military technology, firearms, ordnance, fortifications, increasing numbers of mercenaries and, to a lesser degree, the navy.

Secondly, the expensive development of central and local administration, as well as of Renaissance royal courts, should also be mentioned.

Thirdly, a money economy spread—albeit unevenly—throughout Europe, and emerging state machineries with their taxation systems and growing needs, stimulated that development.

Fourthly, all these developments reflected and made possible a major shift in social forces, i.e. the growth of an urban merchant class (cooperating with the State and supplying it with credit and financial know-how), and even of new land-owning aristocracies (partly of ancient origin, partly upstart families) which now began to join forces; they were primarily interested in exploiting State resources somehow.

I take the liberty of putting the problem in a "nutshell" and treating it rather brutally, disregarding for the moment its legal aspects and even fruitful discussion of the nature of the Renaissance state. The nature of sociopolitical conflicts can be explained as something of a struggle for ownership of the state. The social group which availed itself of state resources could well have been regarded as their owner. Frederick C. Lane has shown the merit of interpreting power, the early state machinery in particular, as a protection-selling enterprise.[2]

Political domination was revealed primarily, although exclusively, in the securing for private use of large shares of state revenues or even of state property. Corporations and groups, i.e. members of the *corpus politicum*, can be defined by the nature and size of the profits they derived from power. However, members of the ruling class could choose among alternative solutions: either to corner their own share of the state and privatize it, so to speak, or to strengthen the existing system of authority, thereby indirectly increasing their own wealth and power by loyally serving the state, the central power. In practice, several factors interfered, such as conflicts among factions of the nobility and clashes of regional interests. But whatever the intention of the nobility's upper stratum, the king and fisc had their own urgent necessities which usually made fast,

[2] F. C. Lane's ideas have been collected in *Profits from Power. Readings in Protection Rent* and *Violence-Controlling Enterprises* (Albany, 1979). Also see N. Steensgaard: "Violence and the Rise of Capitalism: Frederic C. Lane's Theory of Protection and Tribute," *Review*, V, 1, 1981. I attempted to apply the concept to the European 16th and 17th centuries in *Governments and the Governed in Pre-industrial Europe* (soon available in, Wheatsheaf Press, Brighton, Sussex.)

"rough-and-tumble" solutions necessary. However, this only represented a continuation of a trend visible since the reign of Wladyslaw Jagiello (1386–1434), founder and eponym of the dynasty. He tried to secure the succession by massive grants of estates to his powerful subjects, as well as by granting privileges to the Noble Estate as a whole.[3] This forced generosity was very difficult to reverse.

* * *

In the Nordic countries, the Polish parliament had a very poor reputation, and with good reason too. "Poland," wrote Michael Roberts, "was an emotive word," used by discussants in the mid-seventeenth century *riks-råd*. Chancellor Axel Oxenstierna, urging stricter observance of the rules of order in the *Riddarhus*, said:[4]

> "...and not do so as is done in Poland... where when they hold a Diet, one says 'write this,' and another gets up and says 'write that,' and so one after another until at last somebody says 'tear the whole thing up,' and they depart no better than they came..."

Oxenstierna, I believe, repeated the opinion and used the information he had obtained from his former political client, a patrician from Marienburg, Johannes Pfennig, *port parole* of the urban opposition in Royal Prussia. This opposition had been longing for a return of the Royal Prussian regional autonomy which had been abolished in 1569.[5] After 1642, when the chancellor related that horror story to Swedish nobles in the *Riddarhus*, the situation in Poland grew even worse. In 1652, the principle of *liberum veto* was accepted in practice, thereby establishing a portentous precedent.[6]

However, under the last two monarchs of the Jagiellonian dynasty, Sigismund the Old (1532–1548) and Sigismund Augustus (1548–1572), the system worked quite well.[7] Numerous parallels can be drawn with the parliament at Westminster,[8] and most Polish historians agree with Konstanty Grzybowski who dedicated his book *In memoriam Sacrae Regiae*

---

[3] See H. Samsonowicz, "Polish Politics and Society under the Jagiellonian monarchy," in J. K. Fedorowicz (ed.), *A Republic of Nobles*, op. cit.

[4] *Sveriges Riddarskaps och Adels Riksdags-Protokoll*, I series (Stockholm 1855–), vol. III, p. 211; quoted by M. Roberts, "On Aristocratic Constitutionalism im Swedish History, 1520–1720" (1965), reprinted in his *Essays in Swedish History* (London, 1067), p. 48.

[5] The letters of Johannes Pfennig, including a pamphlet on Polish political practices, addressed to Chancellor Oxenstierna during the latter's sojourn in Elbing, have been preserved in the *Riksarkiv, Enskilda Arkiv* IX.

[6] W. Konopczyński: *Liberum veto*, (Cracow, 1918).

[7] See A. Wyczański's paper "The Problem of Authority in Sixteenth Century Poland: An Essay in Reinterpretation" in J. K. Fedorowicz (ed.), *A Republic of Nobles*, op. cit. My own contribution to the same collection of essays is more critical of what may be *sensu largo* called the "structure of politics;" also see A. Mączak, "The Conclusive Years: The End of the Sixteenth Century as the Turning Point of Polish History" in E. I. Kouri & T. Scott (eds.), *Politics and Society in Reformation Europe. Essays for Sir Geoffrey Elton on his Sixty-fifth Birthday* (London, 1987).

[8] This point was stressed by K. Grzybowski, *Teoria reprezentacji w Polsce w epoce Odrodzenia* (Theory of Representation in Poland in the Renaissance), (Warsaw, 1959).

Maiestatis Sigismundi Augusti and strongly stressed Sigismund Augustus' role as a King-in-Parliament.[9]

After the last decade of the 15th century, the *sejm* functioned as a bicameral parliament. The Senate evolved from the royal council and seated all archbishops and bishops, palatines, castellans and, last but not least, even ministers, all of whom appointed for life or until a further promotion. With the exception of lesser castellans, they constituted the kingdom's political elite. Until 1569, the *sejm* only represented Poland; a similar institution in the Grand Duchy of Lithuania was in its infancy. True Lithuanian parliamentarism was only to develop after the last union with Poland (1569). Ministers were thenceforth appointed separately for the two parts of the Commonwealth, but there was only a single, bicameral *sejm*.

Around the middle of the 16th century, the *executio bonorum regalium* was an important internal issue in Poland; it was not extended to Lithuania.[10] The magnitude of the problem can be presented in quantitative terms by calculating the relative size of the royal domain, as it was immediately after the mid-sixteenth century. Its area was estimated at about 30% (the rest belonged to the Roman Catholic Church and to the nobles).[11] It was distributed unequally: about 13% in Masovia and a little more in Greater Poland, 1/3 of the area of Little Poland and Ruthenia-Podolia in the southeast, half of Podlasie and about 60% of Royal Prussia.[12]

Agrarian settlements in Poland differed greatly from the Swedish pattern. Property units consisted of "villages" and "manorial farms" (Polish: *folwark* from the German *Vorwerk*; Latin *praedium*) whose servile labour was supplied by villagers. Royal estates were sometimes distributed in small units comprising single manorial farms but were mainly large "estate" units with from a few to a score or more villages in each. A royal estate (Polish: *królewszczyzna*) was regarded as *panis bene merentium*, some of them as endowments for particular offices. The so-called *starostwa grodowe* (*capitaneatus castrenses*) supported the *starostowie* (Latin: *capitanei*, German: *Amtsleute*) or royal lieutenants who were responsible for enforcing law and order and prosecuting violent crimes.

Jagiello's successors used to mortgage parts of the domain to their creditors, often unpaid military entrepreneurs. This proved to be rather unfortunate for the fisc. Creditors were entitled to deduct their dues from

---

[9] Grzybowski, *Teoria*, op. cit., pp. 141–217.

[10] The statute of 1504 (and Polish legislation in general) did not restrict the actions of the Jagiellons in their position as Grand Dukes of Lithuania where their power was absolute. After the 1569 Union of Lublin, that statute did not apply to Lithuania but was imposed on Royal Prussia which was then recognized as a part of the *Corona* (i.e. Poland) and on parts of the Grand Duchy transferred by its ruler to the *Corona* just before the union was effected in 1569.

[11] The landed estates of the Orthodox Church in the Ruthenian, eastern parts of the *Corona* were negligible; three cities in Royal Prussia, i.e. Gdansk/Danzig, Torun/Thorn and Elbląg/Elbing, had been granted extensive estates in recognition of their involvement and expenses in the war with the Teutonic Order (1454–66).

[12] Based on calculations by J. Luciński, *Rozwój królewszczyzn w Koronie. Od schyłku XIV wieku do XVII wieku* (Poznań, 1970) and A. Sucheni-Grabowska, "Krolewszczyzny" in *Encyklopedia historii gospodarczej Polski do 1945 roku*, (Warsaw, 1981), I, pp. 389–391.

running profits, but there was no system for auditing accounts. The only way to recover an estate under Treasury control was to repay the entire debit. And this was hardly possible in the 16th century.

Students of Swedish history will clearly see traces of parallel developments. The rough Polish equivalent of Magnus Eriksson's Land Law (about 1350) in Sweden was the essays of King Wladislaw I (1305–1333) and his son Casimir (1333–1370) who, after reconstruction of the monarchy, slowly began recovery of the royal estates. Their administration was then closely linked to territorial administration in general, a rather familiar trend in many European states, including the Duchy of Prussia and Denmark. At that time, kings were also able to increase their domains through seizure of landed property. However, this unleashed the fury of the nobles and led to a local covenant in Greater Poland and eventually, in the mid-fifteenth century, a statute which made illegal any seizure imposed without a decree from an appropriate court.

The support of the nobles for a programme of strong administration of the domain began early. In 1440, any appropriation and mortgaging of the domain in the core area of the kingdom (around Cracow) was declared illegal. This was followed by similar acts concerning the *capitaneatus castrenses* (in 1478). Finally, the statute of King Alexander (1504) was enacted; it covered all the royal estates, with the exception of some special cases which were subject to approval by the *sejm*.

In both Sweden and Poland, a kind of political dissociation can be discerned. On the one hand, the kings enjoyed being buttressed by a law prohibiting dissolution of their principal financial resources. On the other hand, they needed a certain amount of elbow room and simply could not do without it. The difference between the situation in these two countries was that the domain issue was an early bone of contention between the upper and the lesser nobility (or the gentry) in Poland. Around the middle of the 16th century, leaders of the lesser nobility became a determined political group, or at least a majority of the county diets were inclined to follow a group of able, "grass roots" politicians opposed to the Senate.

To make a long story short, I conclude that while the great lords profited from the administration, renting and alienation of the royal domain equivalent to the Swedish *förläningar*, the *populus nobilium*, i.e. the gentry, indirectly bore the brunt of all the costs of that activity in the form of taxes. It is true that fifteenth century noble landowners[13] enjoyed greater freedom from taxation than at any time before because their home farms (demesnes),[14] virtually tax-free since 1374, increased at the expense of their peasants' farms. However, heavy taxation would seriously limit their ability to exploit their serfs. The alternatives, i.e. *reduktion eller kontribution*, were deeply rooted in their minds.

---

[13] Feudal property only played a secondary role in Poland; the property of noblemen was usually allodial.
[14] Each medium-sized and large estates usually comprised several desmene farms tilled by servile labour and landless labourers.

The 1504 statute was sandwiched between two other fundamental Acts. The 1501 statute (the Mielnik Charter) was a great success for the Senate which was given the dominant role in the power system. However, this charter was formally abolished by an act of parliament later called the *Nihil novi* (1501). Until the late 1540's, the kings relied mainly on the Senate. King Sigismund's domain policy was internally divided. He did succeed in recovering about 90 towns and almost 800 villages; some debts were cancelled because the creditors had obviously received what was due to them. The Treasurer (Latin: *succamerarius*) was responsible for auditing estate accounts.[15] The incorporation of extinguished fiefs in Masovia (finally in 1526) added about 35 towns and 250 villages. A parallel effort by Queen Bona Sforza led to a build-up of her private domain (15 towns and 160 villages) from 1530–1547 which, after her death in Italy (1557), were incorporated into the royal domain.

This trend came to an abrupt halt after Sigismund Augustus came to power. Along with the successors of Gustavus I in Sweden, the Polish king was involved in costly foreign policy ventures which, incidentally, rather contradicted one another.

Lithuania did not make any massive contributions to the exchequer (in fact, there was no joint exchequer); in many respects it actually threatened to become something of a political and fiscal liability. The circumstance that the king tried to appease the magnates in both his countries is important to my argument. He needed them for his personal plans (his love affair and politically questionable marriage with Barbara Radziwill), as well as for his great political dream: the true union of Poland and Lithuania.

The distribution of royal estates seemed to be a temporary solution to both his financial and political problems. But it was not.

Unlike Gustavus Vasa at Västerås in 1527, neither Sigismund the Old nor his son, Augustus, considered confiscation of Church estates possible even if Augustus was inclined at one point to create a national church and would probably have found it easy to obtain the support of the Archbishop of Gniezno, Jacob Uchański. Incidentally, secularization was never seriously considered by Polish Protestants.[16] It is all the more amazing that wild rumours circulated about the size of ecclesiastical prop-

---

[15] A. Sucheni-Grabowska, *Odbudowa domeny Królewskiej w Polsce, 1504–1548*, (Wroclaw, 1967).

[16] Royal Prussia was a kind of exception. In 1540, the Prussian Council (the upper chamber of the provincial Diet, *Ständetag*) proposed that part of the income from three monasteries, i.e. Oliwa/Oliva, Pelplin and Kartuzy/Karthausen, be transferred to the schools in Elblag/Elbing and Chelmno/Culm. The argument was that only a few monks lived there. King Sigismund agreed to the proposal two years later. See *Urkundenbuch des Bistums Culm*, Nos. 957 and 959. In 1561, Sigismund Augustus mortgaged the holdings of two monasteries and two convents to the city of Gdansk for one hundred thousand thalers. A Mączak in G. Labuda (ed.), *Historia Pomorza*, II, 1 (Poznań, 1976), pp. 405–425.

Protestant cities in Royal Prussia seized the property of some dissolved monasteries and convents. This was an exception, however, and does not change any conclusion about the attitudes of the Protestant nobles. Incidentally, religious issues did not create deep divisions among the Prussian nobility. The Diet (*Ständetag*) was rather concerned about the fate of noble spinsters who were previously placed in convents.

erty holdings. Over a score of scribbled notes preserved in family records repeat terrible news about the allegedly dominant percentage of Church-owned villages. Some of these notes even multiplied the number of villages by an average number of tenants and their taxation. The results allegedly equalled the solution of all financial problems of the realm—if clerics would only start paying taxes properly.

In 1598, an anonymous and well-informed English observer repeated (with some changes) that information, only following the lead of the papal nuncio Girolamo Lippomano.[17] Not unexpectedly, however, the latter cited a different balance: 140,000 villages in the hands of the "nobility" (the royal domain was obviously included in this figure) as opposed to "only" 76,000 ecclesiastical villages plus 560 other villages exempted from military service.[18]

About 1550, the tide of parliamentary politics turned against the holders of royal estates. From 1550 to 1558/59, a kind of political party evolved in the Chamber of Deputies. The "structure of politics" at that time was still rather unclear. In particular, we only know very little about the attitudes of the provincial nobility. Participants in some county diets were still dependent upon or bullied by local magnates. Consequently, they felt safer at *sejm* sessions. The "executionist" movement could not be called a faction, as it had no single, powerful leader. Instead, numerous, skilled, outspoken, well-educated and politically independent (primarily Calvinist) noblemen with great authority were among their brethren.

During the crucial sessions of 1562–1563, they won the support of the entire Chamber.[19] Their watchword, "executio iurium," comprised a long list of demands based on the principle that the king was subordinate to the law. But even if the Noble Estate had constrained the royal prerogative on that basis in the fifteenth century, the same constitutional principle helped the gentry fight the predominance of the magnates. In 1562, the Chamber finally won the support of the king himself.

"Domesday" for the owners of royal estates (as a diarist of the *sejm* session called it) occurred in 1563. Summoned in 1550 for scrutiny of all the deeds they held, the leaseholders had scarcely reacted. Now, however, senators preferred not waiting until compelled and brought their leasehold documents to the king. The *executio iurium* programme as a whole was accepted by the king, and he was granted the taxes he so desperately

---

[17] This is a most interesting and puzzling phenomenon of statistical awareness and, I believe, of skillful propaganda. It merits more detailed analysis. Most of the known copies appear to have been preserved in Royal Prussia. At that time, it was a largely Protestant country. Cf. A Mączak, "El poder y la distribución de la renta social," *Estudios d'História Economica*, 1987, No. 1, pp. 51–53. The English report was edited by C. H. Talbot, *Relation of the State of Polonia and the United Provinces of that Crown, Anno 1598* (Rome, 1968), Elementa ad Fontium Editiones, XIII.

[18] Most estimates of ecclesiastical holdings characteristically contain the same three final digits: "560;" this points to some common source.

[19] I. Kaniewska: "Malopolska reprezentacja sejmowa za czasów Zygmunta Augusta (1548–1572)", *Zeszyty Naukowe Uniwersytetu Jagiellońskiego*, No. 351, 1974: A. Sucheni-Grabowska, "Walka o demokrację szlachecką" in A. Wyczański (ed.), *Polska w epoce odrodzenia* (2nd ed., Warsaw, 1986); J. Maciszewski: *Szlachta polska i jej państwo* (2nd ed., Warsaw, 1987.)

needed for financing the Livonian War. The profits from the domain leaseholds were to be allocated as follows:

- 25 % for the defence of the southwestern frontier (against Tartars and Moldavians);
- 55 % for the king's own treasury;
- 20 % for the leaseholders.[20]

These decisions by Sigismund Augustus were not extended to Lithuania where he, as Grand Duke, was a monocrat. In the heritage land of the Jagiellons, they were unable to gain the support of the lesser nobility. That numerous category only matured very slowly in political respects and did not acquire an independent identity until the late 18th century. Therefore, the high nobility (not necessarily the princes but major landowners in general) were the true beneficiaries of the Union which they had opposed so fiercely in the mid-sixteenth century.

* * *

The entire Polish programme of domain recovery in the 1560's was much harder to implement than the Swedish *reduktion* in the 1680's. These difficulties illuminate the entire Polish *Monarchia mixta* syndrome.[21] The process can be summed up in a few points:

(1) The Chanceries reviewed leasehold and ownership, titles; some titles were cancelled as illegal and therefore became invalid.

(2) Commissioners representing and appointed by the king, the Senate and the Chamber of Deputies were sent to survey the estates *in situ*, check the rights of the leaseholders and subjects (also of town dwellers), adjudicate disputed points and submit proposals for possible improvements.

(3) The *sejm* ruled on the rights of the king's leaseholders-creditors (and, to all practical purposes, the State's), the way the domain should be managed and regular surveys of the royal estates (every five years).

While the victory of the Chamber of Deputies, i.e. of the gentry, was total and complete for the time being, long-term results were not proportional to it.

What was won by the "executionists" and what was retained by the magnates? What happened to the king's revenues?

Ad (1). The job performed by royal secretaries and their staff was impressive enough, even if it was not comparable to the superb clerical work performed in 1680 and subsequently in Sweden. The reason for the

---

[20] In 1567 the last item was extended to 60 % at the expense of the first.
[21] In the 16th–17th centuries, this notion was widely used by Polish constitutional lawyers. Of course, it did not exactly correspond to the Swedish meaning of the term. The question was discussed at the Third Polish-American Conference of Historians in Poznan-Rydzyna in 1978 on the basis of a paper read by Prof. Jaroslaw Pelenski (University of Iowa). The transactions of that conference have yet to be published.

success was probably the genuine enthusiasm of the gentry as a whole and a feeling that serious steps had to be taken in respect to State finances. The fact that lesser royal officers originated from the same social class as the parliamentary "executionists" and that some Chamber of Deputies leaders had close family ties with powerful members of the Senate were characteristic features.[22]

The process of domain alienation was virtually stopped for good. A truly impressive number of settlements (towns and villages) were recovered and somehow incorporated into the domain. The domain amounted to

     36 towns and   382 villages in 1506;
    173 towns and 1,525 villages in 1548;
    197 towns and 1,957 villages in 1565; and
    300 towns and 3,650 villages in 1660.[23]

The question was how much net revenue did they supply to the king and the State?

Ad (2). In 1564 or 1565, the commissioners visited numerous estates and wrote protocols on their surveys which somehow survived the severe damage inflicted on Treasury records in 1944. Most commissioners proved to be highly inquisitive and made a great effort to obtain reasonable estimates of quota units for numerous items, e.g. area sown, grain yield, labour services, prices, employment etc. They checked innumerable documents, questioned tenants about past duties, customary laws etc.[24] Although they were landowners, not professional accountants, they had first-hand knowledge of husbandry. Their enthusiasm was short-lived, however. Nor did the king succeed in stirring the Deputies.

Ad (3). Sigismund Augustus found it necessary to compensate his recent beneficiaries for their losses, chiefly by granting them life-long leaseholds free or on very favourable terms. The old mortgages (dated before 1504) which did not conflict with the law (the so-called "old sums") were also treated very generously. Their possessors were granted full profits for four life-times.

The philosophy underlying that solution was interesting and merits comparison with the 1680 *reduktion* regulations. It was based on the

[22] A Sucheni-Grabowska, "Walka o demokrację szlachecką," *op. cit.*, p. 55f.

[23] In 1660, because of the incorporation of Wołhynia, Podolia and the Ukraine in 1569, these territories had 63 royal towns and about 700 villages. However, it should be remembered that the Southeast underwent dramatic changes: very dynamic growth until the mid-seventeenth century and the disastrous war of 1648. The figures quoted were calculated by A. Sucheni-Grabowska, "Królewszczyzny," *op. cit.*, p. 389.

[24] The late Prof. Jan Rutkowski made pioneering contributions to the analysis of the first survey (Polish: lustracja, rewizja) of the Polish royal estates. This was an introduction to a major synthesis of the distribution of income in the pre-industrial era. However, volume two was destroyed by the Nazis in Poznan during the 1939–1945 occupation. J. Rutkowski, *Badania nad podzialem dochodów w Polsce w czasach nowozytnych* (Cracow, 1938). Cf. even J. Topolski, "El problem del reparto de la renta nacional como medio de sintesis historica," *Estudios d'História Economica*, 1987, No. 1, pp. 107–114. Papers delivered at the International Colloquium on Income Distribution in Explaining History (Poznań, 1986), commemorating the centenary of Jan Rutkowski's birth, will be published in *Studia Historiae Oeconomicae*.

principle that the old leaseholds had not infringed the law, so leaseholders should not be financially penalized. The legislators accepted the strictly legal, not the fiscal, point of view, and it is interesting to note that both the king and the Chamber agreed on that point. While the Executionist leaders struggled rather radically against the alienation of royal estates, they were not greatly concerned about the Treasury's interests. In fact, even after a massive research effort, it would be difficult to arrive at a definitive answer as to whether a power struggle against the magnates or a strong and healthy financial system (based on revenue from the royal domain) was the chief goal of the gentry party. Both aims were probably equally important.

The rank-and-file esquire was probably more directly interested in easing the tax burden on his serfs. This was perceived as a zero-sum game between property tax, on the one hand, and the rent paid to the squire in money, in kind and, not the least, in labour, on the other hand. The tenant's economic potential was understood to be constant.[25] To the gentry it seemed normal and obvious that the king should cover all his and the Commonwealth's expenses from the revenue of the domain, customs duty and salt mines.[26]

It must also be admitted that the direct interests of various strata of the Noble Estates were not necessarily in conflict. The *capitaneus* administering a royal estate often employed deputies (*succapitanei*) and stewards of various kinds who more often than not were lesser, chiefly landless nobles themselves. In the mid-sixteenth century this phenomenon had not achieved full growth; it was also to expand widely in the decades to follow.

Much less attention has been paid to the second survey of the royal estates (1569/1570). It is clearly less reliable and either blindly repeated the 1565 figures or reduced the revenue, in most instances. No major disaster occurred between these dates, and the seventeenth century crisis had not yet been felt. I suspect that the Chamber lost a great deal of its energy. If developments are viewed in terms of *la longue durée*, this unique essay in landowner democracy will be seen to have failed even before the end of the century for a particular constellation of socio-economic and political reasons.

Not unlike the Swedish aristocracy after 1680, the Polish magnates were by no means destroyed or disarmed as a class.[27] The king, in fact no king,

---

[25] Cf. W. Kula, *Theorie économique du système féodal. Pour un modèle de l'économie polonaise 16–18 siécles* (Paris, 1970), pp. 43–54.

[26] Mineral resources did not play any major role. It was an important difference compared to Sweden. Incidentally, examination of the influence of minerals and agrarian products on social and political development in both countries might prove to be fruitful. While massive grain exports and favourable prices in Amsterdam offered Poland a period of economic boom and, most probably, a nice balance of payments towards the end of the 16th century, the Treasury was hardly in a position to profit from it. Nor could the large-estate husbandry easily lead to an economic and technological takeoff.

[27] Henryk Litwin described the process of shaping the magnatery, from the mid-fifteenth to the mid-seventeenth century, in two separate areas, i.e. Little Poland and Great Poland. They had amalgamated just prior to the Swedish War (1656–1660), both in respect to the *connubium* and to public offices without contradicting *ius indigenatus*. H. Litwin, "The Polish Magnates," *Acta Poloniae Historica*, vol. 53, 1986.

could do without them, and the ranks of that elite were swelled by recruits from the most active, prosperous squirearchy. The upper crust of the nobility continued as administrators of the royal domains and made a good living from them. The king and the country had no better reward for a successful M.P. than a senatorial appointment and a leasehold on a royal estate. This corresponded rather closely to the granting of knighthoods in England and of hereditary titles almost everywhere in Europe. In Polish parliamentary democracy, it resulted in a systematic weakening of the Chamber of Deputies as a political force. The gentry clearly made the most of the Renaissance State, as Prof. John Russell Major perceived it. Paradoxically, Poland can be seen in that sense as the most perfect case of the Russell-Majorian Renaissance State.

Even in economic competition, the gentry were unable to oppose their wealthier partners successfully. Not every potential exporter was able to take advantage of the big boom in the grain trade, especially in the 1590's. The existing evidence suggests that the major landlords dominated the market.[28] Moreover, they began to dominate their neighbours, and, consequently, many county assemblies as well.

The administration of and revenue from the royal domain conformed to constitutional development of the Commonwealth as a whole. The growing role of great landowning families was also due to poor communications and transport in the enormous country. This made Poland the largest *Ständestaat* ever. The Commonwealth's political structure in the Free Elections Era (since 1572) could be defined, on the one hand, as the domination of the periphery over the political centre, and, on the other hand, as the predominance of custom and precedent over written law. Political patronage was gaining momentum, as was the principle of political activity, both in the centre and in the periphery. All these phenomena strengthened and encouraged the magnates.

As far as administration of the domains is concerned, the increasing weakness of central administration was destroying the fine foundation of efficiency laid in the 1560's. According to tentative estimates, income from all types of royal estates was divided as follows around the middle of the 17th century:

the military treasury	9.0%
the king's own treasury	9.0%
leaseholders-administrators	82.0%

After the Swedish war, the figures probably amounted to 4.0%, 4.0% and 92% respectively.[29]

---

[28] A. Mączak, "The Conclusive Years," op. cit., pp. 521–525; on the role of a money economy in politics, idem. "Money and Society in Poland and Lithuania in the 16th and 17th Centuries," *The Journal of European Economic History*, V, 1, 1976, pp. 69–104. (Even in Danish, i.e. "Penge of samfund i 1500- og 1600-tallets Polen-Lithauen," *Historisk Tidsskrift*, 76, 1967, pp. 87–112; on the role of the country's dimensions. Cf. my paper read at the conference of Gotlands Fornsal in 1986.
[29] According to A. Sucheni-Grabowska, "Królewszczyzny," *op. cit.*, p. 390.

The royal treasury found three ways of procuring the necessary revenue. First of all, the *sejm* detached (in 1590 and 1641) certain royal estates in Poland and Lithuania and leased them on a short-term basis (the so-called "economies.") This not only helped prevent losses due to the diminishing purchasing power of money, but, secondly, it enabled the king to take advantage of the rivalry of competing magnates and courtiers. Entry fines were not recorded and only went into the king's (or, for that matter, the queen's) own privy purse. No student of domain administration believes that the leaseholders were satisfied with only receiving "the tenth sheaf and the tenth grosch," according to the 1641 Parliament Act. But it still represented undeniable progress in relation to the fate of ordinary domain estates.

The latter became easy prey for the magnates. Domain administration contributed to their political and economic domination. Two extreme but also very different examples may serve to illustrate this point.

Grand Chancellor and Grand Crown *Hetman* (chief military commander of the Crown) Jan Zamoyski († 1605) accumulated 11 towns and more than 200 villages during his life-time plus 12 towns and more than 600 villages as leaseholds from the royal domain.[30]

On the other side of the spectrum, Prussian dignitaries of senatorial rank usually had only scanty allodial goods and derived their incomes from leaseholds of estates, abundantly inherited by the king from the Teutonic Knights. Their strategy rested upon virtual inheritance of leaseholds. In the heat of parliamentary disputes over implementation of the laws, they were referred to as "royal stewards feudal and hereditary."[31]

This situation can be explained by a few statistics. In the period of 1526–1657, the eight most successful and acquisitive families in Royal Prussia possessed 63 royal estates (*capitaneatus*) at one time or another and retained them for different periods of time, 44.3 years on the average. This represented more than 44% of all royal property in that province (32% was held by the four first families). The longest "inheritance" was that of the Czema/Zehmen's Sztum (Stuhm), held for 106 years in a row. Continuous possession for three generations was no exception. This sort of transfer was referred to as *cessio* and required the king's consent; (this consent had to be paid for, of course). For all practical purposes the custom amounted to the sale of offices.[32] It should be kept in mind that this revenue only filled the king's privy purse.

[30] By a formal act of the *sejm*, Jan Zamoyski was granted the huge Dorpat estate (6572 square kilometres) as an allodial property. On his economic prosperity; A. Tarnawski, *Dzialalność gospodarzca Jana Zamoyskiego, kanclerza i hetmana wielkiego koronnego (1572–1605)* (Lwów, 1935).
[31] A. T. Działynski (ed.), *Zródlopisma do dziejów Unii Kor ony Polskiej i W. X. Litewskiego* (Poznan, 1861).
[32] On this subject in Poland, cf. W. Czapliński, "Sprzedawanie urzedów w Polsce w polowie XVII wieku," *Przeglad Historyczny*, 50, 1959; J. Matuszewski, "Sprzedawalność urzedów w Polsce szlacheckiej," *Czasopismo Prawno-Historyczne*, 16, 1964. The above figures were taken from A. Mączak in G. Labuda (ed.), *Historia Pomórza* (see note 15 above), loc. cit.

Swedish historians can easily detect some analogies between the Royal Prussian senators (and other even more important people, i.e. the magnates) and the aristocracy in Sweden during the *stormaktstid*. Fiefs acquired from the Crown, not the allodial goods, provided the basis for the wealth of both groups. This was true, even if the political behaviour of Polish magnates and their attitude towards the Commonwealth was rather different than the attitude of their Swedish counterparts.

* * *

What conclusions can be drawn from these comparisons? Was the constitutional difference between Poland and Sweden abysmal? It probably was. But in my opinion, other factors were of greater importance, for example the structure of the ruling classes, the role of the king, the degree of administrative centralization and what can be vaguely·described as organization of the land.[33] But in order to facilitate comparisons, let me briefly consider a third party: Denmark's *adelsvælde*.[34]

Their common problem was to retrieve, improve or sell the domain.

Sweden eventually chose the first option. It did so chiefly because there were no royal estates in Sweden and Finland which were similar to the continental domains.[35] The revenue from the estates was taxed to some extent. Denmark displayed more features similar to conditions in Poland. In the *adelsvælde*, the Royal Treasury had problems very similar to its Polish counterpart to some extent. The Danes improved their domain revenue rather as Sigismund the Old tried to do but with much greater success. There were important reasons for that success: a more efficient bureaucracy and a different relationship between the king, the *rigsråd* and the nobility as a whole.[36] The contrasting Polish-Lithuanian case clearly illustrates the early development of bureaucratic skills and a bureaucratic code of morals in the Nordic countries. This applied to most or all the countries which ultimately selected the absolutist path of constitutional development. But Sweden of the early Vasas was catching up rapidly and consistently.

This issue, as part of the so-called "Europeization process" in Sweden,

---

[33] This is a most important issue: loyalty to the king and the Commonwealth. It has been the subject of intense discussion by Polish historians. Political comments in correspondence from the early 17th century rarely mentioned the king as the sovereign without simultaneous mention of the Commonwealth. A semantic analysis might well explain the nature of Polish republicanism of that time.

However, I suspect important shifts between several periods in the 16th and 17th centuries and, in particular, a possible difference in attitudes towards the monarch arising after 1573 as the result of the free elections.

[34] I deal with this issue in "Dania i Rzeczpospolita w dobie nowożytnej, problemy i perspektywy badań porównawczych" (German summary: "Dänemark und Polen-Litauen in der Neuzeit. Probleme und Perspektiven der vergleichenden Forschungen,") *Zapiski Historyczne*, 47, 1982.

[35] Cf. note 33.

[36] Citing the literature on Denmark would be irrelevant here; articles by A. Wyczański and A. Mączak in J. K. Fedorowicz (ed.): *A Republic of Nobles*, op. cit. (cf. note 1 above) can serve as an introduction to Polish problematics.

has been duly considered by Prof. Göran Rystad.[37] The gentry in Poland was also aware of the role of officialdom and tried to influence its recruitment. Let me briefly describe some analogies and differences which may help to explain *ex adverso* the development of the power system in Sweden.

Unlike the position in Sweden, where Magnus Eriksson's Land Law was little more than a political *postulatum* in the late 16th century, the county nobility in Poland continued to nominate the king's candidates for appointment to local office. The Swedish *postulata nobilium* of 1594 corresponded to a Polish reality with deep historical roots. However, while the king had to choose his servants from the nobility only, he was not formally required to do so *med råds råde*. Incidentally, it would have been inconceivable for the nobility in Poland of the late 16th century to insist that the king formally consult his *råd* (council), i.e. the magnates. At the time the chief political divide was between the higher nobles, i.e. holders of the principle offices of the realm, and the rank-and-file nobility. However, this was but a phenomenon of brief duration. Yet during the middle decades of the seventeenth century, the gentry ceased to be an independent limb of the *corpus politicum*.

Antagonism between civil servants from the lesser nobility and the aristocrats,[38] the fruit of rapid development of state machinery during the reign of Gustavus Adolphus did not develop on the banks of the Vistula.

From the Polish perspective, the fact that most able-bodied noblemen in Sweden and, for that matter in Denmark as well, had a period of royal service was of great importance. This was due to the small numbers belonging to that Estate. In Poland, every able-bodied and ambitious nobleman strived for an office. However, until they gained ground in the central administration, they were only promoted to positions in the local self-government of that Estate. This provided them with rather different experience and, even more important, rather different civil service training.

One general factor (a big problem in itself) should be taken into account; patronage. When a nobleman entered royal service, he often (if not always) owned his allegiance to his patron rather than to the king himself. Moreover, the Polish solution to domain administration was of direct benefit to the advancing stratum of magnates: both major landowners and high, State officers. Their counterparts in the two Nordic coun-

---

[37] My discussion of appointments to offices are based on G. Rystad's papers: "Med råds råde eller efter konungens godtycke? Makten över ämbetstillsättningarna som politisk stridsfråga under 1600-talet," *Scandia*, 1963; idem., "Ständerna och makten över ämbetstillsättningarna under 1600-talet," *Vetenskaps-Societetens i Lund Årsbok*, 1963, idem, "The King, the Nobility and the Growth of Bureaucracy in 17th-Century Sweden," in G. Rystad (ed.): *Europe and Scandinavia, Aspects of the Progress of Integration in the 17th Century* (Lund, 1983).

[38] The Polish and Lithuanian magnatery could well be compared with western aristocracies: the high social status of the families of magnates was no less continuous here than elsewhere among holders of hereditary titles. And not unlike their Danish and Swedish counterparts, the magnates could be rather sure of their seats on the Council. That upper stratum could be and was referred to as "senatorial families."

tries mentioned above were more closely tied to the State after the late 16th century. They identified with the State as a central organization in the society. In Poland-Lithuania, they constituted an informal but not amorphous body, concentrating on their individual, family or regional interests. This was their strength.

* * *

A comparison between two crucial problems in both countries would also be a comparison of developments crucial to the process of the formation of states in Europe in that period. Such a comparison should be undertaken more systematically than I have been able to do in this brief essay. So I cannot provide an enumeration of all the analogous and differentiating social, economic and/or constitutional circumstances. Facts or factors such as these interfere with one another, and the question is reminiscent (at least for a humanist) of the rather complicated individual operations of a chemist attempting to isolate individual components in a composite substance in an effort to understand their individual functions and effect on the whole. But social components hardly lend themselves to isolation, much less enumeration.

So one cannot disregard the different "shapes" and dimensions in the two countries: the inland nature of the Commonwealth and the crucial importance to Sweden of her Baltic links.[39] To put it briefly, the upper stratum of the nobility found it easier to privatize their share of power at the expense of the central government. They gave the king no chance to enter into long-term alliances with the lesser nobles.

Any comparative study should probably consider a personal factor as well: the failure of Sigismund Augustus (ridiculed as a "wait-and-see" man, i.e. a procrastinator) to destroy the material power base of the magnates.

But was the idea of a "parliamentary democracy" for the nobles realistic? How is a reasonable balance of power achieved in a society based on the ownership of land? How do you limit the build-up of new elites detrimental to that balance? How do you persuade esquires that their local interests are less important than the general needs of the state? Last but not least, let me mention Sigismund Augustus' failure to provide the nation with dynastic continuity. By opening a "vanity fair" of competing foreign princes, the *sejm* probably chose the worst solution at the worst possible time.

A historian prone to discuss the past in social and economic terms might comment that the magnates in Poland-Lithuania did not need to change the law and obviously did not strive to make the State machinery stronger

---

[39] Cf. N. E. Villstrand (ed.): *Kustbygd och centralmakt, 1560–1721. Studier i centrum-periferi under svensk stormaktstid* (Helsinki, 1987), chiefly papers by the editor and the entire "Centralmakt och lokalsamhälle" section. Here, I was not able to profit from Lars-Olof Larsson's paper "Lokalsamhälle och centralmakt i Sverige under 1500- och 1600-talen" in that volume.

and more efficient when trying to derive all possible political benefit from the system. Instead, they simply put their economic assets to good use and developed what could be called the mighty neighbour patronage network.[40] While the country's constitution remained virtually unchanged, the nature of the Commonwealth was transformed into something quite the contrary to the dream once held by Executionist leaders.

[40] Patronage in the Commonwealth is currently the subject of comprehensive study by Polish scholars. The papers by Wojciech Tygielski and Zofia Zielińska, as well as by Gottfried Schramm in A. Mączak (ed.): *Klientelsystem im Europa der frühen Neuzeit* (Munich, 1988), pp. 153–158, 177–210.

POLAND

Only in Italy has the Renaissance – no matter how defined – been treated as a genuine, native phenomenon. When looking for it in other countries (with the possible exception of the Burgundian circle), the first question used to be about Italian influences. The Renaissance civilisation in a European periphery raises the question of cultural, and in particular artistic, transplants. But the discussion in terms of a dichotomy of Italian influences on the one hand, and native elements of Renaissance civilisation on the other, can easily mislead the student of the period, and surely this is not the only way of interpreting the Renaissance in the north.[1]

The influence of Italy, as well as that of other countries prominent in the sphere of fine arts and of letters, is difficult to overestimate. However, in each country the resultant of various cultural factors was different. The new attitude to the classical antiquity was but a part of the cultural restructuring of the sixteenth-century Latin Europe to which it gave a new identity and a new sense of unity. Like Italy of the Quattro and Cinquecento, each society drew both from its own past and from foreign influences. This is particularly clear if we understand the Renaissance not only as an artistic and intellectual trend or style, but as a civilisation including systems of power and authority.

The Renaissance: what's in a name? This question asked with a country like Poland in mind may get answers very different from the ones given by the students of the Italian scene. In each case particular problems should be considered. From the Polish perspective they may be as follows:

- Was the Renaissance the determinant of a period?
- How were Italian (and also German, Netherlandish) influences merged with local traditions, and how were Renaissance symbols understood and interpreted there?
- What did this country bring to the common treasury of the Renaissance civilisation?

There are arguments for regarding the Renaissance as an eponym of a period. This period has been sometimes delineated very broadly, roughly between about 1500 and the 1650s. While the mid–1650s were a major break in Polish political and economic history because of devastating invasions of Russians, Swedes and Transylvanians, the trend now is for a more restricted approach. A recent Renaissance volume of a history of art in Poland embraces the period 1500–1640, but its authors try meticulously to distinguish between works they attribute to the Renaissance (including Mannerism), and to the Baroque.[2] The late Professor Jan Białostocki in his lucid synthesis of the art of the Renaissance in eastern Europe, i.e. in Hungary, Bohemia and Poland, hardly reached beyond the first quarter of the seventeenth century.[3] He underscored diverse asynchronisms:

Humanism – even in Italy, its place of origin – precedes by a few generations the crystallization of artistic phenomena that we classify as Renaissance style. The art of Renaissance was born in Italy; and it took more than a hundred years before it spread all over the Continent . . . before the new merged with the old into an acceptable formula - new enough to satisfy the need for fashionable modernity, yet old enough not to be felt as something foreign.

According to Białostocki, 'in the east, in Hungary, Slovakia or Poland, we can meet the Renaissance – at least in the early stages of its development – in a more original, pure form' than in contemporary France, Germany, Spain and England where late Gothic style was reaching its climax. Adam Miłobędzki writes: 'Pure Renaissance architecture in its Tuscan version was adopted by only two European countries: Hungary and then Poland.'[4] But it was a particular merger of both styles that was characteristic for Poland. The Renaissance art came there as highly elitist: the king and the highest ecclesiastical lord were the first patrons. At that time it was just a transplant of 'pure, original' foreign civilisation. But in one or two generations, Renaissance art would become generally accepted and transformed according to current local needs and tastes.

So the preliminary answer to the above question may be as follows. The Renaissance art, initially known only to a small minority of Poles and created there by foreign hand, became an instant success and already by the second generation, before the middle of the sixteenth century, was privatised by the upper classes. It would shortly be introduced into popular art as well. Active attitude and the taste of patrons were possibly even more important for the development of Polish versions of the Renaissance style than the talents of native artists. All works of art that enriched the national landscape are regarded without much discussion as the national heritage. This was also the case in the early stage of the Renaissance in Poland when, for example – the Sigismund chapel in Cracow – a true masterpiece by any European standards – was designed by Italian masters and hewn in stone by mostly Italian and Hungarian craftsmen, the only noticeable native contribution being the acceptance of the design by the king himself.[5] This is not an unusual attitude both today and in the past. Giovanni 'di Bologna' (or Giambologna) was for example, in his lifetime completely absorbed by his Italian environment and regarded – by foreign visitors at least – as an Italian. And for that matter, Georg Friedrich Handel is now as English as Henry Purcell. Yet in the case discussed here, this was not a balanced exchange of talents and artistic ideas.

Early Renaissance art made Poland particularly and directly indebted to Italy (to Florence but also Venice). Only in painting and particularly in the casting of bronze was the German influence in the early sixteenth century a dominating factor; bronze plaques and slabs from the Vischers' workshop are visible in most prominent places in Cracow churches (156; 158; 161–3). Later, up until the end of the eighteenth century, Poland became a Promised Land for artists from the Lombard Lake District.[6] The active presence of foreign artists remained a constant factor in early modern Polish civilisation at least until the end of the period. And yet, while few Polish artists got any recognition abroad, already around the middle of the sixteenth century there emerged a true native talent, Jan Michałowicz, who was able to absorb and to transform the Italian artistic message.

Particularly characteristic of Renaissance art in Poland was the influence of patrons, chiefly a substantial gentry and magnatery, but also town patriciates. In some later and larger artistic programmes, it is possible to trace a sort of enchantment with works of art that they had seen abroad; this however would be more characteristic of the Baroque.[7] The special demands of lesser sponsors were also important: they compelled artists to follow patterns familiar to them. The Sigismund Chapel and the early tombs created in Cracow, as well as the courtyard arcades of the Wawel Castle were examples of the new artistic style and were reproduced in various scales all over the country.

Already, by mid-century, Renaissance art in Poland was developing clear individual styles. While it constantly drew from foreign sources (Italian, German, Netherlandish), it preserved its identity. Possibly both the timing of Italian influences on Poland and some unfathomable traits of social psychology contributed to the spread of mannerist art. This particular trend would become characteristic of the art on the Vistula and prepare a triumph of Baroque there.

Another peculiarity of the Polish Renaissance was its rural character. Destructions and reconstructions in the subsequent centuries changed the balance: only a few noble residences would resist the portentous challenges of time. One reason for this was that in the sixteenth century stone and brick made up probably less than one per cent of the architecture in Poland. What remains and dominates our image of that art, are tombs and altars in churches, as well as town halls.

Italian urban art had been adapted to the tastes of the nobles, but it also left its imprint on the cities before they became enveloped in the long-term crisis of the seventeenth century. In towns it reflected the growing awareness of urban ruling groups, chiefly merchants who would be plagued by the economic depression somewhat later than the artisans. Town halls, urban parochial churches were being rebuilt, often with visible traces of earlier, Gothic constructions. Direct Italian influence was visible on a greater scale only in Cracow and Poznań, while numerous town houses were being rebuilt and redecorated according to the pattern set by Cracow's principal public buildings. The blossoming of the grain and timber trades in the later sixteenth and early seventeenth centuries also brought about a rebuilding of some towns directly connected with the Baltic: Gdańsk, Elbląg and Toruń. These centres, chiefly Protestant, were greatly influenced by the northern Mannerism; the Italian influence was mostly indirect.[8]

Eventually, this coexistence of rather a somewhat provincial eclecticism of the three styles from the Gothic to the early Baroque, became characteristic of the Polish milieu. Many churches remained partly Gothic, but their constructions were modified by Renaissance chapels and their interiors enriched by, often splendid, sepulchres. These would remain the most characteristic trait of the Polish Renaissance. The likeness in stone of Sigismundus Augustus was located above that of his royal father in the Sigismund Chapel (104, 202), such a 'double-decker' became the fashion with wealthy noble families; the idea itself was older, however (109).[9] If room was available, a family sepulchre could occupy a large space of a wall with its numerous pilasters and arcaded niches. There were even places made for children and babies: some Polish parents seemed to have been particularly prone to commemorate offspring. The great demand for such art found an answer in almost serial production of sculptures by Italian ateliers.[10] Such 'mass-production' tended to level tastes but eventually the quality of that sepulchral art remained impressive indeed. However, it would be wrong to conclude that the general trend was towards uniformity. Both the principal Italian artists and their Polish patrons early on appreciated Manneristic attitudes and decorations. But 'disharmonious, unclassical, incorrect, and unrestrained' forms, as Białostocki described them, coexisted with charmingly quiet, almost sentimental ones (344–61). It was the latter style and taste which eventually dominated sepulchral art. In the Renaissance, Poles did not die: they were merely sleeping and dreaming. Unlike the Valois at St Denis, they never displayed their raw bones and worms did not trouble their bodies or souls. Only a gust of wind raised their fluttering robes or mantles (202–5; but 195).[11]

It would only be a slight exaggeration to suggest that the Polish Renaissance was split according to social classes. The art sponsored principally by the nobility had its roots in Florence. The often flamboyant gable parapet, a decoration most characteristic of town halls and many houses (in fact for a few noble residences as well), came directly from Bohemia and Moravia (235–57; 269; 276). The urban art in the north of the country in the later sixteenth and the early seventeenth century was, however, primarily influenced by Dutch artists. The Gdańsk Armoury, built (1602–05) by Anton van Opbergen [313–15], was strikingly similar – if less extravagant in its construction and decorations – to the Exchange building in Copenhagen and other public constructions from Christian IV's times.

In one sense, Protestantism, the German ethnic identity of the ruling groups in the cities of Royal Prussia, as well as the interaction between merchants who worked their commerce around the Baltic, were creating a special artistic style which strongly influenced the Renaissance in Poland. The ancient capital of the Teutonic Order, Marienburg, later a seat of a royal governor and centre of a royal estate, was given a vast new Renaissance and later a Baroque decoration which, however, did nothing to destroy the core thirteenth/ fourteenth century construction. What was being built anew did not always conform to acknowledged contemporaneous Italian principles of art. Local masters were sometimes influenced by their surroundings; in some parts of the country, like Masovia, parochial churches graciously combined elements of the old and new. Eventually a simple, local type of church was created, usually with one nave and Gothic proportions; distinctive decorations were employed on the gable covering the façade outside the church, and this was followed through internally on the vault. Inspiration might have come from collegiate churches built by Bernardo Morando in Zamość (after 1587–1600) and by Giambattista of Venice in Pułtusk (1560) (275, 330), but the original patterns were imaginatively developed and, eventually, in the first half of the seventeenth century, became the dominant style in central Poland, giving it a unique artistic character.

The coexistence of various styles remained characteristic for Polish architecture and each century added its heritage on top of its predecessors. This is why the Renaissance, while hailed by art historians, has been rather put in the shadow by the quantitatively dominant Baroque architecture. It must be stressed, however, that the Renaissance contributed much to its fast and complete triumph. It was the style alone however that would create an artistic unity of the country and would broaden the western influence on the Ruthenian, and primarily Orthodox, parts of it. The Counter-Reformation – the Jesuits as well as the mendicant orders of St Francis – being the crucial factor.

However, in order to answer the question whether the Renaissance determined a period of the country's history, one has to consider other facets of that life-style. First of all, this is the question of the 'Renaissance state'.

A Renaissance state

It sounds like a paradox but Poland–Lithuania may be regarded as one of the most accomplished Renaissance states, as this term is understood by J.

Russell Major.[12] True, the problem in itself is rather ambiguous because scholars found no consensus about the very notion of the 'Renaissance state'. Professor Major discusses chiefly the France of the Valois kings and stresses its decentralised, consensual structure with representative assemblies playing the crucial role. To such Renaissance administrative-political structures he contrasts the modern state, which is basically absolutist. On the other hand, Federigo Chabod approaches the same general question of the 'Renaissance state' from the Italian perspective, Italy as it was in those days, composed of small states with their old and strong urban ruling elites, as well as with bureaucratic administrative systems which had been introduced there by the Spaniards (Chabod's analytic studies concentrated on Milan).[13]

Now, if France of the later Valois, if Milan, Venice la Serenissima, as well as Naples under the Spanish Habsburg rule, are all to be regarded as Renaissance states, it is not easy to find the common denominator for them all. It may even be concluded that the term does not correspond to a definable reality. However, it is useful to have a term for socio-political structures in which feudal relationships were losing their medieval importance, while the structure of professional bureaucratic administration was only in its prime. Most important for that period, and for the forthcoming power relationships in each particular country, was the nature of post-medieval elites, the role of city patriciates as royal officers, as well as the fate of representative assemblies. Possibly not a roughly uniform solution, but rather the very struggle for identity of the state, was characteristic of what may be called specifically Renaissance power structures. At the risk of a rather gross oversimplification of the Polish constitution, it is possible to say that Poland of the early sixteenth century had drawn somewhat extreme conclusions from common Latin-European dilemmas.

The Kingdom of Poland (since the union of Lublin with the grand duchy of Lithuania in 1569, it had been called the Commonwealth) was an immense *Ständestaat* of almost one million square kilometers (400,000 square miles) and about 11 million inhabitants. Its coherence was neither principally based upon personal ties of *La Féodalité*,[14] nor upon the servants of the crown. Since at least 1501–6 Poland, and since 1569 both parts of the Commonwealth, were one *corpus politicum* with a double corner-stone: the king and the two-chamber diet (Polish: *Sejm*). Unlike the French estates, the *Sejm* met rather regularly, at least once in two years. Provincial parliamentarism, developing during the second half of the fifteenth century, created regional patriotism but only in a few cases (Royal Prussia since 1454/1466, small parts of Silesia) was such political identity based on the awareness of deep historical traditions. In the mid-sixteenth century it was generally understood by the deputies that they represented the country (the nation) as a whole, and not their particular constituencies.[15] In this (and only in this) sense, could the Polish parliamentary system of the Renaissance have satisfied Edmund Burke. It is commonly known, however, that this principle so dear to the politically self-conscious and militant gentry, in particular in the third quarter of the sixteenth century, would be interpreted in a quite opposite manner by their grandsons.[16]

Was that constitutional system directly associated with the Renaissance? There are arguments for that.

Feudal ties had never been very strong and formal in Poland, and the kings of the originally Lithuanian Jagiellon dynasty had to strengthen their disputable rights to the Polish throne and to satisfy the Polish nobles' growing political awareness.[17] The long century of the Jagiellons in east-central Europe ended with the battle of Mohács (1526). Their country of origin, Lithuania, never became a sound dynastic power-base and, finally, as the true victors over the Jagiellons on the international scene (Bohemia and Hungary) emerged the Habsburgs, and on the domestic (Polish-Lithuanian), the nobility.

The latter competitor may be easily misinterpreted, however. During the fifteenth century the estate of the nobility in Poland (but not yet in Lithuania) was given allodial property rights (*possessio iure militari*) which became a strong foundation of civic rights and political independence of that numerous estate. What may be well compared to the habeas corpus – the principle of *Neminem captivabimus nisi iure victum* – was bestowed upon the nobility in a set of statutes as early as 1425–34. In the sixteenth century the nobles could, and did, identify themselves with the nation and the state, developing a quite mature (and in a sense modern) notion of citizenship: unlike their counterparts in many European monarchies, they stressed their *citizen*-and not *subject*-status. The price of these freedoms was to be paid by other prospective political elites – first of all by urban patriciates. It is all too easy to underscore the relatively broad franchise in Poland. At least equally important is the fact that the urban elites were not included in it, and that the upward mobility of the peasantry had been successfully blocked by the statute of 1492 and subsequent royal rulings in which the king (Sigismund I) declined to judge in cases between lords and their serfs (1520). Nevertheless, in the sixteenth and still in the early seventeenth century, the church offered an avenue of advancement for capable and ambitious commoners: bishops were among the principal dignitaries of the Commonwealth and built up their clerical clienteles.

The kings had the right to appoint numerous officers and dignitaries; according to a common estimate of the epoch, up to 40,000 posts, a rule-of-thumb figure which ought not to be taken for granted but which vividly manifests the interest and emotions of the public.[18] Yet the king's freedom of choice was strictly limited by the local self-government of the nobility and by the emerging power of the magnates. In most countries endowed with representative assemblies in early modern Europe, the political polarisation between the prince and the estates was blurred by the system of recruitment of officers. They were socially hardly discernible from the members of the assembly, and often formed a particular, if still informal, estate, or at least had a split identity, with loyalties divided between the prince and their peers.

This was also true of civil officers in Poland but – what was decisive – the kings here were not able to develop their own bureaucracy, here illustrating the 'Renaissance state' of the Italian type as Chabod saw it. Their early attempt to create judicial officers responsible only to the king failed early, and both the fiscal and the judiciary branches of the government became dependent upon the *Sejm* and/or upon the local self-government of the nobility.

A similar trend has been observed in France of the early Valois: each new office originally created to strengthen the king's grip over his subjects and over other already existing offices tended to change itself into a property (or rather leasehold). In Poland–Lithuania all local administrative and judicial officers became so-called 'county *terrestres* officers', i.e. officers representative of their county assemblies of the nobility and partly responsible to an assembly. Most of them were appointed by the king from four nominees of their peers, or upon suggestion of the assembly; *ius indigenatum* was very strictly observed.

Royal power in the provinces was limited by the sheer size of the country and its feeble communications system. This gap was filled by the richest stratum of the nobility, later called the magnatery. The strictly egalitarian ideology and pharaseology of the nobles in Poland–Lithuania was a cover for deep inequalities. A local power-base – that is, a power-base with country assemblies combined with landed wealth – created the position of a magnate house; for all practical purposes peers were created that way. A great noble with a strong local power-base could successfully demand high posts and favours from the king. The latter in turn needed officers loyal to him but also influential with the local gentry.[19]

This all too general description of power networks in Poland shows some traces familiar to a student of French history of that age. Royal power there was deeply shattered during the wars of religion, when aristocratic factions seemed much stronger. However, the outcome of that crisis was eventually different from the fate of the power system in Poland. A few points may be mentioned in this connection. Unlike the *noblesse de robe*, in Poland nobles were not created by virtue of holding office: it was a noble's social status that made him eligible for officers and dignities. Unlike in the west, the commoner or the city could participate in the power game only through the influence of money. The non-noble remained an outsider in the *corpus politicum* of the Commonwealth. Contemporary observers seriously discussed the Polish phenomenon; only in the following century, or for that matter, after the unfortunate reign of Henri Valois, would they wonder about its uniqueness and strangeness.

While it would be difficult to find direct links between the Polish 'democracy of the nobles' and Antiquity, leaders of the gentry at least since the middle of the sixteenth century were profoundly aware of, and interested in, such analogies. At that time everybody in Europe seemed to discover and exhibit with much enthusiasm his ancient roots. Respective myths gained wide currency in Poland as well ('Sarmatian' origins of the Polish nobility), while from the mid-fifteenth century Ruthenian-Lithuanian nobles elaborated their own Trojan myth; particular noble families from Lithuania cultivated their separate Roman ancestors. This was a not uncommon method of cultural modernisation. Another example of the link between current politics and the classical tradition, was a book entitled *De Senatu romano*, written by a future chancellor and *Hetman* (Polish supreme army commander), Jan Zamoyski, during his early studies at Padua University.[20]

More important than these trivialities. of classical erudition were the observations of an anonymous visitor who wrote, in English, 'A relation of the state of Polonia and the united provinces of that Crowne, anno 1598'.[21] The authorship of this treatise is disputed: the editor sees in him Sir George Carew who had indeed visited Poland that year. On the other hand, a distinguished authority, Professor Stanisław Kot, argued for William Bruce, a Scottish scholar who spent long years in the country and had been teaching in Zamość where he could observe Chancellor Zamoyski rather closely. The author, it should be noted, was well informed and obviously close to the chancellor. A hypothesis which seems most probable (while it cannot be proven) is that it was Carew who commissioned a detailed report on the country, and possibly subjected the report to some copy-editing. Bruce's style and/or his Scottish spelling cannot be traced, but the text is strongly Zamoyski-oriented and clearly reflects a long-term familiarity with the country and the chancellor's faction. It also contains numerous allusions to England, so cannot be regarded as a simple translation.

In one of the most spirited chapters of the treatise, the anonymous author compares the Polish polity to the 'Germania' of Tacitus and even to the ancient Roman civic virtue. The common denominator of the ancient and current Polish polities was for him the patron–client relationship:

For that is the common bande of unity between the riche and the poore, bothe by that meanes participating in the benefittes of the lande, the one by commaunde, and the other by dependency of the Commaunders trencher, besides the correspondency of patrone, and Cliente, imitating in that the auncient Rommane state, which by that order was united and kepte in mutuall amity, the Patricians being the patrones of the Plebeians, counselling them, following theire suites, pleading theire causes, and defending them in all cases without fee or reward, and on the other syde the Clientes observing, honoring and with greate respecte wayting on their patrons.[22]

In the next paragraph, the anonym underscores the analogy with the Germanic tribes: 'Tacitus description of the Germane traynes dothe most aptly expresse the Polish.' This comment sounds rather strange because the author was by no means an uncritical observer of Polish politics. He comments with true insight:

In Polonia the condition bothe of suche as serve, and of others, which lyve uppon small revenewes without dependency, is farre better then in Lithuania, being neyther so servile, nor so subjecte to the injuries of the potent. . . .[23]

The principal value of the Polish polity, as the author saw it, was that 'thys dependency makes that the multitude is not so easely drawne to the factions divorces, which some troublesome spirites seeke for the conversion of confusion of the State. . . . ' This was a concern very characteristic of the period.

Alluding to the Aristotelian classification of power systems, the author in question defines the Polish system of rule – with some hesitation – as 'Aristocraticall', and twice compares it to Venice. By '[a]bsurde articles which of a father of the realme make the kinge a pupill', the nobles 'clipt the eagles wynges' and 'seeke dayly to make hys condition worse then any free subiect'.[24] With such opinion the anonymous author anticipates the polity that would develop in the seventeenth century. However, this leads him to a comparison of the King of Poland with the Doge.[25] His elegant, erudite criticism reflects the viewpoint of King Stephen and his principal minister Zamoyski. It is very much in the Renaissance style that our author tries to classify the Polish polity in Aristotelian terms:

. . . some would inferr that this is a Democracy, seeing the Summum Imperium is chiefly in the Nobility, which maketh an huge multitude, those not being excluded, whoe for theire poverty are but serving men.[26]

He also classifies whatever he had learned about Polish history in the same way.

So the political class in Poland drew conclusions from the modern ideas of state. One may even comment that the magnatery shared in practice, if not in theory, that 'predatory' attitude towards the state which Professor Jack Hexter discovered in the political thought of Machiavelli.[27] The result would eventually astound the rest of Europe.

One of the curiosities the anonym touched in his 'Relation', was the multitude of religions in Poland. This was included by him into internal 'inconveniences and dangers of thys state'.[28] He comments 'for religion there is not in any countrey such variety, but that seems better to mainteyne the common peace, then yf the lande were devided into twooe bodies of religion, as France is.' Yet he hails Chancellor Zamoyski for his tolerance, 'whoe seeing the strength of the Common Wealthe to be devided into 3 mayne bodyes of great bulke, viz. Catholikes, Protestantes, and Greekish, knowes

that yf by pursuite, or depression any parte should be mooved to take armes
. . . there would follow the ruine of the State.[29]

Renaissance and the Reformation

Much of the discussion concerning the mutual relationship between the
Renaissance and the Reformation in European countries can be related to
Poland as well. The Reformation has left fewer direct traces on Polish
civilisation than the Counter-Reformation: Catholicism eventually became
very strongly interconnected with Polishness and with the defence of Polish
national identity.

The Reformation, which had already arrived in Poland already by the early
1520s, became a dominating religious and intellectual force during the
following half century.[30] Protestantism – roughly, Calvinism among the
nobility in Poland, Lutheranism among nobles and burghers in Royal Prussia,
and the Polish brethren chiefly in Little Poland – never took violent forms; the
nobility was not given to dogmatic discussion and, until later times, religious
disputes hardly disrupted local communities. Violence by the fanatical mob
would be introduced as a political tool by the Counter-Reformation only,
from the 1570s.

The general problems of the Reformation cannot be discussed here unless
they touch directly on the Renaissance. But in fact, the Reformation was in
many respects an important cultural and innovative factor. Various social
mechanisms were active here. First, after few edicts against the heretics, not
strongly enforced, both the last Jagiellon kings were tolerant of Protestanism;
from the mid-century onwards the Augsburg Confession (but not the
Reformed, that is, Calvinist one) was made legal and equal to Catholicism in
Royal Prussia; Sigismund Augustus even toyed with the idea of a national
church. This made the Commonwealth a haven for persecuted Protestants
and many of them came – Stancari, Blandrata, Fausto Sozzini and some
members of the Czech Brethren being outstanding examples of that immi-
gration. The influx of Protestants increased Poland's contacts with most
intellectually active regions of Europe. It also widened the sphere of western
influence in the country: Lithuanian magnates were mighty and dedicated
patrons of Protestantism. Secondly, confessional competition visibly
enhanced the development of education. Schools based on the Strasbourg
model of Johann Sturm were founded in Protestant centres under the
patronage of great nobles, and in major Prussian towns where they served
both their communities and the landed gentry. Several decades later Catholics
developed two independent networks: Jesuit colleges, chiefly for the gentry,
and seminaries for future priests.

Generally speaking, confessional struggle contributed to the development

of literacy and intellectual awareness in Poland. This happened on several
levels and in many areas: Protestant ministers in the later sixteenth century
were more often than not better educated than the Catholic parochial clergy:
this was at least partly due to the influence of German universities, including
Königsberg (founded 1544) and schools in Royal Prussia.

Journeys abroad were becoming fashionable with the more substantial
gentry; a grand tour became a necessary part of the curriculum for the sons of
magnates. Confessional preference dictated countries and universities to be
visited which included Ingolstadt or Altdorf and Leiden or Louvain/Leuwen,
but Paris and Padua were everybody's favourites. King Stefan Batory,
Chancellor Jan Zamoyski and his secretary, a historian, Reinhold Heiden-
stein – each of them from a different background – were all 'Paduans': that
school became the Alma Mater of Polish youth in of the later Renaissance era.
Foreign travel was important for the development of the Renaissance spirit.
Sadly the universities and schools in Poland could not compete either in
learning or in prestige and popularity with any of the major foreign centres of
learning. The national university in Cracow (founded 1364 but active from
1400) had declined and by the sixteenth century was in a state of crisis. The
Jesuit college in Vilna and the Zamość Academy created by Chancellor
Zamoyski were similarly ill-equipped to attract students.

Confessional struggle was also strongly connected to parliamentary
politics. The election crisis, of 1572–6 contributed greatly to political interest
and awareness amongst the gentry. This has been confirmed by a massive
production of pamphlets, mostly manuscript, collected and transcribed with
interest into family records.

The confessional triangle mentioned by the anonym, that of Catholics,
Protestants and Orthodox or Greek Christians, was a unique phenomenon of
the Commonwealth. It is very plausible that neighbourly coexistence and
mutual understanding between Catholics and Orthodox nobles in the
borderlands of Poland and Lithuania taught them elementary lessons of
tolerance which became principles of parlimentary polity in the second half of
the sixteenth century.[31]

In a long-term perspective, and particularly in comparison with the
following century, the Renaissance state in Poland achieved a delicate
equilibrium. In 1505, the Chamber of Deputies in the *Sejm* had formally
overcome the domination of the Senate and by the 1560s was co-operating
well with the king. Principles of parliamentary polity set deep roots in the
corpus politicum. Citizenship was virtually limited to the nobility which set
up a working self-government with a secure rule of law. Inside the estate the
domination of the upper stratum seemed seriously hampered. During the later
sixteenth century growing western demand for Polish grain and timber
secured economic prosperity; economic thinkers were mostly optimists, even

if they stressed the need for a more consistent foreign trade policy. Notwithstanding anti-urban legislation, many royal towns enjoyed their share in the economic boom and some private ones became thriving centres of landed estates.

This picture however, does not reflect a true state of affairs. The Polish counterpart of Jean Bodin and Jędrzej Frycz Modrzewski (c. 1503–72) advocated alternatives: a stronger royal power, more chances for commoners and, in certain critical cases, like punishment for manslaughter, equality before the law.[32] However, arguing for a strong monarchy would mean political disaster. Even the Jesuits, after an initial setback, changed their attitude and began flattering the gentry. The latter seemed to be the principal winner on the Parliament's floor; they were, however, neither winning in the country's economy nor in county diets.

The final failure of the Renaissance state in Poland was caused by what might be called a contradiction between the egalitarian legislation and political freedoms of the noble estate, and inequality of economic chances between various strata of landowners.[33] The rule by patronage would not save the Commonwealth from factions and civil wars, and factors which still need to be analysed hampered the development of a Polish version of the Jacobean 'rule by the pen'. The domination of the magnatery was enhanced politically by the shattered authority of the sovereign since the free elections, and eventually led to a wide gap between the egalitarian political phraseology and a growing dependence of the gentry upon the magnatery.

Jacob Burckhardt's enthusiasm for the modernity of the Renaissance in Italy has been widely criticised recently.[34] Much of the argument fits Poland as well, but the relationship between the old and the new here took rather particular forms.

The Renaissance in Poland might be presented as an essay in the solution of problems concerned with ethnic-cultural diversity. While the Italian scene was divided into numerous states but in respect of language relatively uniform,[35] the Renaissance culture in the Commonwealth was founded upon a manifold ethnic infrastructure. Polish language and manners were both gaining ground in the Ruthenian and Lithuanian east and struggling with the traditionally dominant German influence in the towns. One is tempted to risk the conclusion that some borderland milieux were likely to have a culturally fruitful soil. Nicholas Copernicus (1475–1543), a scion of a Toruń (Thorn) family originating from Silesia, was exposed to influences from both Germany and Poland – and profited greatly from his studies at Cracow before visiting Italy. Like the whole Varmia/Ermland chapter he was loyal and dedicated to the Polish *raison d'état*. His person and manifold achievements (including a treatise on money with an early formulation of the 'Gresham's Law') show, or rather symbolise, the potential of urban society and its openness to intellectual influences. Ruthenian and oriental (Armenian and other) contributions to the Polish Renaissance were of a different nature. Polish historians agree with Stanisław Grzybowski that long coexistence there of diverse ethnic traditions, and particularly Orthodox and Catholic confessions, contributed to the spirit of tolerance for dissident views and customs.[36]

We have stressed the coexistence and mutual influence of various artistic styles but there were different factors which shaped the literature of Renaissance Poland. Czesław Miłosz wrote: 'to me [the] history of Poland and of its literature seems extravagant and full of incongruities: a Slavic nation whose writers, up to the Renaissance, used only Latin . . . ; a refinement of taste, which produced lyrical poetry comparable to that of Elizabethan England, combined with irony and brilliance but always threatened by drunken torpor and parochial mumblings.'[37] The Renaissance signified both the refinement of Latin and direct contacts with humanists all over Europe (Erasmus was very popular among Cracow intellectuals), and the development of a literary Polish language. The chief works of scholarship were in Latin, of course, like Copernicus' *De Revolutionibus Orbium Coelestium* (1543), Modrzewski's *De Republica emendanda . . .* (1554) and Wawrzyniec (Laurence) Goślicki's *De Optimo Senatore* (1568). There was also an abundant correspondence in Latin of which that of the diplomat, Johannes Dantiscus, was probably the largest.

While Latin – in which, according to common European wisdom, each Pole excelled – built bridges to the intellectual west, the printing-press opened a market for the vernacular. Principal Polish writers published poetry in both languages; a Protestant, Mikołaj Rej (1505–69) enjoyed writing in his native tongue and coined a saying: 'Let the neighbouring nations know that Poles are not geese, but have their own language.' The vernacular literature struggled in the first half of the fifteenth century with inadequacies of vocabulary and with spelling, but already around the middle of the century it was helping to establish a national identity.

Jan Kochanowski (1530–84), both courtier and sincere laudator of the country life, became the symbol of the age. He travelled throughout Germany, Italy, France and was fluent in many languages. He freely translated the Psalms (*David's Psalter*), availed himself of George Buchanan's poems, and often alluded to Horace, while choosing themes from the *Iliad* in his works. The lyrics of his *Laments* which describe the death of his beloved daughter are as moving today as they were in his own period. He also enjoyed composing short verse, which was sometimes obscene, and often directed at his contemporaries. An accomplished contemporary of *la pléiade*, he might also well have written laudatory verse for Thomas Coryat's *Crudities* had he not died too early! In contrast, the next generation got, in Mikołaj Sęp

Szarzyński (1500–81), 'a kind of a metaphysical poet' who was a precursor of Polish literary Baroque and in his poetry greatly resembled John Donne:[38]

> You, who want to find Rome in Rome, pilgrim,
> are unable to find Rome in Rome itself . . .
> Today in vanquished Rome, unvanquished Rome
> . . . lies buried

The second half of the Renaissance age in Poland was as intellectually intense as it was politically dramatic. In 1566 appeared *The Polish Courtier* of Łukasz (Lucas) Górnicki (1527–1603). This was a free translation of *Il libro del corteggiano*, adapted to suit Polish conditions and the lifestyle of the Polish court. Shortly thereafter, during the first free elections of the kings and the confessional struggles, massive production of political pamphlets, in prose and verse, testified to the growing literacy of the gentry. The numerous pirate editions of Jan Kochanowski's poetry signified growing demand for his poetry and for literature in the vernacular in general. The pace of progress during this period was faster than in any time previously or thereafter, but it still could not be compared with that of contemporary England, France, Germany or Spain either in the quantities of books and pamphlets which were printed in or the variety of literary *genres*. In particular theatre in Poland developed slowly.

However, Poland's greatest triumph was in its influence upon the East. The first book in Old Slavonic appeared in Cracow in 1491, followed by books in Ruthenian. The availability of the printing press increased the attractiveness of the Polish language and contributed in part to the Polonisation of the Ruthenian and Lithuanian nobility in eastern parts of the Commonwealth. However, this proved in the end to be a mixed blessing and contributed to dramatic national conflicts from the mid-seventeenth until today.

NOTES

1 In the final stage of preparation for this chapter I profited from conference papers whose proofs Professor Samuel Fiszman kindly gave me for inspection: J. Białostocki, 'Renaissance sculpture in Poland and its European context: some selected problems'; A. Miłobędzki, 'The Renaissance and local "modi": architecture under the last Jagiellons in its political and social context' in S. Fiszman (ed.), *The Polish Renaissance in Its European Context* (Bloomington and Indianapolis, 1988). The reader may turn to that volume chiefly for literary matters. For general information about Poland, see J.K. Fedorowicz *et al.* (eds.), *A Republic of Nobles. Studies in Polish History to 1864* (Cambridge, 1982); also A. Mączak, H. Samsonowicz and P. Burke (eds.), *East-Central Europe in Transition. From the Fourteenth to the Seventeenth Century* (Cambridge, 1985).
2 H. and S. Kozakiewicz, *Renesans w Polsce* [The Renaissance in Poland], 1st edn (Warsaw, 1976), 2nd edn (Warsaw, 1987).

3 J. Białostocki, *The Art of the Renaissance in Eastern Europe. Hungary, Bohemia, Poland* (Ithaca, N.Y., 1976), the following quotations from 1f. Figures in brackets in the text and in notes refer to illustrations in that well-documented book.

4 Miłobędzki, 'Architecture' 291.

5 King Sigismund to the burgomaster John Boner, 1517: 'There has been here an Italian with a model of a chapel he is going to build for us and which we like very much'. H. and S. Kozakiewicz, *Renesans w Polsce*, 37.

6 Białostocki, 'Renaissance sculpture' in Fiszman, *Polish Renaissance*, 281; Miłobędzki, 'Architecture' cit. in *Polish Renaissance*, 291.

7 An outstanding case is the collegiate church in Nieśwież Lithuania, a Baroque-style church under construction at the same time as the building was commissioned by Prince Michael Casimir Radziwill, a Calvinist recently converted by the Jesuits, who had visited Rome during his pilgrimage to the Holy Land.

8 Białostocki, *The Art of the Renaissance*, 82f 311; 313–15; 320. Cf. there comments on the notion of northern Mannerism. Cf. also his comments on houses of wealthy grain-merchants in Kazimierz on the Vistula, 'Renaissance sculpture' in Fiszman, *Polish Renaissance*, 287.

9 More on tomb sculptures in Białostocki, 'Renaissance sculpture in Fiszman, *Polish Renaissance*; H. Kozakiewiczowa, 'Renaissance nagrobki piętrowe w Polsce' [Renaissance double-decker tombs in Poland], *Biuletyn Historii Sztuki*, 18 (1955), 3–47.

10 See H. Kozakiewiczowa, 'Spółka architektoniczno-rzeżbiarska Bernardina de Gianotis i Jana Cini' [Architectural-sculptural firm of Bernardino de Gianotis and Giovanni Cini], *Biuletyn Historii Sztuki*, 212 (1959), 151–74.

11 Białostocki, 'Renaissance sculpture' in Fiszman, *Polish Renaissance*, 288.

12 J.R. Major, 'The Renaissance monarchy: a contribution to the periodization of history', *The Emory University Quarterly*, XIII, 2 (June 1957), 112–24; *Representative Government in Early Modern France* (New Haven, Conn., 1980).

13 F. Chabod, 'Esiste uno stato del Rinascimento?' [1957–8] in his *Scritti sul Rinascimento* (Turin, 1981), 591–623.

14 A. Mączak, 'Vicissitudes of feudalism in Poland' in P. Thane, G. Crossick and R. Floud (eds.), *The Power of the Past. Essays in Honour of Eric Hobsbawm* (Cambridge and Paris, 1984), 283–7.

15 This is one of the principal theses of Konstanty Grzybowski's path-breaking monograph of the *Sejm* in the reign of Sigismund Augustus (1548–72): *Teoria reprezentacji w Polsce epoki Odrodzenia* [Theory of Representation in Poland at the time of Sigismund Augustus], (Warsaw, 1956).

16 This is the question of *liberum veto*, a procedure based on a noble principle but in political reality a virtually anarchic one; in the seventeenth eighteenth century the *liberum veto* became a tool in the hand of many a magnate faction leader. See W. Konopczyński, *Le Liberum veto* (Paris, 1930).

17 See n. 13 and also Fedorowicz, *et al.*, *A Republic*.

18 Cf. C.H. Talbot (ed.), 'Relation of the state of Polonia and the united provinces of that crown anno 1958', *Elementa ad Fontium Editiones* (Rome) 13, 1965. This treatise will be discussed below.

19 These relationships have been presented by the author in 'The conclusive years.

The end of the sixteenth century: the turning point of Polish history?' in E.I. Kouri and T. Scott (eds.), *Politics and Society in Reformation Europe. Essays for Sir Geoffrey Elton on his Sixty-Fifth Birthday* (London, 1987).

20 However, Carolus Sigonius with whom Zamoyski had studied, boasted to Jacques Auguste de Thou that *he* was its author.

21 Talbot, 'Relation', 86.

22 *Ibid.*, 86

23 *Ibid.* 87

24 *Ibid.* 39, 60, 61.

25 Yves Durand was only formally right when he did not classify Poland as a republic. Cf. *Les Republiques au temps des monarchies* (Paris, 1973). Incidentally, Talbot, 'Relation', buttresses our argument that the late sixteenth century was a period decisive for the subsequent two prepartition centuries. See above, n. 19.

26 Talbot, 'Relation', 39.

27 J. Hexter, *The Vision of Politics on the Eve of Reformation* (New York, 1973) 150–72.

28 Talbot, 'Relation' 129.

29 *Ibid.*, 130.

30 For a general overview, see J. Tazbir, *A State without Stakes* (Warsaw, 1973); cf. also G. Schramm, *Der polonische Adel und die Reformation 1548–1607* (Wiesbaden, 1965).

31 The first historian who elaborated this theme was Stanisław Grzybowski. Cf. his 'Mikołaj Sienicki, Demostenes sejmów polskich' [A Demosthenes of the Polish Parliament], *Odrodzenie i Réformaçja w Polsce* 2 (1957).

32 J. Frycz Modrzewski, *Opera omnia*, ed. C. Kumaniecki (Warsaw, 1953–); his principal treatise was *De republica emendanda . . .* (1551).

33 The political rhetorics of that period need a detailed study but it may be symptomatic that in the later sixteenth century when the sovereign as the supreme authority was mentioned, the Commonwealth was added as well.

34 Cf. P. Burke, *The Renaissance* (Atlantic Highlands, N.J., 1987).

35 We are aware of a gross simplification: see C. Dionisotti, *Geografia e storia della letteratura italiana* (Turin 1971), 163. It seems, however, acceptable in order to stress the nature of cultural diversity of both the countries in question.

36 See n. 28, above.

37 C. Miłosz, *The History of Polish Literature*, 2nd ed. (Berkeley, Calif. 1983), xvi ff.

38 *Ibid.*

XII

TACITUS, ARISTOTLE AND THE POLISH POLITY IN THE LATER RENAISSANCE

The Renaissance has discovered the art of diplomatic report. Venetian ambassadors and papal nuntios set high standards of professional competence and literary style. Their diplomatic reports had double character. On the one hand they contained secrets of the state and therefore used to be highly classified. On the other, they developed into a literary genre designed to entertain sophisticated courtiers and princes' councillors. Mastery in political narrative was a perfect first step of a successful career.

While Aristotle offered the perfect framework for defining a polity, Tacitus among classic writers was regarded as the master of political analysis. The report we deal with in this paper is rather unique in that its author is less interested in stereotypic comments and anecdotes than in hard facts on society and political mechanism of Poland-Lithuania. It is also unusual in the manner it uses Tacitus' *Germania* to explain a polity of a contemporary exotic state. Among numerous, chiefly Italian, foreign reports and descriptions of Poland, this one is perhaps the most pertinent and original.

Relation has rather obscure origins. Its manuscript belonged to the royal collection and is now preserved in the British Library. It contains 112 folios.[1] The person of its author has stirred a controversy which so far has hardly been solved. The editor, Charles H.

Talbot, ascribes the relation to Sir George Carew, an experienced English diplomat who indeed visited Poland in 1598. On the other hand, Stanislaw Kot suggested the authorship of William Bruce, a Scottish scholar employed by Grand Chancellor Jan Zamoyski in his Academy in Zamosc. The problem is that the report does not contain any exact information about its author's whereabouts in Poland (he was less familiar with Lithuania). However, clearly it is not a diary or report of an embassy.

More recent papers have brought a wealth of new observations and ideas on *Relation*, but did not answer the question of its authorship.[2] There are strong arguments both for Carew and for Bruce. The text is written in good and even elegant English, which makes an important argument against the Scottish scholar. Bruce would write in 1606 to Lord Salisbury: "Pardon me my Lord that I wrytte to your honor in Scottis. I hade not ane that I might truste quha culde wrytte Inglisse at thys tyme." [p. XIII]

And yet Sir George hardly had time enough in Poland to gather all the data which we find in *Relation*. Dybowski checked the text and found it rather reliable in even close detail; whoever was the author, he had good insider's informations. If this was Carew, he must have availed himself of competent services of a long-time resident. In such case William Bruce would be a perfect informant. Strangely enough the English diplomat would confess to Jacques Auguste de Thou: "Ex illo tempore, qui res serenissimi regis domini mei ibidem [in Polonia] procurarunt, Scoti fuerunt, quibuscum mihi exigua aut nulla consuetudo est."[3]

While the chance is "exigua aut nulla" to solve the question of authorship without some new evidence, the student of the Polish Late Renaissance cannot be but impressed by the writer's familiarity with the Polish politics. For instance, he lists senators according to their religious denomination rather exactly (Dybowski found a few minor errors only). His perspective and views are greatly influenced by Grand Chancellor Zamoyski. The chancellor had been a tribune of the nobility ("inferior Nobility" or "private Nobility" in the author's vocabulary) who thanks to King Stefan Batory (1576–1586) became his principal minister and close collaborator.[4]

*

The best way to introduce the author is to quote a few paragraphs on social divisions of the nobility which follow his presentation of the political elite ecclesiastical and secular. "Of the private Nobility those who are landed men are much respected above the others, for theire capability of honours and helpes, which the Common Wealthe hath from them. And therefore in many cases (as free holders in England are counted Homines legales) Statute theire authority and wittnesse etc weighteth more, as allso in compurgation. [...]

"Bothe the greate Lordes, and private riche gentlemen keepe greate traynes, commonly to the uttermost of theire hability, and some farre beyonde, maynteyning them in that case by badd meanes, suffering, and protecting them in outrages and insolencies. The Lordes also greate guardes of Hayduckes, and Cosackes, so that it seemes the state standes uppon violence, the security being rather in eache mans ability to defende hymselfe, then in the publike protection of the lawe. Thys causeth greate ryotes, and may in tyme devide the State.

Of the poore Nobility having Nec rem nec larem, there is an huge multitude, Which common poverty commes by theise meanes. Fyrst, for that the land possessed by the Nobility is certayne, viz. 140,000[5] villages or Mannours, but the State is dayly wonderfully increased. Secondly, for that Patrimonies oft subdevided at last to nothing. Thirdly the common prodigality of the gentlemen [...] Fowrthly and lastly, For that they may not helpe themselves by trade [...]."

There follows an argument that "bothe spirituall and secular prefermentes allmost onely serve for the mainteyning of greate howses in theire greatnes" and that "the weakelinges can hardly tugge out having but twooe meanes. The first is study which fewe can follow [...]

"The second and ordinary meanes that poore gentlemen are compelled use, is service, which serves them onely to lyve, and not to rise, excepting some fewe which gett speciall favoure with theire lordes and are placed by them in the Leivetennancy of a Castle, or somme bayleywicke, or peradventure are rewarded by them with some peice of lande. This course is held for no disparagement rather because they are not putt to servile drudgery, onely defend theire maisters and wayte on them, though they doe it most submissely, and deiecte themselves by too base adulation." [p. 84 f.]

This raises the question of interplay of humility and pride of the Polish nobility. The topic may seem rather abstract and irrelevant; in fact it is a subject of particular importance for Polish social history and one analyzed hardly closely enough.[6] In other terms, this is a question of how (or whether) a nobleman could maintain his identity and status while serving as his mighty neighbour's client. "For so must they doe that seeke creditt with the Poles," continues the author one of his rare comments on social psychology, "whoe by nature being hygh mynded, love to see theire owne greatnes in anothers humility, and hearing theire owne recommendations from a professory tonge, display theire plumes, and in a vayne seeke by liberall rewarding of suche panegyricall parasites to manifest those vertues which are most harped on."

Such a picture of "multitudinis inopia, et nimiae paucorum opes" lead the Anonym to analogies with ancient Rome. Where "the voyce of every poore servingman being a gentleman weighes as muche in all Conventes and elections as the greatest princes," may easily lead to "tumultes" and "seditions". As compared to the Roman "Lordes of the worlde," their modern Polish counterparts are in better position: in Rome the rich could not well appease "their poore fellowe cittizens" because they had "greate store of slaves and

TACITUS, ARISTOTLE AND THE POLISH POLITY

so could not (as they doe in Polonia) enterteyne theire poore fellowe cittizens." [p. 85]

The fear of imminent riots was characteristic for observers of the English scene of the later sixteenth century. Polish statesmen did not think that way. Our author clearly associated the gentry (i.e., lesser landowners) with ancient Roman citizens recipients of plots of *ager publicus.* He saw a direct analogy to the ancient policy in King Stefan's (1576–1586) distribution of parts of his domain in Livonia, a province which hade been incorporated by Sigismundus Augustus and later defended against the Moscovites by Stefan.

One wonders whether this was the author's own interpretation of what he was seeing in Poland, or rather a comment possibly overheard at the Chancellor Zamoyski's household. One may doubt whether the lesser nobles in Poland were regarded by their more affluent and elitistic brethren as a riotous sort of people. However, the question of their property did exist. In 1596 there appeared a book by Rev. Piotr Grabowski (dead 1625), an early mercantilist Polish writer, which designed a programme of extensive colonisation of South-Eastern borderlands of the Commonwealth. Grabowski explained its double aim: it would be an ultimate system of defense against Tartar incursions, and a solution of a social problem of petty landless nobles.[7] In *Relation* one finds the same idea: "The Poles have good meanes in thys manner to disburden the State, yf there should be any such commotion by placing them in the waste landes of Podolia, and Lithuania, which yf they did afore they be urged, it woulde be a greate securing, enlarging and enriching of the kingdome [...]" [p. 86]

However, if there is no real danger of riots, it is because "thys poorer sorte desyres not any better state": they made the retinues of the great lords. "So that whether the Polish Noblemen keepe such greate and ryotuous traynes in that reason of State, or uppon affectation of pompe, and greatnes, or security of theire persons as being commonly in quarrells, the State cannot well stande without it."

This is what the author cannot explain without alluding to ancient Rome. "For that is the common bande of unity betweene the riche and the poore, bothe by that means participating in the benefittes of the lande, the one by commaunde and the other by dependency of the Commaunders trencher, besides the correspondency of patrone, and Cliente, immitating in that the auncient Romane state, which by that order was united and kepte in mutuall amity, the Patricians being the patrones of the Plebeians, counselling them, following theire suites, pleading theire causes, and defending them in all cases without fee and rewarde, and on the other syde the Clientes observing, honoring and with greate respecte wayting on theire patrons." [p. 86]

Here follows in Latin a substantial quotation from *Germania* because "Tacitus description of the Germayne traynes dothe most aptly expresse the Polish":

"Even in his escort – sayth he – there are gradations of rank, dependent on the choice of the man to whom they are attached. These followers vie keenly with each other as to who shall rank first with the chief, the chiefs as to who shall have the most numerous and the bravest followers. It is an honour as well as a source of strength to be thus always surrounded by a large body of picked youths; it is an ornament in peace and a defence in war. And not only in his own tribe but also in the neighbouring states it is the renown and glory of a chief to be distinguished for the number and valour of his followers, for such a man is courted by embassies, is honoured with presents, and the very prestige of his name often settles a war.

When they go to battle, it is a disgrace for the chief to be surpassed in valour, a disgrace for his followers not to equal the valour of the chief.[8] To defend, to protect him, to ascribe one's own brave deeds to his renown, is the height of loyalty. The chief fights for victory; his vassals [Tacitus: *comites*] fight for their chief. [...][9] Indeed, men look to the liberality of their chief for their war-horse and their blood-stained and victorious lance. Feast and entertainments, which, though inelegant, are plentifully furnished, are their only pay. The means of this bounty come from war and rapine etc. His whole discourse of the German fashions in most thinges fitts the Poles," repeats the anonymous observer.

"To conclude thys poynte, thys dependency makes that the multitude is not so easely drawne to the factious divorces, which some troublesome spirites seeke for the conversion or confusion of the State, and therfore if thys lyncke were loosened by the faulte of eyther party or the cunning of some thirde it would questionles endaunger the State." [p. 87]

So far, this ancient type of patronage is in "Polonia" the foundation of *militia terrestris*, or "the Military estate", i.e., the levy. Once more Tacitus is quoted, and this time the alleged similarity of Polish noblemen to Germanic warriors is used to contrast them all with the ancient Roman military machine.[10]

It seems characteristic that in his description of the levy, the anonymous author presented the nobility of Poland as a feudal society of lords and their followers even while he did not even try to depict any ceremonies so characteristic of the fealty in the West. He does not allude to the Scottish clans: was he not familiar with them or did not wish to involve "Polonia" into such comparisons? On the other hand, he compares the levy in Poland to the Ottoman system, mentioning incidentally the nobles' "villages, or Mannors which are as knightes fees, or *timarres*" [p. 108]. Incidentally, both Carew and Bruce may have been familiar with the Turkish military organization. Yet there was no allusion to Scotts Highlands when this mysterious author described the legal order and the forays so characteristic of the Polish country life. Nor when he analyzes the liberty in that country.

"This impunity", he comments on the homicide among the nobles punished only by a fine and allegedly even encouraged, "is one parte of the Polish liberty, which they thincke, that they onely of all people of Europe enioye,[11] whereas yf we measure the liberty of the greatest parte of the State, we shall fynde that no civill Common-wealthe is so slavish, the commons not being in equall protection of the lawe. For questionless that State which is obnoxious to the violence of another is not free, as it is in Polonia, where iustice is not administered *arithmetically* to all. So that onely the Nobility seemes to be free, which not onely in Geometricall iustice enioyeth all exemptions, and that the honors, and prefermentes, but allso tyrannise over the other [...]" [p. 106] Tacitus, the authority on public morals is once more quoted[12] but the author cannot remain *sine ira et studio*.

The text in question is not only a case of an intelligent and well informed report. It also contributes to the discussion concerning "the state of the Renaissance". In the sixteenth century, peripheric Poland paradoxically can be regarded as a fine case of a Renaissance state, as J. Russell Major sees it.[13] One may say that by comparing Poland directly to most respectful classic patterns, *Relations* made that Commonwealth a particularly clear case of Renaissance polity. Its author is admirable in his untypically balanced attitude towards, and opinions of, his subject. Let me quote a comment on the law and the freedom: "For questionles that State which is obnoxious to the violence of another is not free, as it is in Polonia, where iustice is not administered *arithmetically* to all. So that onely the Nobility seemes to be free, which not onely in *Geometricall* Justice enioyeth all exemptions, and hath the honors, and prefermentes, but allso tyrannise over the other [...]" [p. 106; emphasis is mine, AM].

This seems to be an idea rather freely borrowed from the ancients. The direct original application of the adjective "geometric" (equality) was Plato's *Laws* 757 sq: where *isonomia* was described "arithmetic"; only the geometric (proportional) equality was just, however, because it took account of the virtue (*arete*). Another major classic writer who used that vocabulary was Aristotle. He often opposed the "arithmetic" to the "proportional" when commented upon various forms of friendship (e.g., *Magna Moralia*, 1211b; *Ethica Eudemia*, 1242b; also *Ethica Nicomachea*, VIII 14, 1163a, b; cf. also *Politeia*, V 7, 1301b for proportional equality).

TACITUS, ARISTOTLE AND THE POLISH POLITY

While the Anonym quoted or mentioned neither Plato nor Aristotle, we may ask whether there was any connection between their ideas and his approach to the Polish polity. The terms may have been derived from Plato, but not the conclusion and the political attitude. Unlike Plato, the Anonym used the adjective "geometric" as a negative one, to describe the behaviour of the nobles who "tyrannise over the other" and who in particular were "not aunswerable in lawe, for any outrage against theire owne bawres, and for the lyfe of others [...]". He did not follow any Greek authority as close as he did Tacitus. And yet the student of the clientage is due to him a precious, if indirect, lesson. *Relation* in its more general, theoretical, sections was a study in liberty, power relationships and social balance. The sharpest, most critical, comments were related to the injustice at the courts, when the author discussed the freedom, not the friendship. These ardent phrases were a step beyond Aristotle, towards a new understanding of, and interest in, the notion of freedom. But the historian and social scientist may easily associate the Greek metaphors with Tacitus' *Germania* and Polish magnates and petty nobles: the use of proportional (unequal) friendship is nothing but political patronage. What Aristotle had called "proportional" recently got a much less elegant name of "lop-sided friendship".[14] The Anonym reminds us of the forgotten Aristotelian dimension of this bond.

Notes

1. C.H. Talbot, ed., 'Res Polonicae ex Archivo Musei Britan nici', I pars, "Relation of the State of Polonia and the United Provinces of That Crown 1598", *Elementa ad Fontium Editiones*, XIII, Romae 1965, pp. XI–XII. Later quoted by pages only.
2. E. Mierzwa, "Angielska relacja o Polsce z roku 1598", *Annales UMCS* Sectio F., 17, 1962; Idem, "Na marginesie wydania angielskiego relacji o Polsce z 1598 r.", *Przeglad Historyczny;* J. Dybowski, *"Relation on the State of Polonia...* – stereotypowa czy analityczna wizja szesnastowiecznej Rzeczypospolitej?", 1983, unpublished MA thesis, Institute of History, University of Warsaw.
3. *Relation*, XV; quoted after Thuanus, *Historiarum sui temporis*, VII, V, 28.
4. On Chancellor Jan Zamoyski see W. Tygielski, "A Faction which Could not Lose", in A. Maczak, ed., *Klientelsysteme im Europa der Frühen Neuzeit*, Schriften des Historischen Kollegs. Kolloquien 9, Munich 1988, pp. 177–201; idem, *Politics of Patronage in Renaissance Poland. Chancellor Jan Zamoyski, his supporters and the political map of Poland, 1572–1605*, Warsaw 1990.
5. *Relation* is in the mainstream of Renaissance descriptions of countries and states in that it brings quantitative data on revenues, the army, the levy. He also quotes estimates (current in Poland in the second half of the sixteenth century) of a number of villages owned by noblemen as compared to the (allegedly overwhelming) ecclesiastical property. The figure of 140,000 reappears in connection with the levy. It is an interesting case of a statistical bias and of using alleged statistics in political propaganda. However, we still do not know the number of noblemen's hearths.
6. I discuss this question in relation to the eighteenth century in a volume of essays *Klientela* (at printers, in Polish).
7. P. Grabowski, "Polska Nizna albo osada polska...", in J. Górski and E. Lipinski, eds., *Merkantylistyczna mysl ekonomiczna w Polsce XVI i XVII wieku*, Warsaw 1958.

TACITUS, ARISTOTLE AND THE POLISH POLITY

8. Here follows in *Germania* a sentence deleted in 1598: "And it is an in-famy and a reproach for life to have survived the chief, and returned from the field." (XIV, 1)

9. *Germania,* XIII,3-XIV,3. A sentence is here deleted: "If the native state sinks into the sloth of prolonged peace and repose, many of its noble youths voluntarily seek those tribes which are waging some war, both because inaction is odious to their race, and because they win renown more readily in the midst of peril, and cannot maintain a numerous fol-lowing except by violence and war."

10. *Qui nec tributis contemnuntur, nec publicanus atterit, exempti oneribus et collationibus et tantum in usu praeliorum sepositi velut tela atque arma bellis reservantur.* [p. 107; *Germania,* XXIX, 2]

11. There follows however *altera pars* of the Polish liberty: "that any gentle-man may speake without danger, whatsoever he thinketh, which may cause great stirrs, seditions, troubles, iealousyes etc., howsoever Taci-tus commendes Traians tyme for the liberty which proceeded from the seveare conscience of that Emperor." [p. 106 sq]

12. Unequal protection of the law in Poland had been discussed with much zeal and erudition by Jedrzej Frycz Modrzewski.

13. I make this point in an essay about to appear in R. Porter & M. Teich (eds.), *Renaissance in National Perspective* (Cambridge University press).

14. J. Pitt-Rivers, *The People of the Sierra* [1954], 2nd ed. Chicago 1971.

XIII

The commonwealth of Poland-Lithuania in the late seventeenth century—an essay in interpretation of space

In this essay I do not undertake to explain or to describe in greater detail the economy, civilisation and political system of the state structure that extended over six major river basins (Odra/Oder, Vistula, Niemen/Memel, Dvina, Dniester and Dnieper) and separated Russia from Prussia and Austria—a fact of minor importance for the seventeenth, but crucial for the following centuries. I concentrate on the second half of the seventeenth century, which will be shown as a period when some characteristic traits of the Commonwealth culminated. However, I cannot restrict my argument to the facts and the relationships of these four or five decades sandwiched between two major manifestations of the Swedish *Stormaktstiden*: the Karl Gustav war and the Great Northern War.

What I intend to do is:

1. to discuss the internal divisions of the country and their economic significance;
2. to discuss the importance of the size and the political-administrative composition of the country for the state-building process (if this is a term adequate for seventeenth-century Poland);
3. to determine the importance of the later seventeenth century for both sets of problems.

My questions concentrate on the economy, society and the power structure and on what created that particular civilisation which was in many respects unique in the Europe of the seventeenth century. However, some important topics must be left untouched. This was a country inhabited by various ethnic groups, speaking different languages and having diverse creeds. This was a country where Catholics, Calvinists and Lutherans coexisted, where Czech Brethren had been given a refuge and Polish Brethren had gained cultural importance and acquired the protection of mighty Calvinist magnates and where the Mennonites were valued for their skills and industriousness, and given full religious autonomy. This was the only country in Europe where Catholic and Greek Orthodox communities coexisted; the second half of the seventeenth century was an important period of that coexistence. However, this complex civilisation also acquired its flavour from the Jews, Armenian merchants and Tatars who were being settled in Lithuania. In the heart of that part of the Commonwealth, in Samogitia, heathen traditions and beliefs still influenced the popular culture. All this was possible because the political system was becoming increasingly decentralised because of particular space relationships.

In 1634, after the Polanowa Treaty, *Rzeczpospolita* (which means *the* Commonwealth or *the* Republic) attained its greatest extent: about 990,000 square kilometres. The landscape offered few natural barriers between regions but there were hardly any easy (i.e., fluvial) connections between distant parts of the country. Transport in Lithuania, a country with a continental climate, was difficult during the autumn rains and when the thaw changed roads into muddy pools. For heavy and bulky goods the only possible means of transport was river ships. However, most of the navigable rivers in this part of Europe run northwards to the Baltic and do not facilitate east-west transport connections.

What may be called the "density" of space was very unequally distributed over the whole country. The east was mostly sparsely populated in comparison to the core regions of Poland. While town charters were being granted generously by the kings, the degree of urbanisation was by almost any contemporary standards rather modest. What was a town in the upper Dvina region or, for that matter, even in Masovia, would be hardly recognised as such in many more advanced parts of Europe, including Estonia, Livonia and both parts of Prussia, where urban networks had been designed by the Teutonic Order.[2] Rev. Jan Piotrowski, who wrote his diary of the siege of Pskov in 1581 and also journeyed to Livonia, was delighted by the sight of Livonian towns (even though this country had been destroyed by the Muscovite troops), and compared urban Livonia, not without historical reasons, to Torun (Thorn) in Royal Prussia. A Frenchman, Jean le Laboureur, who tried to impress his compatriots with his image of Poland (where Princess Louise Marie Gonzaga had become

queen in 1646) also remarked that some Masovian towns would have been regarded only as simple villages in France.[3]

Poor transport facilities in this large area were a crucial factor not only in commerce and the economy in general; to a certain extent they also shaped the Polish-Lithuanian power structure which allowed the nobility a degree of local self-government that was unique. In more theoretical terms, the scarcity of administrative officers dependent on the king can also be interpreted as great political distance between the centre of power and the periphery.[4] It is my more general hypothesis, which is confirmed by this discussion of the territory of Poland and Lithuania, that the well-known, even proverbial, weakness of modern Polish kings was caused by a syndrome of extensive privileges acquired by the nobility mainly during the fifteenth century, by a particular property structure (chiefly in Lithuania and the Ukraine) but also by feeble and difficult communications between the court (the king and central offices) and the nobles with their county assemblies (the diets).[5]

In the economy, the spatial factor can be best explained in terms already proposed by H. H. von Thünen (1783–1850) and adapted by the late Professor Wilhelm Abel. Von Thünen wrote in the first paragraphs of his *Isolated State*:

"Man denke sich eine sehr grosse Stadt in der Mitte einer fruchtbaren Ebene gelegen, die von keinem schiffbaren Flusse oder Kanale durchströmmt wird. Die Ebene selbst bestehe aus einem durchaus gleichen Boden, der überall der Kultur fähig ist. In grosser Entfernung von der Stadt endige sich die Ebene in eine unkultivierte Wildnis, wodurch dieser Staat von der übrigen Welt gänzlich getrennt wird. Die Ebene enthalte weiter keine Städte, als die *eine* grosse Stadt, und diese muss also alle Produkte des Kunstfleisses für das Land liefern, so wie die Stadt einzig von der sie umge-

The commonwealth of Poland-Lithuania

Frontiers of the Commonwealth after 1629-1634
(Lauenburg and Bütow, lost 1657, not included)

┼┼┼┼┼ - - - after Andruszów Treaty, 1667

Territory lost to Turkey 1672, recovered 1699

Boundary between Poland and Lithuania

0   100   200   300   400   500 km

benden Landfläche mit Lebensmitteln versorgt werden kann. (...)

Es entsteht nun die Frage: wie wird sich unter diesen Verhältnissen der Ackerbau gestalten, und wie wird die grössere oder geringere Entfernung von der Stadt auf den Landbau einwirken, wenn dieser mit der höchsten Konsequenz betrieben wird."[6]

Abel projected the *Thünenschen Ringe* from that rigorous, dry and formal scheme of the "isolated state" on to the map of early modern Europe.[7] He placed the economic (commercial) centre ("the City") in the area of the Home Counties of England and the Netherlands. It is characteristic of the logic of his-

9

torical research that a theory, a model, is accepted even if one of its premises is disregarded or even contradicted. In this case nobody could accept either the uniformity of soils or the absence of rivers. It has also been noted that numerous "cities" of the sort that have their own hinterlands coexisted, even if none of them constituted such classic cases as Gdańsk (Danzig) and its counterparts on the estuaries of Dvina and Niemen-Pregel.

As far as Poland-Lithuania was concerned, *the City* (in the most exact sense of the term) was Gdańsk, where the demand for foodstuffs was concentrated and where the price of these foodstuffs was usually highest. This was the case in Poland. The Niemen basin had Koenigsberg, and on the Dvina a similar role was played by Riga. The countryside outside the gates of Gdańsk and Elbing resembled Dutch landscapes to a substantial degree. A French diplomat, Charles Ogier, after having visited the Vistula Delta in 1635 (i.e., after ten years of war and/or Swedish and Brandenburg-Prussian military occupation) was visibly impressed by the fertility of the land and the liveliness of its inhabitants. In the second half of the seventeenth century the Vistula Fens, which belonged to the City of Gdańsk, to Elbing and to the Royal domain, were acquiring an even more Dutch character because of extensive Mennonite colonisation. The Mennonites also moved to the south along the Vistula, reclaiming fertile soils as far as Thorn. The relatively high-yield grain and the animal husbandry of the sixteenth and early seventeenth century were at least partly replaced by an even more profitable "Dutch husbandry", i.e., by dairy production.[8] This fits directly the definition of the closest (suburban) circles analysed by the German economist.

The most distant ones were defined by low intensity of animal husbandry (oxen) and a weak demand for grain. The Ukraine has very fertile soils but the proper exploitation of these soils was associated with huge problems. In this region demographic and economic fluctuations had political (in the wide sense of the term) rather than economic origins. This was no less true of the seventeenth century than it is of the twentieth.

It is clear that the Ukraine should not be regarded only from the viewpoint of its relationship with the Baltic. In fact, it was largely beyond the Baltic zone. Some of its cities showed an interest for, and were very actively involved in commerce with, the neighbouring Turkish dominions (Armenian merchants from Kamieniec Podolski; Ukr.: Kamianets'-Podil'skyi). Some importance must also be assigned to trade connections with Russia even though they remain unmeasurable because of the inadequate source base. Incidentally, this is the principal problem encountered when researching the economic history of the Ukraine. However, it is beyond doubt that this country of settlers and warriors was plagued by Tatar incursions.

During the century before the outbreak, in 1648, of the great Cossack uprising led by Bohdan Chmielnicki (Khmel'nyts'kyi), very modest earth-and-timber ramparts and the determination of the defenders were usually sufficient to discourage the Tatar horsemen. This was an extremely wild steppe frontier and there was no accidental coincidence between the acquisition of estates in the Ukraine and political success in the Commonwealth. A great majority of *hetmans*, i.e., chief military commanders of the Polish part of the Commonwealth, had their principal residences and estates in Podolia, Wolhynia or what at that time was called the Ukraine.[9] Only those families which asserted themselves in the south-east were able to establish long-term dominant political positions in the Polish part of the Commonwealth.

After the Cossack uprising and the Karl Gustav war, the history of the south-eastern territories was characterised by a rebuilding process constantly interrupted by Tatar incursions and at least one major Turkish invasion. From 1672 a large part of Podolia was lost for a quarter of a century. The eastern, Cossack part of the Ukraine was taken over by Russia (Perejesław Treaty between Russia and the Cossacks, 1654; Truce of Andruszów between Russia and the Commonwealth, 1667).

However, what was done to reconstruct the agrarian landscape of western Podolia and Wolhynia was very impressive. The reconstruction pattern was different from that followed in central and western Poland at that time. In the Ukraine, landowners had a limited interest in creating demesne farms and they still had chances of attracting settlers from the western part of the country. The principal problem was to find a market for grain and other goods which were part of the rents from manorial (demesne) farms. Surveys of royal estates from the early seventeenth century recorded the fact that demesne farms did not produce any surplus of grain. In the subsistence economy which prevailed, whatever was harvested on the demesne was used to pay the manager, labourers, servants and soldiers. This might not be the whole truth (surveys were based on the testimonies of managers) but there is no evidence of any substantial transport of grain from Podolia and the neighbouring areas until the late seventeenth century. At that time, however, landlords were already trying to transport grain to distant markets, and some of them succeeded relatively well. Their problem was that they were unable to sell their grain and other agrarian and animal products at local fairs and in towns. Small producers of any sort felt more at home at markets, and the small town was to a large extent agrarian in character.

The great landlord had a trump card in the form of his labour force and the timber he owned, this being necessary for building river ships. Great landowners erected in their simple river harbours, called *pale* (verbatim: *pale* means bollards), granaries and warehouses for forest goods (pitch, tar, timber, ashes ect.). There they built river ships and rafts. The south-eastern confines of the Vistula basin became included in the grain-exporting zone. The exact timing of this change remains unknown because trade account sheets from estates and Gdańsk are very scarce. Yet the market mechanism and the long-term trend are clear: the size of the estates and their distance from the principal river estuaries played a crucial role. The whole relationship can be summed up as follows.[10]

1. In the Polish servile system the larger estates were more market-oriented than single manors belonging to the lesser gentry;
2. The farther from Gdańsk, the cheaper the grain and the greater the r e l a t i v e profit from its sale;
3. The farther from Gdańsk, the greater the proportion of large landowners shipping local produce;
4. The farther from Gdańsk, the greater the annual fluctuation in grain exports; in other words while the immediate hinterland took its grain to the Gdańsk market each year, the far-off provinces were only able to send large quantities in particularly fat years. As a consequence of the last two factors, only the greater landlords were able to supply Gdańsk with grain from distant areas on a regular basis.

The cumulative effects of these mechanisms acted almost automatically in favour of the great landowners. They contributed to another socio-economic process, namely to the concentration of landed property.[11] Abundant quantitative data is available on the results of this process in many parts of the country. Property structures can be compared on the basis of the taxation returns of particular counties in several random years. However, the state of land and credit markets in the second half of the seventeenth century is known to us only from the Lwów (Lemberg) area, i.e., from Red Ruthenia.[12] A study of loans and land sales at Lwów fairs leaves little doubt that the magnates (or rather the nobles defined as *magnifici*) were borrowing money from their lesser neighbours (the *nobiles*) and using that money for the purchase of manors. The *magnifici* acted as bankers investing the deposits of their patrons in landed property. Of particular importance is the fact that no manor or substantial village, once acquired by a landlord, had any chance of being sold back to a squire. It simply became an object of transaction between great landowners. On the other hand, many properties, which had been sold by the gentry, were returned to them later (or even immediately) as leaseholds, being parts of the *latifundia* of the landlords.

While this process was characteristic of various regions of Poland and Lithuania, it was probably more intensive in the areas lying far away from sea harbours (i.e., from Gdańsk, Koenigsberg or Riga). A factor of importance there was money circulation: it was far more possible for great landowners to collect cash and shift goods and money from estates in one corner of the country to those in another. Jan Sobieski, later King John III, was able to send oxen and shiploads of various kinds of grain from Ruthenia to the royal domain of Gniew (Mewe) where, because of

the proximity of Gdańsk, there were far better opportunities of selling these goods at advantageous prices.[13]

An additional and (I believe) important aspect of the advantage the great landowners had over their lesser neighbours was the transport services they could offer. As early as in the 1620s the Radziwiłłs used to offer room on board their ships on the Dvina to other landowners, and this sort of a business flourished until the eighteenth century.[14] The evidence from Poland is of a later date but at least in the 1660s this phenomenon was common on the River San in Red Ruthenia.[15] It is highly probable that these transactions gave the squires a unique chance to sell their products at principal markets, use the commercial know-how of their richer neighbours' managers and to bring back industrial and/or luxury goods available in Gdańsk or Riga.

From what has been said, it is clear that the south-eastern estates suffered from one major economic problem: difficult access to the main market, particularly with their grain. In this respect the great property owners had the advantage of size. Local markets were limited in their capacity to absorb basic goods of local origin and these goods were already provided by small-scale sellers. A study of the Lubomirski *latifundium* in the late seventeenth and early eighteenth century has shown that local demand was of no importance for this *latifundium*.[16] Most effort was devoted to the destillation of vodka from grain and, consequently to the establishment of networks of village taverns which from the later seventeenth century were mostly run by the Jews.

Serfs and other economically dependent subjects were obliged to purchase alcoholic beverages in the lord's taverns. Professor Janina Leskiewicz has shown that this was a business which grew steadily from the later sixteenth century.[17] In the late seventeenth century this system was most well developed in the Ukraine, Podolia, Wolhynia and Red Ruthenia. "As much rye should be sown as is possible," ordered Prince Paweł Sanguszko in 1735, "and because there is no purchaser for the grain, let spirits be distilled from it for sale to the Jews [in their taverns] in the Ukraine".[18] At this time the prince's estates in Little Poland still did not rely on the *propinacja* (i.e. forced purchase of alcohol) so much.[19]

A most detailed and interesting piece of technical advice on this matter is that given by Prince Józef Klemens Czartoryski, an experienced landlord with principal estates in Wolhynia, to his son-in-law.

"... without the *propinacja* and money rents there would hardly be a regular cash income. *Propinacja* can be divided into two types: the direct, i.e., run by the owner, and the leased. I advise noblemen living in one or two villages to use direct *propinacja* ( ) because there is no doubt that with great diligence, and by doing the administration himself and not with the help of hired people, it is more profitable than leasing to the Jews or to somebody else. However, a lord with large estates, even if he wished to study husbandry in detail, could by no means administer the *propinacja* directly (this is particularly difficult in towns which are open from all sides) and so he can be best advised to lease it out.[20]"

Prince Czartoryski's advice on the forced purchase of alcoholic beverages was a standard piece of wisdom for landowners. However, he had still more to say:

"*Propinacja* is easy to arrange and does not need (anything more) than, clear common sense; but in addition to common sense agrarian husbandry requires various kinds of economic information and practice... To describe all this information and experience, the largest library would not be adequate; but a lord with large estates should not become engrossed in these subtleties ... because if he wished to farm as the famous economists near

London or Paris and in Switzerland do he would only be able to cultivate 1 % of his land, and the cultivation of one acre would perhaps cost him ten times the value of his harvest. These famous economists do not have more land than that owned by a well-situated tenant here."

Between the "unkultivierte Wildnis" and the agrarian landscape without market outlets on the one hand, and intensive husbandry near Gdańsk on the other, there was a plain that should not be defined in terms of its relationship to grain crops and river transport only. In the core regions of Poland much had changed since the mid-sixteenth century, when the relatively large-scale exportation of grain and forest products started. While there is much dispute among Polish historians about the timing of the agrarian depression in the first half of the seventeenth century, there is a general consensus as to its nature. It has also been accepted that in the regions with tenuous connections to the Baltic, demand for grain survived the early stage of the depression better. I can perhaps explain my viewpoint as follows:

From about the middle of the sixteenth century (sources are scarce and inconclusive for the earlier period) landowners strove to increase their demesne area at the expense of their serfs' farms. Professor Leonid Zytkowicz has shown that this happened not where it was easy to sell grain, but rather where labour was relatively abundant. It is characteristic that in Kujawy (a region of fertile soils on the Vistula south-east of Thorn, where the river provided excellent means of transporting the grain) demesne husbandry was relatively weakly developed. This was, however, a region of substantial peasant farming.[22] The same can be said of Royal Prussia.[23] On the other hand, wherever there was a good supply of labour and other conditions were favourable, this expansion of de-

mesne farming continued and gained momentum simply because there were no legal obstacles to stop it. The nobility was completely free to proceed, virtually undisturbed by the courts of justice.[24] The income per acre from the demesne was higher than rents in money and in kind. The home farm (the demesne) could also profit from the cheap labour of cottars and landless village labourers. From the late sixteenth century the economy and society developed under the continuous pressure of three interrelated trends:
– the increase of home farms (at the expense of the tenantry);
– the increase of rents (the labour rent above all);
– the concentration of landed property (at the expense of the middle-sized owners, mostly one- and two-village squires; the smallest properties were very rarely bought up).

This explains the increase in the grain supply to Gdańsk by the second decade of the seventeenth century, when western demand had dropped.[25] However, much earlier, from the 1580s onwards, there were some clear signs of a poverty crisis among the tenantry: the previously flourishing low-quality clothmaking industry in Great Poland (around Poznań) showed signs of a decline in the demand for its produce in the countryside. Only the centres which had developed regular contacts with more distant markets in eastern Poland and in Lithuania were able to survive. Professor Benedykt Zientara has also proved that a thriving iron industry in Little Poland, run by commoner workmasters on the estates of the nobility, the Church and the Crown, was being largely destroyed by the landowners. This was because forests were damaged by landowners or because in some respects the iron industry was in competition with servile-labour husbandry.[26] The

Karl Gustav war and contemporary incursions by the Transylvanians caught the economy at the worst possible moment. This explains why recovery was so slow and remained so incomplete.[27]

Not without a touch of pedantry, it can be said that here domination of space proved once again to be a principal factor of success or at least of survival. To a certain extent the textile centres of Great Poland and Silesia played the role of industrial suppliers to the more completely agrarian central and eastern regions of Poland. Whereas low-quality produce no longer found any customers, numerous centres of the woollen industry sprang up on the Silesian border. They imitated English jerseys and other kinds of textiles.

In 1660 in a memorandum on the decline of the city's commerce, a merchant of Gdańsk, Johann Koestner, devoted an interesting page to the development of centres of textile production in Silesia and Great Poland.

...Anjetzo hat sich dieser Handel sehr geaendert, fast keine Karasey werden auss Engeland anhero gebracht, feine Lacken aber gegenst die vorigen zu rechnen wenig. Die Ursach ist diese, weil die Lakken zu Fraustadt, Pohlnisch Lissa und anderen Orten der Krohne von denen Tuchmachern, die sich seit dem juengst verflossenen deutschen Kriege daselbst gesasset von Tage zu Tage besser geworden und wohlfeil verkaufet werden, weil auch der pohlnische Adel durch continuirliche Kriege an Mitteln erschoepfet, in Austheilung ihren Dienern guten Libereyen menagieren.[28]

Here I touch on the very important question of the demand for foreign luxury goods. I cannot but remark that, notwithstanding general post-war depression and the difficult reconstruction process, the nobility's demand for luxury goods (silk, cloth, spices etc.) hardly declined at all. In my opinion, this pattern of consumption and the demand for simple industrial goods of high quality at advantageous prices strongly encouraged the nobility to establish direct connections with ports such as Gdańsk.

Political space: by this term, or rather set of terms interconnected by space, I intend to express the territorial dimension of political action and thought.[30] Some examples may explain my point. The squire's interest in national politics differed from the magnate's. The latter had more extensive personal interests and they were hardly ever unconnected with the sphere of politics. His political space was necessarily broader. The squire travelled less than his rich and mighty neighbour. The King and the Court had, by definition, a broader view and an active interest in the country as a whole. The same can be said of the princes of the Catholic Church. So the direction of one's political interests and the range of one's activities, their importance and effectiveness defined one's political space. Yet, the political space of a particular class or group was not determined once and for ever fixed. In the mid-sixteenth century the gentry entrenched in the Chamber of Deputies (or at least their leaders) had reached the level of independent n a t i o n a l politics. Since that time the senatorial families, i.e., the upper stratum of the nobility—the magnates—, slowly but steadily limited any independent political initiatives of their lesser brethren. The more independent of the political centre the county diets were (i.e., for that matter, the larger the county government was), the more limited was the real, and not the imagined, political space of the gentry.

The sphere of action of a politically-minded, active nobleman can be adequately illustrated by the example of Jan Antoni Chrapowicki (1612–1685), a well-off Lithuanian squire who was active not only locally but also as a frequently elected member of the House. He enjoyed the confidence of the House and the Royal Court. In his youth he had made his long Grand Tour of Europe and learned languages (he could later use his Italian at court). However, his principal asset was obviously his political skill and his social charm. He seemed to be irreplaceable on committees, dealing with constitutional, diplomatic (with Russia) and, last but not least, financial affairs. He obviously had a gift for settling disputes and conflicts. He was useful for several political factions and knew how to acquire the favours of kings; he died as a senator, *voivode* of Vitebsk.[31] His journeys were limited to a part of Lithuania (but large parts of this country were occupied by Russian troops for many years of his active life) and to Podlasie. His longer journeys were connected with Sejm sessions or committee duties.

The year 1658 (a relatively quiet one) gives some idea of his mobility. He spent 168 days outside his home, 109 of them at various public conventions and meetings related to his membership of the Sejm. He entertained at home forty guests and groups of guests and paid important visits to seventeen persons (not counting family occasions such as baptisms, weddings and burials). He was ill only five days and hunted eighteen times, mostly in the autumn. He also received 105 letters and despatched 101 (from and to his wife 17 and 13 respectively). Hardly a quiet country life.

For political space, the itineraries are much less important than the area of influence. It seems (because the question remains still largely unresearched) that this is the key to a rationalisation of the unproductive discussion about who was and who was not a magnate. The political interests and the action of the gentry were concentrated on the county diets. Great families had more extensive interests, and the development of this upper

15

social stratum can be interpreted as a gradual increase in the area of influence of each particular family.

From the mid-fifteenth to the mid-seventeenth century major families in Poland (defined as constantly having members in the Senate) increased their areas of influence and successively, if slowly, they merged together into one single Polish magnatery. Henryk Litwin has found evidence for this process in two groups of magnates from Little and Great Poland. He discerned two parallel tendencies: towards contracting marriages with members of major families in the other province, and towards acquisition of offices and dignities there. In the middle of the seventeenth century—this is his thesis—the magnatery was only in the process of becoming a close, relatively homogeneous group.[32] It always remained open to *homines novi*, sometimes clients, or former clients, of major members of the establishment.

The Union with Lithuania in Lublin (1569) presented the problem of a new elite and its role in the Commonwealth. While the Lithuanian gentry had much to learn and entered the political scene of the Chamber of Deputies too late to experience that mature and sublime political movement of *executio iurium*, the Lithuanian magnatery owned much more landed wealth than their Polish counterparts. Thus it was not long before "the Lithuanians" began to acquire leaseholds of royal estates in the Polish part of the Commonwealth.

It would be a rewarding task to sketch the analogies as well as the contrasts between country life in the Commonwealth of Poland and Lithuania and country life in Stuart England. One contrast would certainly be the different relationship between the "county gentry", local elites and the Royal Court in England.

This English pair of notions—"the Court and the Country"—has won little popularity among Continental historians and recently it has even been called into doubt by some British ones too.[33] However, if used a little differently, it seems very useful for interpreting early modern Poland. The difference is that in Poland the Royal Court had a limited force of attraction. The magnates were never strongly tied to the king's residence and from the late seventeenth century that they began to compete in displaying splendour, developing their own "courts"—i.e., households, and enlarging their retinues.

A magnate was really strong when he was constantly aware of what was happening at court and when he was able to control county diets (this could be done directly by his clients) and at the same time take part in local country life. He had to run his own court. In this the way Commonwealth was becoming a federation of country mansions or rather a federation of regional courts.

Most probably the late seventeenth century marked for many parts of the Commonwealth the beginning of a widespread dependence of the gentry on the magnates. Tadeusz Manteuffel has defined this as a Polish type of feudalism, and he has traced it in numerous customs and even ceremonies analogous and not dissimilar to the classic medieval ones. However, this feudalism could perhaps be more properly viewed as a manifestation of the patronage-clientage system.[34] This is not only a question of terminology; the Commonwealth was to become an extreme, and in a sense, classic case of rule by patronage.

In my opinion the terms of this patronage explain best not only what Sir Lewis Namier called "the structure of politics" but also the (very different) nature of government and administration in Poland-Lithuania, at least from the mid-seventeenth century onwards.[35]

Rule by patronage-clientage was completely different in principle from rule by professional or semi-professional royal officers. This is true, I believe, even if one agrees that advanced bureaucracies were also (and, for that matter, are) not foreign to known patronage networks either.[36] It was characteristic of the Polish early modern type of political patronage that the magnates played the role of power brokers. Their weight, power and prestige in the political centre (i.e., in the Sejm and at Court) depended on their kin prestige, wealth, personal assets and last, but not least, on their domination of county diets (dietines, noble constituencies). The diet assembled not only to elect *nuntii terrestres* (members of the Sejm) but it also nominated or elected county officers and dignitaries, elected deputies (members of the jury) to the Tribunal, and was responsible for an increasing number of local issues, including county troops and taxes. After a Sejm session, each diet met once more to listen to and discuss an account of that session. The diet could take a stand on major issues which affected it, decide whether it agreed to new taxes, and whether the behaviour of Sejm deputies was compatible with the instructions they had been given, etc.

This explains why the dominance of the assemblies of the nobility was crucial for the political power of the magnatery. In this game, a carrot was a better incentive than a stick, and a magnate had to court his lesser neighbours rather more intensively than his English counterparts did. The difference lay partly in the fact that in the Commonwealth there were no rotten boroughs and that some constituencies, even if they were politically not very active, were very sensitive and self-conscious. To cut a long story short, we can say that the principal tools used by a magnate to attach the gentry to his person were his court as a focus of social attraction and education for the youth, leaseholds and managerial posts on his estates, and of course brokerage services at Court. Only through a mighty broker could a squire be granted a county dignity, an officer's patent or some other favour from the king. On the other hand, a patron (or a prospective patron) watched carefully the mood of his lesser brethren in order to ascertain who might behave unpredictably and who was self-conscious. No magnate dared to offend his (lesser) brethren.

In the late seventeenth century (and a long time after that) the magnatery still needed noble retinues. It was not until now, or even a little later, that livery became fashionable (it had already gone out of use in England in the early decades). The magnates needed noble crowds to impress and outshine their opponents and rivals. They also needed votes. So the lord's affability and grace was often also in his own direct interest.

However, there were few, but notable, instances where a magnate could be sure of *his* constituency and could relax his control over that neighbourhood. Areas of influence were usually open to rivals, vectors of political influence crossed one another. Whereas the county became more and more a relatively independent legal and political unit, the unity of the Commonwealth as a whole manifested itself chiefly in the common interests and interactions of principal patrons. What is more, paradoxically enough, it seems that the nature and composition of the magnatery was changing. This process began earlier in Lithuania than in Poland. In the late seventeenth century there were only three great competing magnate families in the Great Duchy: the Pacs, the Sapiehas and the Radziwiłłs.[36] The next century, with the Saxon dynasty of the Wettins and, what became even more important, Russian domination of the Polish political scene, saw a change of principal actors.[37]

Does s p a c e explain the particular nature of the Commonwealth? It would be difficult to answer this question in the positive, because the spatial factor was only a geographical, or rather in accordance with our approach, sociogeographical framework in which society developed its institutions and economic relations. Nonetheless, our argument is that the size of this framework was in a sense incompatible with the constitutional system that had emerged out of the fifteenth-century struggle for the freedom of the nobility. It is fascinating to follow how, since its last and dubious victory over the magnates in 1562/63,[38] the gentry had only seen one real danger to their freedom: the king.

Space contributed to the shaping of the Commonwealth in that it created conditions, which were in almost all aspects advantageous to the great landowners, who also played the role of a ruling aristocracy, or even that of a governing oligarchy. Whatever had been devised to increase the political freedom of the nobility as an Estate, space happened to be particularly favorable to this upper stratum. This was not yet fully clear in the early part of the century in question; the second half of the century made it obvious.

NOTES

1. The area of the Commonwealth has never been seriously discussed from this point of view, but I believe Professor Marian Małowist once remarked that the general development pattern of the Commonwealth could be partly explained by its size. Regardless of whether I have remembered his remark properly or not, I am grateful to him for the inspiration while, of course, I take fully responsibility for my argument and conclusions.

2. Regional patterns of urbanisation in the early modern period in north Europe between Lithuania and Ireland were recently discussed comparatively during a conference at the Herzog-August-Bibliothek in Wolfenbüttel (May 1986).

3. J. Le Laboureur, *Histoire et relation du voyage de la Reyne de Pologne et de retour de Madame la Mareschalle de Guébriant...* Paris 1648, p. 179. Le Laboureur wrote about Ciechanów, Mława and Nowe Miasto: they lacked walls and moats, houses there were wretched and disorderly, inhabitants poor, shabby and all of them (?) barefooted.

4. Very little research has been carried out into the relationship between the government and (noble) society with its particular form of Polish self-government. No synthesis similar to *Deutsche Verwaltungsgeschichte* (K.G.A. Jeserich, H. Pohl, G.-Ch. von Unruh, eds.) exists. On the other hand, the distribution of information over the whole country and its use for political purposes by the king, the magnates and the dietines has been discussed recently by Urszula Augustyniak: *Informacja i propaganda w Polsce za Zygmunta III.* Warszawa 1981. On the officialdom see E. Opaliński, *Elita władzy w województwach poznańskim i kaliskim za Zygmunta III.* Warszawa 1981 and L. Buczacki, "Urzędy powiatowe w Wielkopolsce na przełomie XVI i XVII wieku", (résumé français: Les offices dans les districts de Grande-Pologne à la charnière des XVIe et XVIIe siècles), *Przegląd Historyczny*, LXXIV,3, 1983.

5. A. Mączak, "The Conclusive Years. The End of the Sixteenth Century as the Turning-Point of Polish History, in: *Politics and Society in Reformation Europe. Essays for Sir Geoffrey Elton on his Sixty-Fifth Birthday*, ed. by E. I. Kouri and T. Scott, London 1987.

6. H. H. von Thünen, *Der isolierte Staat in seiner Beziehung auf Landwirtschaft und Nationalökonomie.* I (1826). We quote the first paragraphs of Chap. I.

7. W. Abel, "Zur Entwicklung des Sozialprodukts in Deutschland im 16. Jahrhundert. Versuch eines Brückenschlags zwischen Wirtschaftstheorie und Wirtschaftsgeschichte", *Jahrbücher für Nationalökonomie und Statistik*, 173, 1961.

8. Ch. Ogier, *Dziennik podróży do Polski*, I, Gdańsk 1950, pp. 29, 293 (this is a modern edition of the original Latin text with a Polish translation; Polish parts of Ogier's journey only). On husbandry in the Vistula Fens see A. Mączak, *Gospodarstwo chłopskie na Żuławach Malborskich w początkach XVII wieku* (English summary: Peasant husbandry in Vistula Fens at the beginning of the 17th Century),

Warszawa 1962; P. Szafran, *Żuławy Gdańskie w XVII wieku* (deutsche Zusammenfassung: Das Danziger Werder im 17. Jahrhundert), Gdańsk 1981. On the expansion of the Mennonites along the Vistula: K. Ciesielska, "Osadnictwo 'olęderskie' w Prusach Królewskich i na Kujawach w świetle kontraktów osadniczych", *Studia i Materiały z Dziejów Wielkopolski i Pomorza*, IV,2, 1958.

9. W. Dworzaczek, "Kto w Polsce dzierżył buławy?". *Przegląd Historyczny*, XLIII, 1952. There is no up to date survey of the Ukrainian economy in the seventeenth century. A short overview is to be found in Frank E. Sysyn's forthcoming book on Bohdan Chmielnicki's insurrection.

10. Cf. A. Mączak, "Export of Grain and the Distribution of National Income (in Poland) in the years 1550–1650", *Acta Poloniae Historica* XVIII, 1968; idem, "Zusammenhänge zwischen Fernhandel und ungleichmässige Entwicklung polnischer Wirtschaftsgebiete im 16. und 17. Jahrhundert", *Jahrbuch für Wirtschaftsgeschichte*, 1971, Teil III.

11. A. Mączak, "Zur Grundeigentumsstruktur in Polen im 16. und 17. Jahrhundert", *Jahrbuch für Wirtschaftsgeschichte*, 1967, Teil IV.

12. M. Wąsowicz, *Kontrakty lwowskie w latach 1676–1686*, Lwów 1935.

13. Jan Sobieski, *Listy do Marysieńki*, ed. L. Kukulski, II, Warszawa 1973, p. 10; cf. also pp. 83, 95.

14. The shipping activity of the Radziwiłłs has not been adequately researched, although interesting source materials are preserved in the Radziwiłł Archive in the Archiwum Główne Akt Dawnych (Central Record Office), Warsaw. An M.A. thesis by M. Brzozowska on the 1620s (Institute of History, Warsaw University) remains unpublished; Soviet scholars in Minsk have done more work on this commerce in the eighteenth century.

15. J. Burszta, "Handel magnacki i kupiecki między Sieniawą nad Sanem a Gdańskiem od końca XVII do połowy XVIII w.", *Roczniki Dziejów Społecznych i Gospodarczych*, 1955.

16. A. Homecki, *Produkcja i handel zbożowy w latyfundium Lubomirskich w drugiej połowie XVII i pierwszej XVIII wieku*, Wrocław 1970.

17. J. Leskiewiczowa, *Dobra osieckie w okresie gospodarki folwarczno-pańszczyźnianej XVI–XVIII w.*, Wrocław 1957.

18. A. Homecki, o.c.

19. A. Homecki, o.c.

20. W. Kula, J. Leskiewiczowa, eds., "Ks. Józef Czartoryski, 'Myśli moje o zasadach gospodarskich', *Przegląd Historyczny*, XLIV, 1955.

21. Ibid.

22. This is a general conclusion of L. Żytkowicz' *Studia nad gospodarstwem wiejskim w dobrach kościelnych XVI w.*, Warszawa 1962. Żytkowicz, however, studied the 16th and early 17th centuries only.

23. L. Żytkowicz, o.c.; A. Mączak, "Folwark pańszczyźniany a wieś w Prusach Królewskich w XVI/XVII wieku", *Przegląd Historyczny* XLVII, 1956.

24. See *Encyklopedia historii gospodarczej Polski do 1945 roku*, I, Warszawa 1981. under "Folwark" (by M. Kamler).

XIII

25. M. Bogucka, *Handel Gdańska w pierwszej połowie XVII wieku*, Wrocław 1970, p. 69 ff. D. Krannhals' figures on Gdańsk grain shipping are unreliable. This is all the more lamentable since he was the last scholar to consult archival sources destroyed in 1945 (Cf. note 28 and critical comments by U. Wendland in *Weichselland*, 1942, 1/2, pp. 35–45, and *Altpreussische Forschungen*, 20, 1943, pp. 195–197; also Cz. Biernat in Rocznik Gdański, 13, 1954, pp. 224–231).
26. B. Zientara, *Dzieje małopolskiego hutnictwa żelaznego w XIV–XVI w.*, Warszawa 1954, pp. 218sqq.
27. This is a consensus of Polish historians; as a hypothesis it has been proposed by Marian Małowist.
28. Edited by D. Krannhals as an appendix to his *Danzig und der Weichselhandel in seiner Blütezeit vom 16. zum 17. Jahrhundert*, Leipzig 1942.
29. A. Mączak, "Money and Society in Poland-Lithuania in the Sixteenth and Seventeenth Centuries", *Journal of European Economic History*, 1976. On Polish imports in the later seventeenth century cf. A. Manikowski, "Zmiany czy stagnacja? Z problematyki handlu polskiego w drugiej połowie XVII wieku" (résumé français: Commerce de la Pologne entre 1660 et 1700: période de stagnation ou de transformation?), *Przegląd Historyczny*, LXIV,4, 1973.
30. However, the important subject of the space in early modern economic t h o u g h t cannot be discussed here.
31. J. A. Chrapowicki, *Diariusz*, I, ed. T. Wasilewski, Warszawa 1978, p. 7.
32. H. Litwin, "Magnateria polska 1454–1648. Kształtowanie się stanu" (résumé français: Les Magnats polonais, 1454–1648. Formation d'un Ordre), *Przegląd Historyczny*, LXXIV,3, 1983.
33. Cf. papers read at the conference sponsored by Historisches Kolleg on patron-client relationships in early modern Europe (Munich, May 1984). *Klientelprobleme in Europa der Frühen Neuzeit*, ed. by A. Mączak. München. Oldenburg 1988.
34. T. Manteuffel, "Problem feudalizmu polskiego", *Przegląd Historyczny*, 38, 1948; also his "On Polish Feudalism", *Mediaevalia et Humanistica*, 16, 1964.
35. On patronage in Poland, see papers read at the conference mentioned in note 33.

XIV

The structure of power in the Commonwealth of the sixteenth and seventeenth centuries

Though the Polish monarchy retained considerable power in the sixteenth century, there were signs that this power was being increasingly challenged. Perhaps the clearest indication of this lay in the issue of the royal succession. The Jagiellonians had come to the Polish throne in circumstances which required consultation with and approval of the Polish nobility, and virtually every succession thereafter was accompanied by negotiation and concessions. Between the reigns of Jagiełło and Sigismund I, only once did the throne pass from a father to his eldest son; on every other occasion it passed either from one brother to another, or from a father to a younger son. These irregularities were further complicated by the problem of dynastic links with Lithuania, so that by the early sixteenth century it was generally accepted that the Polish monarchy was in fact elective. When Sigismund I attempted to forestall the possibility of an interregnum and renewed haggling with the nobles by having his son crowned during his lifetime, it was already too late to reverse the process. Though the nobility 'elected' the ten-year-old Sigismund II August as their king during his father's lifetime, it was stipulated that this was a unique and unusual case which was not to serve as a precedent and would not prejudice their right to freely choose their king in the future. Clearly, by 1530 the principle of an elective monarchy had entered into the Polish political tradition, and the death of the childless Sigismund II August in 1572 merely meant that the election of a successor would truly be free.

The election came at a time when the lower gentry were at the height of their political power and influence. In the decade preceding, the gentry had spearheaded the movement for the 'execution of the laws', the effect of which was to circumscribe the powers of the greatest magnates while at the same time regularizing the royal revenues. Royal lands illegally alienated after 1504 were to be returned to the king's domain, though this was never completely achieved. These lands were then divided into 'table' lands to meet the expenses of the king's court, and lands which were to be administered for the king by *starostas* who derived an income from them as a reward for services or as payment for their administrative functions. A quarter of the revenues from both types of land was to go for the upkeep of a regular standing mercenary army, known henceforth as the *wojska kwarciane* (from *quarta pars*). By these reforms the gentry felt they has restrained the magnates, regulated the royal income so that no further subsidies would he needed, and generally restored the Commonwealth to the harmonious balance it had enjoyed in some putative past golden age. Though there were radical elements to the movement, on the whole it was a conservative endeavour, as is suggested by its very name. The 'execution of the laws' referred to the gentry's belief that Poland's laws were quite adequate; they merely needed to be executed to the letter in order for the system to work.

The gentry scored other triumphs, among which was the epoch-making Union of Lublin by which the privileges of the Polish nobility were extended to the Lithuanian gentry, thus tempting them against the opposition of the Lithuanian magnates into a close and permanent association with Poland. Further successes came during the reign of Stefan Batory during which the gentry secured control over the Commonwealth's judicial system. All this meant that the gentry were clearly in the ascendant when Sigismund II August died and thereby opened up the question of the manner in which a successor was to be chosen. Because the gentry were organized and confident, because they were led by brilliant men such as Jan Zamoyski, they were able to secure recognition of the principle of *viritim* election – henceforth every single noble in the Commonwealth was to have an equal voice in the election of his king. This took the issue out of the hands of any small group such as the magnates claiming to represent the nobility, and gave it to the entire noble order, which, in theory at least, meant that a royal election might involve assembling several hundred thousand individuals in the fields at Wola outside Warsaw where the election was henceforth to be held.

In effect the royal election of 1573 became something of an auction, with that candidate selected whose representative made the most lavish promises. Indeed, as the nobility went about entrenching their position for all time and ensuring that no king's power would ever threaten them with *absolutum dominium*, two quite distinct documents were drawn up. The first, known as the Henrician articles after Henri of Valois, the first royal candidate to agree to them, became something like the basic law of the Commonwealth. Henceforth every royal candidate was required, before his election, to promise to call the Sejm at least once every two years for no longer than six weeks; to guarantee complete religious freedom to dissident minorities; to consult with the senators resident at his side in questions of war and peace; to consult with the Sejm before calling a *pospolite ruszenie*, which in any case could not be used outside of the borders of the Commonwealth; to consult with the Sejm before imposing new taxes; to accept the elective nature of the Polish monarchy and not to attempt to change it; and finally, in the event that any of these promises were not kept, to recognize the constitutional right *de non praestanda oboedientia* by which the nobility might renounce its allegiance to him. The other document to which any royal candidate had to agree was the *pacta conventa*. Unlike the Henrician articles, the terms of this varied from candidate to candidate and comprised specific promises extracted from them before their election. Some of these conditions obliged the elected king to pay off the debts of his successor, build a Polish fleet out of his own funds, or recover lost territories. They were unrealistic enough to bring discredit upon the whole process of election while at the same time demonstrating the lack of political responsibility among a gentry which sought to solve the state's fiscal and defence problems by shifting the burden onto the king as the price of his election.

The election of 1573 was won by Henri of Valois, largely because he was prepared to promise anything to achieve success and did not entirely believe in the promises which he was making. After five months in Poland, Henri realized that the Poles were quite serious and the prospect of succeeding to the French throne induced him to flée the Commonwealth. The first free election had proved to be a fiasco and an international embarrassment, but in 1576 a somewhat wiser electorate voted for Stefan Batory, the talented and energetic prince of Transylvania. Even this did not go off well, as the magnates preferred a Habsburg and the split election led to a brief civil war marked by Gdańsk's refusal to accept Batory as its king. Ultimately Batory was successful and his reign (1576–86) demonstrated that a strong and courageous king with sufficient personal charisma could still earn the respect of his subjects, carry through reforms, fight successful wars, and effectively punish those like the proud Zborowski family who equated freedom with personal license. Nevertheless the first free elections had not been encouraging and the signs that the political system of the Commonwealth had reached an impasse multiplied: having won their 'golden freedoms', the gentry masses seem to have retreated into a sterile conservatism, terrified of any change in their 'ideal' Commonwealth, obsessed with preventing the king from exercising *absolutum dominium* over them.

Matters came to a head early in the reign of Sigismund III (1587–1632) who, as heir apparent in Sweden and for a brief time its king, was used to considerably more royal authority than the Polish nobility begrudged him. Intent on strengthening his power in the Commonwealth, with an eye to regaining the Swedish crown he had lost in 1599, Sigismund attempted in 1605–6 to introduce reforms which would create a large standing army, increase royal revenues, introduce regular procedures for discussions in the Sejm to curb some of their excesses, and replace the principle of unanimity in the Sejm with simple majority votes. The reforms themselves were quite sensible, but enough of the nobility actually invoked the right of *de non praestanda oboedientia*, and rose in the legal form of rebellion known as a *rokosz* (see glossary), to force the king to shelve the reform program even though he was successful in retaining the Polish throne and defeating the rising. It became obvious after this that the Commonwealth had achieved not so much balance of political forces as a paralysis, which eventually led to stagnation and then catastrophe.

In these circumstances, the magnates of Poland came to play an increasingly important role in the Commonwealth. These were the members of wealthy old families with access to the highest government offices. Some of them could trace their families back to time immemorial, others were descendants of the political elite which had been created by the appointments of Sigismund I and his son, discussed in the last chapter. Office gave them access to royal lands and considerable incomes, which were in turn invested in more land. The shift towards a manorial economy favoured them, and the political deadlock gave them opportunities for manoeuvre. As the gentry masses sank back into sterile conservatism, it was the magnates who emerged as the leaders and organizers of this inchoate political force. The magnates acted as the focus of political activity, as the centre around which factions formed; they were the bridges between the central government and the provincial nobility, the patrons of culture and the agents of its transmission in the absence of a strong royal court, the protectors and promoters of the lower gentry whose political privileges had brought no corresponding economic or social advance. Perhaps it would be no exaggeration to say that in a situation in which centralization at the national level became impossible, the magnates provided something like centralization at the local level; in many spheres of activity they simply replaced the functions of the royal court and the central government. As the following article suggests, by the seventeenth century it was the magnates and the political structures which they created which in some way got around the political deadlock which had developed in the Commonwealth. The republic of nobles had in fact become a republic of a few of the greatest nobles.

Antoni Mączak holds the rank of professor at the University of Warsaw where he specializes in social and economic history. He has also been visiting professor at the University of Illinois and at the British Academy, and has presented a series of lectures at Gothenburg, Uppsala, and various American, German, Italian and Scottish universities. He is co-editor of the *Przegląd Historyczny* (Historical Review), foreign correspondent for the journal *Social History*, and used to be foreign correspondent for the *Urban Yearbook*. Among his published works are studies of various aspects of Poland's economy in early modern times, including the textile industry, agriculture and foreign trade.* He has also co-authored economic and social histories of Poland, edited a history of modern England, and has co-authored a study of the effect of natural resources on European history. Most recently he has prepared a study of everyday life in early modern Europe which will shortly appear in English, and is currently working on a comparative study of European elites in the early modern period.

The contribution which follows represents something of a counterpoint to Wyczański's article. Taking up the thread from the late sixteenth century, Mączak focuses on the concept of social order as it existed in Poland, especially on the order of the nobility which had emerged by the seventeenth century as a social, political and economic elite in the Commonwealth, to the effective exclusion of all other social forces. Rather than concentrating on a weakened central authority, Mączak shifts attention to the exercise of power at the local level, notably by the magnates who organized their own factions and led gentry opinion, providing a degree of centralization in the country which the royal government was no longer able to provide at the national level. In this analysis, the king emerges as little more than just another faction leader, with limited financial resources and with considerably less ability to attract supporters through promotion and advancement than he had exercised in the sixteenth century.

---

* *Sukiennictwo wielkopolskie XIV–XVII w.* (The Textile Industry in Wielkopolska in the XIV to XVII Centuries) (Warsaw 1954); *Gospodarstwo chłopskie na Żuławach malborskich w początkach XVII w.* (The Peasant Economy in Żuławy near Malbork at the Beginning of the XVII Century (Warsaw 1962); *U źródeł nowoczesnej gospodarki europejskiej* (At the Sources of the Modern European Economy) (Warsaw 1967); *Między Gdańskiem a Sundem. Studia nad handlem bałtyckim od połowy XVI do połowy XVII w.* (Between Gdańsk and the Sound. Studies in Baltic Trade from the Middle of the XVI to the Middle of the XVII Centuries) (Warsaw 1972); *Życie codzienne w podróżach po Europie w XVI i XVII w.* (The Everyday Life of European Travellers in the XVI and XVII Centuries) (Warsaw 1978, English edn in preparation); also in preparation, *Governments and the Governed in Pre-Industrial Europe* (Harvester Press). He is also co-author of *Dzieje gospodarcze Polski do roku 1939* (An Economic History of Poland to 1939) (Warsaw 1973); *Społeczeństwo polskie od X do XX w.* (Polish Society from the X to the XX Centuries) (Warsaw 1979); *Geneza nowożytnej Anglii* (The Genesis of Modern England) (Warsaw 1967) and *Encyklopedia historii gospodarczej Polski* (An Encyclopaedia of Polish Economic History), 2 vols. (in preparation); and together with W. N. Parker he has prepared *Natural Resources in European History, Resources for the Future*, Research Papers R-13 (Washington D.C. 1979).

The structure of power in the Commonwealth of the sixteenth and seventeenth centuries

The purpose of the present discussion is to illuminate the essential political evolution of the Polish Commonwealth by analysing its power structure, by which is meant the centres in which power was concentrated and the foundations upon which it rested. To do this, one should perhaps offer an overview of social classes in Poland and their legal position before moving on to a detailed consideration of political institutions and their interaction with key social elements. To begin, some basic definitions are necessary.

One general characteristic of early modern European society was its legal division into distinct estates. The Polish case, though ostensibly similar, in fact manifested certain peculiarities which made it very different. Historically, there was considerable imprecision in Polish political terminology, an imprecision which continues to bedevil historians in their studies of earlier periods in Poland's political evolution. For the distinct English words 'order' and 'estate', the Polish language possessed only one counterpart, *stan* (plural *stany*) which referred both to groups enjoying particular political, social and economic privileges, and to their representatives or representative institutions. The Polish term corresponded to the Latin word *status* and was loosely used up to the eighteenth century to refer to any distinctive, even if legally undifferentiated, group. For example, in the last years of that century, Jędrzej Kitowicz wrote 'A Description of Customs in the Reign of August III' in which he named the clergy, the judiciary (including lawyers and officials in the courts), the military, and the courtiers as distinct orders. Of the courtiers he wrote that those who serve the magnates and wealthy gentry 'can justifiably be termed an order distinct from the others', and he argued that, in its strictest sense, the order of courtiers (*stan dworski*) referred only to 'honourable servants of noble condition, or plebeians ... who pretend to the status of noble by wearing a sword or whose patron passes them off as such'. Clearly a use of the word 'stan' which joins nobles and plebeians under one category transcends any strictly legal definition, and because Kitowicz based his statements on his own experiences and reminiscences rather than following any social theory, we can derive from his social portrait some idea of how these distinctions were regarded in everyday usage. His unfinished work was to have included several other 'professions' including the magnates, lesser landowners, and, finally, the townspeople, peasants, Jews and gypsies. Certainly, in this usage, *stan* and *profesja* (profession) represented particular human conditions rather than orders of society in a strict legal sense.

The Polish language can, however, use the word *stan* in a very narrow sense, as in the case of *stany sejmujące* (the representative estates) of which there were three: the king, the Senate, and the chamber of deputies. Conversely, a broader usage is presented by Marcin Kromer in his *Polonia*, which appeared in 1575 and became western Europe's chief source of information about Poland. This work divided the population of the country in the more traditional European way according to birth into the nobility and the commoners, and according to religious function into the clergy and the laity. In Kromer's work, all other divisions were considered of little importance.

We can admit that the term *stan* reflects considerable ideological and sociopolitical complexity without attempting here to give it a more precise definition than it possessed in the usage of earlier periods under discussion. We shall instead restrict ourselves to the issue of legal privileges in order to compare them to those in other contemporary political systems, and to do this we shall in turn discuss the clergy, the bourgeoisie and finally the nobility as distinct social orders in Poland.

To take the church first, the order of the clergy in Poland, as everywhere else in the Catholic world, was subject to the norms of canon law and enjoyed a clearly privileged status in relation to the rest of society. Catholic archbishops and bishops occupied the first places in the Senate, taking precedence over all temporal senators. They also sat in royal councils where they exercised powers which only time diminished; according to traditional usage, one higher-ranking cleric always exercised the function either of chancellor or vice-chancellor. The clergy was, of course, hierarchically organized and only the tip of this pyramid emerged into full political activity. Unlike the French first estate, the lower clergy in Poland did not have a voice in the representative institutions and even the canons of the church only had a voice in the internal affairs of their own diocese. Even so, intelligent, educated and worldly clerics working through the chancelleries were able to maintain until modern times a considerable part of the influence which they enjoyed in the middle ages. Indeed, this link between the clerical elite and the central institutions of the kingdom generally acted as a stabilizing influence. One example of this occurred when the creation of a national church, independent of Rome, was mooted during the reign of Sigismund II August (1548–72). On this occasion, the close ties between the spiritual and political elites served to reject the proposal and save the country for Catholicism, even though the primate himself was undecided in the matter.

In the Commonwealth as it emerged from the Union of Lublin in 1569, broad political privileges extended only to the Catholic clergy. The Orthodox church in Poland and Lithuania was never able to reach an equivalent legal position nor did the attempted union of the two churches at Brześć in 1596 give the newly created Uniate bishops any seats in the Senate or enhance the political influence of their church. This reflected the temporal power of the Catholic episcopate and was ultimately to have disastrous consequences for the Uniate church in the Commonwealth. Similarly the Protestant clergy, whether Lutheran, Calvinist or other, never possessed any political privileges. Of course, the Calvinists rejected a church hierarchy of this type anyway, and no Catholic bishop had the slightest political reason to be tempted further by the Reformation.

If we turn to the bourgeois order, we find that it lost its political opportunity in Poland at a fairly early date. Cities could still influence royal policy in the fourteenth and fifteenth centuries since they were a major source of credit for the monarchy, but at the beginning of the Thirteen Years' War against the Teutonic Order (1454–66), Kazimierz IV issued privileges to the nobility alone. These privileges of Nieszawa laid the basis for the nobility's parliamentary activities but they did not extend to the towns. Henceforth the bourgeois order was only able to observe from the sidelines as the struggle between the magnates and the gentry gave rise to a new political structure in Poland.

The political emergence of the towns was hampered by a lack of any common institutions or any systematic and permanent contacts among the cities. In fact, every city had its own structure of orders which defined its citizens' relative positions, and there was a hierarchical gradation in the position of the cities themselves. Without adding the city of origin and one's social position within its hierarchy, the bald term *mieszczanin* (town dweller) was of little significance. Indeed it was a negative term signifying a lack of the fiscal and legal privileges possessed by the nobility or its right to the ownership of all land outside the town walls. Still, the town dwellers were distinct from the peasantry and this was of considerable importance to the citizens of smaller towns whose position largely depended on the policies pursued by their overlord – either the city's direct owner, or the *starosta* who administered royal cities. The citizens of royal towns could at least turn to the royal courts or seek the support of royal councillors and this gave them an advantage over private cities which did not enjoy such opportunities.

In fact, when we speak of the bourgeois order we are really speaking of a town's elite. The town councils and urban courts which emerged between the thirteenth and fifteenth centuries deprived the commoners of political rights and left them dependent on, but outside of, the corporate system. There was a new movement in the sixteenth century by representatives of the common people challenging the authority of the urban elites, and the fact that this occurred simultaneously in several Prussian and Polish cities suggests that at least in these towns there was some communication between various opposition groups, a communication which paralleled the spread of Reformation ideology. Sigismund I took advantage of these internal conflicts to strengthen his own authority over the cities by settling their disputes, but none of this had any real impact on the balance of power among the various social orders in the Commonwealth.

It has been suggested by K. Grzybowski that the cities themselves refused to participate in parliamentary activities in the fifteenth century to preserve their independence and avoid domination by the nobility by negotiating directly with the king. Unfortunately the sources offer little evidence of urban elite opinion in this question but, whatever its intention, this failure to take an active political role was fatal to the bourgeois order.

The political possibilities available to Polish cities can be demonstrated by comparison with Prussia. There the conflict between the estates and the Teutonic Knights began in the early fifteenth century and resulted in the domination of the local nobility by the cities. After the second peace of Toruń in 1466 gave final form to the administration in royal Prussia, the great cities of Toruń, Elbląg and Gdańsk shared seats with the nobility in the upper chamber of the regional assembly (the Prussian Council, later the Prussian Senate), while the smaller cities together with the nobles sent representatives to the lower chamber. This largely resulted from the size and strength of the towns and the weakness of the nobility in this small province, but it does illustrate the political opportunity missed by the other cities in the Commonwealth.

The effect of economic strength on political power is best illustrated by the unique case of Gdańsk, which dealt with the Commonwealth as a corporate body though its merchant citizens had individual commercial ties with the grain-producing Polish landowners. Because of its financial strength and commercial links, Gdańsk usually secured advantageous terms in its negotiations, so that Władysław Czapliński has compared its political role in the state to that of a magnate, a more appropriate analogy than the anachronistic description of it as a free city.

The bicameral Polish Sejm which emerged after 1492 contained only a symbolic bourgeois representation from Kraków with an advisory voice in matters specifically affecting that city. After 1569 Wilno was accorded a similar privilege as capital of Lithuania. Without the towns, therefore, political struggles assumed a triangular form involving the king, the magnates and the gentry; the bishops defended their own interests but otherwise they usually sided with the king or magnates. The contest between the gentry and the magnates quickly assumed prominence and manifested itself in the constitutional struggle between the chamber of deputies and the Senate. The royal privilege of Mielnik in 1501 acknowledged the premier role of the latter, but in 1505 the act *Nihil Novi* gave both chambers of the Sejm the right to approve or reject royal legislation. At the time this was a great success for the gentry but, by the end of the century, the system was beginning to operate for the benefit of the magnates. The towns were no longer a significant political factor in a system which had fallen entirely into the hands of the nobility.

The noble order included a substantial proportion of the Commonwealth's population. In the absence of exact data, it is generally estimated that, around the middle of the sixteenth century, the nobility in the Crown alone constituted about 8 per cent of the population, though it was unevenly distributed; in Mazowsze, for example, it was as high as 25 per cent. As early as the fourteenth and fifteenth centuries it was generally accepted that noble status was derived from parents who were both acknowledged by the general consensus of the local gentry to have been nobly born. The testimony of those wearing the same heraldic device was especially noted and, since there was no college of heralds to protect noble coats of arms, such testimony was vital for any court attempting to decide more difficult cases. There were numerous movements to 'investigate and purify' the nobility which often degenerated into quarrels over property and influence, but the Polish gentry as a whole was paradoxically rather generous in according noble status.

For example, after its definitive incorporation into the Commonwealth in 1466, royal Prussia employed a much broader definition of noble status than did that part of Prussia remaining under the control of the Teutonic Order, later to become ducal Prussia. Similarly when the vassal territories of Lębork (Lauenburg) and Bytów (Bütow) were incorporated into the Crown between 1637 and 1657, all freeholders in these areas were deemed noble and were deprived of this status only when the territories went to Brandenburg after 1657. The gentry was similarly indulgent towards those of its brethren who did not own but rented their lands from the magnates or the church.

On the other hand, from 1505, new legislation attempted to limit the incidence of mixed marriage between nobles and commoners by tightening up the requirements for noble descent on the maternal side, and by 1576 the Sejm wrested control over ennoblement away from the king, save in the case of awards on the battlefield. The gentry was determined to resist infiltration into its ranks from a body of energetic and industrious townsmen and it firmly believed in the purity of its own blood. It considered possession of land and personal freedom to be the essence of a noble lifestyle and any noble who did not own land could not take practical advantage of his privileges until he settled on a piece of land either as a tenant or an owner.

The most characteristic form of political activity for the gentry masses were the *sejmiki*, regional assemblies of the nobility which by the end of the sixteenth century in effect decided about the internal affairs of their own districts or provinces. They were summoned by the king, the *wojewoda* (provincial governor) or the *starosta*, and among their functions was the election of deputies to the Sejm to whom the *sejmiki* gave specific instructions and from whom they received reports of the Sejm's deliberations. After 1578, the *sejmiki* also elected

7. A *sejmik* of the regional nobility held in a small town in the eighteenth century, by J. P. Norblin.

representatives to the Tribunal, the final court of appeal in most cases. *Sejmiki* also recommended to the king candidates for provincial office and, beginning with 1672, whenever there was an interregnum the *sejmiki* assumed the highest authority within each province. It was also at the *sejmiki* that disputes were first aired, either between the magnates and the gentry or between the magnates themselves.

Because of the high government offices which they occupied, the magnates together with the wealthiest local landowners were especially influential at the *sejmiki*. Magnates serving as crown officials possessed prestige and considerable wealth, but they were also much more politically involved than the gentry masses. Urszula Augustyniak has pointed out that in a society with very limited circulation of information those with continuous political contacts outside their own region would enjoy considerable authority, while their local opponents without such contacts might have difficulty in influencing public opinion. Thus the provincial gentry might be at a considerable disadvantage in attempting to resist manipulation by the magnates.

The struggle between gentry and magnates also continued at the centre of the political structure, in the Sejm, where customs and regulations emphasized the subordinate role of the chamber of deputies – representing the gentry for the most part – and the superior role of the royal council, that is the Senate, which was by definition composed of the highest officers in the state and therefore the most powerful and influential of the noble order. The deputies formally and ultimately successfully denied this inferior status, yet it was precisely because of their separate status that the deputies could debate issues by themselves under the leadership of a marshal (i.e. speaker) whom they themselves had elected. They were thus able to organize themselves independently and create a centre of political opinion which could radiate out to influence the *sejmiki*.

It was this mechanism which operated during the gentry's movement for the 'execution of the laws'. The most active representatives from the *sejmiki* won a decisive influence in the chamber of deputies and demonstrated this influence during the heated discussions held at the Sejms of 1562 and 1564, dealing with the return of illegally alienated royal land. The mechanics of the movement were illustrated in a bitter speech in the Senate by the magnate Jan Działyński, *wojewoda* of Chełmno, who opposed the activities of the gentry deputies and frequently threatened those from his own seaboard province with reprisals because they 'spoke contrary to the instructions of their own *sejmiki*' and because when meeting in the Sejm they 'resort to royal protection but at home among their neighbours they stay silent and ashamed of what they do here'. This was the lament of a magnate who had lost control over the election of his provincial deputies. It would seem that in the province of Chełmno the gentry were numerous and politically experienced so that in 1563 they were able to elect their own deputy against the will of the region's senators. Elsewhere, as in the province of Malbork, the gentry were not as numerous and the local *wojewoda* continued to control the election of deputies to the Prussian assembly. The representative bodies in royal Prussia were especially active so that the gentry opposition in one *sejmik* could count on the help of its colleagues in the remaining assemblies; for example the grievances of Chełmno province were presented to the Sejm held in 1563/4 in Warsaw by the deputies from Pomorze, since the deputy elected in Chełmno supported senatorial policies.

The above are perhaps extreme examples of the conflict between the gentry and the magnates, taken from a region and period in which the struggle was most intense. Shortly after, during the interregnum beginning in 1572, it became obvious that the senators were able to organize themselves more quickly and effectively than were the gentry, and this was in part because close ties of kinship and friendship amplified their frequent and routine correspondence, whereas communications among the gentry in the *sejmiki* encountered the impediments of distance and unfamiliarity.

Because of the complexity of this two-tiered parliamentary system, the political situation could develop quite differently from what happened in the aforementioned example of royal Prussia between 1562 and 1564. The outcome depended in large part on local conditions in the *sejmiki* as well as on the relations between the king and each house in the Sejm. For example, should the chamber of deputies possess instructions from their *sejmiki* opposing royal tax policy, the monarch might take his appeal directly to the *sejmiki* themselves. Ultimately, however, by the end of the sixteenth century, the *sejmiki* largely became dependent on the will of the magnates and tended to concentrate their attention on local problems which defined their response on any national issue.

The Polish social system made noble privilege accessible to a large proportion of the population and therefore some method of selection was needed to determine who among this numerous class would exercise power. The gentry masses carried on a struggle through the sixteenth century in the *sejmiki* for a role in government, but by the following century these regional assemblies had fallen under the sway of the magnates. Even so, any bald assertion that the magnates alone ruled Poland would represent an oversimplification of seventeenth-century conditions which varied with time, with place, and with the people involved.

If one accepts that a magnate class did emerge to political prominence by the end of the sixteenth century, one must in the first place ask how it came to rise so high above its peers. Great lords had existed for centuries in Poland, but during the sixteenth century a rather newer system of recruitment evolved which depended on selecting the country's leaders from among those royal secretaries whose education and political experience qualified them for further advancement. Andrzej Wyczański has studied the phenomenon of the royal secretaries in detail and has shown how that position groomed candidates to the highest offices in both church and state. Though there was a limited number of places at the top of the socio-political hierarchy, and not every royal secretary achieved a brilliant career, it is true, as Wyczański has shown, that the common element in the biographies of the most prominent leaders of the sixteenth century was service in the chancellery as secretary to the king (see chapter 5).

Another less travelled road to secular advance was through the leadership of the gentry masses. In this milieu, mastery of rhetoric was highly prized and Ciceronian orators well entrenched within their provincial constituency and enjoying the confidence of the *sejmik* had ample opportunity to develop their skills on a national level in the Sejm. Such popular leaders invariably served in numerous delegations, were elected as marshals of the *sejmiki*, were chosen as deputies to the Sejm, and might even crown their careers with an appointment to a senatorial office. It was this latter possibility which posed a hidden threat to the political independence of the gentry which had entrenched itself in the chamber of deputies but which was doomed to continually lose its leadership. Co-optation by royal grants of land and high political appointments to be held for life came to those gentry leaders who had emerged into a position of permanent political influence. Members of the gentry who were too successful politically would find themselves laden with lands and office which served to pull them into the circle of the magnates and weaken their previous commitment to the political aspirations of the gentry masses. By the seventeenth century, many marshals in the chamber of deputies were in fact close to magnate or senatorial status at a time when a majority of the *sejmiki* were also falling under magnate domination. Indeed, by this time it was dependence on the patronage of a magnate which formed the basis of a successful political career.

The advance of the lesser nobles to higher office was fairly complicated, but for the sons of senatorial families the matter was much simpler. Włodzimierz Dworzaczek has demonstrated that by the seventeenth century they 'gained their spurs' and the confidence of the local gentry by acting for a short time as marshals of the *sejmiki* or as deputies to the Sejm, after which they usually managed to secure a permanent position for themselves in the Senate.

The senatorial order of course manifested certain gradations. At the top end were the senators in residence, created by a gentry obsessed with circumscribing the supposed royal pursuit of *absolutum dominium*. They were obliged to reside with the king in order to advise him and scrutinize his activities between sessions of the Sejm which assembled for only six weeks every two years. Władysław Czapliński has shown that because these senators were in fact appointed by the king, in practice a monarch like Sigismund III (1587–1632) used them as a royalist faction to strengthen his own authority. These senators remained in Warsaw rather unwillingly, even though they were only obliged to perform their duties four at a time for half a year, but the task involved expenditures which brought no corresponding remuneration. They were, however, in a position to exercise and enhance their own political influence on the *sejmiki* by sending them letters which paralleled the royal instructions.

At the other end of the senatorial order were the inferior senators (*drążkowi*) whose status was symbolized by the less comfortable chairs in which they sat in the Senate. They were the less important castellans whose opinions were heard only at the end of deliberations and who were often dependent on their more prominent colleagues. They tended to be active in the *sejmiki*, however, and on four occasions between 1570 and 1632 a castellan from the Senate was actually elected as marshal in the chamber of deputies, a short-lived but highly prized honour which gave its holder a decisive influence over the Sejm's activities.

The most peculiar characteristic of the Polish and Lithuanian senatorial magnates was their provincialism which contrasted strongly with the aspirations of the great nobles in more centralized monarchies. Unlike the latter, a Polish magnate's power did not depend on residence in the capital or with the king. Such attendance was important only for young nobles intent on building their careers through service at court to the king or to his ministers, or even to the presumed successor to the king, as in the case of Władysław during the latter part of the reign of his father Sigismund III. The basis of a magnate's activity was in fact domination of the gentry in his own province, especially through the *sejmiki*, as well as acting as an intermediary between his own gentry masses and the royal government. Indeed, to really understand the political mechanisms of the Commonwealth, one must consider the structure not from the centre but from the provincial level.

In a state as extensive and poorly centralized as the Commonwealth, political life could flourish only at the provincial level. Through their *sejmiki*, the gentry could influence the decisions of the king, his ministers, and the Sejm, and this conditioned their political awareness as well as encouraged the central institutions to continually consult with them. The decisions of the *sejmiki* constitute a voluminous and difficult set of sources which still demands much detailed research. These *lauda* contain opinions about both general and particular issues, about taxes, foreign policy, local autonomy, freedom, as well as the individual complaints of prominent or popular local figures and townsmen represented by noble spokesmen. In theory, public and private interests were distinct, but in these documents it is hardly possible to separate the two, and this at least suggests the general view of the gentry that the preservation of individual rights was a public concern. The real problem for the historian is to distinguish between the interests of individual nobles and their interests as a class, and then to consider the historical significance of the contrast between the short-term interests of the noble order and the long-term interests of the Polish state and nation.

As one studies the operations of the *sejmiki* it becomes obvious that, over time, the relationship between patron and client became increasingly its dominant social and political feature and an important link between different levels of the nobility. Zofia Zielińska has examined this relationship in eighteenth-century Lithuania, but her research has led her to warn against seeing its operations in the contacts between the magnates and the poorest of the gentry who were dependent upon them economically. The latter did ritually participate in and vote at the *sejmik* in support of one magnate or another, but Zielińska sees this rather as a 'one-time commercial transaction involving an exchange of their political rights in return for cash advances as well as food and drink at the *sejmik*'. The relations between the magnates and the middling gentry were long-standing and much more complex than this. The magnates would choose the most prominent of the middling gentry to act as the *directores* of their faction in the *sejmik*. Such clients not only carried out their patron's instructions, but they also had an essential function as advisers, agitators and negotiators when dealing with the gentry masses or with opposing factions. By the eighteenth century they also had to deal with the threat of 'exploding' the *sejmik* by the introduction of the *liberum veto* as in the Sejm, though this threat receded after a statute in 1766 introduced majority voting into the *sejmik* for all important issues.

Any faction leader in a *sejmik* could count on his relatives, dependent officials, gentry who served him, and on his 'friends' – temporary allies who supported him as long as he enjoyed the confidence and support of his patron. He frequently had to meet the considerable expense of political activity from his own resources in the hope that, with success, his patron would ensure a lucrative return or intercede to procure land or military office as a reward. If his patron's political interests covered a large area, he might exercise considerable power under the most general of instructions. For example, during a dispute with the king, Krzysztof Radziwiłł, great hetman of Lithuania and one of the most powerful men in the Commonwealth, wrote to Antoni Przypkowski, the administrator of his estates at Mohilev, charging him to have certain matters inserted into the instructions issued by the *sejmik* to its deputies. Rather than commanding his agent, Radziwill made tactical recommendations, using phrases such as 'in my opinion it would be best . . .' and concluded by suggesting that the agent somehow contrive to secure election as one of the deputies.

Individuals like Przypkowski were extremely useful. They administered their patron's estates as the basis of their income, but they also collected information, functioned at their patron's court and organized their own network of agents, called *ductores populi* by the eighteenth century, to agitate among voters and keep an eye on the activities of opposing factions. Such agents were potential competitors who might even inform on the faction leader himself should they manage to get access to the patron. From the best surviving memoirs, such as the detailed diary of Marcin Matuszewicz (1714–73), the provincial faction organizers emerge as almost exact counterparts to the precinct captains in the American electoral system.

A magnate's political ideas, his resources and his family and personal connections were all crucial in the creation of a political faction. The magnates and the Polish parliamentary system as a whole demanded considerable financial investment as well as adroit political activists oriented towards national issues and capable of organizing the gentry. Such individuals were highly prized, for without them the magnates would have been helpless. A professional politician of this sort might never achieve personal independence, but once his reputation was established he could always secure additional advantages by changing factions.

From the viewpoint of the magnates, local political activity might only be part of their total influence within the Commonwealth. For example, the greatest Lithuanian magnates were sometimes able to extend their influence beyond the confines of the Grand Duchy. In the aftermath of the Union of Lublin, their interests reached into the Crown and even into royal Prussia. The Calvinist branch of the Radziwiłł family, to take one case, claimed to protect the interests of Protestants throughout the Commonwealth, though this was only one aspect of their political prominence. In the western areas of the Crown, however, in contrast to Lithuania or the Ukraine, the gentry were less subordinate to the magnates. A classic nineteenth-century study of *sejmiki* in Kujawy by Adolf Pawiński did not detect any examples of magnate interference, and a recent study by E. Opaliński of the elites in the Poznań region between 1587 and 1632 emphasizes the considerable independence of its relatively prosperous gentry.

These regional differences were conditioned by many factors, especially by the economic situation of the nobility. Not every magnate was active in politics, but it was impossible to separate political from economic interests, particularly when it came to defending one's interests in land disputes before a tribunal. Furthermore, the prestige and lifestyle of the magnates demanded that they enhance the education of younger members of the local gentry by employing them in their residences as aides. The local gentry could also demand of their magnate neighbours that they represent their interests before the king, especially when it came to securing judicial appointments and honours. Thus, whether a magnate wanted it or not, economic interests and public opinion tended to push him into political activity.

Such a situation inevitably resulted from the gradual concentration of lands into ever fewer hands, a trend which had accelerated from the end of the sixteenth century. Certainly it has been demonstrated that this was the case for most of the territories of the Commonwealth, though not all areas have as yet been investigated. With the exception of Mazowsze and royal Prussia which lacked the tradition of large hereditary estates, the share of land held by the wealthiest class increased steadily everywhere in the Crown, including the Ukraine. Large landowners were more resistant to disasters, particularly those caused by war, because they could more easily attract new settlers, extend protection to runaways, and weather monetary devaluation. Further research is needed into the circulation of money in Poland, but the great financial crises of 1619 and the 1660s probably contributed to many financial problems resulting in bankruptcies. The magnates could benefit from these since they could easily borrow substantial sums from lesser neighbours with capital, and invest in lands which were up for sale or in any other profitable enterprise. Though the greatest expenses of a magnate were associated with luxury consumption at their chief residences, salaries for their servants and courtiers and political outlays, their major capital investment was in land acquired from smaller landowners. This process has been investigated for estates in the southeast in the second half of the seventeenth century, and further research will undoubtedly show that it began earlier and was more pervasive in the lands of the Crown.

The complex series of interactions between the magnates and their lesser brethren is often unjustifiably interpreted as a one-sided dependency. The relationship could indeed be parasitic, but elements of reciprocity and occasionally even of conflict can also be discerned. For the local gentry, the magnate's residence was the only available cultural centre which might impart some polish to their sons or serve as a marriage market for their eligible daughters. The gentry also expected their local magnate to recommend them for honours and military commissions. In economic matters, the gentry sought administrative posts or leases on their patron's lands and his assistance and protection in legal disputes. If he did not fulfil these expectations, he could not count on the gentry's assistance or loyalty when he needed them, he might be unable to acquire servants, his agents and advisers might transfer their loyalties elsewhere, and he would thereby be weakened vis-à-vis his rivals both in the *sejmiki* and at the royal court.

One should not ignore the social aspects of clientage. Life at the magnate's court introduced the gentry to culture, to music, painting and fashion. It was there, above all, that one could experience the peculiar blend of native, western and oriental traditions which comprised the 'Sarmatian' culture (see glossary) of early modern Poland. In the long run, such cultural leadership merely confirmed the magnate's dominant role, especially in the isolated and poorly developed regions where this cultural milieu was the only intermediary between the residences of the lesser gentry and the outside world.

By the eighteenth century, the continuing concentration of estates and authority had led to a decrease in the number of magnates, that is the number of large landowners who were in a position to conduct independent political action. The independence of the gentry decreased correspondingly, and Witold Kula has observed that by this time most of the gentry held their land on leases rather than by hereditary right. The operation of unvarnished social dependence in such circumstances is best illustrated by the practices of the treasurer of Lithuania, Jan Jerzy Flemming (d. 1771). He was a German whose family had been brought to Poland under August II (1697–1733), and Kitowicz says of him that

he did not like Poles and dealt with them only as much as his interests demanded. It was necessary for him to have friends among the gentry and he maintained their sons as his courtiers, thereby engaging their affections and rendering himself popular. A register of these courtiers included over a hundred names, but few of them were employed at his side; when he took on someone for service, he entered him in the register as a reminder, gave him a pension, food and forage for his horses, and then sent him to one of his estates ... Whenever he needed political support at the *sejmik* or in the tribunal, he instructed his courtiers to assemble at an appointed place.

Flemming hardly knew any of them and had to ask who they were when they arrived. The courtier responded that he was his servant from such and such an estate and when the magnate found confirmation of this in the register, he despatched the new arrival to the marshal for accommodation and other amenities; when he no longer needed their presence, each returned to the estate whence he came.

Admittedly Kitowicz treats Flemming as something of a curiosity within the affable and jovial world of the Sarmatian nobility, but this unintegrated German's blunt realism serves to illuminate the true and pragmatic motives behind the concern of the magnates for their clients.

When compared either with the other social orders in Poland, or with the aristocracy elsewhere in Europe, the Polish nobility as a whole constituted an unusual type of elite. Historians of early modern Europe usually distinguish three different types of elite. A social elite usually enjoyed prestige, high honours and an imposing genealogy; an economic elite included the wealthy who were best able to take advantage of economic opportunities because of the capital available to them; the political elite held important positions in government and thereby controlled political change and the direction of policy. Such distinctions apply to states, but they might also apply to individual cities where there might be a difference between the social prestige of the patriciate and the wealth of the great merchants. Generally speaking, these distinctions were crucial in determining how much power in any society would accrue to the monarchy at its centre.

The Polish Commonwealth seems to confirm this general principle, *ex adverso* as it were, since it is impossible to distinguish specific elite groups within it according to the above criteria. This is because the magnates fused all three forms of status, though in varying proportions. The fundamental condition for membership in the elite was an estate which gave stability to a noble's status, secured the future of his descendants, and facilitated political activity. Capital was also necessary for the maintenance of a suitable residence, as well as for contracting advantageous loans to the state. Offices also demanded considerable financial resources, particularly the office of hetman whose holder often had to settle pay demands by the army without any guarantee of immediate reimbursement. Those attempting to enter the elite would base themselves on grants of royal land to be held in perpetuity, since the acquisition and development of hereditary estates was a slow and costly process in comparison with the short-term efforts needed to obtain a royal land grant, though the number available was limited and competition for them was bitter. In royal Prussia, for example, the elite's hereditary estates were small and one's position largely depended on being given the supervision of royal estates. Between 1526 and 1657 eight families alone held 44 per cent of the *starostwa* in the region, and four of these together held one third of these lucrative appointments. In the end, only two families survived this period, and after the wars of the mid-seventeenth century even this elite disintegrated. Magnates from other regions such as the Radziwiłłs secured control of the Prussian royal estates and local residents became the salaried servants of absentee patrons.

Urban wealth was still able to secure admission into the landed elite in the fifteenth and early sixteenth centuries, but by the seventeenth only a few citizens of Gdańsk with financial links to the royal treasury or to the magnates were able to secure noble status by adoption, and this never brought them further advancement. It was not until the Enlightenment promoted attempts at reforming the Commonwealth in the last years of its existence that pressure was exerted to associate the bourgeoisie of Warsaw with the nobility.

The Polish political elite was closely tied to the magnates, who secured either for themselves or for their protégés all of the key offices in their province. The lower levels of this elite are less well known, but they included local functionaries active in the tribunals and in regional administration which increased in significance as the central institutions of the Commonwealth atrophied. The number of senators and deputies did not increase over time, but local offices, usually of an honorific nature, proliferated beyond measure. By the eighteenth century, because of this inflation of honours, only the obscure, impoverished or feeble-minded remained without some honorary title. The importance of office is illustrated in the memoirs of Jan Chryzostom Pasek, who in 1667 was given the position of *komornik* (bailiff) by the *wojewoda* and other dignitaries of the Rawa province. He wrote that they told him 'this was a step towards higher honours ... even to a voice in the *sejmik* which would be exercised in precedence over those who remained without an office. This was because they very much wanted to raise me *promotionibus* and they promised me that I would be able to rise at the latest within three years. They sent me on delegations to the king, to the archbishop, and to the bishop of Kujawy, all of which enhanced my reputation after which they intended to raise me *ad altiora.*'

Though not wealthy, Pasek possessed considerable personal prestige, a good family, a coat of arms, and the necessary manners, which were quite sufficient attributes to advance him far ahead of even the most brilliant of commoners. They could at best rise to power through the church, though by the seventeenth century even this route became doubtful, not only because of prejudice against the lower orders but also because of the influx of the sons of the lesser gentry into the seminaries.

Among the wealthiest nobles, the length of time a family had been established in a district was a fundamental way of distinguishing membership in the elite, for many individuals of doubtful status attempted to bribe their way into the nobility. Even if such persons were eventually accepted as noble, this rarely led to any further rise in their status, except in cases of unusual ability supported by the protection of a magnate. Among the middling and wealthier gentry social position was tied to the length of settlement in an

area, since ties of marriage and friendship were solidified over several generations and those belonging to a family which had settled in an area only in the
previous generation, or even two generations before, were still regarded as
relative newcomers.

It is therefore somewhat paradoxical that the fact that an admission into
the senatorial order was recent was not a handicap, though one must distinguish here between those for whom such an honour had been achieved with a
patron's help and was the crowning of a career, and those for whom such an
appointment was part of a permanent position within the magnate elite.
This distinction is obviously clearer to a historian familiar with the whole
history of a family than it might have been to the family members themselves
or to their contemporaries. It was, however, easy to discern which senators
'belonged to someone' and which were independent. It is less easy to determine
whether such magnates were tied to the king, and whether indeed such ties
make it impossible to speak of a magnate as independent. Perhaps one should
not regard the Polish king as head of state so much as the head of his own
faction, more or less equal to the others.

The king had many weighty prerogatives among which was the distribution
of royal lands and offices. The higher posts were usually endowed with
commensurate salaries or sustained by the income from estates, but there
were well-known examples of nobles meeting the expenses of their office from
their own coffers. One perceptive observer of Polish affairs, William Bruce,
accused Sigismund III of attempting to destroy the financial position of the
Protestant nobles by systematically appointing them to senatorial office without also giving them any lucrative *starostwa*. Such practices may seem to
contradict the claim made above that the three elite types were fused in
Poland, but it should be noted that contemporaries clearly regarded the
awarding of office without corresponding income as an exception and an
anomaly. The king's position as leader of his own faction depended on the
fact that his prerogatives allowed him to promote and enrich his followers
much more quickly than the magnates could. Therefore any ambitious
parvenu was well advised to initiate his career at the king's side. He did not
need to remain in the royal camp permanently. Once he had achieved a
modicum of success and entered the elite, it was relatively easy to put down
roots. One could usually point to one ancestor or another of senatorial rank
from the fifteenth century; blood ties to the most prestigious families were
also important. This was the purpose of the facade to the palace at Ujazd
built for Krzysztof Ossoliński, then a relative newcomer among the highest
elite. Its inscriptions were devoted to numerous well-known ancestors and
attempted to convince guests of the antiquity of their host's family.*

To distinguish themselves from the gentry masses, the magnates developed

---

* For a more complete description of this palace, see chapter 8.

a taste for fantastic genealogies reaching into antiquity to supplement their authentic roots. Because of its heraldic device, the Krasiński family associated itself with a legend transmitted by Livy involving a raven. The Pac family, which dominated Lithuania in the middle of the seventeenth century, had similar claims. Stefan Pac (1587–1643) visited Florence in 1625 and reported an evening spent at the house of the Pazzi family who suggested that some of their ancestors had fled to Lithuania to escape domestic commotions. He added that he did not deny this 'for I had heard *per traditionem* from my own elders that our house comes from Italy'. Stefan Pac was as yet fairly timid in his genealogical aspirations.

There were a few families with hereditary titles though, with the exception of the Lithuanian dukes specified in the Union of Lublin, these were not officially recognized by the Commonwealth. The Radziwiłłs strengthened a family tree already reaching back into mythology by acquiring the title of 'imperial prince' in 1547. The activities of Jerzy Ossoliński, great-crown-chancellor and brother to the owner of Ujazd, led to a similar honour being bestowed through papal nomination in 1634. There were also a few families who had the title of 'imperial margrave' and their number grew in the eighteenth century. The complexes which such titles aroused is illustrated by a Firlej family tradition which claimed that an ancestor, the *wojewoda* and hetman Mikołaj, refused a title offered him by the emperor during a conference in Vienna in 1515. The family claimed that the emperor dispensed such titles to members of the Polish king's retinue so as not to spend any gold on them. Having thus denigrated those who did hold imperial titles, the Firlejs toyed with the notion that their own title of margrave was the result of a special privilege issued by Kazimierz the Great in 1333!

The contrast between the theoretical equality of all nobles and the sharply defined hierarchy within their society was not just a conflict between theory and practice. Reality demanded both that landownership be the material basis of society and that there be no internal legal barriers within the noble order. Individuals could rise and when they did they took their families with them, but such a rise was incorporated into the social and political system of the Commonwealth in the same way that careers 'from rags to riches' in contemporary society do not alter the nature of fundamental institutions.

Having focused on the structure of regional authority, we should now look once again at Poland's central institutions in order to see more clearly why power shifted away from the centre through the seventeenth and eighteenth centuries. Because of the decay of these central institutions during this period, historians have been relatively unconcerned with the financial administration and resources of the Polish state. The incineration of many archives in 1944 complicates any attempt to fill this gap, and the most valuable recent work has dealt with reform programs and the politics of royal land distribution but offers little information about the real income and expenses of the state. Any attempt to compare Polish data with analogous materials from other states is also problematic since there were great variations in the operation of different fiscal systems. In some states the surviving receipts are so inaccurate that one is left with comparative figures in which only the largest discrepancies are of any significance.

The data which can be used for comparison entail estimates of a state's total revenues or evidence of the sums which actually entered the central treasury. It should be remembered that a considerable part of administrative expenditure was covered immediately by the income from royal estates and tariffs. This and other problems should keep us from any illusion of simplicity in dealing with the profusion of figures to be found in the literature on this subject. On the other hand, differences in the relative financial positions of particular states seem to exceed any margin of error arising from difficulties with the sources.

In order to properly compare the fiscal system of the Commonwealth with that of other states, two questions must be answered: how much revenue entered the royal treasury, and what was its source? One must remember that east central Europe was considerably poorer than the West, and additional problems arise because of the tax and tariff exemptions enjoyed by its nobility. As a result of these exemptions, those sectors of the economy which were most closely tied to the circulation of money managed to escape taxation, and this was even more problematic since a considerable degree of independence was enjoyed by Gdańsk, the chief intermediary in foreign trade.

Early modern European states have been classified according to their fiscal organization as domain states or as tax states. The scheme was first adopted by Joseph Schumpeter and more recently has been taken up by Scandinavian researchers such as Sven A. Nilsson, Brigitta Oden and Erling Ladewig Petersen. According to this classification, the Commonwealth belongs in the first category. No one in Poland suggested selling off the extensive royal estates, and taxation of the nobility did not occur until the introduction of the relatively insignificant capitation tax of 1662, after several unsuccessful earlier attempts. If we compare the Commonwealth with other states which had not yet entered an absolutist stage, such as Denmark or Brandenburg–Prussia at the beginning of the seventeenth century, we can see that the Polish system was characterized by very low productivity on the royal estates. The royal lands underwent an intensive investigation in 1564–5, but subsequent administrators did not manifest similar zeal. Anna Sucheni-Grabowska has shown that by the seventeenth century leaseholders on the royal estates would pay their rents in various ways, as long as they were not liable to any supervision of their current incomes, and this made Poland very different from any state with a developed system of fiscal control.

The result was that the resources of the central government were not great, but also that the nobles who held leases on the royal domains became in some senses the direct and collective owners of the state with an interest in preserving the system. Perhaps this was not so different from the situation in other states with a developed royal domain, but only in the Commonwealth was any challenge to this situation systematically eliminated, whether it came from an urban elite which was a potential competitor for control of state income, or from a monarchy supported by a bureaucracy. In as much as the bureaucracy was growing elsewhere in Europe, its stagnation or even possible regress in Poland is significant enough to warrant further investigation.

Because of this underdeveloped bureaucracy, the central government's operating costs were low, but the income of its treasury was still surprisingly small for what was after all one of the largest and more populated countries in Europe. Around 1580, the income of the public and royal treasury reached around 669,000 *thalers*, which equalled about 17.2 metric tons of silver. During the period of intensive tax pressure between 1649 and 1652, this rose to 1,593,000 *thalers*, or around 38.5 metric tons of silver, which increased again in the next three years to 45.4 tons. After the devastation of mid-century monetary crises and treasury reform, the central government in the Crown collected an average of 43.7 tons of silver annually in the period between 1672 and 1678, while Lithuania's contribution was equal to no more than about 30 per cent of this total. One can also express this as growth in real income by comparing it to fluctuations in the price of grain, the country's main product, and this suggests that the real increase in the treasury's income was much more modest. If we index the price of wheat in Gdańsk between 1576 and 1580 at 100, then prices rose to 195 in the first half of the seventeenth century and then fell back to 137 in the period between 1672 and 1678. Using this reference point, we can observe that the real growth in state income in the Crown was only 15 per cent and 35 per cent in the two three-year periods around the middle of the century when compared with 1580, but it rose to an 85 per cent increase by the beginning of the last quarter of the century.

Detailed comparisons with other states are impossible, but the few figures which we do possess indicate that even the rulers of considerably smaller states enjoyed substantially larger resources. Before 1618, Maximilian I of Bavaria enjoyed an annual income equivalent to something between 26 and 35 tons of silver. In the year 1608, under Christian IV, the Danish state took in 61,000 *thalers* from taxes, 142,000 from the Sound tolls and 207,000 from the royal domains, a total of 410,000 *thalers* or about 10 tons of silver. The Danish royal lands alone brought in about twice as much as the Polish.

Denmark had even less than a tenth the population of Poland. The government of France, on the other hand, ruled twice as many people yet its treasury collected disproportionately larger sums. Its gross revenue in the last quarter of the sixteenth century has been estimated at about 350 tons of silver. The net revenue was somewhere between one fifth and one half the gross, though this probably does not include some hidden state income. Around the middle of the seventeenth century, the net revenues fluctuated between 255 and 425 tons of silver, which are amounts far beyond anything ever to be found in the receipts of the Commonwealth.

Any complete analysis of political power would have to take into account the size of the country's GNP, the extent to which money penetrated through the economy, and other such issues the impact of which is by no means easy to estimate. More obvious, however, are the fatal consequences of its weak fiscal system on the Commonwealth's position in Europe.

There is one final institution which must be considered in this overview of the structure of political power in the Polish Commonwealth, and that is the monarchy itself. The prerogatives of and limitations on royal power were defined by usage and by law. Legal norms alone, however, do not adequately describe the position of the king. For example, even under the Jagiellonians, the Polish monarchy was already legally elective, and therefore the death of Sigismund II August in 1572 did not bring with it any formal change. On the other hand, the passing of the dynasty, regardless of the attempts made to associate Stefan Batory and Sigismund III with it, meant that the elective monarchs who followed lacked the charisma of continuity. In any case, it is doubtful whether the numerous legal limitations on the monarch's power and royal promises to respect the Henrician articles and the *pacta conventa* taken together really defined the true relationship between the king and the Sejm.

It is impossible to distinguish precisely between the effects of a king's personality and the results of institutional conditions on this relationship, particularly since the number of kings involved is too small to allow of any generalizations and each faced unique circumstances. But it is clear that an elected monarch inherited his predecessor's problems without fully benefiting from any advantages which the latter had managed to win through intrigue and negotiation. This element of continuity was taken from the monarchy and assumed to some extent by the Sejm and, in a different way, by the magnates.

Detailed studies of the actions and political ideas of Sigismund III by Władysław Czapliński, Adam Kersten and others has shown how effectively that monarch was able to take advantage of the limited powers left to him by a nobility terrified of *absolutum dominium*. And yet the entirely different personality of Sigismund II August was also able to function effectively though in a completely different situation. A comparison of the two reigns demonstrates the full extent of the changes which had occurred after the first free election, not only in the institutions of the Commonwealth, but in the attitudes of its nobility in the chamber of deputies and in the *sejmiki* and in the great economic transformations which concentrated ever more land in ever fewer hands. Sigismund III, for all his absolutist ideas, could only manoeuvre in matters of immediate policy, and could not transform the basic institutions of the Commonwealth to the advantage of royal power.

Royalists flocked to his court seeking favours, but in rewarding them the king lost his power to control them, and he could never exert any control over his powerful magnate opponents.

It might be fruitful to examine the system of authority in the Commonwealth by considering on whose protection and on whose favour an ambitious noble would most effectively base his career. Everything suggests that the prudent noble tied himself to the magnate family which offered him a modicum of security, an advantage which was ensured by the bureaucracy and the sale of offices in absolutist monarchies. Venality of office also occurred in the Commonwealth, but it did not provide the basis for the rise of a nobility of the robe. Very few of the factors governing political life in the country or the careers of individual nobles depended on the results of a royal election. Leases on royal lands were granted for life with the possibility of exchanging one estate for a larger one, though there was a tendency to give priority to the heirs of the previous holder. By the seventeenth century, the monarch was even accepting surrender of rights to the royal estates as a form of payment. While royal appointments were held for life, this form of tenure did not exist at the courts of the magnates, who had complete freedom to appoint and dismiss their servants, though they did partly heed local gentry opinion. The magnate's court acted as a surrogate for a dynasty in the continuity of relations between patron and client across several generations. Indeed, Tadeusz Manteuffel has compared this to the classical feudal relationship in western Europe.

This leads us to the question of continuity at the royal court, and despite studies of the reigns of Stefan Batory and the Vasas, we cannot yet determine how a perceptive observer might view the continuity of the court's institutions. Certainly Hungarian, Swedish and French servants of the king did not monopolize all places at court and enough opportunities remained for Poles to fill these posts over longer periods of time. In order to understand the operations of the court as a centre for the elite, we must distinguish between its normal functionaries and those who frequently had duties there but prepared themselves for higher goals. The papal nuncio, Fulvio Ruggieri, wrote of the court of Sigismund II August, 'they do not enter this service for money, but rather to leave it in accordance with their talents as prelates, *wojewodas* and castellans'.

By the seventeenth and eighteenth centuries, the magnate courts were playing a similar role to the royal one, and the king had to heed magnate wishes and reward their protégés. Thus, in the matter of promotion the royal court shared its duties with the magnates, though the exact nature of this collaboration undoubtedly depended largely on individual personalities. Certainly the evolution of the royal court did not move in the direction of what Jürgen von Kruedener has described as *Herrschafts- und Machtinstrument*, a court holding a monopoly of all the gentry's social and economic opportunities.

In order to understand the partitions of Poland, it is essential to determine to what extent this system of joint action between the nobility and the monarch through the Sejm and the magnate courts was able to create a modern-state apparatus, capable of competing with other European monarchies. In this regard, the evolution of its social and political institutions from the middle of the sixteenth century might prove to have been of fundamental significance in laying the groundwork for the subsequent tragic fate of the Commonwealth two centuries later.

Relevant Bibliography (for chapters 5 and 6)

J. Bardach, 'Députés à la diète en Pologne d'ancien régime', *Acta Poloniae Historica*, 39 (1979)

'La Formation des assemblées polonaises au XVe siècle et la taxation', *Colloquium Lustrum V. Anciens Pays*, 70 (1977) .

'Gouvernants et gouvernés en Pologne au moyen âge at aux temps modernes', *Recueils de la Société Jean Bodin, 25: Gouvernés et gouvernants*, part 4 (Brussels 1965)

'L'Union de Lublin: ses origines et son rôle historique', *Acta Poloniae Historica*, 27 (1973)

W. Czapliński, 'Licht- und Schattenseiten der Polnischen Adelsrepublik', *Österreichische Osthefte*, 13 (1971)

W. Dworzaczek, 'La Mobilité sociale de la noblesse polonaise aux XVIe–XVIIIe siècles', *Acta Poloniae Historica*, 36 (1977)

'Perméabilité des barrières sociales dans la Pologne du XVIe s.', *Acta Poloniae Historica*, 24 (1971)

S. Grodziski, 'Les Devoirs et les droits politiques de la noblesse polonaise', *Acta Poloniae Historica*, 36 (1977)

K. Grzybowski, 'Les Éléments monocratiques en Pologne (XVe–XVIIIe siècles)', *Recueils de la Société Jean Bodin, 21: La monocratie*, part 2 (Brussels 1969)

A. Kersten, 'Les Magnats – élite de la société nobiliaire', *Acta Poloniae Historica*, 36 (1977)

A. Mączak, 'Money and Society in Poland and Lithuania in the 16th and 17th Centuries', *The Journal of European Economic History*, 5, no. 1 (1976)

'Zur Grundeigentumsstruktur in Polen im 16 bis 18 Jahrhundert', *Jahrbuch für Wirtschaftsgeschichte*, part 4 (1967)

J. Michalski, 'Les diétines polonaises au XVIIIe s.', *Acta Poloniae Historica*, 12 (1965)

E. Opaliński, 'Great Poland's Power Elite under Sigismund III, 1587–1632', *Acta Poloniae Historica*, 42 (1980)

E. Ladewig Petersen, 'From Domain State to Tax State. Synthesis and Interpretation', *The Scandinavian Economic History Review*, 23, no. 2 (1973)

A. Pośpiech and W. Tygielski, 'The Social Role of Magnate Courts in Poland from the End of the 16th up to the 18th Centuries', *Acta Poloniae Historica*, 43 (1981)

S. Russocki, 'Le Système représentatif de la république nobiliaire de Pologne', *Der moderne Parlamentarismus und seine Grundlagen in der Ständischer Representation* (Berlin 1977)

C. H. Talbot (ed.), *Relation of the State of Polonia and the United Provinces of that Crown Anno 1598: Elementa ad Fontium Editiones XIII* (Rome 1965)

A. Wyczański, 'La Structure de la noblesse polonaise aux XVIe–XVIIIe siècles (remarques méthodiques)', *Acta Poloniae Historica*, 36 (1977)

The Conclusive Years:
The End of the
Sixteenth Century as
the Turning-Point of
Polish History

This essay stems from the continuing debate on the background to the partitions of Poland and from my own interest in the no-man's land between the economic and the constitutional development of that commonwealth. My assumptions are very simple. There are, roughly speaking, two extreme attitudes to the 'question of the partitions'. The one assumes that it is a nonsense to study the whole of the early modern period merely as an introduction to the final fate of the Republic, namely its dissolution in 1795. No Czech scholar would think that a book on Czech history before 1620 should merely be a prolegomenon to the White Mountain. To that the other school of thought on Poland's history would argue that the difference between the Czech and Polish cases lies in the fact that the White Mountain, not unlike the battle of Mohács in 1526 for Hungary, was a military contest, whereas the partitions of Poland were the very complex result not only of European international policy but of the country's long-term social and constitutional development as well. While its neighbours followed the general trend towards the centralisation of power and the establishment of a strong army, the Republic of Poland–Lithuania by contrast pursued decentralisation and exalted the civil liberties of the noble Estate.

So much historical and literary effort has been devoted to the partitions, and up to the early part of this century so much energy was expended on identifying certain individuals or social groups as the 'true villains', or rather on exculpating the Poles and indicting the foreign powers, that Polish historians are now reluctant to broach this subject at all. And yet it is not without importance for the course of

European history to understand what caused the disappearance of a state which once divided Russia and Prussia. Poland, as one particular example of a *Ständestaat*, deserves some attention on the part of students of early modern Europe. 'You make it sound as if Polish history were *normal*', a member of Norman Davies's seminar at Harvard remarked with astonishment.[1] This viewpoint has recently been advanced by a German historian of Eastern Europe, Gottfried Schramm, in his comparative study of pre-Mohács Hungary, Bohemia and Poland.[2] In the first two countries the might and the prerogatives of the Estates were crushed during the seventeenth century by the Habsburgs; in Poland they were developing undisturbed by the king. In a sense, the Polish–Lithuanian *Ständestaat* brought the political struggle to its logical conclusion: the Estates all but eliminated the king as a political factor and almost reduced him during the seventeenth century to one amongst many competing magnates. In the fifteenth century the upper echelons of the commons had already been manoeuvred out of the Estates' assemblies.[3] What remained as the ruling force was the nobility, while the clergy was represented in the Senate (the upper chamber) by the archbishops and bishops alone, who socially did not differ from the nobility.[4]

In another brilliant essay on the comparative history of eastern Central Europe Schramm argues that the political weakness of towns and their elites was not a decisive factor in Poland.[5] This was true, he suggests, for Brandenburg–Prussia as well, and it is difficult to find two more dissimilar lines of development than Poland and Prussia. To that my reply would be that in order to compare two neighbouring countries such as these one has to take into account other factors, as for instance their respective sizes, constitutional traditions, and the social and economic position of the aristocracy. Late medieval Poland – up to 1501/5 – may be studied as one of the best examples of a kingdom moulded by *Herrschaftsverträge*.[6] From 1374 the nobility extended its power and personal privileges at the expense of the king; the clergy followed, always viewed with distrust and often countered by the gentry.[7] As a very rough generalisation, the nobility at the close of the fifteenth century had at its disposal a tight network of assemblies, local, provincial and the *Sejm*.[8] By then the principal battlelines in the political and constitutional struggle were drawn between the magnates entrenched in the king's council (the Senate) and the gentry who dominated the Chamber of Deputies (*izba poselska*). The division of the *Sejm* into two separate chambers reflected separate interests and the social conflict which was to lead in

1501 to a privilege granted to the *domini consiliarii* just before his coronation by the future king, Alexander, whereby the sovereign's role was reduced to that of president of the royal council. The *turba malorum vel levium*, the gentry gathered in the Chamber of Deputies, had its day four years later in 1505 when the *Nihil Novi* Act was voted through by the *Sejm* and promulgated by the king: '*statuimus, ut deinceps futuris temporibus perpetuis nihil novi constitui debeat per nos et successores nostros sine communi consiliariorum et nuntiorum terres- trium consensu.*'[9]

Apart from the constitutional problems one might ask why the kings were not able to use the overt hostility between the two levels of the nobility to buttress their threatened position. Why was the lesser nobility, the gentry, in the long run incapable of preserving its political status over against the magnates? Why were the consti- tutional victories of the gentry during the entire sixteenth century scarcely matched by corresponding political success and increasing social independence of their richer neighbours?[10]

In the following analysis I contend that the impressive consti- tutional achievements of the gentry in the Chamber of Deputies, as well as the augmented competence of local nobles' assemblies, went hand-in-hand with the steep rise of the senatorial families as great landowners. So what was being won on the floor of the *Sejm* was being lost through economic competition. Furthermore, I argue that the sheer size of the country, together with its loose network of communications and low density of towns, proved advantageous to the upper and wealthier sections of the nobility. In these respects the close of the sixteenth as well as the early decades of the seventeenth century were of crucial importance. Any hope of establishing strong central power and a thick network of administration was in my opinion by then already doomed, so that the fate of the republic was all but sealed. However, it would be unwise to neglect several other features in a period already rich in significant issues.

Since the constitutional achievements of the second half of the sixteenth century are by now accessible to English-speaking readers, the acts of the *Sejm* sessions in the 1560s as well as the details of the Lublin Union with Lithuania will not be discussed here.[11] However, the principal goal of the politically conscious and active gentry – *executio iurium*, and in particular *executio bonorum regalium* – has rarely been compared with the vicissitudes of the administration of royal domains in other contemporary European countries. The rela- tively strict rules imposed by the *Sejm* on the leaseholders and stewards of the royal estates were intended to solve painful problems of the fisc, indirectly to free the gentry (or rather their tenants) from extraordinary taxation and, not least, to undermine the position of the magnates. One may surmise that for some gentry leaders the last issue was of most importance, but there are few testimonies to that effect. The first *revisio bonorum regalium* compiled in 1564/65 was a masterpiece of inquisitorial control on the part of the representatives of both Chambers and of the king, as the first Estate of the *Sejm*.[12] The next survey in 1569, however, hardly matched the quality of the first one. In the seventeenth century the income figures were more often than not largely of symbolic significance. When badly pressed by the Chamber of Deputies, the *starostowie*, or leaseholders of the royal estates, preferred to pay double or even higher multiples of their original dues rather than submit to some sort of serious survey.[13]

The documents relating to the royal estates have been preserved better than most other early modern archival records, and that is why they are thoroughly studied. However, relatively little has been done to compare the administration of royal estates and its reform in Poland and Lithuania with similar phenomena abroad. For the present argument it is of vital importance that Poland did not transform itself from a domain state to a tax state, to borrow the terminology of Joseph Schumpeter.[14] In that she did not follow Denmark (after 1660) but rather Brandenburg–Prussia and, to a certain extent, Sweden. But notwithstanding the deep differences between these states they were all, barring Poland, well endowed with civil servants and clerical services. In Denmark, Frederick II and Christian IV were able to undertake ambitious reforms of the royal domain. The *lensmand* (vassal) was transformed into a royal official and conditions of leasehold were altered to the benefit of the crown.[15] In Prussia under the rule of Duke Albert former estates of the Teutonic Order were distributed in various forms to the leading nobles and the duke drew little income from his own estates, which were often mortgaged to noble creditors.[16] The early Prussian bureaucracy, however, maintained the high standards of the Order's officialdom and the estate accounts and surveys make an excellent source for students of agrarian economy and administration.[17] Furthermore, the *reduktion* in Sweden in the 1680s was made possible because of the excellent job done by civil servants since the sixteenth century.

I wish to stress the administrative factor because in Poland it hardly applied. The study of Poland's administration and civil service from the Middle Ages to the eighteenth century is still in its infancy, reflecting both the historical situation and the current lack of understanding for this topic among Polish historians. Tax records used to be kept quite carelessly and no one normally dared inquire about tax declarations. In the seventeenth century, when a series of emergencies called for higher taxes, it was easier to change the taxation system from land tax to hearth tax and later to poll tax than to secure a reasonable degree of reliability on the part of noble taxpayers. All the instances of highly efficient and dependable civil servants date from the sixteenth century.[18] Whereas in most countries that embraced absolutism a network of civil servants had already developed in the fourteenth century (France is the best example), in Poland after 1388 the nobility struggled against the office of *iusticiarius* and succeeded in eliminating it altogether before 1481.[19] The function of the *iusticiarii* had been to arrest suspects and bring them before royal judges. It is therefore highly probable that the conflict between noble autonomy and central authority had already begun just after the extinction of the Piast dynasty in 1370.

But why were the nobles so successful against the monarchy? Numerous charters granted by Jagiełło (1386–1434) and his descendants were more often than not simply arrogated by various groups within the nobles' Estate. Historians have failed to analyse carefully which groups profited directly therefrom, but the crucial Statute of Nieszawa, extracted from the king under blackmail by the noble levy gathered for the campaign against the Teutonic Order in 1454, clearly shifted the political balance within Poland to the advantage of the middling gentry and so paved the way for its subsequent domination of the *Sejm*.[20] In the fifteenth and even in the early sixteenth century there was still no clear division between magnates and the rest of the nobility: the aristocracy as a whole was powerful in every public sphere from local assemblies to the *Sejm*. Nevertheless, between 1521 and 1538 the deputies tried to outlaw the prevailing custom which allowed senators to elect part of the deputies' number in the local nobles' assemblies. Yet the gentry still felt more at ease and less dependent when on their home territory.

In the mid-sixteenth century the situation changed sharply as the Chamber of Deputies became a refuge for politically conscious deputies who felt unsafe on their home territory. On the *Sejm* floor in 1563/64, the session which culminated in the formally decisive victory of the 'executionists', the palatine of Chełmno, Jan Działyński, in protesting against the *executio iurium*, which in his opinion was contrary to Prussian liberties,[21]

> most of all cursed those deputies from the Pomeranian lands who in addressing the Chamber exceeded their mandate, calling them light-minded and malign, who hide here behind the king's protection, but who back home keep silent and ought to remain silent and be ashamed of what they instigate here.[22]

Notwithstanding the impressive achievements of the deputies in the 1560s their cause had a fairly slim chance of success in the long run. In the first place the gentry was losing the economic battle with the great landowners; secondly, its members became increasingly enmeshed in relations of clientage with their mighty neighbours; thirdly, adherents of the *executio iurium* movement lacked adequate organisation: they could not form a faction because there was no powerful leader,[23] and each successful politician, if he did not scorn personal advancement, sooner or later was granted a senatorial title and so was lost to the movement.

The great boom in the grain trade in the second half of the sixteenth century, especially in the 1590s, could not be turned to direct account by all potential exporters. What we know about the distribution of market opportunities for various groups of grain producers may be summed up as follows:[24] in Baltic ports prices were usually much higher than in the hinterland. That has been demonstrated in detail for the whole Vistula basin, as well as for Danzig's hinterland. The only economical means of transport was river boats; road transport of bulky, heavy commodities (grain, timber, ashes, etc.) was very expensive, and large loads in any case imposed too great a strain on draft animals. Within Poland–Lithuania heavy tolls were not levied and for all practical purposes goods belonging to the nobility were exempt. However, feasible transport by no means came cheaply for every nobleman. The rafting or floating of goods was a relatively complex business which needed skilled and experienced managers and hands and was only worthwhile when a sufficient quantity of goods had been assembled. The quantitative sources available suggest that size and distance played a crucial role.

1. In the servile labour system the larger landed estates were more market-oriented than single farms belonging to the lesser gentry.

2. The further from Danzig the cheaper the grain and, in turn, the greater the relative profit from its sale.[25]
3. The further from Danzig the greater the share of large landowners in rafting local produce.
4. The further from Danzig the greater the annual fluctuations in grain exports, which meant that while the immediate hinterland brought its grain to the Danzig market each year the far-off provinces were able to send considerable quantities only in particularly fat years. As a consequence of the last two factors only the greater landlords were able to supply Danzig with grain from distant areas on a regular basis (see Tables 1 and 2).

The cumulative effect of all these variables redounded to the advantage of the magnates, and one may hazard that the further from the Baltic the more inequal became the opportunities of access to a profitable market. Active involvement in the grain, oxen or timber trade did not imply any diminution of status for the nobility. Records

Table 1   Landowners in the Vistula grain trade (1555–76)

Province of origin	Masovia		Little Poland		Ruthenia and Wolhynia	
Quality of harvest	High	Low	High	Low	High	Low
Average total transports*	35,648	17,144	18,505	6,092	14,813	1,845
Landowners' share (%)**	53	63	84	89	83	92
Percentage of landowners' share among:						
magnates	52	58	69	72	69	76
rich gentry	24	24	18	18	25	13
medium gentry	24	18	13	10	6	11

Note   In order to show the contrast between fat and lean years four medium-harvest years for each province from the twelve years for which data are available have been disregarded. Masovia was nearest to, and Ruthenia–Wolhynia furthest from, Danzig.
*Commercial loads (for rye *circa* 2.2 metric tonnes).
**Other shares taken by merchants and the clergy.
Source   A. Mączak, 'Export of Grain and the Problem of Distribution of National Income in the Years 1550–1650', *Acta Poloniae Historica*, XVIII (1968), p. 82.

Table 2 Assessment of gross profits from the grain trade by exporters from different provinces

Province of origin	Masovia		Little Poland		Ruthenia and Wolhynia	
River shipments	High	Low	High	Low	High	Low
Average price of rye in Danzig*	25,6	35,1	36,2	17,13	27,10	27,13
Gross profits of great landowners*	78,000	50,000	107,000	20,000	81,000	9,000
Gross profits of other vendors*	138,000	79,000	65,000	13,000	54,000	4,000

*In Prussian marks and groschen (20 groschen = 1 mark). In each case three years of high and low river shipments from the mid-sixteenth century have been chosen, when corresponding statistics of rye prices obtained by the royal estate of Malbork (Marienburg in Prussia) are available.
Source Mączak, 'Export of Grain', p. 83.

of the toll-house in Włocławek on the Vistula, where goods belonging to the nobility were duly registered but only in rare cases also charged, clearly reveal numerous partnerships buying up grain and other products from their localities in Masovia and sending them down to towns on the Lower Vistula in Royal Prussia or directly to Danzig.[26] That type of enterprise did not occur in the Upper Vistula basin. There, at least from the early seventeenth century onwards, great landowners offered space in their river boats to their lesser neighbours and oversaw their goods in Danzig. That practice went hand-in-hand with the buying-up of marketable goods at local markets or indeed from the lords of small estates direct.[27]

After 1579 even sample quantative data are lacking but the figures which we have for the total shipments of grain down the Vistula from beyond Warsaw show that they were rising fast. It is safe to assume that this increase was due primarily to the cumulative effect of the nobles' shift to domain farming at the expense of their tenants' holdings and to the increase in the number of great estates as a result of the purchase of gentry estates on a massive scale. Whatever evidence exists suggests that greater landlords were dominating the market and that they were spending money on consumption rather than on covering the operating costs of their estates (which were minimal), as well as developing their courts and buying land. The concentration of landed property during the late sixteenth and early seventeenth century was a very striking phenomenon (see Table 3). In his recent thesis on the land market in Greater Poland, a region beyond the immediate orbit of Danzig trade, Dr Andrzej Pośpiech has shown that this market became active during boom periods. Concentration of property required a nucleus of great estates, and that may be the reason why it did not occur in Masovia – the proverbial region of petty nobles – or in Royal Prussia, where local magnates at a provincial level rested their social standing and influence upon the royal estates which they held effectively by inheritance.[28] In the south and south-west of Poland, by contrast, the growth of estates owned by the leading magnate families was truly impressive: several noblemen launched their families in the space of one lifetime into the ranks of the highest aristocracy and richest landowners.

Among that group Sebastian and Stanisław Lubomirski increased their estates between 1581 and 1629 in the palatinate of Cracow alone from four to ninety-one villages (alongside twenty-three royal ones). Whoever was shrewd enough to strike roots in the Ukraine could be sure of multiplying his estates and revenues thanks to the rapid colonisation of that vast region. The extreme case was Prince Jeremi

Table 3 Distribution of noble property in the Palatinate of Cracow

Size of property	Percentage of owners		Percentage of villagers		Villages per owner	
	1581	1629	1581	1629	1581	1629
Less than 1 village	36.1	43.9	20.3	6.6	0 9	0.3
1	38.6	29.6	25.6	18.3	1.1	1.0
2–4	20.0	19.6	31.1	30.5	2.6	2.6
5–9	4.6	4.8	14.4	19.8	5.2	6.9
10 or more	0.7	2.1	8.7	24.8	20.3	19.9
Total (absolute figures)	849	771	1399	1268	1.7	1.7

Source A. Mączak, 'Zur Grundeigentumsstruktur in Polen im 16. bis 18. Jahrhundert', *Jahrbuch für Wirtschaftsgeschichte*, 1967, part IV, p. 148 (with corrections).

Wiśniowiecki who in 1630 according to inventories of his property owned six hundred hearths on the left bank of the Dnieper, which by 1647 had risen to the incredible figure of 38,460 (or around 230,000 souls).[29] The Wiśniowieckis originated from Ruthenia but several genuinely Polish families were also able to profit from the estate and colonisation boom in the wake of the incorporation into Poland of what had been the southern part of the grand duchy of Lithuania. The most interesting case of spectacular growth is that of Jan Zamoyski. 'Parvum parvo additur' was his acquisitive principle, but from 1589 he was also able to acquire even large domains comprising fifteen or more villages. During his lifetime he increased his property from four villages in 1572 to over two hundred villages and eleven small towns. In addition, he administered six hundred royal villages and a dozen other towns.[30] The case of Zamoyski is especially important because he had been a very influential leader of the 'executionist' gentry and became the premier nobleman only on account of his role during the first interregna (1572–76) and because of the grace of King Stephen Báthory. As grand chancellor and grand hetman of Poland (there were counterparts for Lithuania) Zamoyski disposed of a large network of clients.[31]

While the chancellor-hetman (chief military commander; both posts held for life) was probably unique in his political career and general success, the establishment of clienteles was quite characteristic of Poland and Lithuania in these years. In that the republic was by no means unique in Europe, but generally patronage was changing its form wherever absolutism was on the rise, as in France and Spain, or where a rapid process of modernisation was involved, as with the Dutch United Provinces. At issue here is the traditional patronage exercised by the high nobility, a phenomenon which remained greatly in evidence wherever central power and modern bureaucracy could not reach.[32] Poland–Lithuania was to become the promised land of rural clientage and to remain so until the partitions of the late eighteenth century. That is the second reason, in my view, for the helplessness of any independent political movement of the gentry, and it leads on to the third.

How could a political party be run which set itself against the magnates? No network of communications existed comparable to that of the church, the king and the intensive personal contacts between high noble families which had emerged even before the sixteenth-century interregna when between sessions of the Sejm the leading senators were able to communicate much more quickly and easily than the squires. There was little prospect, therefore, of a balanced and efficient polity based upon true 'gentry democracy'. This explanation differs somewhat from the one advanced by Perry Anderson for what he defines as Polish 'anarchy, impotence and annexation'.[33] According to Anderson 'the paradoxical size of the *szlachta* and formal absence of titles within it produced a self-destructive caricature of a representative system proper within the gentry'. Neither the size of the privileged Estate nor the absence of formal titles by themselves explain anything: Denmark acquired its first counts only after the absolutist *coup* of Frederick III, while in the Spanish kingdoms *hidalgos* were roughly as numerous as the *szlachta* in Poland.[34] But Anderson is right that 'no immanent mediation of interest was practicable within the noble class' – at least on a scale of some 700,000 to 900,000 square kilometres. Another, though small, country with a relatively numerous and modestly endowed nobility, barely organised into 'a vertical hierarchy of ranks' – the Piedmont of Duke Emmanuel Philibert – became from 1559 onwards a model case of absolutism.[35]

It is not easy to pinpoint the overriding cause of a phenomenon so baffling as the Polish 'golden liberty'. Perhaps a solution to this dilemma will help resolve some more general questions about the possible relationships between rulers and their Estates in other European countries. The social fabric cannot be compared with molecular structures, so that historians would be well advised not to resort to the analytic principles governing chemical combinations which operate by the subtraction of individual components. There is no need to apologise, therefore, for the lack of a precise historical explanation.

Numerous and far-reaching fiscal and jurisdictional liberties were not uncommon in Europe before the era of absolutism. Bohemia–Moravia, Hungary, Sweden–Finland and Denmark–Norway all had elective monarchies. For Poland what mattered was that the 'normal' tug-of-war between the prince and the Estates was played out in such a vast country, and that the legacy of the Jagiellon dynasty – Lithuania – was in a sense a geopolitical liability: it brought little in rents and taxes, involved Poland in conflicts with Muscovy and the Tartars, and bequeathed an economic, social and seigneurial power structure which favoured the owners of immense estates. Despite such an obvious overstatement[36] the point serves to stress the difference between the situation of the Jagiellons and that of the Hohenzollerns, who were able to play off Brandenburg officials against Prussian subjects and vice-versa, or that of the Oldenburg dynasty who knew how to use the duchies of Schleswig and Holstein to strengthen their sway over Denmark.

It is too easy to say that Jagiełło and his descendants were weaklings, whereas the Hohenzollerns are commonly regarded as a particularly gifted dynasty. The Jagiellons found themselves in a precarious situation roughly determined by three central factors: they inherited and had to develop a society of Estates with poorly developed towns; as a consequence the money economy was primitive, which gave little scope for intensive taxation; and Poland's geopolitical position afforded little chance of concentrating their efforts in one direction, so for all practical purposes no important goal was attained during the sixteenth century. Moreover, there was little internal consensus about the priorities of domestic and international policy. For Greater Poland the Tartars were a very remote danger, while Prussia and Livonia were of little interest to Little Poland. All the same, it is easy to underestimate the role of various deeply-rooted customs in public life. Traditionally offices (including leaseholds of royal estates) were granted for life, which gave the king little opportunity of creating a truly dependable civil service. It was characteristic that once a *homo novus* had been appointed he did not usually feel any obligation of long-lasting loyalty towards his benefactor and sovereign. Sigismund III tried to be determined and peremptory in his appointments' policy,[37] but while he was able to disregard Protestant candidates after 1592 he could never introduce even minimal changes in the institutional and constitutional system.

After the first free election it was too late for any kind of *absolutum dominium*. Recently Professor Andrzej Wyczański has praised highly the movement for the execution of the laws, suggesting that it 'led not to a weakening but rather to a strengthening of royal power ... and improved the efficiency of the central bureaucratic organs'. It also 'weakened the political influence' of lay and ecclesiastical magnates and 'gave the monarchy greater freedom of manoeuvre'.[38] I agree that the co-operation of the last Jagiellon, Sigismund Augustus (1548–72), with the Chamber of Deputies was for a time exemplary, but apart from changing the royal electoral system I do not see any real chance of establishing an efficient government based on the monarch and the gentry, but not on the magnates. It is difficult to overstate the gentry's disapproval of heavy taxation and the crown's active policy against Poland's neighbours. Were Polish nobles so distrustful of their monarchs only because of their poor experience with Henry of Valois?

It can be taken for granted that since those years royal authority had greatly diminished. If the Reformation provided a chance for an independent political movement of the gentry (and most of its parliamentary activists before 1572 were Protestants of various denominations), no acceptable Protestant candidates for the throne could be put forward. Nothing was done, moreover, to institutionalise co-operation between the king and the deputies. This leads me back to certain social changes that were taking place in the nobles' Estate. Its upper stratum – senatorial families – was never a closed caste; outstanding members of the gentry were acceptable as marriage partners and thus they were able to enter the more exclusive circles of the high aristocracy. A recent study of deputies from Báthory's reign (1576–86) has shown that a relatively large number would become senators under Sigismund III.[39] The sharp conflict between both chambers in the 1550s and 1560s was to be forgotten. During the *rokosz* of 1606–9 some radical overtones against the magnates could still be heard, but sixty years later, when the nobility once more took up arms against the monarch, those voices were silent. The *populus nobilium* was unable to keep what may be called the balance of social powers. Its internal cohesion was nationally provided almost entirely by its topmost stratum, the magnates. Genuine grass-roots gentry activity after 1600 was no longer possible and with it any long-term alliance with the king.

Dr Anna Sucheni-Grabowska, who has rightly stressed the last Jagiellon's skill in government and his sound choice of political allies, points out the crucial weakness of his situation: Sigismund Augustus lacked any close ties with financiers.[40] However, that obviously did not derive from personal neglect on his part but from the country's general situation. Poland's financial centre was Danzig, which remained beyond the king's sphere of influence. What is more, Danzig had good reason to distrust any Polish efforts towards administrative centralisation and was perfectly satisfied to co-operate politically and economically with individual magnates.[41]

To envisage the Polish Commonwealth run by true servants of the crown remains entirely conjectural. In Sigismund Augustus and Báthory's day royal secretaries had been both efficient and competent, and many of them enjoyed glittering careers.[42] But in Poland 'rule by secretaries', as in Sweden under Eric XIV, John III and Charles IX, was out of the question. By the time it was technically possible both the aristocratic elite and the politically conscious gentry had become too powerful. And, last but not least, Polish towns, which had already been ignored as allies by the early Jagiellons, never produced potential royal counsellors.

Nothing was ever simple in Polish affairs. But in seeking to determine the latest date at which the fate of the state was still in balance I would draw particular attention to the 1560s. A free-for-all by foreign princes vying for the Polish throne from 1572 onwards must have been detrimental to any sensible reform, even if the Vasas were able to survive for more than eighty years. The decentralisation of power and administration which was already under way under Báthory was likely to destroy any effective financial reforms. But at the root of the structure of the state lay the distribution of property throughout the vast countryside. The power of the local lords was much more real than that of the distant king. They were both patrons and the only available power brokers. And since the king was to be freely elected, was his person or rather the particular patron the proper mainstay of security and stability? In a kingdom without hereditary monarchy the true dynasties were those of the magnates.

Notes

1. N. Davies, *God's Playground. A History of Poland*, vol. I (Oxford, 1982), p. xi.
2. G. Schramm, 'Polen – Böhmen – Ungarn: Übernationale Gemeinsamkeiten in der politischen Kultur des späten Mittelalters und der frühen Neuzeit', *Przegląd Historyczny* (forthcoming). Paper read at the 3rd Conference of Polish and West German historians, Mainz, July 1984.
3. J. Bardach, 'La formation des assemblées polonaises au XVe siècle et la taxation', *Standen en Landen*, LXX (1977), p. 281. Royal towns took their stand on their particular charters, but the privileges granted by King Casimir to the noble Estate in 1454 formally prejudiced the fiscal immunities of the towns, and the *Sejm* did not hesitate to tax them without their consent.
4. In formal terms no 'upper' and 'lower' House existed in Poland, and the gentry strongly objected to such epithets. There were, on the other hand, numerous procedural similarities between the respective relationships of both Houses of Parliament at Westminster and of the Senate and Chamber of Deputies in Poland.
5. G. Schramm, 'Adel und Staat. Ein Vergleich zwischen Brandenburg und Polen-Litauen im 17. Jahrhundert', in M. Biskup and K. Zernack (eds), *Schichtung und Entwicklung der Gesellschaft in Polen und Deutschland im 16. und 17. Jahrhundert. Parallelen, Verknüpfungen, Vergleiche* (*Vierteljahrschrift für Sozial- und Wirtschaftsgeschichte*, Beiheft LXXIV) (Wiesbaden, 1983), p. 61. The point in question comes out somewhat indirectly in the text, but it was stressed by Schramm in discussion.

6. Cf. collections of papers on *Herrschaftsverträge* which omit the Polish case, in *Schweizer Beiträge zur Allgemeinen Geschichte*, X (1952), and R. Vierhaus (ed.), *Herrschaftsverträge, Wahlkapitulationen, Fundamentalgesetze* (Veröffentlichungen des Max-Planck-Instituts für Geschichte, LVI) (Göttingen, 1977).

7. Cf. Bardach, 'Formation', p. 280, with full bibliography on early Polish parliamentarianism. Parallel to Bardach cf. S. Russocki, 'Le système représentatif de la république nobiliaire de Pologne', in K. Bosl (ed.), *Der moderne Parlamentarismus und seine Grundlagen in der ständischen Repräsentation* (Berlin, 1977); also cf. a series of papers in *Acta Poloniae Historica*, XXXVI (1977).

8. This is the point stressed by Bardach, 'Formation'. One may add that local assemblies were an excellent stage for noble, and particularly freshman, politicians; their traditions and conventions formed in the fifteenth and sixteenth centuries paved the way for the system of government and administration which prevailed in the later seventeenth and eighteenth centuries.

9. *Volumina legum*, vol. I, p. 299; cf. Bardach, 'Formation', p. 291.

10. The expression 'magnate' is a late coinage and rather pejorative. Recent discussions on the nature and definition of the magnates are of secondary importance; here the expression is used to describe great landowners, senators (with the exception of backbenchers or lesser castellans) and members of their families.

11. Cf. Davies, *God's Playground*; J. K. Fedorowicz (ed.), *A Republic of Nobles. Studies in Polish History to 1864* (Cambridge, 1982); A. Mączak, H. Samsonowicz, and P. Burke (eds), *East–Central Europe in Transition from the Fourteenth to the Seventeenth Century* (Cambridge, 1985), chs. 1 and 10.

12. The 1564/65 survey has been thoroughly analysed by Jan Rutkowski in his *opus* on income distribution in early modern Poland *Badania nad podziałem dochodów w Polsce w czasach nowożytnych*, vol. I (Cracow, 1938).

13. A. Sucheni-Grabowska, 'Walka o wymiar i przeznaczenie kwarty w końcu XVI i na początku XVII wieku', *Przegląd Historyczny*, LVI (1965). Recently K. Chłapowski has assessed the overall results of the *executio bonorum regalium* in *Realizacja reform egzekucji dóbr, 1563–1665* (Warsaw, 1984), concentrating on estates pawned in Little Poland.

14. E. Ladewig Petersen, 'From Domain State to Tax State', *Scandinavian Economic History Review*, XXIII (1975).

15. Idem, *Fra standssamfund til rangssamfund, 1500–1700* (Copenhagen, 1980), pp. 219, 291.

16. H. Schweichler, 'Das Domänenwesen unter Herzog Albrecht in Preußen (1525–1568)', *Mitteilungen der Literarischen Gesellschaft Masovia*, XVII (1911), pp. 119–20. On fraud cf. C. von Nostitz, *Haushaltungsbuch des Fürstenthums Preußen 1578*, ed. K. Lohmeyer (Leipzig, 1893), p. 155.

17. M. North, *Die Amtswirtschaften von Osterode und Soldau* (Berlin, 1982).

18. Much has been done and is being done on this subject by Professor Andrzej Wyczański. Cf. his general conclusions in both edited volumes *cit.* n. 11.

19. J. Bardach, *Historia państwa i prawa Polski*, vol. I, 2nd edn (Warsaw, 1964), p. 476f.

20. This was the conclusion of S. Roman in his *Przywileje nieszawskie* (Wrocław, 1957).

21. Since 1466 the western part of the former territory of the Teutonic Order belonged directly to the Polish kings and with the Union of Lublin in 1569 was incorporated into Poland.

22. A. T. Działiński (ed.), *Zródłopisma de dziejów Unii Korony Polskiej i Wielkiego Księstwa Litewskiego*, vol. II, part 1 (Poznań, 1856–61), p. 386.

23. Cf. D. J. Roorda, *Partij en factie* (Groningen, 1961), pp. 1–36.

24. Cf. W. Kula, *An Economic Theory of the Feudal System. Towards a Model of the Polish Economy, 1500–1800* (London, 1976). Lack of space prevents the inclusion of adequate evidence on prices and market conditions.

25. Comparable evidence has been collected from the first survey of royal estates in 1564/65. Cf. A. Mączak, 'Preise, Löhne und Lebenshaltungskosten in Europa des 16. Jahrhunderts. Ein Beitrag zur Quellenkritik', in I. Bog *et al.* (eds), *Wirtschaftliche und soziale Strukturen im säkularen Wandel. Festschrift für Wilhelm Abel zum 70. Geburtstag*, vol. II (Hanover, 1974), pp. 322–5, 340–1.

26. S. Kutrzeba and F. Duda (eds), *Regestra thelonei aquatici Wladislaviensis saeculi XVI* (Cracow, 1915), *passim.*

27. The same practice was used by the Radziwiłłs in Lithuania, but probably only later.

28. A. Mączak in G. Labuda (ed.), *Historia Pomorza*, vol. II, part 1 (Poznań, 1976), p. 204. Eight leading noble families between 1526 and 1657 held 44% of royal estates (four of them as much as 32%); Bratian remained in the hands of a single family for 123 years; another family held Sztum (Stuhm) for over 106 years. Dr Pośpiech's thesis is on the property market in the county of Kalisz in the 16/17 c., University of Warsaw, 1984.

29. W. Tomkiewicz, *Jeremi Wiśniowiecki (1612–1651)* (Warsaw, 1933), ch. 5.

30. A. Tarnawski, *Działalność gospodarcza Jana Zamoyskiego, kanclerza i hetmana wielkiego koronnego* (Lwów, 1935).

31. W. Tygielski, 'A Faction that could not lose'. Paper read at a conference on *Patronat-Klientel-Beziehungen in der frühen Neuzeit*, Historisches Kolleg, Munich, October 1985 (forthcoming).

32. On various types of clientage in early modern Europe see the papers presented to the conference, above, n. 31.

33. P. Anderson, *Lineages of the Absolutist State* (London, 1974), p. 298.

34. M.-C. Gerbet, *La noblesse dans le royaume de Castille* (Paris, 1979), pp. 149–53. Cf. also J. Meyer, *Noblesses et pouvoirs dans l'Europe d'ancien régime* (Paris, 1973), pp. 28–9 and *passim.*

35. Recent publications by Professor Enrico Stumpo suggest that there is

much misunderstanding about the numbers and economic potential of the Piedmont nobility. Cf. his *Finanza e stato moderno nel Piemonte del seicento* (Rome, 1979), pp. 278, 290; idem, 'I ceti dirigenti in Italia nell' età moderna. Due modelli diversi: nobilità piemontese e patriziato toscano', in A. Tagliaferri (ed.), *I ceti dirigenti in Italia in età moderna e contemporanea* (Udine, 1984), pp. 167–8.

36.   I cannot here embark upon the knotty subject of the long-term consequences of the Polish–Lithuanian unions. However, having recently read numerous examination papers by students on roughly this topic, I detect the blossoming in present-day Poland of a stereotyped argument which goes: Lithuania was the mainstay of the magnates: the latter were detrimental to Poland's fate: *ergo*, Lithuania was somewhat of a curse for Poland. Only a few candidates ventured, for instance, that without the Lithuanian buffer Poland would have been swallowed by Russia even earlier.

37.   On royal power cf. Wyczański's papers in the edited collections *cit.* n. 11, and below, n. 38. Greater detail on Sigismund III is given by W. Czapliński, 'Rządy oligarchii w Polsce nowożytnej', *Przegląd Historyczny*, LII (1961); A Kersten, 'Problem władzy w Rzeczypospolitej czasu Wazów', in *O naprawę Rzeczypospolitej XVII–XVIII wieku* (Warsaw, 1965).

38.   A. Wyczański, 'The Problem of Authority in Sixteenth-Century Poland. An Essay in Reinterpretation', in Fedorowicz, *Republic of Nobles* (as n. 11), p. 99. The author's final remark that 'these conclusions fly in the face of existing opinion' is not altogether accurate, for most students of the period agree that in Sigismund Augustus' reign both government and administration still worked well.

39.   Witold Rodkiewicz's paper on deputies' careers is to appear in *Przegląd Historyczny*. Membership of the Chamber played different roles in the informal *cursus honorum* of the various strata of the nobility. For squires multiple membership was compatible with higher county offices and dignities; young magnates hardly bothered to run for it more than once, if at all.

40.   A. Sucheni-Grabowska, 'Badania nad elitą władzy w latach 1551–1562', in A. Wyczański (ed.), *Społeczeństwo staropolskie*, vol. I (Warsaw, 1976), p. 96. This paper (with a French summary) is a thorough and balanced appreciation of Sigismund Augustus' government and administration.

41.   For the role of Danzig in the Polish–Lithuanian Republic W. Czapliński's paper, 'Problem Gdańska w czasach Rzeczypospolitej szlacheckiej', *Przegląd Historyczny*, XLIII (1952) is still valid. Czapliński calls Danzig 'a collective magnate'.

42.   A collective biography of Báthory's secretaries by Leszek Kieniewicz will appear in A. Wyczański (ed.), *Społeczeństwo staropolskie*, vol. IV (1986). On their predecessors from Sigismund Augustus' times cf. idem, 'Problem of Authority', pp. 106–7.

INDEX OF PERSONS AND PLACE NAMES

[Contemporary author's names are given in *italics*]

INDEX

For Product Safety Concerns and Information please contact our EU
representative GPSR@taylorandfrancis.com Taylor & Francis Verlag GmbH,
Kaufingerstraße 24, 80331 München, Germany

Printed and bound by CPI Group (UK) Ltd, Croydon, CR0 4YY
01/05/2025
01858437-0001